The Evolution of Logic

The Evolution of Logic examines the relations between logic and philosophy over the last 150 years. Logic underwent a major renaissance beginning in the nineteenth century. Cantor almost tamed the infinite, and Frege aimed to undercut Kant by reducing mathematics to logic. These achievements were threatened by the paradoxes, like Russell's. This ferment generated excellent philosophy (and mathematics) by excellent philosophers (and mathematicians) up to World War II. This book provides a selective, critical history of the collaboration between logic and philosophy during this period.

After World War II, mathematical logic became a recognized subdiscipline in mathematics departments, and consequently but unfortunately philosophers have lost touch with its monuments. This book aims to make four of them (consistency and independence of the continuum hypothesis, Post's problem, and Morley's theorem) more accessible to philosophers, making available the tools necessary for modern scholars of philosophy to renew a productive dialogue between logic and philosophy.

W. D. Hart is currently Professor of Philosophy at the University of Illinois at Chicago, where he chaired the philosophy department for twelve years. He has also taught at the University of Michigan, University College London, and the University of New Mexico. He is the author of *The Engines of the Soul*, now available in paperback (Cambridge, 2009), and the editor of *The Philosophy of Mathematics* and has published more than seventy articles and reviews in academic journals.

T0372703

THE EVOLUTION OF MODERN PHILOSOPHY

General Editors:
Paul Guyer and Gary Hatfield *(University of Pennsylvania)*

Published Books in the Series
Roberto Torretti: *The Philosophy of Physics*
David Depew and Marjorie Greene: *The Philosophy of Biology*
Charles Taliaferro: *Evidence and Faith*
Michael Losonsky: *Linguistic Turns in Modern Philosophy*
W. D. Hart: *The Evolution of Logic*

Forthcoming
Paul Guyer: *Aesthetics*
Stephen Darwall: *Ethics*
William Ewald and Michael J. Hallett: *The Philosophy of Mathematics*
Adrian Moore: *Making Sense of Things: The Evolution of Modern Metaphysics*

Why has philosophy evolved in the way that it has? How have its subdisciplines developed, and what impact has this development exerted on the way that the subject is now practiced? Each volume in "The Evolution of Modern Philosophy" will focus on a particular subdiscipline of philosophy and examine how it has evolved into the subject as we now understand it. The volumes will be written from the perspective of a current practitioner in contemporary philosophy, whose point of departure will be the question: How did we get from there to here? Cumulatively the series will constitute a library of modern conceptions of philosophy and will reveal how philosophy does not in fact comprise a set of timeless questions but has rather been shaped by broader intellectual and scientific developments to produce particular fields of inquiry addressing particular issues.

For my wife, Faith

The Evolution of Logic

W. D. HART

CAMBRIDGE
UNIVERSITY PRESS

CAMBRIDGE UNIVERSITY PRESS
Cambridge, New York, Melbourne, Madrid, Cape Town,
Singapore, São Paulo, Delhi, Tokyo, Mexico City

Cambridge University Press
32 Avenue of the Americas, New York, NY 10013-2473, USA

www.cambridge.org
Information on this title: www.cambridge.org/9780521747721

First published 2010
Reprinted 2011

A catalog record for this publication is available from the British Library.

Library of Congress Cataloging in Publication Data

Hart, W. D. (Wilbur Dyre), 1943–
The evolution of logic / W.D. Hart.
p. cm. – (The evolution of modern philosophy)
Includes bibliographical references and index.
ISBN 978-0-521-76681-4 (hardback) – ISBN 978-0-521-74772-1 (pbk.)
1. Logic – History. I. Title.
BC15.H37 2010
160.9–dc22 2010028908

ISBN 978-0-521-76681-4 Hardback
ISBN 978-0-521-74772-1 Paperback

Contents

Preface

In high school I read a book from the school library called *Introduction to Mathematical Thought* by E. R. Stabler. Early on he described a pattern in which he displayed a conditional, its antecedent, and its consequent. I stared at this display, trying to get the point. Then the penny dropped: this is a way the mind *moves*, from the first two to the third. That was my first experience of explicit logic, and it was eye-opening.

I took my first logic course at university from W. V. Quine. He lectured by mumbling at his stack of three-by-five cards, but the textbook was the second edition of his *Methods of Logic*, which I still think is the best baby logic book I have seen. As I learned gradually who Quine was, I was too awestruck to approach him again. Instead, I did a lot of work with his former student Burt Dreben. Dreben described himself as a logical positivist, but he was really a philosophical nihilist. He once said in lecture, "Rubbish is rubbish, but the history of rubbish is scholarship." The rubbish was all of philosophy, and the scholarship was where he wanted me directed. He taught us a lot of logic and early analytic philosophy. He first taught me Gödel's incompleteness theorem from Rudolf Carnap's *The Logical Syntax of Language*, and he later taught it from Gödel's original paper. Both now seem to me perverse pedagogy, especially the first, but it reflected his historical taste.

I never succumbed to Dreben's philosophical nihilism. He once told me I had a twelfth-century mind, and though I have never been able to penetrate scholastic philosophy, I still understood what he meant and pretty much agreed with him. I got from him a taste for the history of modern logic and analytic philosophy, but I wanted to do philosophy too, so I wanted to argue about whether authors we were working on are right or wrong. The first five chapters that follow grew out of the kind of training I got from Dreben. They go from Dedekind and Cantor up to Gödel's incompleteness theorem, but they are a selective history, and it is critical – I allow myself to do some philosophy as we go along.

I continued to work with Dreben as I moved on to graduate school, but that was when Hilary Putnam joined the faculty of Harvard. Putnam is no philosophical nihilist. He reminded me a bit of Russell earlier on: both were amazing sources of a wealth of new philosophical ideas. Perhaps one sometimes wanted to try to do a second draft oneself, but that could be very instructive. Putnam taught a wonderful course in Gödel's and Cohen's (then recent) results on the consistency and independence of Cantor's continuum hypothesis. That course marked me for life.

In my first job after graduate school, I met Fred Goldstein, who had come to Michigan from the logic program at Stanford. Somewhere along the way I had developed the notion that only people with theorems named after them were logicians, so Russell and Quine were not logicians. Fred saw how silly and self-destructive this notion was. He thought that modern logic was distinguished by certain methods. After Gödel's method of arithmetization, which was like basic literacy, these distinctive methods were constructible sets, forcing and generic sets, and the priority method. Fred said a logician knows at least some of these methods. Fred's idea was liberating, and since I had seen constructible sets and generic sets with Putnam, Fred gave me a yen to learn the priority method. I regret to say that Fred was soon diagnosed with leukemia and died very young.

At that same university, Michael Morley had been denied tenure a few years earlier. He had then gone on to prove Morley's theorem, which inaugurated the second great age of model theory. That story shows there can be triumph after rejection. I think Fred died too early to see that Morley's theorem belongs with Fred's three distinctive methods. It took a while for the recognition of it to begin to percolate out from the specialists. The point of Chapters 6 through 9 is to present versions of Fred's four monuments to philosophers.

In the early 1990s, Paul Guyer asked me to write the logic and philosophy volume for a series of books he was editing for Cambridge University Press. I was intrigued by the project and wrote a proposal, but I was then taking up administrative chores that made sustained thought difficult, so the project hung fire for a long time. Then, as I was giving up administration, Paul asked whether I was still interested in the project. You and I can be grateful to Paul for what you hold in your hands. There can be intellectual life after administration. I am grateful to Beatrice Rehl of Cambridge University Press and especially to Russell Hahn for their skillful shepherding of my manuscript through production.

In the early stages I had invaluable advice and support from my friend and former student Matthew Moore, now at Brooklyn College. Another friend and former student (the first one to retire), Andrew Lugg, also gave me useful comments. I wish to thank my able colleagues and friends Daniel Sutherland and Walter Edelberg for their insightful discussions and suggestions. As I was writing, Daniel organized a reading group on the philosophy of mathematics. That group was kind enough to discuss some of the earlier chapters, and I am grateful for their criticism and help. I must confess that I lost track of which graduate students dropped in or out, but I must acknowledge Sean Paul Morris (who also read the page proofs) and my astonishing former student Mihai Ganea. And I am grateful to Robert Fischer for preparing the four diagrams for publication.

My wife, Faith, is not mathematical, and she regards philosophy, especially my twelfth-century version of it, as pretty bizarre. She once told me that I think numbers get up and dance around. She edits and designs books, mostly in the history of art. I write longhand, and she types and edits what I write, and doing that with symbols is a labor of love. She also prods me to keep me going. Marrying Faith was the best thing I ever did.

✦

ONE

Cantor's Paradise

Cantor's quarry was the infinite. The mathematics of number had always been about objects of which there are infinitely many, like natural numbers, or objects of which not only are there infinitely many but each is also itself infinite, like real numbers with endless decimal expansions. The infinities of geometry, like the infinity of points on a line or triangles in a plane, had always been there, but the applications of the calculus in geometry made its infinities more salient. The recognition of the infinity of its subject matter was always a reason not to test the conjectures of mathematics by checking the examples but rather to prefer proof. Aristotle urged that the infinite could only ever be potential, like a process with no fixed end, but that completed actual infinite wholes were ruled out. Such views look to countenance possibilities that could not be actual, which sounds contradictory, but even Gauss, the prince of mathematicians, had a *horror infiniti*. Cantor swam against the tide.

To work out a theory of the infinite per se, Cantor needed to figure out which things are classified as finite or infinite. That is one source of his interest in sets. For this purpose sets should be any old collections, whether unified by having something in common or not, like the Walrus's shoes and ships and cabbages and kings. Sets should be an utterly general sort, so whether there are infinitely many such and suches can always be re-asked as whether the set of such and suches is infinite. As horses are the kind that divides into stallions and mares, so sets are the kind that divides into finite and infinite.

Cantor distinguished between two sorts of infinity, one where order is front and center, and another where it is less obvious. (Order can often be taken as process finished and complete.) Since order is an extra, let us first put it aside. We want to articulate what it is for two sets to be the same in size. There are as many digits on your left hand as on your

1

right. One way to check this is to count each and get the same answer, five, in both cases, but that procedure assumes number, something we also want to articulate. Another way is to match your digits one-to-one, so that each is matched with just one partner. This you can do without counting or numerical claims. Order does not matter. Palm to palm, you can match thumb to thumb, index finger to index finger, and so on. But you can also invert one hand and match thumb to pinkie, index to ring finger, and so on. And there are obviously many (120, in fact) ways to tie each digit to a unique digit on the other hand.

The general idea is that a set A has as many members as a set B exactly in case there is a way to match the members of A with the members of B one-to-one. The phrase "one-to-one" may make you worry that numbers like one are being smuggled in surreptitiously. The honest way to allay this worry is to lay out the set theoretic nuts and bolts of matching one-to-one so it is clear no numbers have snuck in. Laying out these nuts and bolts is also a way of illustrating how sets have become the arena in which logic, mathematics, and more are conducted. Sets are not just the natural kind of infinity; they are also a natural kind across logic, mathematics, and beyond. Frege's aim was to reduce the mathematics of number to logic. To do so, he treated extensions (of predicates, properties, or concepts) considerably more systematically than the comparatively casual use traditional logic had made of extensions for centuries before Frege. His treatment of extensions got into enough trouble that it is at least doubtful whether the mathematics of number is reducible to logic. But Frege's systematic treatment of extensions is an important stage in sets becoming the arena of mathematics and logic.

There are two primitive predicates in our exposition of basic naïve set theory. (We'll see later what the naïveté is.) We want a predicate for the relation of, say, a senator to the set of senators. This is called the membership, or elementhood, relation, and is usually written for short as similar to the small Greek letter epsilon, or $\in$. So if S is the set of states and A is the state of Alabama, then $A \in S$ says that Alabama is a member of the set of states. If our theory were to be a theory of nothing but sets, $\in$ could be our only primitive, and in that way set theory is the laws of the membership relation. But if we want to allow room for application to things like people and rocks that we don't think of as sets, so that we can have the set of people and the set of rocks, then we should also take identity as a primitive. We write this, as usual, as the double bar, =. To say that 7 + 5 = 12 means that the number 12 is the same thing as the sum of 7 and 5.

It is central to sets that they are identical when they have the same members. There aren't two totalities of all and only the shoes. The principle that sets with the same members are identical is called extensionality. Were we discussing nothing but sets, we could take membership as our only primitive predicate and use extensionality to introduce identity. But if we include things like the Rock of Gibraltar and Peter Abelard that presumably are not sets, then since only sets have members, Gibraltar and Abelard will have the same members, namely none, and yet not be identical. So when sets are applied, it is natural to assume identity as well as membership. Extensionality distinguishes sets from predicates and properties. Two predicates like "is directly over Big Ben" and "is directly above Big Ben" are true of all and only the same things, and yet are different predicates. Being spelled the same suffices for predicates to be identical. Properties can be had by the same things and yet differ. Easy instances are empty properties like being a centaur and being a griffin. But instantiated properties, like having a heart and having a liver, also seem to differ even if all and only the animals with hearts have livers. Some say that necessary coextensiveness suffices for property identity; others reply that necessity is unclear (without making it clear what clarity requires). Whatever the rights and wrongs of that dispute, there is more worked-out and settled lore about sets than about properties, so logicians and mathematicians favor sets over properties.

There are two systematic ways to name sets. If a set is finite and we have names for its members, then curly brackets enclosing a list of those names separated by commas is a name for that set. So

$$\{Mercury, Venus, Earth\}$$

is the set of the three inmost planets of our solar system. Since Cantor's quarry was the infinite, such names would not have satisfied him. Suppose we have a predicate like "Ralph gave x a present." Here the variable "x" marks a blank that may be filled by singular terms (proper names, definite descriptions, demonstratives) denoting things that are or are not targets of Ralph's generosity. Abbreviate this predicate as "Px." Then

$$\{x \mid Px\}$$

is read "the set of all things, say x is one, such that Px" and in our case would be the set of all and only the recipients of Ralph's generosity. This set is called the extension of the predicate "Px," uniqueness here being justified by extensionality. The assumption that every predicate has a set that is its extension is called comprehension. Naïve set theory is the theory whose axioms are extensionality and comprehension, and as we shall see, comprehension is thought to be its naïveté.

The notation $\{x \mid Px\}$ is called set abstraction. List terms can be replaced by abstracts on the model of

$$\{x \mid x = \text{Mercury or } x = \text{Venus or } x = \text{Earth}\},$$

so we can make do with abstraction if we wish to be economical. The abstraction notation was introduced by Giuseppe Peano. Like the definite description operator, it applies to predicates and yields singular terms. Such terms may occur in yet further predicates, whence intricate nesting may ensue. Abstraction and membership are like inverses of each other. When Pa, the predication factors into a being a member of the set of Ps; Quine calls this the principle of abstraction. When a is a member of the set of Ps, membership and abstraction cancel out, and so Pa; this Quine calls concretion.

Comprehension says there is a set of all those things not identical with themselves (or a set of all unicorns), and extensionality says it is unique. This set is called the empty set, and it is denoted by $\emptyset$, which is not the Greek letter phi, but similar to the Danish and Norwegian slashed O. Some people who think of sets as somehow constituted out of, or dependent for their existence on, their elements have metaphysical qualms about the empty set. But an empty set need be no more troubling than an empty glass. Extensionality says that a set's members suffice to fix its identity, but this is neither to say the set is constituted from its members nor to say it depends for its existence on them. Besides, the hypothesis that there is an empty set has proved its utility time and again, and confirmation need not be cowed by metaphysical intuitions.

For any objects a and b, there is a unique set $\{a, b\}$ whose members are a and b. Since $\{a, b\}$ and $\{b, a\}$ have the same members, extensionality says they are identical. So $\{a, b\}$ is called the unordered pair of a and b. When a is b, their unordered pair is the set whose sole member is a; this is written $\{a\}$ and is called the unit set or singleton of a. If a is itself a set with none or many members, it will not have the same members as its singleton, so in general a should be distinguished from its singleton. (But in what might seem an excess of economic zeal, Quine favored identifying a non-set with its unit set, as he showed how to do consistently.)

The empty set and unordered pairs assure us some sets outright. There are also operations on sets that assure us their values given their arguments. The Boolean operations, named for George Boole, correspond to truth functions. Thus the union of a and b, written a ∪ b, is the set of all x such that x ∈ a or x ∈ b. (The notation "∪" is Peano's.) With ∅ and unit sets, repeated union gives us all finite sets. The intersection of a and b, written a ∩ b, is the set of all x such that x ∈ a and x ∈ b. (The notation "∩" is also Peano's.) The intersection of the set of all odd numbers and the set of all even numbers is the empty set. Such sets are called disjoint. Without the empty set, disjoint sets would have no intersection, and we could not form a ∩ b without checking that a and b meet; the convenience of always being able to form a ∩ b is an example of the utility of ∅. The complement of a, written variously whence we pick ā, is the ∅ of all things not in a. Complements, as we shall see, are a mark of naïveté, and sophistication sometimes favors differences, written a − b and explained as the set of all x such that x ∈ a but x ∉ b. (The ∈ with a stroke is denial of membership.)

In addition to Boolean operations, we also have the subset, or inclusion, relation. A set a is a subset of a set b, written a ⊆ b (like a softened less-or-equal sign), just in case all members of a are members of b. If b is also a subset of a, then they have the same members and so are identical. Note that when a ∈ b, then every member of {a} is a member of b, so {a} ⊆ b. Thereby may, but need not, hang a tale. Some people picture a layered world. On the ground floor, or layer 0, are the non-sets, the shoes and ships and so on. On layer 1 are the sets of things on layer 0. On layer 2 are either the sets of things on layer 1 (if, like Russell, you like your layers exclusive) or the things on layer 0 or layer 1 (if you like your layers cumulative). And so on for longer than you might expect. On this picture, Plato and everybody else is on layer 0, while the set of people and Plato's unit set are on layer 1. Then ∈ relates *across* layers (Plato is a member of his unit set and the set of people), while ⊆ relates *within* layers (the singleton of Plato is a subset of the set of people). It took a long, long time for us to learn to distinguish between ∈ and ⊆. The distinction was drawn clearly and driven home only in the nineteenth century. The premisses and conclusions of traditional syllogisms were either universal (All men are mortal) or particular (Some dogs are terriers). Singular premisses (Socrates is a man) were recognized, as in the old textbook inference from our universal and singular premisses to a singular conclusion (Socrates is mortal), but the effort to assimilate the singular to the universal or particular encouraged a confusion between ∈ and ⊆, as if Socrates were a tiny species.

The picture of layers helps distinguish between ∈ and ⊆, which is a virtue of it. Some people think it is the only right, or possible or coherent, way to picture the world. Maybe, but that view carries substantial commitments, so be wary of buying into it thoughtlessly. We will see larger issues later, but here is a smaller one. Consider propositions and self-reference. Russell (and probably Leibniz) thought of propositions as extensions of sentences as sets are extensions of predicates and as its denotation is the extension of a name. For example, the proposition that Socrates is bald would be the ordered pair <s, B> whose first member, s, is Socrates and whose second member, B, is the set of bald people. (We will get to ordered pairs very soon, but for now the important thing is that when a is different from b, the ordered pair <a, b> with a first and b second is a different thing from <b, a> with b first and a second.) This proposition <s, B> is true just in case s ∈ B, which opens a natural story about truth. Now consider a self-referential proposition like

This proposition can be expressed in eight words.

Let E be the set of propositions expressible in eight words, and let p be the proposition we are now considering. On Russell's conception, p is <p, E>, the doubling being the self-reference. We will soon construe ordered pairs as sets, and on the layered picture, an ordered pair will lie two layers above its members. On a layered picture, a set lies on a layer higher than its members, which would forbid self-referential propositions. But proposition p seems in order, indeed true, and we will later see more systematic reasons for reluctance to give up self-reference. It would not be shrewd to commit fully to the layered picture unreflectively, even if it is the conventional wisdom.

The set of tigers is the extension of the predicate "is a tiger." This predicate is unary (Latin) or monadic (Greek), both of which mean that it has one blank or empty space that on being filled with a singular term (like "Tony") yields a sentence. Each predicate has a number of blanks, filling all of which with singular terms yields a sentence. This number is called the predicate's polyadicity (Greek) or, much more rarely, its arity (Latin). The predicate "love" is binary (or dyadic) since it has two blanks for names, as in "Regina loved Søren," and "give" is ternary (or triadic) since it has three blanks, as in "The president gave the contract to his brother-in-law." The Greek and Latin of logicians give out and they speak instead of 5-adic (or 5-ary) predicates. (Some predicates, as in "Andrew united Bob, Curt, David, and Ed in a conspiracy," seem to lack a unique polyadicity, but they are rare.) In reckoning the polyadicity of a predicate in a sentence, one may count as many of the occurrences of singular terms as one wishes. For example, in

Richard gave the diamond to Elizabeth

one may count three singular terms filling the blanks in a ternary predicate, but one may count any two filling blanks in a more complex binary predicate, and one may count any one filling the blank in a yet more complex unary predicate. The logician is prescinding from grammatical roles (like direct or indirect object) and, as it were, counting several singular terms all as several subjects of a polyadic predicate.

The set of tigers is the extension of the monadic predicate "is a tiger." We would also like extensions for polyadic predicates. As tigers one by one fill out the extension of "is a tiger," we expect pairs to fill out the extension of a dynadic predicate like "loves." But we notice immediately that order matters. Regina seems to have been a normal person and to have loved Søren, but we owe Kierkegaard's works at least in part to his inability to make up his mind that he loved Regina. Unrequited love shows that the members of the extension of "loves" cannot be unordered pairs. We write ordered pairs with angle brackets, so the ordered pair whose first member is Regina and whose second is Søren is $\langle r, s \rangle$. This pair is in the extension of "loves," but $\langle s, r \rangle$ is not, so it had better turn out that $\langle s, r \rangle \neq \langle r, s \rangle$. This illustrates a central aspect of order: when $a \neq b$, $\langle a, b \rangle \neq \langle b, a \rangle$; order alone suffices to distinguish ordered pairs. More generally, $\langle a, b \rangle = \langle c, d \rangle$ if and only if $a = c$ and $b = d$ (while, by contrast, if $a = d$ and $b = c$, then $\{a, b\} = \{c, d\}$). This principle articulates what Tarski in the 1920s will call a material adequacy condition, that is, a condition an account of something (in Tarski's case truth, in ours, order) should meet to be adequate. In the 1910s, Norbert Wiener and Kazimierz Kuratowski each showed a way to explain the ordered pair in the primitive terms of set theory so as to satisfy the adequacy condition. (Quine said this work is a philosophical paradigm.)

We mostly follow Kuratowski, whose later account explains $\langle a, b \rangle$ as $\{\{a\}, \{a, b\}\}$. It would be a mistake to stare at this hoping for insight into order. Such insight as there is to be had was already articulated in the adequacy condition. Kuratowski's account is adequate (as is Wiener's different one) if it proves to satisfy the adequacy condition.

There is no enlightenment to be found in the proof that Kuratowski's account works, but students always ask to see a proof, so here goes. Suppose <a, b> = <c, d>. Then, by Kuratowski's account, {{a}, {a, b}} = {{c}, {c, d}}. Since {a} is a member of the set on the left, it is in the one on the right, so it is {c} or {c, d}. In the first case, a is c, while in the second both c and d are a. So in any case, a = c. Next we distinguish two cases. For the first, suppose a = b. Since {c, d} is in the second set, it is in the first, so it is {a} or {a, b}; if it is {a}, then d is a, which is b; while if it is {a, b}, then d is a or b, which are identical, so d is again b. Hence if a = b, b = d. So for our second case, suppose a ≠ b. If b = c, then since a = c, a = b, so since we're supposing a ≠ b, b ≠ c. Then b ∈ {c, d}, so since b ≠ c, b = d. Hence, in any case, b = d, as we were to show. This argument is a welter of unmemorable cases, so don't worry if your attention glazed over; what matters is that it works. Russell called Kuratowski's (and Wiener's) construction a trick.

Once we have ordered pairs, we may take an ordered triple <a, b, c> as <<a, b>, c>, an ordered pair whose first member is an ordered pair. An ordered quadruple <a, b, c, d> is <<a, b, c>, d>, and so on through all the ordered n-tuples. Then we may take the extension of an n-adic predicate to be a set of ordered n-tuples. We should work an example to fix ideas. The extension of the binary predicate "a is n years old at noon today" (where the blanks in the predicate are marked with the variables "a" and "n") is the set of ordered pairs <a, n> such that a is n years old at noon today. This one could also think of as (the noon today time slice of) the age relation. Let us focus on people: let P be the set of people (alive at noon today) and let N = {0, 1,...} be the set of all natural (i.e., non-negative, whole) numbers. The set of all ordered pairs <a, b> whose first member a is an element of P and whose second member b is an element of N is called the Cartesian or cross product of P and N. It is written P × N. It is called Cartesian in memory of rectangular Cartesian coordinates for the points on a Euclidian plane; it is called cross because if A has n members and B has k members, then A × B has n times k members (which hints at reconstructing arithmetic in set theory). A binary relation between people (alive at noon today) and natural numbers is any old subset of P × N. A relation between members of A and members of B is a subset of A × B. Age is a relation between people and numbers; age (at noon today) is

{<p, n> | p ∈ P and n ∈ N and p is n years old at noon today}, which is a subset of P × N. An n-ary relation among members of n sets $A_1, A_2, \ldots, A_n$ is a subset of $A_1 \times A_2 \times \ldots \times A_n$, the set of ordered n-tuples whose first member is in A_1, whose second is in $A_2, \ldots$, and whose n^{th} is in A_n.

Of course, a relation may hold between some members of a set like P and others. Such a relation is a subset of P × P. For example, parenthood (at noon today) is a subset of the set of all ordered pairs <a, b> of people (alive at noon today). We use exponential notation for cross products whose factors are identical: P^2 is P × P; P^3 is P × P × P; and so on. Let R be the parenthood relation just mentioned. Let W be the set of all women (alive at noon today). We might want to restrict the first members of a relation S to elements of a set A; we would write S ↿ A for the set of pairs <x, y> in S such that x ∈ A. Then the motherhood relation is R ↿ W. To restrict the second members of pairs in S to A, we write S ↾ A. Then the daughterhood relation is R ↾ W. To restrict both to A, we write S ↑ A, so R ↑ W is the mother–daughter relation.

Aristotle's syllogistic logic is geared for unary predicates. It had long been recognized that there are arguments whose conclusions clearly follow from their premises but where syllogistic cannot certify these arguments because the arguments' success turns on polyadic predicates. Here is an example from Augustus De Morgan in the nineteenth century:

All horses are animals.
Hence, all heads of horses are heads of animals,

where the dyadic predicate "x is a head of y" is crucial. It was not until the nineteenth century that a systematic account of relations began.

In addition to De Morgan, Charles Sanders Peirce and Ernst Schröder were central in the articulation of relations. Notation like R ↑ W is just one fruit of their work. The fact that ordered pairs were worked out set theoretically pretty much at the end of the articulation of relations shows how hard it was to command a clear view of relations.

In the seventeenth century, Newton and Leibniz focused our attention on functions. The path of a particle in, for simplicity, the plane rather than space is a continuous curve, and using Cartesian coordinates the ordinates of points along the curve can often be given as mathematical functions of the abscissae. The speed of this particle at a point along its path will be given by the derivative of such a function, and conversely, the path is given by the integral of the particle's velocity; anyone who has done some calculus knows that differentiation and integration are the meat and potatoes of Newton's and Leibniz's calculus. At school we were all programmed in algorithms for computing the sums and products of natural numbers, and addition and multiplication are also functions. Such education inclines us to think of functions in terms of ways of calculating the output, or value, of a function at its inputs, or arguments. A somewhat less intentional image of a function pictures it as a bunch of arrows, one *from* each argument *to* the value of the function for that argument; the collection of its arguments is called the function's domain, while the collection in which its values lie is called the function's range, so on this picture a function is a collection of arrows arcing from its domain into its range.

As late as Kant at the end of the eighteenth century, curves were the leading image of functions. Through the nineteenth century, people worked out an extensional conception of a function. The calculus is infinitary, and the geometrical imagination trusted since Euclid began to go awry in the infinities of the calculus. Much of nineteenth-century mathematics was given over to a process called the arithmetization of analysis, which is what calculus grows up into. The aim of this process is to replace geometry, especially in analysis, with the mathematics of number, or later, set theory. An extensional conception of a function arises by starting from the picture of a bunch of arrows arcing from its domain to its range, and then discarding everything except the ordered pairs whose first members are the arguments and whose second are the values; only input and output remain, and we don't worry about how what goes in becomes what comes out.

We write $f : A \rightarrow B$ to mean that f is a function whose domain is a set A and whose range is a set B. But we have just seen that on the extensional conception this means that f is a set of ordered pairs whose first members lie in A and whose second lie in B; that is, it is a relation between members of A and B. There are two special conditions that such a relation must meet in order to be a function. First, for every member a of A, there is at least one member b of B such that <a, b> is in f, that is, f relates a to b. Second, for each a in A, there is at most one b in B such that <a, b> is in f. In the crochets of logic, the first condition is that

$$(\forall a)(a \in A \rightarrow (\exists b)(b \in B \land < a, b> \in f)),$$

while the second is that

$$(\forall a)(a \in A \rightarrow (\forall b)(\forall c)((b \in B \land c \in B \land$$
$$<a, b> \in f \land <a, c> \in f) \rightarrow a = c)),$$

both of which use only notions built up by logic from primitives of set theory. Motherhood, for example, is not a function from women to people, since, first, some women have no children, while, second, others have several. But age (at noon today) is a function, since (at noon today) everyone is one and only one number of years old.

Once we have the extensional conception of a function, we revert from <a, b> ∈ f to the customary notation f(a) = b; the existence and uniqueness conditions underpin the singular term f(a). Like relations, functions have polyadicities. Age is unary, while addition and multiplication are binary. Remember that a unary function is a binary relation (between the domain and the range). Addition and multiplication are said to commute (or be Abelian, for the nineteenth-century Norwegian mathematician Niels Abel) because a + b = b + a. But exponentiation does not commute, since $2^3 = 8$ but $3^2 = 9$. So the domain of a binary function should be a set of *ordered* pairs. So in general the domain of an n-ary function will be an n-fold Cartesian product $A_1 \times \ldots \times A_n$, and if the range is A_{n+1}, the function is a set of ordered (n+1)-tuples $<a_1,\ldots, a_n, a_{n+1}>$ such that $a_1 \in A_1,\ldots, a_n \in A_n$ and $a_{n+1} \in A_{n+1}$ (that meet the existence and uniqueness conditions). Remember that an n-ary function is an (n+1)-ary relation; addition, which is a binary function, is the extension of the ternary predicate "x + y = z" and so a ternary relation.

A relation is a function only if each argument bears the relation to a unique value; each of us has (at noon today) a unique age in years. But a number may be the age of many different people; there are lots of five-year-olds. To rule out functions sending different arguments to the same value we require the function to be one-to-one (or injective). This means that when f : A → B and a and b are different arguments in A to f, then f(a) is different from f(b). Each natural number n has a unique successor, so the relation of a number to its successor is a function; moreover, different numbers have different successors, so the successor function is one-to-one. When a function is one-to-one, it never happens that different arguments collapse into the same value, so there are at least as many things in the range as in the domain. This fails with the age function since it is not one-to-one; there are fewer than two hundred ages but billions of people.

A relation is a function only if for each argument there is a value to which the argument bears the relation; for each of us there is a number that is our age. But a number may be the age of no one; there are no 2,000-year-old men. To rule out functions sending no argument to some member of the range we require the function to be onto (or surjective). This means that when f : A → B and b is in B, then there is an a in A such that f(a) = b. The successor function is not onto, since 0 is a natural number that is not the successor of any natural number; among the integers positive, zero, and negative, however, successor is onto. When a function is onto, it never happens that a member of the range is missed out by the function, so there are at most as many things in the range as in the domain (and there could be fewer if the function were onto but not one-to-one). Our mortality prevents age from being onto. Every wife has a unique husband, but there are also bachelors, so the husband-of function from wives to men is not onto, and there are more men than wives.

A set A has as many members as a set B just in case there is a function that maps A one-to-one onto B. Such a function is sometimes called one–one correspondence, and f : A $\xrightarrow[\text{onto}]{1\text{–}1}$ B means that f is a one–one correspondence from A to B. Having seen one–one correspondences built up from scratch, you know that no notion of number was smuggled in surreptitiously; in particular, though a beginner might worry about the number one in one-to-one, you have seen it is about identity rather than number. Besides, it makes sense that a grasp of the as-many-as relation need not presuppose number, since it is clear that there are as many brains as spines (or as vertebrates) even when you are not clear on how many vertebrates there are.

It is an immense virtue of a number-free understanding of the as-many-as relation that it allows us to make sense of as-many-as questions about collections too big to count using 0, 1, 2, and so on. It allows us to compare infinite sets. It was not Cantor but Richard Dedekind who articulated the infinity of a set as its being in one–one correspondence with one of its proper subsets. (A proper subset of A is a subset of it to which some member of A does not belong.) Galileo observed the natural one–one correspondence between the natural numbers and their proper part, the even numbers. This looks like

$$0 \to 0$$
$$1 \to 2$$
$$2 \to 4$$

and so on; if you like arithmetical specifications, let f(n) = 2n. An axiom in Euclid says that the whole is always greater than any of its (proper) parts, and Galileo appealed to Euclid's authority to infer from the correspondence that there is no completed infinite totality of the natural (or even) numbers. Leibniz extended Galileo's reasoning to conclude that there are no infinite numbers either. Dedekind was inverting this reasoning. Like Cantor, he is committed to infinite sets (or systems, as he called them). So he concludes that Euclid's axiom is false, despite millennia of idolatry as *a priori*, and takes being the same size as a proper part as the hallmark of infinity. His courage inaugurates a grasp of the infinite per se.

A set with as many members as there are natural numbers is said to be countably (or sometimes denumerably) infinite. The even numbers are countable. (Some use "countable" to mean finite or countably infinite, so one needs to check how it is meant in a given text.) There are countably many integers. Interleave the integers and count them thus:

$$0 \to 0$$
$$1 \to 1$$
$$-1 \to 2$$
$$2 \to 3$$
$$-2 \to 4$$
$$\vdots \to \vdots$$

We don't have to, but we can arithmetize this picture by sending an even number 2n to n, and an odd number 2n + 1 to –n. Between any two rational numbers a and b there is a third, $\frac{(a+b)}{2}$; $\frac{3}{2}$ lies between 1 and 2. The rationals are thus said to be dense, and density can make one think there are more rationals than naturals. Cantor showed this is not so. Make a table of the non-negative ratios (we can put the negatives back in later by interleaving as we did with the integers). In the top row put the ratios with 0 in the numerator, in the next those with 1 in the numerator, and so on.

$\frac{0}{1}$	$\frac{0}{2}$	$\frac{0}{3}$	...
$\frac{1}{1}$	$\frac{1}{2}$	$\frac{1}{3}$	...
$\frac{2}{1}$	$\frac{2}{2}$	$\frac{2}{3}$	...
$\vdots$	$\vdots$	$\vdots$	

(We don't allow division by zero. This is not an arbitrary fiat among schoolteachers. The point is rather that $\frac{a}{b}$ should be the unique c such that a is b × c. But if a is positive and b is zero, there is no such c, while if a is zero, then any c will do. So division will have a unique value and be a function only if we don't divide by zero.) We next stitch the beads in this box together along the lines indicated by these arrows.

$$\frac{0}{1} \rightarrow \frac{0}{2} \quad \frac{0}{3} \rightarrow \cdots$$

$$\frac{1}{1} \quad \frac{1}{2} \quad \frac{1}{3} \cdots$$

$$\frac{2}{1} \quad \frac{2}{2} \quad \frac{2}{3} \cdots$$

$$\vdots \qquad \vdots \qquad \vdots$$

Grab the thread at end $\frac{0}{1}$ and jerk it out straight and then count the beads as follows, eliminating duplicates of earlier beads.

$$0 \quad 1 \quad 2 \quad \tfrac{1}{2} \; \cdots$$

$$0 \quad 1 \quad 2 \quad 3 \; \cdots$$

(We could arithmetize this correspondence too, but we need not.) A short line segment has as many points as a long. Put them parallel with their left ends on a perpendicular.

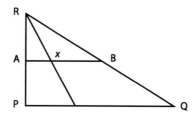

The line joining B and Q meets the perpendicular at a point R. If we map any point x on AB to the point where the line through R and x meet PQ, we have a one–one correspondence.

Cantor's great discovery is that some infinite sets are not the same in size. Each real number from zero up to but not including one has a decimal whose integer part is always zero, so we will ignore it. Suppose there were a one–one correspondence between these decimals and the naturals.

$$0 \leftrightarrow .a_1\, a_2\, a_3\, \cdots$$

$$1 \leftrightarrow .b_1\, b_2\, b_3 \cdots$$

$$2 \leftrightarrow .c_1\, c_2\, c_3\, \cdots$$

$$\vdots \qquad \vdots$$

where each of the as, bs, and so on is a digit, that is, among 0, 1,..., 9 (except that in order to have unique decimals we rule out those eventually constantly 9, so .250... is allowed but not .249...). We form the decimal for a real somewhere from 0 up to but not including 1 by going down the diagonal indicated by the arrows. Its first digit, α_1, is 2 if a_1 is 1, but 1 if a_1 is not 1. Its second digit, α_2, is 2 if b_2 is 1, but 1 if b_2 is not 1. And so on. The general idea is that if the natural k is assigned to the decimal $.n_1n_2n_3...$, then α_{k+1} is 1 if n_{k+1} is 2, but 2 if n_{k+1} is 1. Let α be the real whose decimal is $.\alpha_1\alpha_2\alpha_3...$. Then α differs from the real assigned to 0 in its first digit, from the real assigned to 1 in its second digit, and so on. This α is not a value of our supposed correspondence. We have shown that no function maps the naturals onto the reals from zero up to but not including one. This argument of Cantor's is called a diagonal argument after how we described α. Since then there have been many diagonal arguments, but Cantor's was the first.

If any infinite set had as many members as any other, the arithmetic of infinity would be boring. Cantor's proof that there are more reals than naturals hints that it is not. But first we should explain "more." A set A has fewer members than or as many members as B just in case A has as many members as a subset of B, or equivalently, some function maps A one–one into B. (If you noticed that we sometimes omit "to" from "one-to-one," recall Emerson's apothegm that a foolish consistency is the hobgoblin of little minds.) Then B has more members than A just in case A has fewer members than or as many members as B, but it is not true that B has fewer members than or as many members as A. This is equivalent to requiring that A can be mapped one–one into B but A cannot be mapped onto B (or B cannot be mapped one–one into A).

Cantor proved that there are many more than two different infinite sizes. For any set x, the power set of x, written P(x), is the set of all subsets of x. Here we want to be careful about the distinction between members and subsets. So to illustrate, let x = {a, b} be a set with two members. The subsets of x are $\emptyset$ (since vacuously any member of $\emptyset$ is a member of x), the singletons of a and b, and x. So P(x) has four members. If x is a finite set with n members, then there are 2^n subsets of x, since for each of the n members there are 2 possibilities, in or out of the subset. It is an easy induction on natural numbers to show that 2^n is always greater than n ($2^0 = 1 > 0$, and if $2^n > n$, $2^{n+1} = 2 \times 2^n = 2^n + 2^n > n + 2^n \geq n + 1$; it is natural that anything to the zero power is one, for since $\dfrac{a^5}{a^3} = \dfrac{a \times a \times a \times a \times a}{a \times a \times a} = a \times a$, $\dfrac{a^n}{a^k} = a^{n-k}$, and then $a^0 = \dfrac{a^n}{a^n} = 1$).

Cantor's theorem says that for any set x, its power set P(x) has more members than x. First we have to show that we can map x one–one into its power set. We do so by sending each member of x to its unit set: this is a function, and it is one-to-one because by extensionality distinct things have distinct singletons. (In our example we send a to {a} and b to {b}.) Next we show that no function maps x onto P(x). So suppose for reductio that f does map x onto P(x). Let y be the set of all members z of x such that z ∉ f(z). We show that y is not a value of f. But y is Cantor's big idea here, so we should pause to digest it. Suppose in our example f were

$$x: \quad a \quad b$$

$$f: \quad \searrow \quad \searrow$$

$$P(x): \quad \varnothing \quad \{a\} \; \{b\} \quad x$$

Then y is the set of things in x *not* members of what is at the end of their f arrows. In this case both a and b are, so y is ∅, and presto majesto, f does not hit ∅. Let's try again. This time

$$x: \quad a \quad b$$

$$f: \quad \downarrow \qquad \searrow$$

$$P(x): \quad \varnothing \quad \{a\} \quad \{b\} \quad x$$

Here a is not in what's at the end of its f arrow, so a is in y, but b is in what's at the end of its f arrow, so b is not in y. Hence y is {a}, and again f does not hit {a}. Once more

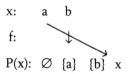

$$P(x): \quad \varnothing \quad \{a\} \quad \{b\} \quad x$$

Check that only b is in y, so y is {b}, and f does not hit {b}. Try other examples yourself. In general, suppose f did hit y, so for some z, f(z) = y. Either z ∈ y or z ∉ y. If z ∈ y, then since y = f(z), z ∈ f(z), so z ∉ y by how y is defined. If z ∉ y, then since y = f(z), z ∉ f(z), and then z ∈ y again by how y is defined. So both possibilities are impossible. Hence there is no map f taking x onto P(x), so P(x) is bigger than x. (If the members of x were a, b, c,..., consider the array of conditions

$a \in f(a)$ $a \in f(b)$ $a \in f(c)$ ...

$b \in f(a)$ $b \in f(b)$ $b \in f(c)$ ...

$c \in f(a)$ $c \in f(b)$ $c \in f(c)$ ...
  $\vdots$ $\vdots$ $\vdots$

Go down the diagonal indicated by the arrows taking negations thus

$a \notin f(a)$ $b \notin f(b)$ $c \notin f(c)$ ...

Then y is the set of members of x meeting these negative conditions. Cantor's proof that P(x) is bigger than x is also a diagonal argument.)

Now let A_0 be an infinite set, say the set of all natural numbers. Let A_1 be $P(A_0)$. Let A_2 be $P(A_1)$, and so on, so $A_{n+1} = P(A_n)$. Then for every n, A_n is an infinite set bigger than A_k for any k less than n. So we have as many infinite sets, no two of the same size, as there are natural numbers; we have an infinity of different infinite sizes. But there is more. Let A be the union of A_0, A_1, and so on. If A is not bigger than all of them, it has fewer members than or as many members as some A_n. (This should seem obvious, but it calls for an interesting argument.) Then it has fewer members than A_{n+1}. But A_{n+1} is one of the sets unioned to form A, so it is a subset of A and thus A_{n+1} is not bigger than A. So A is another infinite set, this one bigger than all of A_0, A_1, and so on. Don't stop now. Let B_0 be A, iterate power set through the naturals again, and again union all the B_n. Mixing power set and union in this way, a plethora of infinite sets, no two of the same size, emerges.

There is a natural correspondence between the reals from zero up to but not including one and the sets of positive integers. (The successor function from n to n + 1 is a one–one correspondence between the naturals and the positive integers, so there is a one–one correspondence between sets of naturals and sets of positive integers.) A decimal is fixed by a function whose arguments are positive integers and whose values are digits, that is, among 0, 1,…, 9, except that we exclude those f eventually constantly 9. Then for any real r from zero up to but not including one, there is a unique f of this sort such that

$$r = \sum_{n=1}^{\infty} \frac{f(n)}{10^n}.$$

But there is nothing magic here about 10 and the digits 0, 1,..., 9. Suppose we took 2 and the digits 0, 1. Then excluding those f eventually constantly one, for any real r from zero up to but not including one, there is a unique f of the new binary sort such that

$$r = \sum_{n=1}^{\infty} \frac{f(n)}{2^n}.$$

For any set S of positive integers, let c_s be the function (from positive integers to $\{0, 1\}$) such that for any positive integer k, $c_s(k) = 0$ if $k \in S$ but $c_s(k) = 1$ if $k \notin S$. In effect, taking 0 as truth and 1 as falsehood, $c_s(k) = 0$ says it is true that k is in S, while $c_s(k) = 1$ says it is false that k is in S; c_s is called the characteristic function of S. For any set S of positive integers, let

$$r = \sum_{n=1}^{\infty} \frac{c_s(n)}{2^n}.$$

This fixes a one–one correspondence between sets of positive integers and reals from zero up to but not including one; S goes to the binary real whose n^{th} digit says whether n is in S. This correspondence shows a way Cantor's theorem generalizes his proof that there are more reals than natural numbers.

Lines, planes, and space are continua. The idea is that a continuum has no gaps. An old tradition distinguishes so firmly between the continuous and the discrete that, while of course accepting that a point may lie on a line, it insists that a continuum is not granular and so does not consist of points. But Descartes founded analytic geometry on the assumption that there is a one–one order-preserving correspondence between the points on a line and the real numbers. "Order-preserving" means that if f is the correspondence and point p on the line lies to the left of point q, then the number f(p) is less than the number f(q); the left-to-right relation is reflected in the less-to-greater relation. Actually, it is perhaps an anachronism to state Descartes's assumption in terms of the real numbers. If pressed, Descartes might have explained his coordinates geometrically as lengths (and so numbers) of segments. The real numbers were not isolated from geometry until the arithmetization of analysis during the nineteenth century. But once the real numbers were liberated from geometry, good conscience recognized analytic geometry as centered in the assumed correspondence just mentioned. The range of the correspondence is the set of points on the line, and since the nineteenth century we have ceased to see much difference between a line and the set of points on it. It has become customary, especially in discussions focused on size, to call the reals and the power set of the natural numbers continua too. (The function that sends x to $\frac{x}{(x-1)}$ shows that there are as many non-negative reals as reals from zero up to but not including one.)

Cantor proved that there are more reals than natural numbers. This leaves open whether there is a set with more members than there are natural numbers but fewer members than there are reals; is there a size between those of the naturals and the reals? Cantor conjectured that there is not; this has come to be called the continuum hypothesis. There is also a generalized continuum hypothesis conjecturing that for no infinite set A is there a set larger than A but smaller than P(A). In 1900 the German mathematician David Hilbert, addressing the powers of mathematics that then were, put the continuum hypothesis at the head of the agenda for twentieth-century mathematics. In the 1930s, Kurt Gödel proved that if prevailing set theories are consistent, the continuum hypothesis is not refutable in them, and in the 1960s, Paul Cohen proved that if prevailing set theories are consistent, neither is the continuum hypothesis provable from them. Gerald Sacks called the generalized continuum hypothesis a rock of undecidability. Hugh Woodin has an elaborate program for winkling out plausible axioms to settle (probably by refuting) the continuum hypothesis.

So far we have talked about fewer, as many as, and more, relations that suggest number, but we have not considered how to get from such relations to numbers. Cantor himself thought that we abstract a number as something common to all and only those sets any one of which has as many members as any other. The notion of such abstracting has a very long history, but that does not make it clear. Sometimes it sounds perceptual, as if we saw a single thing common to all these sets, but it feels silly to look for the number five both in the digits on one's left hand and in the digits on one's right. Sometimes it sounds more intellectual, as if we infer to the existence of a single thing common to all these sets. Then one wants to see the logic of the inference.

The irony is that set theory lays out this logic (and Frege, unlike Cantor, uses it). The as-many-as relation is called an equivalence relation, which means that it is reflexive, symmetric, and transitive. So next we explain these terms. Recall that a (binary) relation is a set of ordered pairs. Let R be a binary relation. The field of R is the set of all those things that either bear R to something or to which something bears R, so the field of the parent-of relation is the set of living things, while the field of the gravitational attraction relation is all massive bodies. To get the idea of an equivalence relation, keep in mind examples like as-tall-as and as-hot-as. (In Welsh, in addition to the three standard degrees absolute [hot], comparative [hotter], and superlative [hottest], there is a fourth [as hot as].) A relation R is reflexive just in case every member of its field bears R to itself; each of us is as old as himself. R is symmetric just in case for any a and b in its field, when a bears R to b, b bears R to a; if a is as old as b, b is as old as a. R is transitive just in case for any a, b, and c in its field, when a bears R to b and b bears R to c, then a bears R to c. It should be clear that our as-many-as relation has all three properties and so is an equivalence relation.

Now suppose A is a set. By a partition of A we mean a collection P of subsets of A with two features: first, for any member a of A there is a set X in P such that a is in X; and, second, different members of P are disjoint. You might liken a partition to a tiling of A that covers it completely (first feature) without any tiles overlapping (second feature). Let A be a set and let R be an equivalence relation whose field is A. For example, A might be the set of people, and R, the as-old-as relation. We will see ages as members of a partition of A reflecting R. For any member a of A, let [a] be the set of all b in A such that a bears R to b. Then [a] is called the equivalence class of a. If several equivalence relations with field A are in play, we say [a] is the equivalence class of a under R and sometimes write $[a]_R$ to make the connection with R explicit. Let P be the set of all these equivalence classes, one for each a in A. We will show that P is a partition of A. To establish the first feature, note that since R is reflexive, each a in A bears R to itself, so a is always in [a], which is a member of P. The reflexivity of an equivalence relation reappears as the first feature (full coverage) of its corresponding partition. Next, suppose that [a] and [b] are different members of P. Since they are sets, this means that some c in A is in one but not the other. That can happen in two ways; we will look at one and you can do the other to fix ideas. So suppose c is in [a] but not in [b]. By how we defined equivalence classes, this means that

(1) a bears R to c

and

(2) b does not bear R to c.

We have to show that [a] and [b] are disjoint, that is, no d in A is in both. So suppose for reductio that some d is. Then

(3) a bears R to d

and

(4) b bears R to d.

Since R is symmetric, it follows from (3) that

(5) d bears R to a.

Then since R is transitive, it follows from (4) and (5) that

(6) b bears R to a

and from (6) and (1) that

(7) b bears R to c.

Since (7) contradicts (2), we have reached an absurdum. Symmetry and transitivity in the equivalence relation reappear as the second feature (nonoverlap) of its corresponding partition. An equivalence relation is said to induce the corresponding partition of its field. Conversely, if we start from a partition P of a set A and define a relation R with field A such that for a and b in A, a bears R to b just in case a and b are both in some member of the partition, then we can show R is an equivalence relation. Equivalence relations and partitions are different ways to package the same information.

In *Our Knowledge of the External World*, Russell urges a principle he says could as well be called the principle that dispenses with abstraction. The idea is that we give up metaphysical worries about what, say, the age five-years-old might be and instead go with the set of all people as old as any given five-year-old. He sometimes calls this replacing inferring to entities by logical construction, but that is an excess of enthusiasm; sets are entities to whose existence we infer. But equivalence classes give us a uniform and articulate setting for ages, weights, heights, and so on. Frege thought they would also do for numbers (though our setting is not his). Frege and Russell founded a constructional tradition in philosophy that includes Carnap, Goodman, David Lewis, and others. But the core, and perhaps sum total, of that tradition is that one object the bearers of an equivalence relation have in common is their equivalence class.

When A has as many members as B, what they have in common is their number of members. So (roughly) Frege and Russell took the number of members of A as the set of all B with as many members as A.[1] (This is rough because Frege did not think of himself as working with sets and because Russell layered his sets, so his numbers are not unique.) An object is a number just in case for some A it is the number of members of A. Then 0 is the number of members of ∅, 1 is the number of members of {0}, and 2 is the number of members of {0, 1}. A number n is less than or equal to a number k, n ≤ k, just in case there are A and B such that n is the number of As, k is the number of Bs, and there are fewer As than Bs or as many As as Bs. Define a function s so that when n is a number, s(n) is the number of numbers k ≤ n. If we follow Frege and Russell and focus on familiar numbers beginning with the natural numbers, we may isolate them as the members of all sets A such that 0 ∈ A and s(n) ∈ A when n ∈ A. Among the naturals, s(n) is the number of members of {0, 1,..., n} and is, as one expects, n + 1. But if n is the number of members of an infinite set, then s(n) = n; Cantor's generalized continuum hypothesis conjectures that the power set of an infinite set is of the next, or successor, infinite size.

These numbers are cardinals. As Frege puts it, a cardinal number is an answer to the question how many. There are (or would be if Greek mythology were true) twelve Muses. This does not depend on the Muses being arranged in some special order; there are twelve Muses even if Erato (lyric poetry) has no priority over Clio (history) nor Clio over Erato. But if we are going to count the Muses, we pick a first Muse to match with "one," a second to match with "two," and so on up to "twelve." When we count Muses, either we pick Erato before Clio or we pick Clio before Erato, and while we can do so without favoritism, we must pick one first. The terms "first," "second," "third," and so on reflect positions in an ordering; this is the central idea behind ordinal (rather than cardinal) numbers.

It is set theory, and more specifically the theory of relations, that articulates order. Let R be a binary relation with field A. We say that R

---

[1] In *Labyrinth of Thought*, 2nd ed. (Basel: Birkhäuser, 2007), 87, José Ferreirós says that by the 1850s, Dedekind was using equivalence classes, and that Gauss and Riemann had done so earlier. But when Dedekind came to define the natural numbers (*Essays on the Theory of Numbers* [New York: Dover, 1963], 68, article 73), he did so in terms of abstraction, like Cantor, not in terms of equivalence classes, like Frege.

partially orders A just in case R is irreflexive and transitive. Irreflexivity means that nothing in A bears R to itself. The ancestor-of relation partially orders a family tree, and the order is partial because siblings (and spouses) are incomparable in the ordering. The proper-subset-of relation partially orders a set's power set, and the order is partial because when the set is {a, b}, its subsets {a} and {b} are incomparable in the ordering. A partial ordering is total just in case any two members of its field are comparable, that is, either a is R to b, or b is R to a, or a is b. (These alternatives are exclusive.) So the less-than relation totally orders the natural numbers, and with larger fields "it" totally orders the integers, rationals, and reals. (The "it" is in scare quotes here because each of these relations is from the extensional point of view an extension of, and so different from, the orders mentioned earlier.)

There are no infinite descending sequences of natural numbers, for if the sequence starts with n, then since there are only n natural numbers less than n, there aren't enough naturals to fill out an infinite sequence descending from n. Another way to put this is that any nonempty set of natural numbers has a least member. A total order well-orders its field just in case any nonempty subset B of its field has an R-least member, that is, there is a b in B such that for any a in B different from b, b bears R to a. So less-than well-orders the natural numbers. But it does not well-order the integers, since there is no least negative number, nor does it well-order the rationals or the reals, since there is neither a least positive rational nor a least positive real.

Let R be a binary relation with field A and let S be a binary relation with field B. Let f be a one–one correspondence mapping A onto B. Then we say f preserves R (in S) just in case for any x and y in A, x bears R to y just in case f(x) bears S to f(y). When we count the Muses, we lay out an ordering of the Muses and a correspondence of them with the numerals from "one" to "twelve" that preserves the usual ordering of the numerals in our ordering of the Muses, and the ancestor-of relation between family members is preserved between their names in the family tree. Relations are said to be similar when there is a one–one correspondence between their fields that preserves one relation in the other. Similarity is an equivalence relation, so it partitions (binary) relations into equivalence classes, and the equivalence class of a relation under similarity is called its type.

Cantor named the types of some total orders. He used ω for the type of less-than on the natural numbers. He used $^*\omega$ for the type of less-than on the negative integers. We can add types of the total orders by concatenating an order of the first type with a copy of the second chosen so they have disjoint fields. So he used $^*\omega + \omega$ for the type of less-than on the integers. An order of type $^*\omega + \omega$ has no end points, while an order of type $\omega + {}^*\omega$ has a terminus at either end, so such an addition does not commute. Cantor used η for the order type of less-than on the rationals, a dense total order without end points of a countable set. The names $^*\omega$ and η are no longer much used in mathematics, but a philosopher might do well to remember them.

An ordinal number is the order type of a well-ordering. So ω, the type of less-than on the naturals, is an ordinal number because less-than well-orders the naturals. It is the smallest infinite – or, as Cantor put it, transfinite – ordinal number. But "smallest" makes sense here only if we have an ordering of the ordinal numbers. We say that a well (or even just total) order R with field A is an initial segment of a well (or total) order S with field B just in case A is a subset of B, R is S restricted to A (which we called S ↑ A earlier) and when a ∈ A and bSa for some b ∈ B, then b ∈ A (so R omits nothing S-below anything in its field; R has no S-gaps). Your pre-Revolutionary ancestors are an initial segment of your ancestors, and the naturals less than 100 are an initial segment of the naturals, though the even numbers are not. R with field A is a proper initial segment of S with field B just in case it is an initial segment and A is a proper subset of B. An ordinal number α is less than an ordinal number β just in case there is a well-order R of type α with field A, a well-order S of type β with field B, and R with A is similar to a proper initial segment of S with B.

The less-than relation, $<$, well-orders the ordinals. Cantor's arguments here are a bit sketchy, so we will fill in some blanks. We do so using principles that come with well-orderings. Let R be a well-order with field A. Suppose that whenever all b in A such that b is R to a are in a set C, then a is in C too; then all members of A are in C. For otherwise let a be the R-least member of A not in C; then everything in A R-below a is in C, so by the supposition a is in C after all. This is proof by R-induction. We can also explain expressions by R-induction. Suppose that we state conditions on whether a member a of A, for example, satisfies a predicate in terms of how satisfaction of the predicate distributes across a's R-predecessors (if a has no R-predecessors, we state outright whether a satisfies the predicate); then we have satisfaction conditions for the predicate over all of A. For otherwise let a be the R-least member of A on which the predicate is unsettled; then it is settled on everything R-below a, so by the supposition it is settled on a after all.

Less-than partially orders the ordinals. Suppose $\alpha < \beta$ and $\beta < \gamma$. Then there is a well-order R with field A of type α, a well-order S with field B of type β, and a well-order T with field C of type γ, and there are functions f and g such that f shows R similar to a proper initial segment of S and g shows S similar to a proper initial segment of T. For any a in A, let $h(a) = g(f(a))$; h is called the composition of g on f. Then h shows R similar to a proper initial segment of T, so $\alpha < \gamma$. Next we show that < is irreflexive. For any set A, let i_A be the function whose value on any a in A is a. We show that for any well-order R with field A, i_A is the only function that shows R similar to an initial segment of R. For any member a of A, let A_1 be the set of members of A R-below a, let R_1 be $R \upharpoonright A_1$, and suppose that i_{A_1} is the only function that shows R_1 similar to an initial segment of R_1. To extend i_{A_1} to a similarity with domain $A_1 \cup \{a\}$, we have to assign to a a member of $A - A_1$, and to avoid gaps, the only choice is a itself. So if A_2 is $A_1 \cup \{a\}$ and R_2 is $R \upharpoonright A_2$, then i_{A_2} is the only function that shows R_2 similar to an initial segment of R_2. Our claim follows by R-induction. If $\alpha < \alpha$, a well-order of type α is similar to a proper initial segment of itself, and this is ruled out by the claim just established. We can show that only one function can show a well-order similar to an initial segment of another. It is perhaps worth noting that while an infinite set is always the same size as many of its proper subsets, the only initial segment of a well-order to which it is similar is itself, which is not a proper initial segment.

To show that less-than totally orders the ordinals, we show that $\alpha < \beta$, or $\alpha = \beta$, or $\beta < \alpha$. Let R be a well-order with field A of type α and let S be a well-order with field B of type β. To get started, suppose first that A is empty. Then the empty set shows A similar to the empty initial segment of S. So if B is empty, $\alpha = \beta$, while if B is not empty, $\alpha < \beta$. Likewise, if B is empty, $\alpha = \beta$. So if either A or B is empty, α and β are comparable. If neither A nor B is empty, suppose we have a binary relation $F \subseteq A \times B$ that is a similarity between an initial segment R_1 with field A_1 of R and an initial segment S_1 with field B_1 of S. If $A_1 = A$ and B_1 is a proper subset of B, then $\alpha < \beta$. If A_1 is a proper subset of A and $B_1 = B$, then $\beta < \alpha$. Otherwise A_1 is a proper subset of A, and B_1, of B. Let a be the R-least member of $A - A_1$, and b, of $B - B_1$. Then $F \cup \{<a, b>\}$ is a similarity between the initial segment of R with field $A \cup \{a_1\}$ and the initial segment of S with field $B \cup \{b_1\}$. We thus define by R and S inductions a relation F that is either a similarity between R and S, so $\alpha = \beta$, or between R and a proper initial segment of S, so $\alpha < \beta$, or between S and a proper initial segment of R, so $\beta < \alpha$. (Showing cardinal numbers comparable is more demanding.)

To show that less-than well-orders the ordinals, let A be a nonempty set of ordinals. We must show there is a least ordinal in A. If not, there is a sequence $\alpha_1, \alpha_2, \ldots$ of ordinals in A such that for all n, $\alpha_n > \alpha_{n+1}$. Then for each n there is a well-order R_n with field A_n of type α_n such that R_{n+1} is similar to a proper initial segment of R_n. Taking compositions of these similarities, it follows that for each n there is a well-order R_n with field A_n such that for all n, R_{n+1} is a proper initial segment of R_n and of R_1 where A_{n+1} are nonempty. For each n, let a_n be the R_1-least member of $A_n - A_{n+1}$. Then the set $\{a_1, a_2, \ldots\}$ of all these a_n is a nonempty subset of A_1 with no R_1-least member, which is impossible since R_1 well-orders A_1.

Every ordinal is the type of an initial segment of the ordinals. In particular, α is the type of $< \upharpoonright \{\beta \mid \beta < \alpha\}$. (If R is a relation, the field of $R \upharpoonright A$ is always A, so we need not mention the field of $R \upharpoonright A$ separately. Indeed, since the field of a relation is always uniquely determined by the relation, we never need mention a relation's field separately. But it is often easier to follow what is going on if we do so.) For any well-order R with field A we may sort members of A into three kinds. A member of A may have no R-predecessors; there are never two members of A of this kind. Otherwise a member a of A has R-predecessors. One sort of this kind has an immediately predecessor, so there is a b that is R to a but there is no c such that b is R to c and c is R to a. Another sort has predecessors, but no immediate predecessor, so there is a b that is R to a and for any b R to a there is a c such that b is R to c and c is R to a. Members of A of the first kind are R-successors, and members of A of the second kind are R-limits. It follows by R-induction that if a member of A with no R-predecessors is in a set C, if the R-successor of a member of C is in C, and if R-limits are in C when all their R-predecessors are in C, then all members of A are in C. Among ordinals, 0 is the type of $< \upharpoonright \varnothing$. Since $< \upharpoonright \varnothing$ has no proper initial segments, there is no ordinal $\alpha < 0$. So $\{\alpha \mid \alpha < 0\} = \varnothing$, and thus 0 is the type of $< \upharpoonright \{\beta \mid \beta < 0\}$, as expected. For any ordinal α let $s(\alpha)$ be the type of $< \upharpoonright \{\beta \mid \beta \leq \alpha\}$. Suppose α is the type of $< \upharpoonright \{\beta \mid \beta < \alpha\}$. The relation $< \upharpoonright \{\beta \mid \beta < \alpha\}$ is a proper initial segment of $< \upharpoonright \{\beta \mid \beta \leq \alpha\}$. Thus $\alpha < s(\alpha)$, which separates s on cardinals from s on ordinals. No proper initial segment of $< \upharpoonright \{\beta \mid \beta \leq \alpha\}$ properly extends $< \upharpoonright \{\beta \mid \beta < \alpha\}$. Thus α is the immediate predecessor of $s(\alpha)$, and $s(\alpha)$ is the successor of α. Moreover, $s(\alpha)$ is the type of $< \upharpoonright \{\beta \mid \beta < s(\alpha)\}$, as expected. Now suppose λ is a limit ordinal and that for all $b < \lambda$, β

is the type of $< \uparrow \{\gamma \mid \gamma < \beta\}$. $< \uparrow \{\beta \mid \beta < \gamma\}$ properly extends $< \uparrow \{\gamma \mid \gamma < \beta\}$ for all $\beta < \lambda$, but no proper initial segment of $< \uparrow \{\beta \mid \beta < \lambda\}$ properly extends $< \uparrow \{\gamma \mid \gamma < \beta\}$ for all $\beta < \lambda$. So the type of $< \uparrow \{\beta \mid \beta < \lambda\}$ is the least type greater than the types of $< \uparrow \{\gamma \mid \gamma < \beta\}$ for all $\beta < \lambda$, and since each of these types is β, the type of $< \uparrow \{\beta \mid \beta < \lambda\}$ is λ, as expected. So, as we said, for any α, α is the type of $< \uparrow \{\beta \mid \beta < \alpha\}$. In particular, each ordinal is greater than every member of the initial segment of the ordinals of which it is the type.

The finite ordinals are the members of all sets A such that the ordinal $0 \in A$ and $s(\alpha) \in A$ when $\alpha \in A$. Let F be the set of finite ordinals. Then ω, the least transfinite ordinal, is the type of $< \uparrow F$, and the transfinite ordinals are the ordinals $\alpha \geq \omega$. Let N be the set of natural numbers. Set $f(\omega) = N$. When $s(\alpha)$ is transfinite, let $f(s(\alpha))$ be $P(f(\alpha))$ and when λ is a limit, let $f(\lambda)$ be the union of the $f(\beta)$ for $\beta < \lambda$. Then when α is transfinite, $f(\alpha)$ is an infinite set, and when $\alpha < \beta$, $f(\beta)$ is larger than $f(\alpha)$. For each transfinite α, let c_α be the cardinal number of $f(\alpha)$. Since we can map the transfinite ordinals one–one into the infinite cardinals, there are at least as many infinite cardinals and transfinite ordinals. To show the converse, we use a new principle, the axiom of choice. This says that if A is a set of nonempty sets, there is a function f with domain A such that for any x in A, $f(x) \in x$. The idea is that f picks from each x in A a member of x; f is called a choice function for A. When A is finite, we can prove it has a choice function, so we need a new axiom only when A is infinite, and then only when the members of A are opaque to us. Russell makes this point by saying that when A is an infinite set of pairs of shoes, we can pick the left one uniformly, but when A is an infinite set of pairs of socks, we need the axiom of choice.[2] It follows from the axiom of choice that every set can be well-ordered, that is, for any set A there is a well-order whose field is A. Let P be the set of nonempty subsets of A, and let f be a choice function for P. Suppose we have a one–one function g whose domain is an initial segment S of the ordinals and whose values lie in A, and let B be the range of g on S. If B is a proper subset of A, let $g' = g \cup \{<\alpha, b>\}$ where α is the type of $< \uparrow S$ and $b = f(A - B)$, while if $B = A$, let $g' = g$. Then g' is a one–one function

[2] Russell's less felicitous version occurs in "On Some Difficulties in the Theory of Transfinite Numbers and Order Types," reprinted in his *Essays in Analysis*, ed. Douglas Lackey (New York: George Braziller, 1973), 157–58. This essay was first published in 1905. His more felicitous version (using socks) occurs in his *Introduction to Mathematical Philosophy* (London: George Allen & Unwin, 1919), 126.

whose domain is the initial segment $A \cup \{\alpha\}$ of the ordinals and whose values lie in A. By induction there is a one–one g from an initial segment s of the ordinals and whose range is A. Since g maps S one–one onto A, h = {<a, α> | g(α) = a} maps A one–one onto S. Let R be {<a, b> | a, b ∈ A, and h(a) < h(b)}. Then R well-orders A. (To go the other way, let A be a set of nonempty sets, and let U be the union of the sets in A. If R well-orders U, for any x ∈ A let f(x) be the R-least member of x. So if any set can be well-ordered, the axiom of choice follows.) For any infinite cardinal c, let S be a set in c (and so of size c), let R be a well-order of S, and let α_c be the type of R. If c is less than k, a well-order of a set of size c is similar to a proper initial segment of a well-order of a set of size k, so $\alpha_c < \alpha_k$. So we can map the infinite cardinals one–one into the transfinite ordinals. Hence there are as many infinite cardinals as transfinite ordinals.

We can also that show there are at least as many ordinals as cardinals without choice. For any cardinal c, let L_c be the set of ordinals with fewer than c predecessors. Then L_c is a segment, and if we let α_c be the type of $< \uparrow L_c$, then sending c to α_c maps the cardinals one–one into the ordinals. But it was as well to have been introduced to choice, and, as we shall see, we have already used it elsewhere.

Let us also sketch maps between cardinals and ordinals that will have later reflections. For any cardinal c, let L_c be the set of ordinals with fewer than c predecessors. L_c is a segment. If we let α_c be the type of $< \uparrow L_c$, then α_c is the least ordinal with c predecessors, and sending c to α_c maps the cardinals one–one into the ordinals. To go the other way, first let S_c be the set of ordinals with c or fewer predecessors. Then S_c is a segment, and if we let v_c be the type of $< \uparrow S_c$, then v_c is the least ordinal with more than c predecessors. So if we let σ(c) be the cardinal of the set of predecessors of v_c, then σ(c) is the least cardinal greater than c. (So the generalized continuum hypothesis says that if c is infinite, the power set of L_c has σ(c) members.) Let z be the cardinal of ∅ and let ζ be the type of $< \uparrow ∅$. Let f(ζ) = z, and f(s(α)) = σ(f(α)); when λ is a limit, for each β < λ, let $A_β$ be the segment of ordinals less than $\alpha_{f(β)}$, and let f(λ) be the cardinal of $\cup_{β<λ}A_β$. Then f maps the ordinals one–one into the cardinals. John von Neumann used α_c to rethink the cardinals in the aftermath of the paradoxes.

When a function maps a set A one–one into a set B and another function maps B one–one into A, there is a function that maps A one–one onto B. This claim is sometimes called the Cantor–Bernstein–Schroeder theorem. All its proofs are interesting, so it is not obvious or trivial. We use the axiom of choice to show that cardinal numbers are comparable, that is, that for any cardinals c and k, c is less than k or c is k or k is less than c. To do so, let A be of size c and B be of size k. Use choice to get an R that well-orders A and an S that well-orders B. Our proof that ordinals are comparable yields a relation $F \subseteq A \times B$ that is either a similarity of R to an initial segment of S, so c is less than or equal to k, or a similarity of S to an initial segment of R, so k is less than or equal to c. This shows c and k comparable. We have often assumed cardinals comparable without saying so. The first time was when we said that if the union of the set of naturals, its power set, and so on is not larger than all these sets, it is smaller than or the same size as one of them. It follows from the comparability of cardinals that any set can be well-ordered, which yields the axiom of choice. For any set x let h(x) be the set of ordinals α such that $\{\beta \mid \beta < \alpha\}$ can be mapped one–one into x. Then h(x) is a segment of ordinals. Let α be the type of $< \restriction h(x)$. Since α is greater than all members of h(x), $\alpha \notin h(x)$. So by comparability there is an f that maps x one–one into $\{\beta \mid \beta < \alpha\}$. Let R be $\{<a, b> \mid a, b \in x,$ and $f(a) < f(b)\}$. Then R well-orders x.

David Hilbert called Cantor's realm of infinite cardinals and transfinite ordinals a paradise. Such praise might have made Cantor nervous (though he was seven years dead when Hilbert gave it). Cantor distinguished three kinds of infinity: potential, actual, and absolute. By the potential infinite Cantor meant variables. He wrote long before Frege's scrupulous syntax sank in, and by variables he meant things that vary, like lengths. But, he said, variables always have ranges of variation (like non-negative reals for lengths), such ranges are sets, and an infinite set is an actual infinity; the potential infinite presupposes the actual. Another way to imagine a potential infinity might be a sequence $u_1, u_2, \ldots$ of possible worlds each accessible to all its successors, all containing only finitely many inhabitants, but each containing more inhabitants than its predecessors; then no possible world is infinite, but however many things there might be, there could be yet more. Cantor would grant all this, and observe that it requires an actual infinity of possible worlds. What we might call Cantor's thesis, that there won't be a potential infinity of any sort unless there is also an actual infinity of some sort, deserves more attention than it has received. Cantor said that only God is absolutely infinite. He was anxious that his set theory not poach on absolute preserves, and many of the theologians he cited on the infinity of divinity were Catholic (like Origen, Augustine, Aquinas, and Frs. Magnon, Saguens, and Libertore). For Hilbert to call it a paradise might have seemed to threaten his theological discretion. But most philosophers find the infinite so irresistible that they are likely to agree with Hilbert.

But there was a serpent in Eden, and there were three in Cantor's paradise. Three paradoxes arise in Cantor's naïve set theory. The first to be published appeared in 1897 and is due to Cesare Burali-Forti. Let On be the set of ordinals guaranteed by comprehension as the extension of "is an ordinal." Then < well-orders On, so let Ω be the type of < ↾ On. On the one hand, since Ω is the type of the segment On, Ω is greater than all ordinals in On, but on the other hand, Ω is an ordinal, so it is a member of On. Then $\Omega < \Omega$, which is impossible since < is irreflexive. The second was first described in a letter Cantor wrote to Dedekind in 1895. Let U be the universe, the set of everything, guaranteed by comprehension as the extension of "is self-identical." On the one hand, by Cantor's theorem, U is strictly smaller than its power set P(U), but on the other hand, everything in P(U) is self-identical and so a member of U, and then P(U) is smaller than or the same size as U. The third struck Russell while thinking about diagonal arguments, and he sent Frege a letter describing it in 1902. Some sets, like the set of all lions, are not members of themselves (since it is not a lion), while others, like the set of all sets, are members of themselves. Let R be the set of all sets of the first sort, that is, not members of themselves. R is the extension of "$x \notin x$" guaranteed by comprehension. Then any set is a member of R just in case it is not a member of itself. So R is a member of R just in case R is not a member of R, which is a contradiction.

When Hilbert spoke of Cantor's paradise, what he said was that no one shall be able to drive us from the paradise that Cantor created for us. That trope might well have made Cantor very nervous of Rome's judgment. But Hilbert's point was that Cantor's theory of sets had for the first time made systematic sense of the infinite per se, so even if in its naïve state that theory was beset by paradox, still, what it reveals is such a joy that we will insist on sophisticating it to avoid paradox while retaining its insight into the infinite. But if naïveté is often unreflective, sophistication deliberates.

TWO

✦

Die Urwahrheiten

We are all post-Kantians, not perhaps because we believe the space in which we live and move and have our being is created by the action of our senses, but because Kant set an agenda for philosophy that we are still working through. Kant says (at 260 in his *Prolegomenon to Any Future Metaphysics*) that it was Hume who first interrupted the dogmatic slumbers into which Leibniz and Wolff had lulled him. Hume had argued that nothing in the idea of causation can guarantee that for each event there exists an earlier one that caused it; ideas do not guarantee that anything answers to them. But if it is not a relation of ideas that every event have a cause, then, if it is true, it can only be a matter of fact, and so known, if known at all, by experience. This conclusion was an affront to the dogma that the principle of sufficient reason is known and justified independently of any appeal to experience.

Kant composed his agenda for overcoming skepticism in terms that endured. Assume the anachronistically labeled traditional analysis according to which a person A knows that p (where "p" marks a blank to be filled by an indicative sentence) just in case A believes that p, it is true that p, and A is justified in believing that p. The point of the justification clause is that for A to know that p, his belief's being true should not be just a lucky guess. The focus of epistemology, or theory of knowledge, has usually been more on the nature of justification than on details in the analysis of knowledge. Kant divides knowledge into two sorts that differ according to how the belief is justified. He calls knowledge *a posteriori* when it is justified, even in part, by appeal to sense experience. Knowledge is *a priori* when it is indeed knowledge but not *a posteriori*, that is, when it is justified but not justified even in part by sense experience. Note two points here. First, the account of *a priori* knowledge is wholly negative; it says only how *a priori* knowledge is not justified. This raises the question how *a priori* knowledge is justified, and a refinement of that question will become the first agendum of Kant's critical philosophy. Second, while nearly all parties agree that some knowledge is justified by sense experience, it may not be equally evident that there is *a priori* knowledge. This issue was on the philosophical agenda before Kant, and is still there two centuries after his death (in 1804). Kant himself thought we know *a priori* that for every event there is a prior event that caused it, and he worked hard to elaborate this thought. That principle was, he thought, necessary for natural sciences like physics, and while much of the physicist's knowledge of nature is *a posteriori*, he could not have that *a posteriori* knowledge unless he knew *a priori* that every event has a cause. But Kant also believed that there are whole, systematic bodies of knowledge that are entirely known *a priori*. The two leading examples were logic and mathematics. We will return in a moment to what Kant thought logic was. From the Greeks to Kant, mathematics was first and foremost geometry. Geometry was not just Euclid's system of figures in the plane, but also the solid geometry of the space in which we live and move and have our being. Kant is quite explicit that there is only one space; the idea of lots of spaces is later and thoroughly un-Kantian. In his *Elements*, Euclid's Book IX is about number theory, like the infinity of primes. But the Greeks thought of number geometrically, and the mathematics of number achieves independence from geometry only in the arithmetization of analysis during the nineteenth century. It was central for Kant that our geometrical knowledge is *a priori*.

In addition to distinguishing between *a posteriori* and *a priori* knowledge, Kant also distinguished between synthetic and analytic judgments. Analyticity in Kant's system plays a role like that of relations of ideas in Hume's (or trifling propositions in Locke's). Leibniz seems to have been the first modern philosopher to focus on sentence-sized units that he called propositions. (Among ancients, the Stoics had sentence-sized units, but the Empiricists among the moderns focused on word-sized units like ideas.) These have played at least three roles. Stuff like grass and colors like green are neither true nor false, but it is true that grass is green. One role of propositions is as what is true or false; since Frege, this has also been put as being the bearers of the truth values (truth and falsity). Second, many mental states are attributed to people using a verb (thinks, hopes, fears, believes) completed with "that" followed by a sentence. Around 1900, G. E. Moore and Bertrand Russell described such mental states as attitudes (like thinking, hoping, fearing, believing) toward a proposition expressed by the sentence in the verb's complement. (Such verbs are still called verbs of propositional attitude even by philosophers who do not take propositions very seriously.) A second role of propositions is as objects of the propositional attitudes. Kant speaks more of judgments than of propositions; for him the objects of the attitudes seem themselves to be mental, while for Moore and Russell (and perhaps Leibniz) propositions were more like abstract entities expressed (as the jargon goes) by sentences in much the same way as numbers are abstract objects named by numerals. The third role of propositions is as meanings of sentences, but this does not become prominent until the twentieth century when Russell inadvertently starts the philosophy of language by declaring that some sentences (like "Everything is identical with itself") that seem utterly in order are meaningless and express no proposition. There were pieces now counted as philosophy of language published before the theory of types, but it was Russell's outrageousness that got the rhubarb going. In addition to Russell's platonic propositions and Kant's mental judgments, around 1930 Alfred Tarski took the bearers of the truth values to be linguistic items, sentences. What is true is articulated into subpropositional bits, like a subject (grass) and a predicate (green), whose relation makes it true. Sentences wear on their inscribed faces an articulation into subsentential units, words; and the structures of either platonic propositions or mental judgments always seem to be read back into them without argument from the sentences used to express these propositions or judgments. Around 1950, John Austin, observing that one and the same sentence (like "I am hungry") can be true at one time but false at another, or true in one man's mouth but false in another's, said that it is not sentences but statements, acts performed by speakers using sentences, that are the bearers of the truth values. Around 1970, Donald Davidson noted that by adding places in a truth predicate for context, like speaker and time, we could accommodate Austin's observation and still follow Tarski in predicating truth of sentences. It is still not settled whether to favor platonic propositions, mental judgments, or sentences.

One way to approach analyticity is through examples. An example of Moore's is the proposition that all bachelors are unmarried. Someone might make an extensive survey asking bachelors whether they are married, and, on tallying his results, advance the hypothesis that all bachelors are unmarried. But this would be a waste of effort because, so the story goes, being unmarried is part of what it means to be a bachelor, so understanding the proposition that all bachelors are unmarried suffices to justify belief in it. It seems plausible that there is some sort of difference between the proposition that all bachelors are unmarried and the proposition that all bachelors are more prosperous than husbands. Controversy sets in when we try to articulate the difference. Kant gave two (or perhaps three) accounts of analyticity. On one, the predicate of an analytic judgment is contained in its subject. Note three (or perhaps four) points about this account. First, it assumes that all judgments are of subject–predicate form. The assumption is very old and persisted into the twentieth century. It distorts Leibniz's system, and it marks how long and hard the struggle was to make sense of relations and (polyadic) quantification. Whatever grammarians say (and the assumption is enlightening in understanding grammar), Russell was excited by the revelation in the logic forming around him of other forms, especially quantificational, of proposition. We follow Russell, so Kant's assumption seems too narrow to us. Second, the distinction between subjects and predicates is a grammatical distinction at home in discussions of sentence structure. Kant is reading this structure back into the structure of judgments. Mental states, or mental objects of propositional attitudes, may have anatomies, but we should know by what sort of dissection these anatomies are revealed, and why there is a coincidence between the anatomy of judgments and the grammar of sentences. Third, Kant's trope of a predicate contained in a subject is clearly a metaphor; if the predicate of a written sentence were literally contained in its subject, the sentence would be illegible. The metaphor leaves us without a literal account of analyticity. (Fourth, Kant says that analytic judgments are not ampliative, and some wonder whether this is another account of analyticity. But the idea seems to be that a judgment is ampliative when its predicate adds something new not already in its subject, so not being ampliative would amount to the predicate being contained in the subject, which was the first account.) As for Kant's other account, he says (at B190) that the truth of an analytic judgment can always be adequately known in accordance with the principle of contradiction. The somewhat odd phrase "be adequately known in accordance with" seems to make best sense if taken as "be adequately justified from." As the Kneales observe, the principle of contradiction would be better named the principle of noncontradiction: no contradiction is true.[1] It is probably best to read "the principle of contradiction" as a synecdoche for the laws, or at least the basic laws, of logic. The

---

[1] William Kneale and Martha Kneale, *The Development of Logic* (Oxford: Clarendon Press, 1962), 367n2.

question, then, is to what we may appeal in justifying from laws of logic. If we may appeal to anything we know, then anything we know will turn out to be analytic, which is not what Kant wants. If we may appeal only to logic, then only logic will be analytic, since from logic only logic follows by logic. Nowadays we count as logic quantification theory perhaps with identity. The judgment that all bachelors are unmarried is represented in that system by the form: All Fs are Gs. Taking Fs as numbers and Gs as even numbers, this form comes out false, so it is not a law of logic. So taking justification as purely logical would make judgments analytic on the first account, not analytic on the second. We can reverse this result if in justifying from laws of logic we may appeal to logic and judgments analytic according to the first account. It is important to note that on the second account it turns out that, and may even be analytic that, logic is analytic. If the two accounts are to agree at least in extension, logic should then be analytic on the first account. A logical example Kant often cites is the law of identity, which he puts as A is A, and here he might have thought the predicate coincides with the subject, giving us analyticity on the first account. This reasoning may seem a bit peculiar to us. We expect the identity predicate to be flanked by singular terms (like proper names, definite descriptions, or demonstrative phases) or variables of quantification, but we do not expect predicates to be either singular terms or variables of quantification. But Kant wrote at the low-water mark in the history of logic. He thought that logic was over, finished, and complete in Aristotle's theory of the syllogism. This is to neglect both Stoic propositional logic and the scholastic logical achievements swept away in the enthusiasm of Renaissance humanism. Supposedly the judgments in syllogisms were either universal, as in "All men are mortal," or particular, as in "Some men are mortal," or singular, as in "Socrates is a man." But syllogistic had no way of treating singular terms as distinct from general terms or predicates; all its "variables" marked places thought of as predicate positions. Socrates might be thought of as a tiny little species. Then, instead of "Socrates is a man" saying that an individual is a member of a set or species, it says that one species is a subset of, or is included in, another. (It is not until the nineteenth century that we get clear about the distinction between the membership and subset relations.) In this way, probably the most famous textbook example of an inference –

All men are mortal
Socrates is a man
Therefore, Socrates is mortal –

is assimilated to the syllogisms the Schoolmen nicknamed Barbara: if all As are Bs and all Bs are Cs, then all As are Cs. (The subject and predicate of Barbara herself are not so easy to make out.)

For much of the twentieth century, the quick gloss on analyticity was that a sentence (proposition, judgment) is analytic if it is true by virtue of the meanings of the words in the sentence (used to express the proposition or judgment). This gloss needs to be taken with at least a grain of salt. For one thing, while a word like "bachelor" in Moore's example has a stereotyped definition ("unmarried adult man") on which dictionaries generally agree, many words, like "if," "all," "are," and "and," are at best assigned synonyms or examples in dictionaries rather than analyzed into simpler components. If we try to update Kant by saying Barbara is true by virtue of the meanings of these words like "all" and "are," we should admit that we have no access independent of Barbara to the meanings of these words from which we could deduce Barbara without begging the question; if we could tell a story about the meanings of "all" and "are," Barbara would be the judge of whether the story were true. But the lump of salt is that analyticity is at best a mode of justification, not of truth. It is an ancient and honorable view that truth is correspondence to fact; in order for a sentence to be true, the world should be as the sentence says it is. Tarski showed us how to do without facts here. Consider a formal language; call it L. In addition to logical signs (for truth functional connectives, punctuation, and quantification including variables), L may have extralogical signs – individual constants (or dummy names), predicate signs (each with a positive integer attached giving the predicate's polyadicity), and function signs (also with polyadicities) – but it must have at least one predicate if it is to have any formulae. To give an interpretation or reference-scheme for L, Tarski has us start with a domain D. He builds a theory of interpretations, or what he called models, by drawing on set theory, so he requires that D be a set. It is an enormous convenience to assume D is not empty, but if we wish, we may allow D to be empty. To interpret a constant of L in D, assign it a member of D to act as its denotation. To interpret a n-ary predicate letter of L, assign it a set of ordered n-tuples of members of F to act as its extension. To interpret an n-ary function letter of L, assign it a function whose value for each ordered n-tuple of members of D is a member of D. Tarski then shows how to reduce truth for sentences of L to the references under an interpretation of L. For example, if S is a simple subject–predicate sentence in which a unary predicate P is predicated of a constant a and the scheme assigns d from D to a and subset A of D to P, then S is true just in case a is a member of A; the sentence "Socrates is bald" is true just in case Socrates is a member of the set of bald men. The reduction gets hairier for sentences of L of other forms, but the simple subject–predicate case illustrates the idea. Given a sentence, or even discourse, in a natural language, it can often be factored into syntax and a reference scheme. First, there is often an obvious formal language in which to represent the sentence's form (or a range of such languages, depending on how much of the sentence's structure we want to represent). With "All bachelors are unmarried," the obvious choice is a language with two unary predicates F and G, making

$$(\forall x)(Fx \to Gx)$$

the form of the sentence. Then there is often a salient reference scheme. Let D be the set of people, and assign to F the set of people who are bachelors and to C the set of unmarried people. Then (telescoping Tarski's details) our form is true under this scheme just in case all bachelors are unmarried, so we have recovered our original sentence and shown that our factorization of it was adequate. When we can factor a sentence into a form and a reference scheme, the reference scheme gives us a generally reliable way of saying what the sentence is about (thus shielding us from, for example, the sort of dust Nelson Goodman raises in the two papers in section VI of *Problems and Projects*). For our present purposes the thing to see is that

All bachelors are unmarried
All bachelors are richer than husbands
All bachelors are bachelors

are each just as much about bachelors as the other two. Each is true just in case the flesh-and-bone bachelors out there in the world are, respectively, unmarried, richer than husbands, and bachelors. Truth is univocal, which is why the conjunction of two truths about subject matters however disparate is nonetheless true. What, if anything, is distinctive about claims attracting the label "analyticity" is at most epistemic, a matter of justification rather than a distinctive variety of truth. The proposition that bachelors are unmarried would then be analytic if knowledge of the meanings of the words used to express the proposition sufficed without experience of its subject matter to justify belief in the judgment. That account would explain the doctrine that analytic truths can be known *a priori*. (Those who wanted mathematics to turn out analytic and so true by meaning rather than correspondence to fact wanted thereby to dodge the metaphysics of an abstract subject matter for mathematics. They were confused.)

Among truths, Kant contrasts those that are analytic with the rest, which he calls synthetic. Analyticity wears the trousers (as Austin put it) in this distinction, as being *a posteriori* did in its; such truths get a positive account, and their opposites are defined by negation. It is usually difficult to settle interesting examples (which is why we focused on Moore's). Kant said it is synthetic that all bodies are heavy. The example would be plausible if we were reluctant to build gravitational attraction into the meaning of the word "body." But were we, for example, to want to deny that a sphere of radius one yard in a region of space utterly devoid of matter is a body, we might want to insist that a body be ponderable, and then weight is at hand. Kant said it is analytic that all bodies are extended. This is an odd example for Kant to give. Like any eighteenth-century intellectual, Kant admired Newton. Indeed, part of Kant's objective was to secure certainty for much of Newton's physics, and Kant was not innocent of that science. Anyone familiar with Newton knows how much he makes of mass-points. Did Kant mean to exile the mass-points from the bodies by definition? Is he defining mass-points out of existence? (Kant seems to have been aware of such issues and to have addressed them in *The Metaphysical Foundations of Natural Science*.) Respect for the Cartesian doctrine that extension is the essence of matter is one thing, but Newton thoroughly denies that Cartesian doctrine; for him mass is central to matter. Here analyticity merely confuses the issues.

With two binary distinctions, we get four compounds. Kant ruled out *a posteriori* knowledge of analytic truths. He may have thought that anyone seeking empirical evidence for an analytic judgment did not understand the judgment and so would not acquire knowledge of it. This seems to assume a transparency of meaning that ill accords with the opacity of whether it is analytic that all bodies are extended but synthetic that all bodies are heavy. Besides, it seems clear that a door-to-door survey of bachelors would provide evidence that they are unmarried even if there is an easier way to justify the claim; meaning does not prescribe justification. Synthetic *a posteriori* knowledge would include most of the natural science, the physics, astronomy, and chemistry, emerging in Kant's time. Since such knowledge is justified by experience, we have at least the beginnings of a story about how such science is known. But, as noted earlier, since *a priori* knowledge is picked out by how it is not justified, there is a question about how it is justified.

Kant thought that logic is known *a priori* but is analytic, and so on our gloss is justified by the meanings of the logical particles central in stating its laws. At the low-water mark in the history of logic, that opinion was perhaps more plausible than after the revival of logic beginning in the nineteenth century.

Kant's focus was on *a priori* knowledge of synthetic truths. Such truths are not justified by experience, nor are they justified from the meanings of the words used to state them, so how are they known? How, Kant asks, is synthetic *a priori* knowledge possible? This question is the pretext for Kant's critical philosophy. But it has purchase only if there is synthetic *a priori* knowledge. To appreciate an example, controversy about which goes back a way, we make a third distinction, this time between necessary and contingent truths. People usually do not read for a long time standing up, so you are probably not standing as you read this. If so, it is true that you are not standing. But you could have been, so that truth is contingent. You are also identical with yourself, and that is not something you could fail to be, so that is a necessary truth. The contingent truths could have been otherwise, but the necessary ones could not. Leibniz thought that our actual world is only one world among a vast range of other merely possible worlds: a necessary truth is true in all possible worlds; a possible truth, in at least one. At B3 in the first *Critique*, Kant says that experience teaches us that a thing is so and so, but not that it cannot be otherwise. In the ways we can see color and shape, or feel shape and texture, we have no experience of necessity or (nonactual) possibility, only of actuality. To expand slightly, perception is by its nature causal,[2] and causality does not hold between what is actual and what is merely possible, so we have no experience of what is going on in other possible worlds, and thus modal knowledge (knowledge of what is necessary or merely possible) is not *a posteriori*; Kant thought that knowledge of necessity is *a priori*.[3] The standard example is that nothing could be red all over

---

[2] Cf. H. P. Grice, "The Causal Theory of Perception," reprinted in part in *Perceiving, Sensing, and Knowing*, ed. Robert J. Swartz (Garden City, N.Y.: Doubleday Anchor, 1965), 438–72, and W. D. Hart, *The Engines of the Soul* (Cambridge: Cambridge University Press, 1988; paperback ed. 2009), 54 ff.

[3] In *Naming and Necessity* (Cambridge, Mass.: Harvard University Press, 1980), Saul A. Kripke observed that we can sometimes infer a necessary truth from two premisses, one known *a posteriori*, so if (as we said) *a priori* knowledge rules out any justification by experience, then some necessary truths are known *a posteriori*. Fair enough; these examples Kant missed out, but even in them the necessity in the conclusion comes from the premiss known *a priori*, which vindicates Kant somewhat.

and green all over at the same time and place. That these colors exclude
each other does seem to be a necessary truth; in general, determinants
(for example, being six feet tall and being seven feet tall) of a determinable (for example, height) exclude one another necessarily. We cannot
imagine an object having both, and the imagination is the royal road to
knowledge of possibility and necessity. Granted that it is necessary that
nothing is at once red all over and green all over, knowledge of it would
be *a priori*. But, the story continues, the colors red and green are simple and basic enough that no definitions of their names in more basic
terms are available, so there are no definitions from which to show this
necessity analytic. It is then a synthetic necessity known *a priori*. This
example has been much discussed, and no definitions of the names of
the colors that would show it analytic have been generally accepted.[4]
On the other hand, it bucks the trend in most twentieth-century analytic philosophy that necessity is our creature, that there is no necessity
out there in nature independent of us.

That simple determinants of the same determinable exclude one
another necessarily yields a relatively scattered fund of examples, so
if that were the only synthetic *a priori* knowledge, it would have been
less front and center on the post-Kantian philosophical agenda. But
Kant thought that mathematics is all of it synthetic *a priori*, and that
would be a large and systematic example. Mathematicians do not look
to perform experiments on triangles or prime numbers, nor do they
make expeditions to examine exotic ones; they look to sit around and
think, and what could be more *a priori*? Kant says that truths of pure
mathematics carry with them necessity, which cannot be derived from
experience. It is indeed an ancient and honorable view that all the
truths of pure mathematics are necessary, so if necessity can be known
only *a priori*, the necessity of pure mathematics would be so known.
But Kant seems to mean that the necessity of a mathematical truth is
inseparable from that truth, as if there were no difference between there

[4] See, for example, Arthur Pap, "Logical Nonsense," *Philosophy and Phenomenological Research* 9 (1948): 262–83; Pap, "Are All Necessary Propositions Analytic?" *Philosophy Review* 50 (1949): 299–320; Pap, *Elements of Analytic Philosophy* (New York: Macmillan, 1949), chap. 16b; Hilary Putnam, "Reds, Greens, and Logical Analysis," *Philosophical Review* 65 (1956): 206–17; Pap, "Once More: Colors and the Synthetic A Priori," *Philosophical Review* 66 (1957): 94–99; Putnam, "Red and Green All Over Again: A Rejoinder to Arthur Pap," *Philosophical Review* 66 (1957): 100–03. An earlier discussion occurs in Russell, *The Principles of Mathematics* (London: George Allen & Unwin, 1903; 2nd ed. 1937), sect. 440.

being exactly five regular solids and its being necessary that there are exactly five regular solids. In that case, mathematical knowledge would be modal knowledge, so if modality is known *a priori*, so is mathematics. He argues that the mathematics of number is synthetic from the example that 7 + 5 = 12. He says that the concept of the sum of 7 and 5 contains nothing save the union of the two numbers into one, and in this no thought is being taken as to what that single number may be which combines both. Instead, we must go outside the concepts of 7, 5, and addition and call in examples like intuitions of fingers or points to see the number 12 emerge. Perhaps children do first learn that 7 + 5 = 12 by imagining fingers or points in ways at which Kant here hints. But our grasp of meaning or concepts seems too shaky to settle whether in so doing they are or are not going outside the concepts of 7, 5, and addition.

But Kant could give a better argument that much of pure mathematics is synthetic. As we saw at the outset of this chapter, when Hume woke Kant from his dogmatic slumbers, it was by convincing him that no existence proposition (for example, for every event there exists a prior event that caused it) is analytic. In Hume's terms we would say that existence is always a matter of fact, never a relation of ideas. Hume appeals to this principle in giving uncharacteristically short shrift in Part IX of the *Dialogues Concerning Natural Religion* to analytic arguments like Anselm's for the existence of God. You cannot make things exist just by how you mean terms purporting to denote them. The thesis that no existence proposition is analytic is one of the few constants in philosophical consciences. Note next that there are many existence claims in mathematics: witness the infinity of primes, the five regular solids, and the undecidable propositions of *Principia Mathematica* and related systems. Just about any axiomatization of a branch of mathematics includes some existence axioms. It would follow that some mathematical truths are synthetic, so granting that they are known *a priori*, mathematics would provide a fund of synthetic *a priori* knowledge. The central question for Kant's critical philosophy is how synthetic *a priori* knowledge, whether in geometry or sufficient reason (every event has a cause), is possible.

Kant died in 1804, and eighty years later Frege published *The Foundations of Arithmetic*. Though it was hardly noticed at the time, it is to this day perhaps the single best book ever written in the philosophy of mathematics. It was a philosophical aim of Frege's to undermine part of Kant's critical agenda. He agreed with Kant that geometry is synthetic *a priori* (though it is not clear that he thought space transcendentally ideal). But he would argue that the mathematics of number is analytic. (This project assumes a split between geometry and the mathematics of number. Even as late as Kant's time, a Greek geometric conception of number prevailed, and Kant might have had difficulty understanding Frege's project. But, as Frege notes, the arithmetization of analysis, a major endeavor of nineteenth-century mathematics, had severed geometry and the mathematics of number. Going the other way, one of Hilbert's aims in *The Foundations of Geometry* was to eliminate number [as measure of lengths and angles] from geometry.) Frege's argument would take over from Kant the premiss that logic is analytic. The bulk of his effort would go into showing that the mathematics of number is reducible to logic, that is, that the primitive terms of the mathematics of number are definable in logical terms and that the laws of number are deducible from these definitions and the laws of logic. Other philosophers have made claims of reducibility, that is, that such and suches (like values) are nothing but so and soes (like desires), but Frege wrote out in detail chapter and verse of his reduction. In doing so he began a constructional tradition in analytic philosophy that includes Russell, Carnap, Goodman, and David Lewis. Frege's thesis that the mathematics of number is reducible to logic may be called logicism (of a narrower sort). From it and the premiss that logic is analytic, it follows that the mathematics of number is analytic, which also may be called logicism (of a broader sort). Logicism is meant to deny Kant a datum.

Frege states his understanding (in 1884) of analyticity and the *a priori* in article 3 of *Foundations*. In a footnote he says he does not mean to assign a new sense to these terms, but only to state accurately what earlier writers, Kant in particular, have meant by them. This is a stretch. Frege says that the distinctions between *a priori* and *a posteriori*, analytic and synthetic, concern not the content of the judgment but the ground for making the judgment. Part of Frege's purpose is to liberate the inquiry from psychology; Kant's grounding the synthetic *a priori*, including the mathematics of number, in transcendental psychology is a nonstarter for Frege. But even framing the distinction in terms of judgments may misrepresent Frege's mature view. Eight years after *Foundations* he published his distinction between sense and reference. Part of what happened then was that Frege recognized nonphysical, nonmental abstract objects expressed by sentences. These he called thoughts, but that label is misleading, since they are not psychological but more like propositions in Leibniz or Russell. As singular terms like "7 + 5" and "15 – 3" may have different senses but refer to the same thing, Frege says the sentences "7 + 5 = 12" and "15 – 3 = 12" also express different senses or thoughts but denote the same thing, the truth-value truth. Thoughts are senses of sentences, and senses are not psychological. It is as if the grammatical composition of a sentence out of words were projected both into a platonic composition of a thought out of senses and a psychological composition of a judgment out of ideas. Where Kant framed his distinctions in terms of judgments he took as mental, the mature Frege would frame his in terms of thoughts he took as abstract, unsullied by the grubby fingers of subjectivity.

Frege may have been working his way toward this sharp separation of the psychological from the logical, the subjective from the objective, even in 1884. He says that when a proposition (*Satz*, translated as "proposition" by Austin) is called *a posteriori* or analytic in his sense, this is a judgment not about how we might form the content of the proposition in our consciousness or about how one might come to believe it, but about the ultimate ground (*tiefsten Grunde*) upon which rests the justification for holding it to be true. Notice the impersonal definite articles: *the* ultimate ground, not yours, mine, or God's; and *the* justification, the one and only. Frege says that to settle whether a truth is analytic or synthetic, *a priori* or *a posteriori*, we must find the proof of the proposition and follow it right back to the primitive truths, *die Urwahrheiten*, that have such a ring in German. Frege initiated the analytic style of philosophy, a style that thinks itself distinguished by the clarity of its exposition and the care of its argument. He takes the figure of foundation, the axiomatic method writ large among philosophers, perhaps more seriously than any other philosopher. A trend in analytic philosophy has been a loss of confidence in the notion that knowledge has foundations, in what Nelson Goodman called epistemic priority. For one thing, Gödel showed that no consistent axiomatic system proves all mathematical truths, and for another, Quine convinced many of us that the failure of Carnap's reduction of physical objects to sensory Gestalts shows that we justify belief not so much by reasoning from theorem to theorem as by seeing which system of theorems best fits (or explains) our experience. But Goodman's adjective "epistemic" may fail to express quite how radical Frege's conception is. Many of us are content to believe that there is out there independent of us, of our beliefs and our conceptual schemes, a world of galaxies and glaciers, of quarks and quasars, and maybe even of numbers and spheres. These objects are subject to laws we do not just make up but, if we are lucky, learn. But beyond this, Frege thinks there is a single right deductive order of the truths. This is not an epistemic order, a sequence in which we at our best, or Kantian rational beings smarter than we, or God, would justify later from earlier truths. It is not an epistemic order, but the logical order, and it is our job to arrange our beliefs in this order if we can make it out.

Consider Euclid's geometry. After Hilbert and others, we might think of it as an historically given collection of sentences from which we can in several ways select some and deduce the rest from them. But assuming, as Frege did, that Euclid's geometry is true, Frege thinks that just one of these deductive organizations is right. Euclid's axiom of parallels says that if a line L intersects two lines A and B so that the interior angles 1 and 2 on one side of L make less than a straight angle,

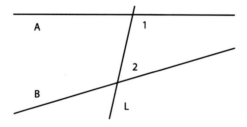

then A and B intersect on the side of L on which 1 and 2 lie. Many of us were taught what is called Playfair's postulate (after an eighteenth-century editor of Euclid, though Heath says the axiom goes back to Proclus in the ancient world): Given a line L in a plane and a point P in the plane not on L, there is one and only one line in the plane through P parallel to L. Given the rest of Euclid's axioms, his postulate is equivalent to Playfair's (and the reasoning from Playfair to Euclid is interesting). Frege seems committed to saying that in the logical order of geometry, either Playfair's postulate comes before Euclid's, or Euclid's comes first. Heath reports Dodgson as preferring Euclid's because it is positive and finitary, while Playfair's is negative and infinitary. Playfair's frames a familiar comparison between Euclid (unique parallel) and spherical geometry (no parallel) and saddle geometry (several parallels). One might prefer learning lots of connections to being forced into a single Procrustean order. Another example centers on similar figures, those of the same shape if not size. Triangle ABC is similar to DEF if their corresponding angles are equal (say A to D, B to E, and C to F) and their corresponding sides are proportional (say AB is to DE as BC

is to EF, and BC is to EF as AC is to DF). Euclid inquires into how much
of this suffices for the rest. He proves, using the postulate of parallels,
that if an angle in each equals the other (say A and D) and the enclosing sides are proportional (so AB is to DE as AC is to DF), then ABC is
similar to DEF. George Birkhoff and Ralph Beatley showed that we can
also axiomatize plane geometry by assuming this principle of similarity and deducing the parallels postulate.[5] Frege seems committed to at
least one of these axiomatizations misrepresenting the logical order of
geometry, while seeing connections in opposite directions deepens one's
grasp of the subject. It is not clear what would individuate the unique
logical order of truths.

A conclusion follows from premises and may figure among other
premises from which yet further conclusions follow, and logical consequences may burgeon without end. Now consider the converse relation,
that is, the relation which a conclusion bears to premises from which
it follows and which may themselves follow from yet further premises.
Frege assumes that the converse of the logical order stops. He says that
to settle whether a truth is analytic or synthetic, *a priori* or *a posteriori*,
we must find the proof of the proposition and follow it right back to
the primitive truths. These *Urwahrheiten* are the stopping points of the
converse of the logical order. We will return to the question whether
there must be *Urwahrheiten*.

Frege says that if the primitive truths from which the proof of the
proposition proceeds are nothing but general logical laws and definitions, then the truth is analytic. (Presumably, he means what looks like
a conditional as a biconditional; this is common mathematical practice.) In the same sentence he reminds us to take into account all the
propositions upon which the admissibility of the definitions depends.
Note that this account of analyticity assumes that general logical laws
are *Urwahrheiten*. But let us first ask which logical laws are general,
and what it is for the admissibility of a definition to depend on a
proposition.

Tyler Burge takes "general" to mean that all the quantifiers in the
Urwahrheiten should be universal.[6] If singular terms and function
signs are eliminated in favor of predicates, then a truth all of whose

[5] George David Birkhoff and Ralph Beatley, *Basic Geometry*, 3rd ed. (New York: Chelsea, 1959).
[6] Tyler Burge, *Truth, Thought, Reason: Essays on Frege* (Oxford: Clarendon Press, 2005), 367, 370.

quantifiers are universal in the prenex is true if there is nothing at all. Looked at that way, Burge's reading of "general" would accommodate the precept that no existence claim is analytic. But, as Burge recognizes, this is not a very plausible understanding of Frege.

It is distinctive of how the natural numbers were axiomatized (in the second half of the nineteenth century by Grassmann [1861], Peirce [1881], Dedekind [1888], and Peano [1889])[7] that axioms about which natural numbers exist are front and center: there is a natural number zero, which is the successor of no natural number, and every natural number has a successor. (Mathematical induction, also known as the inference from n to n + 1, says that these are the only natural numbers; it is a limitative principle.) While Frege did not have Tarski's term "material adequacy condition," these axioms of natural numbers play the role of conditions of material adequacy on his definitions of "zero," "successor," and "is a natural number." To establish the adequacy of his definitions, he must deduce these axioms from general logical laws and his definitions. Only then will he have demonstrated logicism (of the narrower sort). Frege knew he had to get existence results, so if the general logical laws could only be universally quantified, the existence results would have to come from the definitions. (Making things exist by definition already sounds a bit dodgy.)

A definite description, like "the first dog born at sea" (Strawson's example), is admissible only if two propositions are true: first, there exists a dog born at sea before any other; and, second, there were not two dogs born simultaneously at sea before any other. The first is an existence condition; the second, uniqueness. This line of thought is prominent in Russell, but Frege had it too. Similarly, an n-ary function sign is admissible only if for each n-tuple of arguments, there is at least (existence) and at most (uniqueness) one value. Existence and uniqueness conditions may be among what Frege meant by propositions on which the admissibility of definitions depends.

In reducing the mathematics of natural numbers to logical laws and definitions in his *Grundgesetze* (1892 and 1903), Frege gets his existence results from his Basic Law V, which he hoped would pass muster as an *Urwahrheit* (though, as Burge argues, he was less sure of it than of his other basic laws). Using notation more like ours than Frege's, V says that

---

[7] Geraldine Brady, *From Peirce to Skolem* (Amsterdam and New York: North-Holland/Elsevier, 2000), 13–14.

$$\{x \mid Fx\} = \{x \mid Gx\} \leftrightarrow (\forall x)(Fx \leftrightarrow Gx),$$

where "$\leftrightarrow$" is short for "if and only if." We should pause to see how Frege took this. Frege rethought properties as functions he called concepts. A function, as always, assigns values to arguments. A concept is a function that assigns to each object a truth value. So instead of the color green, the concept:*green* assigns truth (or the true) to each green thing, but falsity (or the false) to anything else. Frege took the right-hand side of V to say that the concepts F and G have the same truth values at the same arguments. Our notation for sets comes from Peano, but Frege did not read the left-hand side of V in terms of sets. Instead he assigns to each concept F a *Wertverlauf*, or course-of-values. He likens the course-of-values of a concept to the graph of a function. So the course-of-values of the concept:*green* would be the curve passing through truth over each green thing, but falsity over anything else. The members of our set of green things would be the objects under truth along the course-of-values of the concept:*green*.

In the *Grundgesetze*, Frege's version of our notation $\{x \mid Fx\}$ is primitive. This means it is not defined, so it has no definition concerning whose admissibility we may take into account propositions on which it depends. But the notation, even if primitive, converts predicates into singular terms, in fact, definite descriptions. For each predicate of his system there is such a definite description, and such a definite description is admissible only if an existence condition and a uniqueness condition are met. Such definite descriptions are admissible only if for each concept there exists a course-of-values of it, and there are never two different ones. The first condition we have seen before, where it was comprehension; and the second, extensionality. It is not clear that V all by itself will individuate $\{x \mid Fx\}$. As far as V goes, $\{x \mid Fx\}$ could be the course-of-values of F, but it could also be the set of Fs, or even the equivalence class under coextensiveness of F. Assuming these are distinct, we use the discussion in which Frege embeds V to distinguish $\{x \mid Fx\}$. But whatever $\{x \mid Fx\}$ is exactly, V requires there to be an object that is it. For given F, it is immediate that $(\forall x)(Fx \leftrightarrow Fx)$, whence by V, $\{x \mid Fx\} = \{x \mid Fx\}$, and thus $(\exists y)(y = \{x \mid Fx\})$. Granted that $y = \{x \mid Fx\}$ if and only if $(\forall z)(z \in y \leftrightarrow Fz)$, it follows that for any F there is a y such that $(\forall z)(z \in y \leftrightarrow Fz)$, which certainly sounds like comprehension. Comprehension, which is an existence proposition, is a proposition upon which the admissibility of (not the definition but) the notation for course-of-values (or sets or extensions) depends. Even if the quantifier

visible in V is universal, the propositions on which the admissibility of
the notation in it depends include existence claims.

This suggests contrasting "general" in Frege's account of analyticity
not with particular (existential) but with singular. Traditional logic distinguished universal (all) judgments, particular (some), and singular. An
open sentence in which predicates are the only extralogical primitives
may be closed either by quantifying the free variables or by substituting
singular terms for them (or by a mix of both stratagems). If on closing by
quantification of either sort we get a logical law, it is general, while if we
use singular terms, we must look to the existence and uniqueness propositions on which depends the admissibility of those terms to tell whether
we have a general logical law.[8] So construed, Frege's account of analyticity would not immediately preclude the analyticity of the existence axioms for natural numbers that Frege aims to show analytic. But it would
subvert the precept that no existence claim is analytic, since it would
require comprehension, which is an existence claim, to be analytic.

The stress on logic in Frege's account of analyticity reminds one of
Kant's second account of analyticity and its stress on the law of contradiction. There had been discussion of extensions in traditional logic for
ages, but the use Frege made of basic law V would not have been logic
familiar to Kant and is the most dramatic example of how Frege's logic
differed from the impoverished logic of Kant's time. But Kant would do
well to be skeptical about counting V as logic.

Next Frege explains what he counts as synthetic. If the proof of the
proposition requires some truths, presumably *Urwahrheiten*, that are
not of a general logical nature but come from a special science, then the
truth is synthetic. So the contrast between analytic and synthetic comes
to a contrast between general logical laws and special sciences. Hume
had long before argued that the laws of nature are matters of fact. For
Frege the natural sciences are special, but so is geometry. After Frege's
Grundgesetze and Russell's and Whitehead's *Principia*, the constructional tradition in analytic philosophy turned to doing for the extra-
mathematical world something analogous to what logicism had done
for number. Russell's *Our Knowledge of the External World* (1914) is

[8] When we define a predicate of equivalence classes in terms of a condition of a member of the class, we have to show the predicate is well defined, that is, that the condition is met either by all members of the class or by none. This independence of the
defining condition from which member of the class we might pick may be a proposition on which the admissibility of the definition of the predicate depends. Similar
remarks apply to functions of equivalence classes.

an earlier sketch of constructing the external world from sense data. Carnap's *Der logische Aufbau der Welt* (1928) is one of the most detailed efforts to construct matter, other people, and society from one's experience, in Carnap's case Gestalt rather than sense data. In 1951 in "Two Dogmas of Empiricism," Quine observed that in Carnap's initial step in the *Aufbau* into the external world, ascribing a quality q to a spacetime point p, Carnap makes the ascription not so much in terms of a specific bit of experience peculiar to it as in terms of which overall system of ascriptions of qualities to points most smooths turmoil (minimizes action). This means that if any one bit of experience remains the same while others vary, the ascription of q to p may change, so the presence of q at p is not reduced to any specific bit of experience. Quine's observation was a philosophical crux at which founding empirical knowledge in sense experience on the model of Frege's logicism began to give way to more holist conceptions of confirmation. This is a retreat from the figure of foundations and the logical order.

There are examples of comparative fundamentality among the natural sciences that many people find attractive. Chemistry is more basic than biology; and physics, than chemistry. This traces a reduction in size (animals to molecules, and molecules to atoms), and we often try to explain a larger thing in terms of laws relating its smaller parts. But biology has an historical aspect in evolution, and there seems to be a loss of confidence that, given the extent of accident in history, evolution can be reduced to chemistry as Frege aimed to reduce the mathematics of natural numbers to logic. Besides, the program of explaining the bigger in terms of the smaller can sap one's confidence that there are *Urwahrheiten* in the special sciences. In Frege's day, molecules were controversial enough that Ernst Mach did not believe in them. We have gone from molecules to atoms, atoms to electrons and protons, protons to quarks, and perhaps from quarks to strings. At each moment smallest bits are fashionable, but difficulties eventually seem to drive us to yet smaller bits. Were such composition to descend infinitely, perhaps there would be no *Urwahrheiten* in the natural sciences.

Frege says that for a truth to be *a posteriori*, it must be impossible to construct its proof without including an appeal to facts, that is, to truths that cannot be proved and are not general, since they contain assertions about particular objects. The *a posteriori* is here described as a sort of truth, not as a sort of knowledge, and there is no mention here of justification of beliefs by experience. One might wonder here about assertions about particular objects. Perhaps Frege is reverting to singular propositions but contrasting these singular propositions with the ones to which he alluded in describing analyticity. There the existence and uniqueness propositions on which depends the admissibility of the singular terms had to be general logical laws. In a singular *a posteriori* truth one expects that the singular terms will depend for their admissibility not on general logical laws but on something else. Perhaps in some cases the existence and uniqueness conditions are shown to be met in ostensive definitions of the singular terms. Since what is ostensible is open to view, this might be a way to work experience into Frege's version of *a posteriori* truth. But Frege does not say this. Kant's conceptions of *a posteriori* knowledge as knowledge justified by experience remains the dominant notion.

Finally, Frege says that for a truth to be *a priori* its proof should proceed exclusively from general laws that neither need nor admit of proof. To this sentence he appends a footnote arguing for primitive general laws on the grounds that from "mere individual facts" alone, nothing general follows; so if there are generalities in the logical order, some of the *Urwahrheiten* must be general. Of course existential truths follow from individual facts by existential generalization, so in this note Frege doubtless means "universal" by "general." But since the basic laws of arithmetic include existential claims, arithmetic can be analytic and *a priori* in Frege's sense only if the general laws from which they are proved are in part existential. This note also shows that Frege thinks a conclusion can be justified only by premises from which it follows; he makes no room for inductive justification short of deduction. While the *Urwahrheiten* beneath analytic truths must be general logical laws, those beneath *a priori* truths must be general laws; logical roots are not required for *a priori* truths. The difference allows for geometry to be *a priori* but synthetic rather than analytic. On the other hand, for geometry to be *a priori* it must be derived exclusively from general laws, while for it to be synthetic it should require for its proof truths of a special science. This looks to require a special science composed of general (nonlogical) laws, and one wonders how such speciality and generality fit together.[9]

---

[9] Dummett and Burge observe that while Frege counts truths proved exclusively from general logical laws as analytic and *a priori*, he does not say that these laws themselves are analytic and *a priori*. They agree this is an oversight, which seems right. Presumably the distinctions among truths should be exhaustive, and Frege should count general logical laws as neither synthetic nor *a posteriori*, for if they were proved from special sciences or facts, then so would anything proved from them, which would make arithmetic synthetic or *a posteriori*.

General laws that neither need nor admit of proof are vivid in this account of the *a priori*. These negations seem to underscore the ultimate fundamentality, the *Ur*, of *Urwahrheiten*. Frege's account of the *a priori* is almost as negative as Kant's, except for Frege's mention of generality. One wants to know how *a priori* truth, whether analytic or synthetic, is possible.

Maybe it isn't. The *a priori* was in retreat in analytic philosophy during most of the twentieth century. In the natural history of belief, some claims leave us cold. Considering the claim that it was snowing at the peak of Mount Kilimanjaro at noon on 1 April 1600, a person lacking implausibly specialized historical access does well neither to believe nor to disbelieve it. But the claim that everything is identical with itself has another natural history; by and large, people believe it. These are remarks in the natural history of belief, not epistemology. Call cases like acquiescence in the universality of self-identity cases of saying is believing. This mnemonic does not refer primarily to a quick or easy way to belief. Although the notion of the *a priori* would probably have less purchase if saying is believing were not often quick and easy, there can be instances of prolonged uncertainty or acrimonious exchanges. The mnemonic denotes primarily the absence of a way to belief at all. This lacuna has its social side. It is not just that people to whom it occurs on their own that everything is identical with itself believe it. Perhaps even more so, it is that if one says it to others, they just agree; they do not ask for argument. That is a way experts in a field settle on axioms. That one can just get away with a claim encourages the idea that it does not need proof. The rage that tends to greet the eccentric who asks how we know in cases where saying is believing reinforces the status of such claims as neither needing nor admitting of proof. But this is still just sociology, not epistemology.

Experience justifies suspicion of the idea that saying justifies belief. Here are three cases in point. Geometry was Kant's leading example of synthetic *a priori* knowledge. During the nineteenth century, considerable mathematical attention was focused on the postulate of parallels. By then this was usually put in the form named for Playfair, that is, given a line L in a plane and a point P in the plane not on L, there is one and only one line in the plane through P that is parallel to L. The mathematicians determined that (except in an uninteresting minor way) there is no proving the parallels postulate from the rest. They began to work out what space would be like were there no parallel through P to L (spherical geometry) or were there several (hyperbolic geometry). As curvature was understood and generalized, the differences among these cases were seen as differences in the curvature of space, and Riemann in particular worked out how the curvature of space could vary from here to there. In his General Theory of Relativity (1916) Einstein used Riemann's techniques to relate gravity explicitly to the curvature of (not space but) spacetime. The physicists hijacked the word "cosmology" from the philosophers in the 1920s, and physical cosmology has had a rich history since Einstein. But since 1916 the smart money has bet that geometry is an *a posteriori* empirical science. In particular, even if saying were believing for the parallels postulate, our best judgment seems to be that it is false of the spacetime in which we live and move and have our being, and there is no other. (The postulate would be true if spacetime were empty.) It would be difficult to overstate the effect this example had on epistemology during the twentieth century.

Our second example comes from infinity. Euclid's fifth axiom says that the whole is greater than the part, and his intellectual authority was unsurpassed for millennia. We have seen how Galileo appealed to the axiom to infer from there being as many natural numbers as even numbers that there could not be a completed infinite totality. We have also seen how Dedekind inverted Galileo's reasoning and converted the denial of Euclid's axiom into a definition of infinite sets. Set theory has its difficulties, but a set theoretic theory of the infinite is the tree of knowledge in the paradise from which Hilbert said no one will be able to drive us. One might hazard that we have been making an experimental intellectual choice between Euclid's axiom and Dedekind's definition. Frege notwithstanding, conclusive proof is the exception, not the rule, but the upshot of the experiment is that even if for millennia saying that the whole is greater than the part sufficed for belief, it was false.

Our third example comes from Frege. As we have seen, he needs comprehension to be a general law of logic and so *a priori*. But as we have also seen, Russell's paradox is a deduction of a contradiction from comprehension, and so a proof by *reductio ad absurdum* that it is not *a priori* true but false. The same is true of Burali-Forti's paradox and Cantor's paradox. But these are paradoxes looking to arise in the infinite: Frege was more focused on the natural numbers than the transfinite ordinals, and Cantor had written up the paradox around his theorem in a private letter to Dedekind. It was Russell's letter of 1902 that shattered Frege. He lived until 1925 and he continued to write philosophy after 1902 that still attracts philosophers, but his great days as a logician were over.

In these three cases – the parallels postulate, Euclid's fifth axiom, and comprehension – saying was believing at least for a while, but what was said was false. Such evidence should make a shrewd philosopher skeptical about whether there is *a priori* knowledge at all. Once saying is believing goes arguably wrong, it is prudent to test its other deliverences against experience. But it is not knockdown conclusive proof (which Frege thought was all there is to justification) that *a priori* knowledge does not exist, and the phenomenology of saying is believing is a strong incentive to revive rationalism – mostly, the doctrine that there is *a priori* knowledge. The real monuments of philosophy are its problems, like how *a priori* knowledge is possible (if it is); they never get solved, which can look to civilians as if there is no progress, but progress lies in the memorable extensions of the dialectic, the conversation back and forth, they generate.

Early in the twenty-first century, rationalism is reviving in some quarters, and Tyler Burge is one of its most creative exponents. In *Truth, Thought, Reason*, he writes:

> [Frege] holds that justification for holding logical laws to be true rests on and follows from primitive laws of truth. He spells out this dependence of epistemic justification on the laws of truth in two ways. He thinks that laws of truth indicate how one ought to think "if one would attain to truth". But a judging subject necessarily would attain to truth, insofar as it engages in judgment. So any judgment by a particular person necessarily is subject to prescriptive laws set out by the primitive laws of logic. One is justified in acknowledging them because doing so is necessary to fulfilling one's aim and function as a judging subject.
>
> Frege's second way is: acknowledgment of certain laws of truth is necessary for having reason and for engaging in non-degenerate thinking and judging. One is rationally entitled to judge the primitive laws of logic to be true because the nature of reason – and even non-degenerate judgment – is partly constituted by the prescription that one acknowledge at least the simple and basic laws of truth. To put it crudely, reason and judgment – indeed mind – are partly defined in terms of acknowledging the basic laws of truth....
>
> ... Frege's line is to hold that, although the laws of truth are independent of judging subjects, judging subjects are in two ways not independent of the laws of truth. First, to be a judging subject is to be subject to the prescriptions of reason, which in turn are provided by the laws of truth (logic). For judgment has the function of attaining truth; and the laws of logic – which are constituted by atemporal thoughts and atemporal subject matter – provide universal prescriptions of how one ought to think, given that one's thinking has the function of attaining truth.

Second, being a judging subject is to have or have had some degree of reason. Having or having had some degree of reason requires acknowledging, at least implicitly in one's thinking, the simplest, most basic logical truths and inferences.[10]

These sentences have a formal air reminiscent of some passage of Kant. There is no prospect of proving the primitive laws of logic from something more primitive, since there are no more primitive premises. Instead, belief in these laws is justified because commitment to them is part of what justification is. The strategy seems to be to combine phrases (like "how one ought to think," "judging subject," "attain to truth," "having reason") in a description of justified belief in basic logic whose special status (analytic, necessary, *a priori*, self-evident?) is to settle belief that such belief is justified. This description expands on what is at issue, and if so, perhaps should not justify anyone not already on board in embarking.

It is over the top to say that acknowledging Frege's Basic Law I is necessary for having reason and for engaging in nondegenerate thinking and judging. In our notation this law goes

$$A \rightarrow (B \rightarrow A).$$

Law I articulates part of a truth-functional understanding of conditionals. On such understanding, the truth value of a conditional is determined by and (this is the crux) *only* by the truth values of its antecedent and consequent. Sometimes a true conclusion follows from true premises, and sometimes a true conclusion follows from false premises (All dogs are reptiles, and all reptiles are mammals: therefore, all dogs are mammals). When a conclusion follows from premises, the conditional whose antecedent is the conjunction of the premises and whose consequent is the conclusion is true. So some conditionals with true consequents and either true antecedents or false antecedents are true. It follows that the conditional is a truth function only if all conditionals with true consequents are true. Frege says that the reference of a predicate is a concept, which is a function whose value is always a truth value. Then the reference of an atomic sentence is its truth value, a doctrine he extends to all sentences, so the reference of a sentence connective is a truth function, and Basic Law I is inevitable. (There is thus available to Frege an argument for a basic law not admitting proof.) But not all sentence connectives are truth functional: some truths are

[10] Burge, *Truth, Thought, Reason*, 315–16.

necessary, and some are not; some truths are probable, and some are not. If a predicate is to have a reference, it need not be one of Frege's concepts, but might be the set of things of which the predicate is true. Then, if one wishes, one may specify set theoretic versions of Russellian propositions to be denoted by the sentences of a formalized language like Frege's.[11]

The dictum that all conditionals with true consequents are true and its companion that all conditionals with false antecedents are true are fighting words in some quarters. They are known there as paradoxes of material implication, another title for taking the conditional truth functionally. The conditional so construed is also called the philonian conditional, after Philo of Megara, one of its ancient advocates. The debate over whether the conditional is truth functional is ancient, endless, and acrimonious. Charles L. Stevenson parodied the material conditional by using it to prove the existence of God.[12] If prayer works, the best explanation is that God hears it and answers. This entitles us to the first premiss: God exists if heaven on earth obtains if Lenin prays for heaven on earth. The second premiss is the biographical fact that Lenin never prays. It follows from the second premiss that the conditional "Heaven on earth obtains if Lenin prays for heaven on earth" has a false antecedent and so is true. It then follows from the first premiss by *modus ponens* that God exists. (The trick here is not to get suckered into arguing about the first premiss.)

There is a story (perhaps apocryphal, but one should never let truth spoil a good story) that when Russell told his audience in Boston in 1914 that all conditionals with false antecedents are true, he was asked whether he really meant that if one plus one is one, then Russell is the Pope. On the spot Russell answered that he did indeed mean it. For if one plus one is one, the union of the unit set of Russell and the unit set of the Pope is a unit set, so Russell is the Pope. Clever as it is, Russell's answer concedes the objection to the material conditional. Those opposed to it, sometimes called relevance logicians, say a conditional is true only when the antecedent adequately supports the consequent because, for example, there is a good argument from the antecedent to the consequent.

---

[11] For details of one version, see my "The Syntax of the World," *Crítica* 28 (April 1996): 13–24.

[12] Charles L. Stevenson, "If-iculties," in *Logic and Art: Essays in Honor of Nelson Goodman*, ed. Richard Rudner and Israel Scheffler (New York: Bobbs-Merrill, 1972), 279–309.

There are things to be said in behalf of the truth-functional conditional. Paul Grice first introduced conversational implicature to defend taking the conditional truth functionally.[13] There are interpolation theorems that provide a kind of local anesthetic against the sting of irrelevance.[14] But the main thing is the simplicity and perspicuity of the truth table for the conditional. Years of experience in regimenting (formalizing and axiomatizing) extensive bodies of reasoning have accustomed us to the axioms, laws, and rules for the conditional corresponding to its truth table, which include the paradoxes of material implication. Salient among the rules are *modus ponens*, a license to infer from a conditional and its antecedent to its consequent, and conditional proof, a license to infer a conditional from a deduction (a relevance logician would insist that it be a *good* deduction) of its consequent from its antecedent. For all we know, an ingenious relevance logician will devise a perspicuous semantics for the conditional perhaps only slightly more complex than its truth table, which is not truth-functional but which legitimates *modus ponens*, conditional proof, and all the other good reasoning with conditionals but invalidates the paradoxes of material implication. Frege's Basic Law I is an old standard now in axiomatic organizations of logic, but our ingenious relevance logician's new semantics for the conditional might well justify us in dropping Basic Law I. It seems injudicious to say that relevance logicians lack reason and engage only in degenerate thinking and judging. Reason is not even partly defined by belief in the paradoxes of material implication.

Burge is enlightening on how Frege is a traditional rationalist for whom self-evidence is central to the *a priori*. But it is not self-evident what self-evidence is. Burge says the basic truths

> carry their justification intrinsically, in that their truth can be justifiably recognized from the nature of those truths, in justificational independence of consideration of other truths. On this conception self-evidence is an intrinsic property of the basic truths, rules, and thoughts expressed by definitions.[15]

One longs for an intellectual analogue of a color chart to guide one in recognizing this intrinsic property. Presumably the property does not

[13] Grice, "Causal Theory of Perception," 438–72. (Some editors omit the material on conversational implicature when reprinting this paper.)
[14] For example, Wilfrid Hodges, *Logic* (Harmondsworth: Penguin, 1977), 141–42, and my "Interpolación y relevancia," *Análisis filosófico* 13 (May 1993): 55–56.
[15] Burge, *Truth, Thought, Reason*, 350.

come in degrees, but perhaps its detectability varies. Perhaps there are laws of self-evidence that could be exploited to figure out improved ways to recognize it. The reflexivity of self-evidence purports that a self-evident truth is justified from itself, and if this justification is independent of all other truths, the circularity is especially flagrant; circular justification is an oxymoron.

Burge embeds Frege in the rationalist tradition. He writes:

> Descartes' appeals to self-evidence were not meant to receive immediate approbation from anyone who would listen. Self-evident propositions are self-evident to anyone who adequately *understands* them. Descartes and other traditional rationalists did not assume that understanding would be immediate or common to all mankind, or even common to all socially accepted experts. Understanding was something more than mere mastery of the words or concepts to a communal or conventional standard. It involved mastering a deeper rational and explanatory order. Acknowledgment of the truth of self-evident propositions would be immediate and non-inferential, only given full understanding in the relevant deeper sense.
>
> Frege is relying on this tradition.[16]

Suppose two sects each claim exclusive insight into the *Urwahrheiten*. The claims of each sect are incompatible with those of the other, but as in the familiar stories of underdetermination of theory by data,[17] each canon accounts for the conventional wisdom equally well. When they confront each other, each side says its own doctrine is self-evident and offers no argument for it but says the other side has failed to master a deeper rational and explanatory order. A person steeped in the hypothetico-deductive method and inference to the best explanation would be justified in being skeptical; so far there is no telling which, if either, sect holds at least true beliefs, and there need never be.

Are there any *Urwahrheiten* at all? Discussing not proof but definition, Russell once wrote:

> Since all terms that are defined are defined by means of other terms, it is clear that human knowledge must always be content to accept some

---

[16] Ibid., 354.

[17] W. V. Quine, "Two Dogmas of Empiricism," reprinted in *From a Logical Point of View*, 2nd ed. rev. (Cambridge, Mass.: Harvard University Press, 1961), 44–46 and references cited there. One available in English is Pierre Duhem, *The Aim and Structure of Physical Theory*, trans. Philip P. Wiener (Princeton: Princeton University Press, 1954), chap. 6.

terms as intelligible without definition, in order to have a starting point
for its definition. It is not clear that there must be terms that are *incapable*
of definition: it is always possible that, however far back we go in defining, we always *might* go further still.[18]

One might expect an infinite regress of proof to be bound up with an
infinite regress of definition. Where once the natural numbers and their
laws seemed basic, undefinable, and unprovable, Cantor, Frege, and
Russell worked out systems of objects (sets, courses-of-value, classes)
in terms of which they claimed to define the numbers and to prove
the laws of numbers from laws of the objects of their systems. To be
sure, their systems had problems, but we have revised their systems
so as to preserve versions of their reduction (or modelings) while, we
hope, avoiding those problems. Some have claimed that sets should in
turn be rethought in terms of still more basic things, categories.[19] For
mere mortals the actual regress will at each moment always be finite,
and the infinite regress will be potential, as Russell says. But our grasp
of the logical order might always be superficial, and the logical order
an actual infinite regress. It is not self-evident that it must stop, and
nothing Frege says proves that it does. For every proposition, there is a
stronger one from which it follows.

[18] Bertrand Russell, *Introduction to Mathematical Philosophy* (London: George Allen
      & Unwin, 1919), 3–4.
[19] F. William Lawvere, "The Category of Categories as a Foundation for Mathematics,"
      in *Proceedings of the Conference on Categorical Algebra, La Jolla*, ed. S. Eilenberg
      et al. (New York: Springer, 1966), 1–21.

THREE

✦

Expeditions

Which Sets Exist?

The Burali-Forti paradox was a crisis for Cantor's theory of ordinal numbers; Cantor's paradox was a crisis for his theory of cardinals; and Russell's paradox was a crisis for Frege's logicism. Had the crises been local, sets (and courses-of-values) might have gone the way of phlogiston, the stuff thought in the eighteenth century to be lost from something burning (and supplanted by oxygen taken up in burning). But sets (or their kissing cousins) were not going to go without a fight. We can make out at least four reasons for this resilience. Among philosophers, logicism retained a fascination that gave it room to evolve. Among mathematicians, Cantor's theory of infinity retained a fascination that Hilbert, for one, would not abandon. Also among mathematicians, set theory became the framework, the lingua franca, in which – by and large – modern mathematics is conducted. Finally, there are the applications of set theory, of which those in logic are central for us.

Frege layered functions. A first-level function assigns objects to objects: doubling is a first-level function that assigns six to three; and the concept:*green* is a first-level function that assigns truth to all and only the green things. The derivative of the square function is the doubling function, while that of the sine is the cosine, so differentiation is a second-order function. In another example, Frege reads "There are carrots," so its subject is the concept:*carrot* and its predicate is the concept:*existence*. Existence is thus a second-level concept whose value is truth at all and only the first-level concepts under which something falls.[1] This allows Frege to refine Kant's criticism of the ontological

---

[1] Perhaps more generally a quantifier is a second-level function whose value at an (n+1)-ary first-level concept is an n-ary concept, unless n is zero, in which case its value is a truth value, an object. In that case, quantifiers would be second-level functions sometimes having first-level concepts as values and sometimes objects as values. When the

argument for the existence of God. Kant said that existence is not a predicate, which is heroic, or even quixotic, grammar. Frege could say that since existence is a second-level predicate, it is at the wrong level to be a defining feature of an object like God.

But Frege did not layer objects. Russell rocked Frege with Russell's paradox in a letter dated 16 June 1902. Less than two months later Russell wrote, on 8 August 1902: "The contradiction could be resolved with the help of the assumption that ranges of values are not objects of the ordinary kind; i.e., that $\varphi(x)$ needs to be completed (except in special circumstances) either by an object or by a range of values of objects or by a range of values of ranges of values, etc. This theory is analogous to your theory about functions of the first, second, etc. levels."[2] In the next year, 1903, Russell sketches in Appendix B to *The Principles of Mathematics* what types of objects might look like. In type 0, the lowest, would go the nonclasses like Heinrich Heine and the moon. In type 1 would go the classes of objects of type 0; in type 2, the classes of objects of type 1; and generally in type n + 1 would go classes of objects of type n. These types of objects are not cumulative, since Heine is not of type 2, and if types are classes, type n is an object of type n + 1.

Typing orders objects so that the members of a class of type n + 1 are of type n. This rules out self-membership. If there were a universe, a class of all objects, then since classes are objects, it would be a member of itself. So the universe does not exist. But we have just seen that nothing is a member of itself, so if there were a set of all non-self-members as in Russell's paradox, it would be the universe. So since the universe does not exist, neither does Russell's paradoxical set of all non-self-members. As Russell wrote in August 1902, we can suppress his paradox if we layer objects rather as Frege layered functions; where being-an-argument-to raises level among Frege's functions, being-a-member raises type among Russell's classes. It also suppresses Cantor's paradox. There the problem was that the power set of the universe had to be both bigger than the universe (by Cantor's theorem) and not bigger (since it is a subset of the universe), and the absence of the universe obviates the problem. If we allowed ourselves only segments of ordinals all of the same type, the order type of a segment would

value of a first-level concept at an object is truth, Frege says the object falls under the concept. Perhaps the concept:*falls-under* is a binary second-level concept whose first argument is an object and whose second is a first-level concept. In that case, second-level concepts could also have arguments of different levels.

2 Published in Gottlob Frege, *Philosophical and Mathematical Correspondence*, ed. Gottfried Gabriel et al., trans. Hans Kaal (Oxford: Basil Blackwell, 1980), 144.

always be of higher (Russellian) type than the ordinals in the segment, so there would be no segment of all ordinals, which would suppress the Burali-Forti paradox too. But suppressing these paradoxes costs us the universe. And suppressing the familiar arguments of these paradoxes does not ensure that other arguments for these, or even arguments for other paradoxes, will not pop up elsewhere.

Russell's theory of types was vastly more complex than this sketch suggests. For one thing, since Russell had no reductions of n-ary relations to classes of ordered n-tuples, he also typed relations. But the mare's nest grows up around propositions, meaning, ramification, and predicativity. After Russell's paradox, Frege largely withdrew from the more mathematical side of logic. During the decade in which Russell was working out *Principia Mathematica* with Alfred North Whitehead, the great French mathematician Henri Poincaré became one of Russell's main adversaries. Poincaré denied that mathematics could be reduced to logic. Mathematical induction, the central law of the natural numbers, says that when 0 has a property and n + 1 has it when n does, then all natural numbers have it. Poincaré read this as an infinity of instances of *modus ponens*: we are given that 0 has the property; by the second premiss, if 0 has it, so does 1; so by *modus ponens*, 1 has it; again by the second premiss, if 1 has it, so does 2; so again by *modus ponens*, 2 has it; and so on ad infinitum through all the natural numbers. The transcendence of the mathematics of number over logic lies, thought Poincaré, in this infinity. A logicist might define the natural numbers as the members of all sets of which 0 is a member and of which n + 1 is a member when n is, thus telescoping Poincaré's infinity of *modi ponens* into a second-order definition. Hostility to mathematical logic from one so eminent as Poincaré discouraged study of logic in France for a long time.

But however much Russell and Poincaré may have disagreed about other things, they agreed that Russell's paradox and the Burali-Forti paradox[3]

---

[3] Cantor described his paradox in a letter to Dedekind in 1899. Ernst Zermelo first published this letter in Georg Cantor, *Gesammelte Abhandlungen mathematischen und philosophischen Inhalts*, ed. Ernst Zermelo (Hildesheim: Georg Olms, 1962; reprint of 1932 ed.). Patrick Suppes, *Axiomatic Set Theory* (Princeton: Van Nostrand, 1960), 9, says that Cantor's paradox was not published before Zermelo's 1932 edition of Cantor. It is difficult to believe it was not more generally known before 1932. There is a recognizable version of Cantor's paradox in section 344 of Bertrand Russell, *The Principles of Mathematics* (London: George Allen & Unwin, 1903; 2nd ed. 1937), 362, and Russell says in a footnote that he discovered his own paradox thinking about Cantor. But Russell omits Cantor's paradox from the budget of paradoxes with which he begins "Mathematical Logic as Based on the Theory of Types" in 1908 (see the next note). (My student Sean Paul Morris brought section

are not isolated but belong with other paradoxes.[4] The oldest of these is
the ancient paradox of the liar. This centers on a proposition that says
of itself that it is not true. The reasoning is that if this proposition is
true, it has the property it ascribes to itself and so is not true, while if it
is not true, it has the property it ascribes to itself and so is true after all.
Russell's response is to type propositions. This requires that each proposition be of higher type than those it is about. But the proposition at
the center of the liar paradox is about itself, and so cannot be of higher
type than the proposition it is about. "This solves the liar," says Russell
in his brisk fashion.[5] As Russell layers sets above their members, so he
layers propositions above their subject matter. The first rules out the
universe, while the second has the consequence that there are no propositions about all propositions. This consequence is a counterexample to
itself. At 3.332 in the *Tractatus*, Wittgenstein writes, "No proposition
can make a statement about itself, because a propositional sign cannot
be contained in itself (that is the whole of the 'theory of types')."[6] It
is obvious that 3.332 is a counterexample to 3.332, but Wittgenstein
just grins and bears it, for this antinomy is the center of his distinction
between saying and showing.[7]

344 of *Principles* to my attention.) When in 1925 Frank Ramsey distinguishes the
logical paradoxes (including Russell's and Burali-Forti's) from the linguistic paradoxes (including the liar and the least indescribable ordinal), he adds to paradoxes
from Russell's 1908 budget of paradoxes Grelling's paradox about heterologicality.
(An adjective like "long" that is not true of itself is heterological; is "heterological"
heterological?) But Ramsey does not mention Cantor's paradox (and neither had
Russell). See F. P. Ramsey, "The Foundations of Mathematics," reprinted in his
The Foundations of Mathematics and Other Logical Essays, ed. R. B. Braithwaite
(Paterson, N.J.: Littlefield, Adams, 1960), 20. Ramsey credits the heterological paradox to Hermann Weyl's 1918 book on the continuum, but in *Set Theory and Its
Logic* (Cambridge, Mass.: Belknap Press of Harvard University Press, 1963; rev.
ed. 1969), 254n6, Quine says it is due to Kurt Grelling and L. Nelson in a paper of
1907–08. But Hilbert and his colleagues at Göttingen seem to have learned a version
of Cantor's paradox from Cantor; see Volker Peckhaus, "Paradoxes in Göttingen,"
in *One Hundred Years of Russell's Paradox*, ed. Godehard Link (Berlin: Walter de
Gruyter, 2004), 502.
4 See Bertrand Russell, "Mathematical Logic as Based on the Theory of Types,"
   reprinted in his *Logic and Knowledge: Essays, 1901–1950*, ed. Robert Charles
   Marsh (London: George Allen & Unwin, 1956), 57–102. This 1908 classic begins
   with a budget of paradoxes and is a milestone of modern logic.
5 Ibid., 79.
6 Ludwig Wittgenstein, *Tractatus Logico-Philosophicus*, trans. D. F. Pears and B. F.
   McGuinness (London: Routledge & Kegan Paul, 1961; 1st German ed. 1921), 31.
7 See my "The Whole Sense of the *Tractatus*," *Journal of Philosophy* 68 (6 May
   1971): 273–88.

But we must not miss out Berry's paradox. Let us dismiss all special marks and insist that all definite descriptions be written out using only the twenty-six letters of our alphabet, the hyphen, and the blank (so that we can distinguish "button" from "butt on"). So there are at most 28 descriptions one letter long. Similarly, there are at most 28^2 descriptions two letters long, so there are at most $28 + 28^2$ descriptions one or two letters long. In this way there are at most

$$28 + 28^2 + \cdots + 28^{79}$$

descriptions with no more than 79 letters. This number is big, but it is finite. But there are infinitely many natural numbers, so there are numbers denoted by no description of fewer than 79 letters. By the least number principle,

> the least number denoted by no description of fewer than seventy-nine letters

exists. On the other hand, we just referred to it using a description of 77 letters. In an infinitary version, there are at most countably many descriptions of finite length to be formed from a finite, or even countable, alphabet. But there are uncountably many ordinals, so there are ordinals without finite descriptions, and thus a unique least one. But "the least ordinal without a finite description" is a finite description of it.

Russell says,

> Thus all our contradictions have in common the assumption of a totality such that, if it were legitimate, it would at once be enlarged by new members defined in terms of itself.
>
> This leads us to the rule: 'Whatever involves *all* of a collection must not be one of the collection'; or, conversely: 'If, provided a certain collection had a total, it would have members only definable in terms of that total, then the said collection has no total'.[8]

Russell and Poincaré think of defining an object in terms of a class of which it is a member as a vicious circle, and a prohibition against doing so is sometimes called the vicious circle principle. Russell ramified in order to obey this prohibition. To illustrate what this means, suppose we are considering which classes there are of type 1. Classes are extensions of acceptable predicates. Suppose we have accepted some primitive predicates true of some nonclass objects of type 0 and false of the rest. We allow truth-functional combinations of these primitive predicates

[8] Russell, "Mathematical Logic," 63.

and we allow quantification into them, but only over objects of type 0. Call such a compound formula predicative. Within type 1 there will be classes that are extensions of predicative formulae. A restricted version of comprehension would have it that for each predicative formula F(x)

$$(\exists y)(\forall x)(x \in y \leftrightarrow F(x))$$

(where "y" may not occur in F(x)). Such classes in type 1 are said to be of order 1. But next we might allow predicates still of objects of type 0 but in which quantification over both such objects and classes of order 1 is allowed. Another restricted version of comprehension would have it that each such formula also has an extension, a class in type 1 of order 2. And so on ad infinitum. Each type of class ramifies into an infinity of orders.

Poincaré was a bit of an idealist, except that where Berkeley said that to be is to be perceived, Poincaré flirted with the idea that to be (in mathematics) is to be defined, and thus in a way made by us. It is natural to think that a brick from which a house is made comes before, not after, the house. (Mathematical houses do not wear, so even if the house were a brick factory, no bricks made in it would replace worn bricks from which it is made.) The ordering (like that of orders) required by the vicious circle principle and ramification is congenial to a certain kind of idealism in the philosophy of mathematics. Ramifying is also sometimes called a requirement of predicativity. One who thinks of mathematical objects not like houses we build of bricks but more like galaxies composed of stars out there independent of us will be untroubled if our only way to pick out a star is in terms of features of the galaxy it inhabits. Russell's philosophical views varied, but he was not much drawn to mathematical idealism after he took up serious logic.

As early as Appendix B to *The Principles of Mathematics*, Russell also thought of types as ranges of significance. This is an idea that caught on later in nontechnical philosophy. So one used to hear it called a category mistake to apply or deny the predicate "is red" of the number seventeen. Such neurasthenic negation was sometimes prompted by dreamings of defining metaphysics away. But seventeen is a number, numbers are not physical, and only physical things are red, so seventeen is not red. A vigorous metaphysician will defend not only a robust negation and an extensive law of the excluded middle, but also categorical claims such as that numbers are not physical. Chomsky argues that there are grammatical but meaningless sentences from the famous example

Colorless green ideas sleep furiously.

This example seems meaningful (especially compared to deliberate nonsense like Lewis Carroll's poem "The Jabberwocky"). First, since green is a color, nothing green is colorless, so since it is natural to take Chomsky's example as universally quantified, it is true by vacuous antecedent, and so meaningful. (If it were ambiguous and could be existential, it would be false, and so again meaningful; and were it ambiguous, it would have two meanings rather than none.) Second, consider

Ideas sleep furiously.

Since only animals sleep and ideas are not animals, ideas do not sleep, and so neither do they sleep furiously; the claim is false and so meaningful. Grammarians should not be allowed to parse metaphysics away.

Back to Russell. Significance grows teeth when Russell declares self-membership meaningless; the membership predicate must be flanked by terms of consecutive type. This obliterates the instance of comprehension

$$(\exists y)(\forall x)(x \in y \leftrightarrow x \notin x)$$

responsible for Russell's paradox. But we have already seen that typing denies it, so obliteration seems like overkill. As long ago as Plato's *Cratylus*, philosophers had written about meaning, but they usually did not thereby elicit dialectic from their peers. Russell did. It might seem like common sense that the class of senators is not a senator and thus is not a member of itself. Nevertheless, Russell said, solving contradictions in basic logic requires us to deny not that it is true, but that it is meaningful. Technical results can reveal failures of meaning in what seemed to make good sense. This was a moment in philosophy of language becoming a recognized specialty within analytic philosophy.

The vicious circle principle is a principle about definitions, and since some think definitions present relations among words, they might expect a discussion of signs and expressions. Again, if types are ranges of significance, then since some think words carry significance, they too might expect a discussion of notation. But as Gödel notes, there is no precise syntax in *Principia Mathematica*.[9] Russell's handling of

---

[9] Kurt Gödel, "Russell's Mathematical Logic," reprinted in his *Collected Works*, vol. 2, *Publications, 1938–1974*, ed. Solomon Feferman et al. (Oxford: Oxford University Press, 1990), 120. Gödel describes *Principia* as a considerable step backward in precision from Frege.

comprehension is a locus of such infelicity. He never actually states comprehension. It is instead assumed in his syntax when for any acceptable formula F(x) he allows the singular term we would write as $\{x \mid F(x)\}$. He tends in the basics to concentrate more on F(x) than on $\{x \mid F(x)\}$. While Frege's concept:*bean* is the function whose value is truth at all and only the beans, Russell's corresponding propositional function sends each object (of suitable type) to the proposition that it is a bean. When Russell is writing philosophy and dodging commitments to the existence of things, propositional functions tend toward linguistic expressions like open sentences, but when he is writing mathematics and committing to the existence of things, they tend toward extra-linguistic abstracta like attributes.[10] Articulate, precise syntax makes it harder to mix up an expression and what it stands for. Mixing them up is called confusing use (of the expression to talk about what it stands for) and mention (of the expression to talk about it), and while one is unlikely to confuse a man and his name, the risk of such confusion increases with the abstractness of one's subject matter.[11]

The elements of Russell's theory of types are of forbidding difficulty, and commanding a perspicuous view of them is a daunting prospect. Then there are his existence axioms. Of these the most novel is his axiom of reducibility. Let P be a property whose range of significance is the natural numbers. One might take being an odd perfect number. (A perfect number is one like 6 equal to the sum $1 + 2 + 3$ of its proper divisors; the next is 28; and the next, 496. There are infinitely many even perfect numbers; no one knows whether there are any odd perfect numbers.) The characteristic function c_p of P is such that

$$c_p(n) = \begin{cases} 0 \text{ if } P(n) \\ 1 \text{ if not } P(n) \end{cases}$$

so c_p is like a Fregean concept with 0 for truth and 1 for falsity. For each natural number n, let $e_p(n)$ be

$$c_p(0) \times c_p(1) \times \cdots \times c_p(n),$$

[10] W. V. Quine, "Logic and the Reification of Universals," reprinted in his *From a Logical Point of View*, 2nd ed. rev. (Cambridge, Mass.: Harvard University Press, 1961), 122–23.

[11] On use and mention, see W. V. Quine, *Mathematical Logic*, rev. ed. (New York: Harper Torchbooks, 1962; reprint of 1951 rev. ed. of 1940 ed.), sect. 4. Anyone who works through chapter 7 of this book will become proficient at use and mention.

the product of the first n + 1 values of c_p. Then the numbers $e_p(0)$, $e_p(1)$,... form an infinite sequence of natural numbers; if there is an odd perfect number, this sequence is 1 for a while but 0 ever after, while if there is no odd perfect number, this sequence is always 1. We do not know how it settles down. But we know that the sequence never increases, and that 0 is a number less than or equal to each member of the sequence. This last is put by saying 0 is a lower bound for the sequence. The greatest lower bound, or limit, of the sequence is the lower bound than which no other lower bound is greater. The principle that any nonincreasing sequence of real numbers bounded below has a greatest lower bound is a version of the completeness axiom of the real numbers, a sine qua non of analysis. But the greatest lower bound of $e_p(0)$, $e_p(1)$,... is among them, which flouts the vicious circle principle. Russell would not have reduced the mathematics of number to logic without securing the completeness axiom of the reals. To do so he assumed that the propositional function of being the greatest lower bound of $e_p(0)$, $e_p(1)$,... is coextensive with a predicative propositional function, and so one in which this totality to which the greatest lower bound belongs is not mentioned. That is a characteristic instance of Russell's axiom of reducibility. In effect the axiom of reducibility erases ramification and the orders; circles are virtuous when you need greatest lower bounds.

In 1925 Frank Ramsey urged splitting Russell's 1908 budget of paradoxes in two.[12] In one group would go paradoxes like Russell's and Burali-Forti's; we would add Cantor's paradox, though neither Russell nor Ramsey mentions it, and it is not clear that they knew of it in 1925. In the other group would go the liar, the least indescribable ordinal, and one heterological paradox, not in Russell's budget. Ramsey calls the paradoxes in the first group logical. We might say they are paradoxes around the membership relation, and since we now distinguish between logic and set theory, we call them set theoretic paradoxes. He says the others turn on "thought, language or symbolism, which are not formal but empirical."[13] Tarski taught us to call relations between thought, language, or symbolism and (not its meaning but) its subject matter semantic, and we count truth, description, and truth-of as semantic in this peculiar usage, so we call paradoxes in the second group semantic. We could rephrase Ramsey's point in our terms by saying that while

[12] See Ramsey, "Foundations of Mathematics."
[13] Ibid., 20.

set theory must address the set theoretic paradoxes, it can ignore the semantic paradoxes. Then types without orders suffice, and we can dispense with ramification and the axiom of reducibility.[14]

The axiom of reducibility says that for each propositional function there is a coextensive predicative propositional function. Russell could not bring himself to count such an existence assumption as analytic. Another existence assumption was the axiom of infinity, which says there are infinitely many individuals in type 0. This puts a class of each finite cardinality in type 1, and thus (an exemplar of) each finite cardinal in type 2. It is then clear that the natural numbers will repeat in each type from 2 on, which is a bit embarrassing. (Frege's zero, the cardinal of the empty set, occurs in type 2 also, but his one, the cardinal of the unit set of zero, occurs in type 4, so his natural numbers do not lie in a single type, and thus there is no class of Frege's natural numbers.) Russell does not assume infinity outright, but makes theorems for which he uses it into conditionals with infinity in the antecedent. The axiom of choice is also an existence assumption, since it says that for any set A of nonempty sets, there exists a function f such that for any x in A, f(x) is a member of x. Russell called (the equivalent he used of) the axiom of choice the multiplicative axiom, since he used it to ensure that infinite products were nonempty. The axioms of reducibility, infinity, and choice are existence claims, and Russell was not happy about calling existence claims analytic; one might invert Frege's argument and reason that since the mathematics of number is synthetic and reducible to logic, logic is synthetic. Comprehension is also an existence assumption and belongs with reducibility, infinity, and choice even if Russell did not put it into words.

When Russell (and Whitehead) published *Principia Mathematica* in 1910, he said in the preface:

> the chief reason in favour of any theory on the principles of mathematics must always be inductive, *i.e.* it must lie in the fact that the theory in question enables us to deduce ordinary mathematics. In mathematics, the greatest degree of self-evidence is usually not to be found quite at the beginning, but at some later point; hence the early deductions, until they

---

[14] John Myhill proved in "The Undefinability of the Set of Natural Numbers in the Ramified *Principia*," in *Bertrand Russell's Philosophy*, ed. George Nakhnikian (New York: Barnes & Noble, 1974), 19–27, that without the axiom of reducibility there is no definition of the set of natural numbers while ramification remains. The basic problem is that we cannot define the natural numbers as the members of *all* sets to which zero belongs and to which n + 1 belongs when n does.

reach this point, give reasons rather for believing the premises because true consequences follow from them, than for believing the consequences because they follow from the premises.[15]

When Russell deduced from Frege's *Urwahrheiten* the existence of a set that both is and is not a member of itself, this was not the discovery of an amazing new sort of object, but a refutation of Frege's Basic Law V. If Frege or Russell laboring long at their derivations had deduced that $7 + 5 = 13$, it seems clear that this would not have shown that Kant was wrong and that $7 + 5$ is after all 13 but rather that there are mistakes in the assumptions from which the derivations begin. Where Russell says the reason in favor of the principles, the assumptions, is inductive, we might amplify his epithet in terms of the hypothetico-deductive method or inference to the best explanation.[16] Later Quine will argue that the self-evidence even of the middling is an epistemic illusion; while saying is believing is a psychological quirk of ours, *a priori* knowledge is not to be taken seriously, and such justification of knowledge of unseen things like numbers as we have is in terms of how best to explain our experience overall.

Russell published "Mathematical Logic as Based on the Theory of Types" in 1908. In that same year Hilbert's student Ernst Zermelo published "Investigations in the Foundations of Set Theory I," in which he began what became the dominant set theory of our time. Russell needed many sorts of variables restricted in range to single types (and orders), which made for a cumbersome notation. Zermelo followed mathematical practice and minimized the sorts of variables he used. An early order of business was to restrict comprehension in hopes of suppressing the paradoxes. Zermelo assumes not that every predicate has an extension but rather that given a set we may separate out from it those of its members satisfying the predicate. This is called separation (*Aussonderung*). Suppose the predicate is non-self-membership and we have a set z. Then by separation

$$(\exists y)(\forall x)(x \in y \leftrightarrow (x \notin x \land x \in z)).$$

The fateful step in Russell's paradox is instantiating "x" by the value guaranteed for "y," whence

$$y \in y \leftrightarrow (y \notin y \land y \in z).$$

[15] Alfred North Whitehead and Bertrand Russell, *Principia Mathematica*, 2nd ed. reprinted (Cambridge: Cambridge University Press, 1935), v.

[16] See Peter Lipton, *Inference to the Best Explanation* (London: Routledge, 1991).

This is truth-functionally equivalent to

$$y \notin y \land y \notin z.$$

So for any set z we get a non-self-member, which is boring, and a non-member of z, which is interesting. The second conjunct tells us that for every set there is an object not in it. Once again, the universe does not exist. That points a way toward suppressing Cantor's paradox, though that paradox may not have been generally known in 1908. The Burali-Forti paradox becomes a proof that there is no set of all ordinals (so "is an ordinal" has no extension); we can separate from any set the ordinals in it, but the Burali-Forti paradox shows that no such set contains all the ordinals.

Zermelo's separation is usually read second-order. This looks like

$$(\forall z)(\forall F)(\exists y)(\forall x)(x \in y \leftrightarrow (Fx \land x \in z))$$

(where "y" cannot occur in "Fx"). The quantifiers binding the variables "x" and "y" are first-order: their substituents are singular terms, like proper names, definite descriptions, and demonstratives; their values include, but are not exhausted by, the denotations of their substituents. The quantifier binding "F" is second-order, and it is the presence of this quantifier that makes Zermelo's separation second-order. The substituents for "F" are predicates, and its values are often controversial.[17] Frege thought they are concepts, and Russell thought they are propositional functions.

Zermelo states separation thus: "Whenever the *Klassenaussage* Fx is definite for all members of a set z, z has a subset y containing as elements precisely those elements x of z for which Fx is true."[18] "*Klassen*" is the plural of the word that translates "class," and "*aussage*" translates "expression." The latter might make one think a *Klassenaussage*

---

[17] We do not allow the same variables in both singular-term position and predicate position, for otherwise we might put

$$F(X) \leftrightarrow \neg X(X)$$

whence

$$F(F) \leftrightarrow \neg F(F),$$

a version of Russell's paradox, and the heterological paradox.

[18] Ernst Zermelo, "Investigations in the Foundations of Set Theory I," trans. Stefan Bauer-Mengelberg, in Jean van Heijenoort, ed., *From Frege to Gödel: A Source Book in Mathematical Logic, 1879–1931* (Cambridge, Mass.: Harvard University Press, 1967), 202. I have paraphrased Bauer-Mengelberg.

is a predicate and that Zermelo is quantifying over predicates in some language. In a language with an at most countable alphabet and in which expressions are of finite length, there are at most countably many predicates. So when z is countably infinite, taking separation as quantifying over predicates would allow it to assert the existence of at most countably many subsets of z. But by Cantor's theorem, z has continuum many subsets, and for each such subset y of z, the attribute of membership in y, if definite, could be expected to yield a subset of z by separation. It makes separation richer if we take definite class-expressions as substituents for "F" and something like definite properties as its values.

Zermelo's notion of definiteness attracted attention. He seems clearly to say that "is definable by means of a finite number of words" is not definite (so the paradox of the least indescribable ordinal vanishes), but he does not tell us what is indefinite about it. What he does say is that a question or assertion is definite if the fundamental relations of the domain, by means of the axioms and the universally valid laws of logic, determine without arbitrariness whether it holds or not; likewise a class-expression F(x), in which the variable term x ranges over all individuals in a class z, is said to be definite if it is definite for *each single* individual x of the class z.[19] This might be more lucid, but he does seem to be contrasting definiteness, the absence of arbitrariness, with vagueness.

Thinking about substituents for "F" we might make a few observations. Otto Jespersen calls a noun a mass word when it has no plural, does not take numerical adjectives, and does not take "fewer." Some mass nouns include "molasses" and "moonlight." Quine contrasts mass nouns with count nouns, which he says divide their reference.[20] It is part of the nature of tigers and virtues where one leaves off and another begins. Sets are always sets of objects; there is no set of all molasses nor is there a set of all moonlight. (There is a set of all shoes and another of all ships but none of sealing wax.) This may make one wonder how naturally a set theoretic semantics can account for the validity of syllogisms like

(a) All percale is cotton
     All cotton is vegetable
     So all percale is vegetable.

[19] Ibid., 201.
[20] W. V. Quine, *Word and Object* (Cambridge, Mass.: Technology Press of the Massachusetts Institute of Technology, 1960), sect. 19.

(b) All counterpoint is harmony
     All harmony is music
     So all counterpoint is music.

One wishes we had some theory of stuff as we have theories of sets. One dodge here is to insert dummy units like "piece of percale" and "passage of counterpoint." This yields count nouns, but one wonders whether they are definite enough for Zermelo. Adjectives like "green" and "wooden" yield predicates like "is green" and "is wooden" but do not divide their reference and lack sets as extensions. A dodge here is to add a dummy count noun like "thing" as in "green thing." Are there continuum many green things in a single pea? "Green thing" is a count noun (phrase), but one wonders whether it is definite enough for Zermelo. Then there are the count nouns like "cloud" that can be vague. On a cloudy day when it is not completely overcast and the clouds are roiling, sometimes touching briefly before parting, and sometimes merging or splitting, it may be unclear where one cloud ends and another begins and how many clouds there are at a given moment. One wonders whether Zermelo would have thought these questions can be settled without arbitrariness. As we shall see, Skolem will later resolve the issue of definiteness by making set theory first-order.

Zermelo of course assumes extensionality. But separation yields sets only from sets in hand; with just extensionality and separation, there need be no sets at all. In an astronomical application we might assume the set of galaxies (and select for special attention individuals like the Milky Way, sets like the spiral galaxies, and functions like one assigning each galaxy its closest neighbor). We can apply sets to objects as long as there are not too many of them. But set theory need not be applied to non-sets. We assume the empty set outright (and later we will assume an infinite set). For Boolean operations we assume that any two sets have a union, an intersection, and a difference; we do not want complements, since the complement of the empty set is the universe, which we have already shown does not exist. We also assume big unions, that is, for any set z of sets there is a set y which is the union of the sets in z (so $x \in y$ if and only if $x \in u$ for some $u \in z$). For stepping up we assume that everything has a unit set. Unit sets and unions suffice for ordered pairs. Since Cantor's theorem is the glory of set theory, no axiomatization of sets would be adequate (in Tarski's sense) unless it ensures that every set has a power set, so we assume so.

Let H_0 be the empty set, let H_{n+1} be the power set of H_n, and let H be the union of all the H_n. H is the set of hereditary finite (pure) sets; every member of H is finite, and so are its members, and so on ad infinitum. If we restrict the relation $\in$ of membership on both sides to elements of H, we get a structure in which all the axioms of pure set theory we have so far assumed come out true. H has infinitely many members, but none of its members is infinite. So we cannot prove in the theory we have so far that there is an infinite set.[21] An infinite set is a sine qua non of Cantor's theory of the actual infinite, so we add an assumption, infinity, that there is one. This is usually put by saying there is a set x such that $\varnothing \in x$ and $y \cup \{y\} \in x$ when $y \in x$. Once we have infinite sets, we want the axiom of choice.

Frege's number zero is the set of all sets with as many members as the empty set, which is the singleton of the empty set. His number one is the set of all sets with as many members as the unit set of zero, which is the set of all unit sets. The (big) union of one is then the universe, which we proved does not exist. Zero would be the only one of Frege's natural numbers to exist. The present theory preventing us from deducing ordinary mathematics, we need a new account of cardinal and ordinal numbers. Hilbert's student John von Neumann worked one out in the 1920s that became standard. His basic decision was to start with the ordinals, and to treat the cardinals as a special sort of ordinal. When there is a one–one correspondence between the set of As and the set of Bs, there are as many As as Bs. When there are well-orders of the As and the Bs and the one–one correspondence preserves these well-orders, say that the As are as long as the Bs. (The usual term for this is "being cofinal with.") Both as-many-as and as-long-as are equivalence relations, and borrowing a device of Frege's, we took Cantor's cardinals as the equivalence classes of as-many-as and his ordinals as the equivalence classes of as-long-as. When the universe goes, so do Cantor's cardinal one and his ordinal one. So von Neumann replaces each of Cantor's ordinals with a standard representative chosen from it. Cantor's ordinal zero is the unit set of $\varnothing$ (which has no proper initial segments), so von Neumann's zero has to be $\varnothing$. From Cantor's ordinal one, von Neumann takes $\{\varnothing\}$, and

[21] Dedekind argues in article 66 of "The Nature and Meaning of Numbers," in his *Essays on the Theory of Numbers* (New York: Dover, 1963), 64, that since for each of my thoughts I have a thought of it, but there are things in my mind (like my ego) that are not thoughts, my mind is infinite. Russell flounders in this argument: *Introduction to Mathematical Philosophy* (London: George Allen & Unwin, 1919), 138–40.

the element of his one is his zero, its predecessor. From Cantor's ordinal two von Neumann takes $\{\varnothing, \{\varnothing\}\}$, and its elements are his zero and one, its predecessors. More generally, if von Neumann chooses α from an ordinal of Cantor's so that the predecessors of α are its elements, then $\alpha \cup \{\alpha\}$ will be a choice he can make from the successor of that ordinal of Cantor's, and its predecessors will be its elements, and von Neumann can take a limit to be the set of its predecessors.

To make a theory, say that a set x is transitive if all members of members of x are members of x. A set α is an ordinal if and only if it is transitive and $\in \upharpoonright \alpha$ well-orders α. (A set x is $\in$-connected if and only if for any members y and z of x, $y \in z$ or $y = z$ or $z \in y$. Since $\in$ well-orders an ordinal, it is $\in$-connected. We will later consider an assumption called foundation [or regularity]. In the presence of that assumption, $\in$-connection may replace well-ordering by $\in$ in the definition of ordinals.) What follow are some things we can show about ordinals; showing them is a way to help the reader acquire an active understanding of how von Neumann understood ordinals. First, the empty set is an ordinal; and if α is an ordinal, so is $\alpha \cup \{\alpha\}$. A transitive proper subset of an ordinal is a member of it; this exercise is a bit more challenging. Any member of an ordinal is an ordinal. For any ordinals α and β, α is a subset of β or β is a subset of α; so $\alpha \in \beta$ or $\alpha = \beta$ or $\beta \in \alpha$. If x is a set of ordinals, the union of x is an ordinal. An ordinal α is the set of all *ordinals* that are members of α. If x is a nonempty set of ordinals, then the intersection of all ordinals in x is an ordinal in x; the ordinals are well-ordered. We define $\alpha < \beta$ to mean that $\alpha \in \beta$; this is one of the glories of von Neumann's theory. Then $\alpha < \beta$ if and only if α is a proper subset of β. Also, $\alpha < \beta$ if and only if $\alpha \cup \{\alpha\} \leq \beta$. We define $s(\alpha)$, the successor of α, as $\alpha \cup \{\alpha\}$. The union of $s(\alpha)$ is α. But α may be either the successor of the union of α or the union of α; successors are of the first sort, while $\varnothing$ and limits are of the second. So α is a limit if and only if α is not $\varnothing$ and $\alpha = \cup \alpha$. Any property had by any ordinal when all its predecessors have it is had by all ordinals; otherwise some α lacks it, and the ordinals $\leq \alpha$ without it are a set (by separation), so the intersection of this set is the least ordinal without it, contrary to the hypothesis. We define an ordinal α as a successor if and only if $\alpha = s(\beta)$ for some β; no limit is a successor, and if $\alpha < \beta$ where β is a limit, then $\alpha < \gamma < \beta$ for some γ. Any property had by $\varnothing$, had by $s(\alpha)$ when had by α, and had by a limit when had by all predecessors of the limit, is had by all ordinals.

The axiom of infinity with separation yields a least limit ordinal. It is called ω. For any set x there is an ordinal α and a function f that maps α one–one onto x. We use the axiom of choice for this. The details get messy, but the idea is simple. Let g be a choice function for the nonempty subsets of x and let a be an object not in x. Let f(0) be g(x) if x ≠ ∅ but a otherwise. Let f(α) = g(x − {f(β) | β < α}) if x − {f(β) | β < α} ≠ ∅, but a otherwise. We just pick members of x in accord with g as long as they last. Since x is a set but there is no set of all ordinals by the Burali-Forti paradox, there is a least ordinal α such that f(α) = a. Then f maps α one–one onto x. Call sets x and y similar if and only if there is a function mapping x one–one onto y; this is a notion familiar from Cantor and Frege. We have shown that for any set x there is an ordinal similar to it. Call the least such ordinal the cardinal of the set, and say that an ordinal is a cardinal if and only if it is the cardinal of some set. Then ∅, s(∅),... and ω are all cardinals but s(ω), s(s(ω)),... are not. Every cardinal ≥ ω is a limit.

Von Neumann's successor is the union with the singleton, but Zermelo's was just the singleton. So von Neumann's natural numbers are ∅, {∅}, {∅, {∅}},... while Zermelo's are ∅, {∅}, {{∅}},.... These two different structures are isomorphic models of the laws of natural numbers, so if one is focusing just on natural numbers there is not much to choose between them. It has been argued that if natural numbers really are sets, then there should be a unique answer to which set is 2, so since there is nothing to choose between von Neumann's {∅, {∅}} and Zermelo's {{∅}}, numbers are not really sets at all.[22] Perhaps natural numbers are sui generis. But someone like Quine after a perspicuous cosmology of the abstract reaches of the world might want not so much to reduce numbers to sets as to replace natural numbers with one among several systems of set theoretic candidates. It is also easier to see how to generalize von Neumann's finite ordinals into the transfinite. All of Zermelo's nonzero finite ordinals are singletons, but if ω were a singleton it is hard to see how it could fail to be the successor of its member and so not a limit. By now von Neumann's theory has become so established that one might suspect von Neumann discovered which sets the natural numbers are.

Our proof that for every set x there is an ordinal α and a function f that maps α one–one onto x actually escapes from Zermelo's set theory. The problem emerges if we are out beyond ω and we have assigned members of x to all of

$$0, 1,...; \omega, \omega + 1,...$$

22 See Paul Benacerraf, "What Numbers Could Not Be," reprinted in *Philosophy of Mathematics: Selected Readings*, ed. Paul Benacerraf and Hilary Putnam, 2nd ed. (Cambridge: Cambridge University Press, 1983), 272–94.

but there are still members of x to deal with. We need a limit to ω, $\omega + 1,\ldots, \omega + n,\ldots$ as an argument to which f can assign the next chosen member of x. But Zermelo's set theory does not guarantee one. To see what is going on here, let R_0 be $\varnothing$, let R_{n+1} be the power set of R_n, let $R\omega$ be the union of R_0, $R_1,\ldots$, and let $R_{\omega+n+1}$ be the power set of $R_{\omega+n}$, and let R be the union of R_ω, $R_{\omega+1},\ldots$. The structure whose domain is R and whose membership relation is $\in \upharpoonright R$ is a model for all Zermelo's axioms. Each ordinal α among $0, 1,\ldots; \omega, \omega + 1,\ldots$ crops up in $R_{\alpha+1}$ but there is no ordinal in R greater than ω, $\omega + 1,\ldots$. In particular, $\omega \in R_{\omega+1}$, so its power set is a member of $R_{\omega+2}$, but its cardinal, the cardinal of the continuum, is much too big to be a member of R. Hence it is not true in R that every set has a cardinal number of members, and so neither is it provable in Zermelo's set theory. A set theory that allowed sets with no number of members would be crippled. We need a new assumption.

Let Q be a relation and let x be a set. Suppose that for each member y of x there is a unique z such that Qyz. Then replacement says there is a set u such that for all z, z is in u if and only if Qyz for some y in x. For example, the axiom of infinity gives us the set ω of natural numbers. Let Q be the relation that holds between y and z just in case y is a natural number and z is the set $R_{\omega+y}$ we considered in the last paragraph. Then by replacement there is a set u of all those sets $R_{\omega+n}$, and the (big) union of u is the set R mentioned lately. The ordinal $\omega \times 2$ is the limit of ω, $\omega + 1$, $\omega + 2,\ldots$, and it is a subset of R, so separation provides the ordinal we were missing before.[23] Separation follows from replacement.

---

[23] Ordinal arithmetic is curious. The sum $\alpha + \beta$ is the ordinal of an α-sequence followed by a β-sequence (adjusted so that these are disjoint). So $1 + \omega$ is the ordinal of

$$-1, 0, 1,\ldots,$$

which is order-isomorphic to

$$0, 1, 2,\ldots,$$

so $1 + \omega = \omega$. But $\omega + 1$ is the ordinal of

$$0, 1,\ldots; -1$$

which is *not* isomorphic to $0, 1, 2,\ldots$. Hence $1 + \omega \neq \omega + 1$, and ordinal addition does not commute. The product $\alpha\beta$ is the ordinal of a β-sequence in which each point has been replaced by an α-sequence (adjusted that so any two are disjoint). So 2ω is the ordinal of

$$1, -1, 2, -2,\ldots,$$

which is order-isomorphic to $0, 1, 2,\ldots$, so $2\omega = \omega$. But $\omega2$ is the ordinal of

$$0, 2,\ldots; 1, 3,\ldots,$$

which is not order-isomorphic to $0, 1, 2,\ldots$. Hence $2\omega \neq \omega2$, and ordinal multiplication does not commute.

Let z be a set and let F be a definite property. If no members of z have F, the required set y exists by null set. Otherwise, let v be a member of z with F. Let Q be the relation that holds between any member w of z and either w if w has F or else v. Then the set u assumed by replacement of those t such that Qwt for some w in z is the subset y of z required by separation. Replacement tells us that only collections smaller than the universe can be sets.

This derivation is a derivation of second-order separation from second-order replacement, and one imagines that Zermelo would have wanted second-order replacement restricted to definite relations. Replacement was proposed independently in 1922 by Abraham Fraenkel and Thoralf Skolem.[24] Perhaps because Fraenkel was German and Skolem was Norwegian, and Germany was still an intellectual powerhouse in 1922 despite the devastation of World War I, Zermelo's set theory has come to be known as Zermelo–Fraenkel set theory (ZF for short, or ZFC when the presence of the axiom of choice is being stressed), but in considering the neglect of Skolem we should remember that he was no advocate of axiomatized set theory as a foundation for mathematics. Both Fraenkel and Skolem reconsidered definite properties. In his proof of the independence of the axiom of choice from the rest of set theory with non-sets (a formalization of Russell on socks), Fraenkel reworked definite properties as certain functions, but this did not catch on. But Skolem's idea did (even if Zermelo did not like it).[25] Skolem focused on the substituents for the second-order variables. A language designed for pure set theory will include a primitive predicate for membership and, if the designer is kind, a primitive predicate for identity. The formulae will be built up from these predicates and variables using truth-functional connectives and quantifiers. Skolem uses only first-order variables and quantifiers (intended in the pure case to range over sets). Each such formula seems definite enough, and Skolem frames one separation axiom with each such formula. Zermelo had in effect said,

It is an axiom that for each definite property

followed by the rest of his separation. Skolem by contrast says,

For each formula it is an axiom that

[24] See van Heijenoort, *From Frege to Gödel*, 291.
[25] See Gregory Moore, "The Emergence of First-Order Logic," in *History and Philosophy of Modern Mathematics*, ed. William Aspray and Philip Kitcher, (Minneapolis: University of Minnesota Press, 1988), 126.

followed by the rest of separation. Reversing the scopes means that where Zermelo assumes a single second-order axiom, Skolem assumes an infinity of first-order axioms, all conforming to a simple pattern. Skolem's formulation is called an axiom schema, and for decades schemata for first-order axioms have replaced second-order axioms in set theory (and elsewhere).

Replacement too is put as an axiom schema, and first-order separation axioms are derivable from first-order replacement axioms. It is worth noting that if in a separation axiom

$$(\exists y)(\forall x)(x \in y \leftrightarrow (Fx \wedge x \in z))$$

the formula F is already known independently of the separation axiom to have a set u as extension, then the separation axiom is redundant because the required set y is the intersection of z and u. A separation axiom is useful when the formula F is not known to have a set as extension, and a replacement axiom is useful when the two-place formula R is not known to have a set as extension. The schemata of first-order axioms are weaker than the second-order axioms, but they obviate questions of definiteness and they allow a tractable logic, as second-order forms do not.

In the 1920s John von Neumann described a structure; others had noted it, but von Neumann's work eventually took root. Let R_0 be $\varnothing$, let $R_{\alpha+1}$ be the power set of R_α, and when λ is a limit let R_λ be the union of the R_β for $\beta < \lambda$. The sets R_α are called the ranks, and if x is in R_α for some α, then the least such α is called the rank of x. So, for example, each ordinal α has rank $\alpha + 1$. One might think of ranks as like types made cumulative and extended into the transfinite along the ordinals. We can define a predicate V by saying that $V(x)$ if and only if $x \in R_\alpha$ for some α. No set is the extension of this predicate, for since $V(\alpha)$ for every ordinal α, if V had an extension, we could separate a set of all ordinals from it, which would land us in the Burali-Forti paradox. But suppose that $(\forall x)V(x)$. Then whenever $x \in y$, x would be of lower rank than y, so sets would be layered, as Russell thought. In 1929 von Neumann argued that within a world in which the axioms of ZFC are true there is an inner world in which all those axioms are still true and so is $(\forall x)V(x)$.[26] This became known as an inner model construction or argument; in the

[26] John von Neumann, "Über eine Widerspruchsfreiheitsfrage in der axiomatischen Mengenlehre," *Journal für reineund angewandte Mathematik* 160 (1929): 373–91. See also Thoralf Skolem, "Some Remarks on Axiomatized Set Theory," sect. 6 (298–99), in van Heijenoort, *From Frege to Gödel*.

1930s Gödel used inner models to show that if Zermelo–Fraenkel set theory is consistent, it remains so on adding the axiom of choice, and if Zermelo–Fraenkel set theory with choice is consistent, it remains so on adding the generalized continuum hypothesis (though Gödel actually worked with another set theory we will describe soon).

The title of von Neumann's 1929 paper was "On a Consistency Question in Axiomatic Set Theory," which does not advertise a claim that $(\forall x)V(x)$ is an *Urwahrheit*. But many people find it congenial. Where replacement, power set, big union, and infinity give us sets we think we need, the assumption that $(\forall x)V(x)$ throws away sets some think we do not need, like a set a such that a = {a} or a sequence $a_0, a_1, \ldots$ of sets such that for all n, $a_{n+1} \in a_n$. As we saw, if S is the set of propositions expressible in seven words, assuming that $(\forall x)V(x)$ would forbid taking the proposition

> This proposition is expressible in seven words

as the ordered pair p = <p, S>, which might seem a bit preemptory.[27] The assumption that $(\forall x)V(x)$ is sometimes called the axiom of regularity and, sometimes, the axiom of foundation. Gödel says foundation "is not indispensable, but it simplifies considerably the later work."[28] But in the second half of the twentieth century there emerged an opinion that foundation is the heart of *the* way to do set theory.[29] The core

[27] Such propositions are put to work by Jon Barwise and John Etchemendy in *The Liar: An Essay on Truth and Circularity* (New York: Oxford University Press, 1987). The set theory they use is described by Peter Aczel in *Non-Well-Founded Sets* (Stanford: Center for the Study of Language and Information, 1988), and in my "On Non-Well-Founded Sets," *Crítica* 24 (December 1992): 3–21. With foundation, settling the identity of members of sets x and y suffices to settle that of x and y by extensionality. But if a = {a} and b = {b}, the identities of the members of {a} and {b} cannot be settled without settling that of these sets; extensionality needs to be extended when self-membership happens, and there is more than one way to extend it. Aczel shows that the intended world of well-founded sets includes a model for non-well-founded set theory.

[28] Kurt Gödel, *The Consistency of the Axiom of Choice and of the Generalized Continuum Hypothesis with the Axioms of Set Theory* (Princeton: Princeton University Press, 1940), 6.

[29] A seminal exposition of this view is by George Boolos in "The Iterative Conception of Set," reprinted in his *Logic, Logic, and Logic*, ed. Richard Jeffrey (Cambridge, Mass.: Harvard University Press, 1998), 13–29. A pivotal source here is Dana S. Scott, "Axiomatizing Set Theory," in *Axiomatic Set Theory: Proceedings of Symposia in Pure Mathematics*, ed. Dana S. Scott XIII.2 (Providence: American Mathematical Society, 1974), 13: 207–14.

idea is to assume the ordinals, build up the ranks, and then prove most of the axioms of ZFC in the resulting structure. This approach has its pedagogical charms. Its pretext is Gödel's remark in 1947 that

> This concept of set, however, according to which a set is anything obtainable from the integers (or some other well-defined objects) by iterated application of the operation "set of," and not something obtained by dividing the totality of all existing things into two categories, has never led to any antinomy whatsoever; that is, the perfectly "naïve" and uncritical working with this concept of set has so far proved completely self-consistent.[30]

But that the iterative sets suffice for most of ZFC does not show they are necessary, nor is it evident that the set of operation has no fixed points (as 0 is a fixed point of the square-of operation) and no infinitely descending chains (as negative integers are an infinitely descending chain of the successor function).

Besides, we may not be restricted either to thinking of sets as objects got by iterating "set-of" or to thinking of them as all ways of splitting the universe in two. John Venn pictures them as something like loops, though extensionality forbids two loops enclosing the same objects. This image may give us a way of thinking of replacement, the assumption of ZFC that eludes justification from the iterative conception. Picture a function as arrows, one and only one leading from each point in the loop that is the domain of the function. Replacement says that the range of this function is a set, and to lasso the range, either reel in the arrows (to fit the range in the loop around the domain) or slide the loop around the domain along the arrows to loop around the range. One supposes it was some such image that led Fraenkel to call replacement "replacement."

The usual statement of foundation is not that $(\forall x)V(x)$, but that any nonempty set has a member disjoint from it. This phrasing is ordinal-free and closer to the primitives of the language of ZFC. The idea is that were $a_0, a_1, \ldots$ a sequence such that $a_{n+1} \in a_n$, then the set $a = \{a_0, a_1, \ldots\}$ would have no member disjoint from it, since $a_{n+1} \in a \cap a_n$. (If $b \in b$, let $b_n = b$ for all n, and then $b_{n+1} \in b_n$.) First-order logic is compact. This means that any logical consequence of a set (finite or infinite) of first-order sentences is a logical consequence of a finite subset of those

[30] Kurt Gödel, "What Is Cantor's Continuum Problem?" reprinted in his *Collected Works*, vol. 2, *Publications, 1938–1974*, ed. Solomon Feferman et al. (New York: Oxford University Press, 1990), 180.

sentences. Suppose ZFC, which is first-order, is consistent. Add to its language an infinity a_0, a_1,... of new constants and the sentences $a_{n+1} \in a_n$. For any finite set of these new sentences, let n be the largest number such that a_n occurs in a sentence in this finite set. Let a_n denote $\varnothing$, a_{n-1} denote $\{\varnothing\}$,..., and a_0 denote the n-fold iterate of unit-set starting from $\varnothing$. Then all the sentences in the finite set come out true in a model for ZF. Hence no contradiction follows from ZFC plus all of $a_{n+1} \in a_n$. So first-order ZFC cannot rule out infinitely descending $\in$-chains. (This argument is due to Leon Henkin.) A second-order foundation might look like

$$(\forall F)((\exists x)(Fx) \to (\exists y)(Fy \wedge (\forall z)(z \in y \to Fz))).$$

Second-order logic is not compact.

From 1925 to 1940 Hilbert's students John von Neumann, Paul Bernays, and Kurt Gödel worked out a set theory now called NBG after them. Often in set theory, "class" and "set" are mere stylistic variants, but NBG distinguishes sets among classes. Its basic objects are classes. Often it is exposited with capital letters as variables ranging over classes, but these are first-order variables. A set is defined to be a class that is a member of a class. The German for "set" is "*Menge*," so this definition is often written

$$M(X) \leftrightarrow (\exists Y)(X \in Y).$$

Lowercase letters are used as variables restricted to sets. Let $\varphi(X, X_1,...,X_n)$ be a (first-order) formula of this language; as indicated, it may contain class variables "X_1",..., "X_n" besides "X," but all its quantifiers must be restricted to sets (and it may not contain "Y").[31] The NBG version of the comprehension schema reads

$$(\exists Y)(\forall X)(X \in Y \leftrightarrow (M(X) \wedge \varphi(X, X_1,...,X_n))),$$

which says that $\varphi(X)$ has as extension a class Y of all and only the *sets* x such that $\varphi(x)$. A class that is not a set is called a proper class. Comprehension says for non-self-membership that

$$(\exists Y)(\forall X)(X \in Y \leftrightarrow M(X) \wedge X \notin X),$$

---

[31] Gödel does it this way on page 8 of *Consistency of the Continuum Hypothesis* (cited in note 28), but Monk allows quantification over classes. See J. Donald Monk, *Introduction to Set Theory* (New York: McGraw-Hill, 1969), 16. This is called Bernays–Morse set theory by C. C. Chang and H. Jerome Keisler in *Model Theory* (Amsterdam: North-Holland, 1973), 510–11.

so there is a class Y of all non-self-membered sets. The fateful step in Russell's paradox is instantiating "X" for this Y. Here this yields

$$Y \in Y \leftrightarrow M(Y) \wedge Y \notin Y,$$

which is, as with separation, truth functionally equivalent to

$$\neg M(Y) \wedge Y \notin Y,$$

so

$$\neg M(Y).$$

Russell's paradox turns into a proof that Y is a proper class (whence it is a member of no class, and thus not a member of Y). Ordinals are sets, and there is a class of all ordinals, but the Burali-Forti paradox turns into a proof that the class of all ordinals is proper. There is a class V of all sets, and every set has a power set larger than the set by Cantor's theorem, but Cantor's paradox turns into a proof that V is not a set but is a proper class. V would be a member of its power class, so since it is proper, it has no power class. V might look like an ersatz universe, but it omits all the proper classes, so there are things not in V.[32]

The other axioms of NBG are extensionality for classes, power set just for sets, pairing (for all sets x and y there is a set z whose elements are x and y), big union (the union of a set of sets is a set; there is a class of unit sets, and if its union were a set, V would be a set), foundation, infinity (there is an infinite set), choice, and replacement. Some restrict choice to sets and others allow it for classes. Replacement may be put

$$(\forall R)(\forall x)((\forall y)(y \in x \to (\exists!z)Ryz) \to$$
$$(\exists u)(\forall z)(z \in u \leftrightarrow (\exists y)(y \in x \wedge Ryz))),$$

so a single first-order class quantifier does duty for the infinity of instances of the axiom schema of replacement in ZFC. The comprehension schema of NBG can be derived from finitely many of its instances, so NBG needs only finitely many axioms about classes.

Every theorem of ZFC is a theorem of NBG. Conversely, Joseph Shoenfield stated in 1954 an algorithm that, given a proof in NBG of a theorem just about sets, yields a proof in ZFC of that theorem.[33] So

---

[32] A model in Tarski's sense is a tuple or sequence whose first member is its domain, so according to NBG there is no model whose domain is V.

[33] Joseph R. Shoenfield, "A Relative Consistency Proof," *Journal of Symbolic Logic* 18 (1954): 21–28.

there is nothing to chose between ZFC and NBG as far as sets on their own go. There is another way to look at this. Some who think there are more sets than are dreamt of in ZFC or NBG might propose an ordinal α such that R_α with $\in \upharpoonright R_\alpha$ as its membership relation is a model for ZFC. When ZFC is first-order, such an ordinal is called weakly inaccessible. It is inaccessible since, by Gödel's second incompleteness theorem, we cannot prove in first-order ZFC that there are such ordinals because ZFC cannot prove ZFC consistent if it is consistent.[34] Such a model yields a model for first-order NBG if we take the classes as the subsets of R_α; the sets are the members of R_α, and the proper classes are its subsets that are not elements of it. A cardinal α such that R_α yields a model for second-order ZFC is called strongly inaccessible[35] and would yield an analogous model for second-order NBG.

The theory of types suppresses the universe by requiring a set to be of higher type than its members, while the universe is a member of itself and yet is forbidden to exceed its own type. The axiom of foundation suppresses the universe in much the same way, but even without foundation, ZFC and NBG have their own ways of omitting the universe. Quine went another way. He says he "disliked the lack of a universe class in Zermelo's system, and the lack of complements of classes, and in general the lack of big classes."[36] The result was the system of his paper "New Foundations for Mathematical Logic"; that system is now known as NF.[37]

One way to see NF is in contrast with the theory of types. Let us forget orders. In the theory of types, each variable takes its values from the members of a single type. Types are ticked off using arabic numerals,

---

[34] A cardinal α is singular if and only if it is the union of fewer than α cardinals each less than α; a singular cardinal can, as it were, be reached from below by addition. A cardinal is regular if and only if it is not singular. Let $\aleph_0$ be ω, let $\aleph_{\alpha+1}$ be the least cardinal greater than $\aleph_\alpha$, and let $\aleph_\lambda$ be the union of the $\aleph_\beta$ for $\beta < \lambda$. The $\aleph_\alpha$ are the infinite cardinals. A cardinal is weakly inaccessible if and only if it is regular and $\aleph_\lambda$ for some limit λ. The cardinal of the continuum could be weakly inaccessible, which would make it big where Cantor's continuum hypothesis makes it small.

[35] A cardinal α is strongly inaccessible if and only if it is uncountable, regular, and for any set x of cardinal less α, the power set of x is also of cardinal less α (so α cannot be reached from below by power set).

[36] W. V. Quine, "The Inception of 'New Foundations,'" reprinted in his *Selected Logic Papers*, enl. ed. (Cambridge, Mass.: Harvard University Press, 1995), 288.

[37] W. V. Quine, "New Foundations for Mathematical Logic," reprinted in his *From a Logical Point of View*, 2nd ed. rev. (Cambridge, Mass.: Harvard University Press, 1961), 80–101. This essay dates from 1937.

and which type a variable ranges over may be indicated by an arabic numeral superscript attached to occurrences of the variable. For example, "x^7" ranges over type 7. To describe features common to many types, Russell allows himself a merely heuristic device he calls typical ambiguity, according to which he will write terms like "x^n" in which the superscript might look like a variable ranging over the natural numbers. But Russell does not mean these superscripts as variables accessible to quantification within the formulae of *Principia Mathematica* lest the universe sneak back in as

$$\{x \mid (\exists n)(x^n = x^n)\}.$$

Officially the type superscripts are confined just to particular arabic numerals. We have to understand an indefinitely, indeed infinitely, extensible range of these expressions, which would invite variables to occupy their niches, and we use a predicate "is a type" that is true of what these expressions seem to denote, but the quantified talk about types these would facilitate is censored from the formulae of *Principia*.

Quine's set theoretic roots are more in *Principia* than in ZFC or NBG, and much of his set theoretic work lay in cleaning up *Principia*. In NF he uses only a single style of variable. Membership is his only primitive predicate (and he defines the identity of x and y by saying that for all z, x is in z if and only if y is in z). His question is how to restrict comprehension in hopes of suppressing the paradoxes. His answer is stratification. The formula A is stratified if and only if there is a way to go through A replacing variables (free and bound) by arabic numerals so that every occurrence of $\in$ is flanked by consecutive (not just increasing, but *consecutive*) numerals. These numerals say nothing about the world; they do not label types into which objects fall but just mark a pattern in the syntax of A. But suppose A is stratified and the variable "x" occurs free in A ("y" may not). Then it is an axiom of NF that

$$(\exists y)(\forall x)(x \in y \leftrightarrow Ax).$$

For example, the formula "$x \notin x$" is not stratified, so it is not an axiom of NF that

$$(\exists y)(\forall x)(x \in y \leftrightarrow x \notin x),$$

which is how NF dodges the usual argument of Russell's paradox. On the other hand, the formula "$x = x$," which spelled out in primitive terms reads

$$(\forall y)(x \in y \leftrightarrow x \in y),$$

is stratified; just replace "x" with "0" and "y" with "1." So it is an axiom of NF that

$$(\exists y)(\forall x)(x \in y \leftrightarrow x = x).$$

So NF admits the universe. The only other assumption in NF about sets is extensionality.

Since NF allows the universe, which is a member of itself, it rejects foundation. Without foundation, the von Neumann ordinals are the transitive sets well-ordered by membership. A well-ordering is a partial ordering, which is irreflexive. But irreflexivity of membership is non-self-membership. So as stratified comprehension failed to yield the pivotal set of Russell's paradox, it also fails to yield the set of von Neumann ordinals (or cardinals either).[38] On the other hand, the obvious formula saying either that set A has as many members as set B or that well-order R is as long as well-order S is stratified, and stratified comprehension yields the sets of their equivalence classes, that is, the set of cardinals and the set of ordinals in the style of Cantor.

The existence of the universe and the set O of all ordinals will make a philosopher nervous about Cantor's paradox and the Burali-Forti paradox. Cantor's paradox arises when Cantor's theorem is applied to the universe. We need a bit of articulation to say how the Burali-Forti paradox arises when O is about. Recall that a segment of ordinals is a set S of ordinals such that for an α in S, if $\beta < \alpha$, then β is in S too; segments have no gaps. When S is a segment, let $\sigma(S)$ be the ordinal (type) of $< \uparrow S$. Let us say that S is *capped* if and only if $\sigma(S)$ is the ordinal (type) of $< \uparrow \{\alpha \mid \alpha < \sigma(S)\}$. It was a theorem in Cantor's paradise that every segment of ordinals is capped, and the Burali-Forti paradox arises when this theorem is applied to O. When the universe and O are around, both these theorems will have to give, at least somewhat, and thus so will their proofs.

Already in 1937 Quine remarked an effect of stratification on the proof of Cantor's theorem. At the crucial juncture, after we have

---

[38] Transitivity looks like

$$(\forall y)(\forall z)((z \in y \wedge y \in x) \to z \in x).$$

A numeral replacing "x" in the antecedent could not be consecutive with one replacing "z," but would have to be in the consequent. So transitivity is not stratified. Neither is $\in$-connection.

assumed for reductio a function f that maps the set x onto its power set, Cantor asks us to consider the set

$$y = \{z \in x \mid z \notin f(z)\};$$

this move is the diagonalization. Quine observes that the condition

$$z \notin f(z)$$

is not stratified. It requires the existence of a subset a of x (the value of f at z), a set b (the unit set of z), a set c (the unordered pair of z and a), and a set d (the unordered pair of b and c) such that

$$z \in b \wedge z, a \in c \wedge b, c \in d \wedge d \in f \wedge z \notin a.$$

To stratify this, the same numeral would replace "z" and "a" in the second clause, while by the last clause this is forbidden. The loss of the diagonal set will make a mathematician nervous about losing Cantor's theorem, which would be tantamount to expulsion from his paradise. But suppose we raise the arguments of f a stratum. Suppose, that is, the domain of f is not x but the set of singletons of members of x. Then the condition for the diagonal set would require a subset a of x (the value of f at $\{z\}$), a set b (the unit set of x), a set c (the unordered pair of $\{z\}$ and a), and a set d (the unordered pair of b and c) such that

$$\{z\} \in b; \{z\}, a \in c; b, c \in d; d \in f; \text{ and } z \notin a.$$

Here the second and last clauses require that the numeral in lieu of "a" be consecutive with the numeral in lieu of "z." So the condition is stratified, and stratified comprehension yields the diagonal set.

The upshot is that Cantor's theorem acquires an antecedent. For each set x, stratified comprehension yields the set u(x) of all unit sets of members of x. Rosser calls a set x cantorian if x has as many members as u(x).[39] Then Cantor's theorem says that if x is cantorian, it is smaller than its power set. Cantor's paradox becomes a proof that the universe is not cantorian. Note that the condition for a one–one correspondence between objects and their singletons would require the existence of an object x, a set a (the unit set of x), and a set b (the unordered pair of x and a) where the members of the correspondence are the sets c (the unordered pairs of a and b) such that

$$x \in a; x, a \in b; \text{ and } a, b \in c.$$

[39] J. Barkley Rosser, *Logic for Mathematicians* (New York: McGraw-Hill, 1953), 347.

To stratify this, the same numeral would have to replace "x" and "a" in the second clause, while in the first the numeral replacing "a" must be consecutive with the one replacing "x." So the condition is not stratified, and NF does not show all sets cantorian (if it is consistent).

In 1950 Hao Wang and J. Barkley Rosser proved that NF has no models in which identity obeys its usual laws, less-than for cardinals well-orders the natural numbers, and less-than for ordinals well-orders them.[40] We should preserve identity, so if the natural numbers are well-ordered, the set O of all ordinals is not well-ordered, there is no ordinal for less-than on O, and the Burali-Forti paradox is obviated, but at a considerable cost. Now suppose that the set O of all ordinals has an ordinal Ω, the type of <. But although O is a segment, it is not capped, because Ω is a member of O. (This suggests that Ω is its own successor, which would prevent getting above Ω.) When in Cantor's paradise we proved that every segment is capped, we did so by transfinite induction, a consequence of the well-ordering of O by <. That a relation R is a well-ordering with field A is usually explained by saying that every non-empty sub*set* of A has an R-least member; well-ordering is a principle about sets. So understood, transfinite induction may be put

$$(\forall x)((\forall \alpha)((\forall \beta)(\beta < \alpha \rightarrow \beta \in x) \rightarrow \alpha \in x) \rightarrow (\forall \alpha)(\alpha \in x))$$

(where the Greek letters are variables restricted to ordinals). It is not plausible that NF yields a transfinite induction schema

$$(\forall \alpha)((\forall \beta)(\beta < \alpha \rightarrow F\beta) \rightarrow F\alpha) \rightarrow (\forall \alpha)F\alpha$$

good for all formulae F even unstratified. To argue by transfinite induction we need a set to show that all ordinals belong to a set. To show all segments are capped, this set would be

$$\{\alpha \mid < \uparrow \{\beta \mid \beta < \alpha\} \in \alpha\},$$

and to get this set by stratified comprehension, the condition

$$< \uparrow \{\beta \mid \beta < \alpha\} \in \alpha$$

should be stratified. This requires *of* the set x such that when $\beta, \gamma < \alpha$ and $\beta < \gamma, < \beta, \gamma > \in$ x, *that* x $\in \alpha$. The clause that $\beta, \gamma < \alpha$ puts all three in the same stratum (as it were), while the clause that $<\beta, \gamma> \in$ x puts β and γ below x, and the clause that x $\in \alpha$ puts x in below α. Hence the

[40] J. Barkley Rosser and Hao Wang, "Non-standard Models for Formal Logic," *Journal of Symbolic Logic* 15 (1950): 113–29.

condition is not stratified, and the induction is blocked. But capping is so central to ordinals that we do not want to abandon it entirely.[41]

The theory of types is now a thing of the past. As far as sets go, there is nothing to chose between ZFC and NBG, and they are now the mass market for sets.[42] NF is a more specialized taste, but if one wants the universe, NF is a place to look.[43]

Quine did not rest with NF. In NF we need a set a to apply mathematical induction,

$$(0 \in a \wedge (\forall n)(n \in a \to (n + 1) \in a)) \to N \subseteq a,$$

where N is the set of natural numbers. In general the way in NF to get a is as the extension of a stratified formula. This obstructs proving in NF that $\{k \mid k < n\} \in n$, which is a big loss. So Quine devised ML.[44] As in NBG, in ML everything is a class, and sets are classes that are members of classes, but in ML, V is a set. The axioms of ML are extensionality, a comprehension schema for classes according to which for every formula $F(x)$ there is a class of all sets x such that $F(x)$, and a comprehension schema for sets according to which for every stratified formula $F(x)$ in which all free and bound variables are restricted to sets there is a set of all sets x such that $F(x)$.[45] ML and NF have the same sets, and each is consistent if the other is. But in ML the a in induction may be a class, and there is a class of all n such that $\{k \mid k < n\} \in n$. But ML has difficulties with infinite ordinals and with real numbers.[46]

---

[41] Rosser, *Logic for Mathematicians*, 474.

[42] For a sample of the devotion the iterative conception of sets inspires, see D. A. Martin's review of W. V. Quine's *Set Theory and Its Logic*, rev. ed., in the *Journal of Philosophy* 67 (26 February 1970): 111–14; it is remarkable that Quine replied to Martin, in the *Journal of Philosophy* 67 (23 April 1970): 247–48.

[43] NF is not the only place to look for the universe. See T. E. Forster, *Set Theory with a Universal Set: Exploring an Untyped Universe*, 2nd ed. (Oxford: Clarendon Press, 1995). There is a charming exposition of such a theory in M. Randall Holmes, *Elementary Set Theory with a Universal Set*, Cahiers du Centre de Logique, vol. 10 (Louvain-la-Neuve, Belgium: Academia, n.d.). Available online: math.boisestate. edu/~holmes/holmes/head.pdf.

[44] W. V. Quine, *Mathematical Logic*, rev. ed. (New York: Harper Torchbooks, 1962). The system of this book is called ML.

[45] The restriction of bound variables to sets is crucial and is due to Hao Wang, "A Formal System of Logic," *Journal of Symbolic Logic* 15 (1950): 25–32.

[46] See Joseph Ullian, "Quine and the Field of Mathematical Logic," in *The Philosophy of W. V. Quine*, ed. Lewis Edwin Hahn and Paul Arthur Schilpp (La Salle, Ill.: Open Court, 1986), 569–89.

FOUR

✦

The Universe and Everything

Here is a picture of a simple instance of truth.

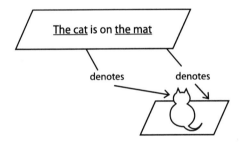

The example is John Austin's. The picture has two parts: what is true, and what makes it true. As we have mentioned, the things that are true or false are articulated into smaller bits that are neither true nor false but pick out the subject matter that makes for truth. Even if one favors abstract propositions or mental judgments as bearers of the truth values, still, sentences wear their articulation into such smaller bits, words, on their inscribed faces, and that articulation seems to get read back into propositions (as concepts) or judgments (as ideas). Tarski took the sentences themselves as the truth bearers.

Traditional grammar teaches that every sentence has a subject and a predicate. While that dictum remains a basic principle of composition, the logicians reconceived it in several ways. In the first place, one of the major achievements of nineteenth-century logicians like Peirce and Schröder was to begin a systematic taxonomy of relations. It is basic here that while earlier only unary properties (like being red or being round) received sustained attention, now binary relations (like loving or being above), ternary (like a giving b to c), and so on got equal billing.

It was as if where traditional grammarians had assumed each sentence has a unique subject, now logicians ignored declension (subject, direct object, indirect object, possessive, and so on) and treated the two, three, or however many singular terms to which a binary, ternary, or whatever polyadicity predicate is applied to make a simple sentence, all as several subjects of that single predicate. In Austin's example, the predicate is "is on" for the binary relation of superposition, and the two subjects are "the cat" and "the mat."

As Hartry Field urged, Tarski can be viewed as having reduced truth to reference or denotation.[1] In our example, given that "the cat" denotes the creature below with the ears, "the mat" denotes the supine object below, and the superposition relation is the extension of the binary "is on" predicate, then the sentence "The cat is on the mat" is true just in case the eared creature bears the superposition relation to the supine object. That might seem like a thicket of verbiage, but all it does is to put our picture into words. More generally, if a sentence S is composed of a binary predicate P applied to singular terms a and b, then given that a denotes x, b denotes y, and relation R is the extension of P, it follows that S is true if and only if $<x, y>$ is a member of R. It is clear that the reduction generalizes across predicates of all polyadicities.

Articulation of inferences requires the recognition of sentence structures besides subjects–predicate form. Modus ponens, for example, licenses inferences from a conditional and its antecedent to its consequent, and conditional proof licenses inferences to a conditional from a deduction of its consequent from its antecedent. An n-place sentence connective is a word or phrase that, applied to n (occurrences of) sentences, yields a sentence.[2] So "not" is a 1-place sentence connective for negation, and "and" is a 2-place connective for conjunction. The conditional is a 2-place sentence connective. Let * be any n-place sentence connective. We say that * is truth functional if and only if for any n sentences $S_1,..., S_n$, the truth value of the sentence $*(S_1,..., S_n)$ is determined by and (this is the important bit) *only* by the truth values of $S_1,..., S_n$. The truth value of the negation of a sentence is the opposite of the truth value of the sentence, so negation is truth-functional. A conjunction is true if both conjuncts are true but false otherwise, so conjunction is also truth-functional. It is more controversial whether the conditional

[1] Hartry Field, "Tarski's Theory of Truth," *Journal of Philosophy* 64 (1972): 347–75.
[2] The point of this talk of occurrences is to allow the different places in a 2-place connective to be filled by one and the same sentence. "Grass is green and grass is green" is a grammatical conjunction.

is truth-functional, but the material conditional is a way of reading it truth-functionally (so that a conditional is true unless its antecedent is true and its consequent is false). So read, modus ponens transmits truth, and sound deduction makes for true conditionals inferred by conditional proof.

Call sentences got by applying an n-ary predicate to n (occurrences of) singular terms atomic. So far we have described how to reduce truth for atomic sentences to the extensions of their predicates and the denotations of their singular terms. We can then extend this account to sentences built up by (even deeply nested) applications of truth-functional connectives. It takes a bit of reasoning, but we can show that any truth-functional connective can be built up from applications of negation and conjunction; the material conditional, for example, amounts to not (A and not-B). So we need only extend to negations and conjunctions. Clearly, the negation of a sentence is true if and only if the sentence is not true, and the conjunction of two sentences is true if and only if both conjuncts are true. So we have extended our account of truth from atomic sentences to all truth-functional compounds of atomic sentences. These used to be called molecular sentences.

Let us describe the structure of molecular sentences a bit more explicitly. Say that an atomic sentence is a molecular sentence of depth 0, and that a molecular sentence of depth n + 1 is either the negation of a molecular sentence of depth n or the conjunction of molecular sentences of depth at most n, and at least one of depth n. Then a molecular sentence is a molecular sentence of some depth. The depth of a molecular sentence measures the nesting of connectives in it, so the material conditional as described in the last paragraph is of depth three if A and B are atomic. We have given what is called an inductive description of the molecular sentences. When we say the atomic sentences are molecular, this is called the basis clause, and it sets out a way to start building up molecules. When we say negations and conjunctions of molecules are molecules, this is called the inductive clause, and it sets out ways to build more-nested molecules from less. We implicitly assume what is called an extremal clause, which says that only sentences so built up from atoms by negation and conjunction are molecules. The basis and inductive clauses say what goes into the molecules, while the extremal clause says that nothing else (like the moon) goes in.

Our inductive description might look circular, since it says in the inductive clause that the negation of a molecule is a molecule. This looks to describe molecularity in terms of molecularity, and thus to make a circle. But depth makes the apparent circularity benign. Each molecular sentence has a unique depth, and from the sentence we can read off its construction from atomic sentences by negations and conjunctions. The basis clause stipulates that the atoms are molecules of depth 0, and once the molecules of depth n are settled, the inductive clause settles those of depth n + 1. Every inductive description or definition requires an underlying order like that by depth so as not to be viciously circular. The order of molecules by depth is like a well-order except that it is not total; different molecules may have the same depth, so comparability fails.

Our account of truth is also inductive and traces the order of molecules by depth. Suppose that A is an atom composed of an n-ary predicate P applied to n terms $t_1, \ldots, t_n$. Suppose the denotations of $t_1, \ldots, t_n$ are $d_1, \ldots, d_n$ and the extension of P is an n-adic relation R. Then in the basis case, we say that A is true if and only if $d_1, \ldots, d_n$ (in that order) stand in the relation R. In the inductive case, let S be a molecule of depth n + 1. S is either a negation not-A or a conjunction (A and B), and since A and B are of lesser depth than S, we may suppose their truth conditions already accounted for. Then if S is not-A, S is true if and only if A is not true, while if S is (A and B), S is true if and only if A is true and B is true. (This account will work only for those who already understand negation and conjunction, and for that matter, standing in a relation.)[3]

We have made no suggestion that all sentences of, say, English are truth-functional compounds of atomic sentences.[4] Necessity, for example, seems to be a 1-place sentence connective. But it is not truth-functional. For both "Three is odd" and "Napoleon died at St. Helena" are true, but while the first could not be false, the second could (since Napoleon could have escaped from St. Helena too and died in, say, Corsica). So "It is necessary that three is odd" is true, but "It is necessary that Napoleon died at St. Helena" is false. So the truth value of a sentence S does not all by itself settle the truth value of "It is necessary

[3] Some writers call such inductive accounts of truth recursive. But the main usage of "recursive" ties it intimately to decidability. A property P is decidable if and only if there is a finite list of rules that, applied to any given object a, settles in finitely many mechanical steps whether a has P. The basis clause in our account of truth does not require that the extensions of the predicates be decidable, and truth is undecidable in most interesting cases. So it is illiterate to call an inductive account of truth recursive (unless one can show decidability).

[4] But Wittgenstein seems to have claimed this in his *Tractatus*. Ludwig Wittgenstein, *Tractatus Logico-Philosophicus*, trans. D. F. Pears and B. F. McGuinness (London: Routledge & Kegan Paul, 1961), prop. 5.

that S," and thus necessity is not truth-functional. Some followers of Leibniz think that in addition to this, the actual world, where Napoleon died at St. Helena, there are other possible worlds where Napoleon died in Corsica. Were we to relativize truth to possible worlds, we could say "Necessarily S" is true at one world if and only if S is true at all worlds.[5] But the metaphysics and epistemology of possible worlds are controversial. Note too that the inductive form of our account of truth requires that both the truth of S and its necessitation be relativized to a world, while one may have expected necessary truth not to be so relativized.

Many mental states are attributed by saying of a person (like Ann or Beth) that she hopes, or fears, or believes, or whatever, that the moon is cubical, or that 12 is prime, or whatever. A sentence attributing such a state will have a subject denoting someone, a verb (often called a verb of propositional attitude), and a that-clause filled out by a sentence. If we treat "hope," "fear," "believe," and other verbs of propositional attitude as binary predicates in atomic sentences, then we cannot assume that all the atomic sentences are available prior to nesting for embedding in sentences of positive depth; sentences of any positive depth might, for all we know, fill out the that-clause in an ascription of a propositional attitude in a (supposedly) atomic sentence. If atoms do not precede molecules, our inductive structure is at risk, so for the sake of that structure, we should not take verbs of propositional attitude as making atomic sentences. One might leave such verbs bound to proper names (denoting a person said to have the attitude) and take these compounds as 1-place sentence connectives. To do so would be to assimilate "John believes that" to negation and necessity. But then, since we all believe some, but not every, truth, it is clear that belief is not truth-functional. Neither is necessity. But while in the case of necessity there is a systematic, albeit controversial, metaphysics of possible worlds that suffices to organize some opinions about necessity, the case of belief and the other propositional attitudes is less settled. No thesis that all English sentences are truth-functional compounds of atomic sentences has been made out.

When the revolution in logic began in the last third of the nineteenth century, most of the revolutionaries (like Cantor, Frege, Peirce, and Peano) were focused primarily on the reasoning that occurs in mathematics. Philosophers may talk of necessity in their commentary about mathematics, but necessity (unlike numbers and functions) has little

---

[5] See Brian F. Chellas, *Modal Logic* (Cambridge: Cambridge University Press, 1980).

place in the statements of mathematics. If there is mathematics to be made of belief (subjective probability)[6] or desire (utility in economics),[7] it was not made until the twentieth century. But ever since Aristotle, there had been a focus in logic on universal and particular sentences (or judgments or propositions). A universal sentence tells us about everything, as in all men are mortal, while a particular sentence tells us about something, as in some dogs are terriers. The two operators are called quantifiers because they specify the extent to which a claim holds. Quantifiers had also figured in mathematics at least since Euclid, as in his axiom that for *any* two points, *there is* a unique straight line passing through both. Logic for mathematics may not need necessity or belief, but it certainly needs quantifications.

When Aristotle described syllogisms (for example, if all men are mortal and some men are vegetarians, then some vegetarians are mortal), he sometimes used capital letters to give the forms of the premises and conclusion (for example, if all As are Bs and some As are Cs, then some Cs are Bs). The idea is that the syllogism is dependable no matter what (grammatically acceptable) substituents go in for the dummy capital letters marking blanks for substitution. The substituents for these capital letters are typically predicates. But Aristotle has no systematic way to represent the polyadicity of predicates. Indeed, until the nineteenth century there is something of a prejudice against relations and in favor of properties.[8] But during the nineteenth century, logicians like Augustus De Morgan argued (1859) that there are impeccable inferences that turn on relations but that, for this reason, elude Aristotle's syllogistic.[9] Two favorite examples of the same form are

All horses are animals.
Hence, all heads of horses are heads of animals,

and

All circles are figures.
Hence, all who draw circles draw figures.

---

[6] See Richard C. Jeffrey, *The Logic of Decision*, 2nd ed. (Chicago: University of Chicago Press, 1983).

[7] See John von Neumann and Oskar Morgenstern, *Theory of Games and Economic Behavior*, 2nd ed. (Princeton: Princeton University Press, 1947), Appendix, 617–32.

[8] This prejudice is intense in Leibniz. See Bertrand Russell, *The Philosophy of Leibniz*, 3rd ed. (London: Routledge, 1992), 4 and elsewhere throughout.

[9] Augustus De Morgan, "On the Syllogism IV," reprinted in his *On the Syllogism and Other Logical Writings*, ed. Peter Heath (London: Routledge & Kegan Paul, 1966), 208–46.

The first turns on the binary relation of being-the(or a)-head-of, while the second turns on the relation (also binary) of drawing. One upshot of observations like De Morgan's is a recognition that we need a systematic account of relations, and De Morgan, Charles Sanders Peirce, and Ernest Schröder begin working out such an account.[10]

But once one begins to take relations seriously, one comes to want dummy letters besides Aristotle's capitals. Consider, for example,

Every boy loves some girl or other.

Here we have two quantifiers, one universal for the boys, and another particular (or, as we now say, existential) for the girls. These quantifiers show a kind of dependence, since the example means that each boy bears the loving relation to some girl, but that different boys may very well love different girls, and no one girl is loved by all the boys, so which girl (or girls) is loved depends on which boy we start with. So the example says that

For every boy, there is a girl such that he loves her.

Here we have two unary predicates ("is a boy" and "is a girl") for which Aristotle might happily substitute capital letters. But we also have the two pronouns, and their convenient genders tie "he" back to "every boy" and "she" back to "every girl" so that we can tell which bears the relation to which. But there are only three grammatical genders, while the polyadicity of relations and the nesting of quantifier are boundless, so a more systematic notation would be helpful. Mathematicians use variables, like the little x, y, and z of algebra, for this sort of purpose. Logicians sometimes call their little letters individual variables (in contrast with Aristotelian capitals, thought of as variables ranging over properties or sets) or variables of quantification.

The substituents for individual variables are singular terms, and these variables may occupy places in atomic sentences filled by singular terms. So as well as "John is a boy" and "Mary is a girl," we also have "x is a boy" and "y is a girl." But while a singular term like "John" or "Mary" has, or purports to have, a unique denotation of which the predicate in an atomic sentence is either determinately true or determinately false, a variable like "x" does not even purport to have unique denotation in, say, "x is a boy." Instead we think of variables as having a range or universe of values, and the predicate will be true *of* some of these values

[10] See William Kneale and Martha Kneale, *The Development of Logic* (Oxford: Clarendon Press, 1962), 427–34.

perhaps, and may be false *of* others. This means that an atom like "x is a boy" is like "that is a boy," where the demonstrative pronoun lacks an antecedent. Such an atom has no determinate truth value (until we are told what that is). We expect sentences to have truth values, so we call atoms with variables without a specified value not sentences but formulae. We can still build up truth-functional compounds with atoms containing variables; then the atoms are called atomic formulae, and the compounds, formulae. So, for example,

y is a girl and x loves y

is a formula. Note how the recurrence of "y" shows that it is a girl who would be loved rather than do the loving.

Quantifying a variable (or binding a variable with a quantifier) should be sharply distinguished from substituting a singular term for the variable. When we quantify a variable, we do not specify a unique value for it, but instead specify an extent (all or some) of which the predicate in which the variable occurs is true. Suppose, for example, we want to say of x (whatever that might be) that x loves some girl. In Aristotelian logic, the universal and existential quantifiers (all and some) always seem to come attached to a monadic predicate, as in "every boy" or "some girl"; it is as if there were as many quantifiers of either kind as there are monadic predicates. We break this attachment. We have only two quantifiers, one universal for everything, and the other existential for something. But these quantifiers come with individual variables attached so we can keep track of where what extent is being attributed. Our shorthand for the existential quantifier is a capital backwards "E." When this is attached to the individual variable "y" as in "(∃y)...," where a formula fills the ellipsis, then it should be construed as "There exists an individual, call it y, such that...." One should not read it as "There exists a y such that...," which would attach a monadic predicate to the quantifier; the predicates will come in the formula filling the ellipsis. We can then put "x loves some girl" as

(∃y)(y is a girl and x loves y).

Now we return to our original example: every boy loves some girl. In addition to the existential quantifier, we also have the universal quantifier, nowadays usually written for short as an upside-down capital "A" with an individual variable attached. We take our example as: For any individual, call it x, if x is a boy, then there is an individual, call it y, such that y is a girl and x loves y. Or for short

$(\forall x)$(if x is a boy, then $(\exists y)$(y is a girl and x loves y)).

(Here we want the formula governed by the universal quantifier to be a conditional rather than, say, a conjunction because we do not mean that everything is a boy.)[11]

Now that we have quantifiers and their variables we are going to have to rethink truth. But first, we pause to consider whether we have enough grammar and vocabulary to represent mathematical discourse and reasoning adequately. We associated the variables of quantification with singular terms like the name "0" for the number zero. Since the nineteenth century, mathematicians have devoted a great deal of attention to functions (like addition on natural numbers, differentiation of real functions, and the powerset operation on sets), and it is natural to want signs for functions to represent mathematical discourse. A function sign, like a predicate, has a polyadicity. That is, there is a fixed number of terms to which a function sign is applied to yield a term. Addition is binary, while powerset is unary. So we specify the terms inductively. At the basis step, we say that any individual variable or name (or constant, as we shall call them) is a term. At the induction step, if f is a function sign of polyadicity n and $t_1,\ldots, t_n$ are terms, then $f(t_1,\ldots, t_n)$ is also a term. At the extremal step, we say that an expression is a term only if it can be built up from the basis step by finitely many uses of the induction step. Note that if we start with only one constant, c, and only one unary function sign, f, we get an infinity of terms:

$$c, f(c), f(f(c)),\ldots$$

by repeated use of the induction step.

We replaced pronouns with individual variables because there are not enough pronouns to make all the distinctions predicates of arbitrarily large polyadicity require. But there are also only finitely many

[11] The post-Aristotelian conception of the quantifier seems to have been worked out three times, each independent of the other two: once by Frege, once by Peirce, and once by Peano. See W. V. Quine, "Peirce's Logic," in *Selected Logic Papers*, enl. ed. (Cambridge, Mass: Harvard University Press, 1995), 258–65. There is an enlightening description of the contribution of Peirce's student Oscar Mitchell in Randall R. Dipert's "The Life and Logical Contributions of O. H. Mitchell, Peirce's Gifted Student," *Transactions of the Charles S. Peirce Society* 30 (1994): 515–42. The backwards "E" for the existential quantifier descends to us from Peano through Russell; they used "(x)" for the universal quantifier. The upside-down "A" seems to come from Alfred Tarski's students in the second half of the twentieth century.

little letters from the end of the alphabet. So, at least officially, our variables are the letter "x" with positive integer subscripts: x_1, x_2,.... Since subscripts can be annoying, unofficially we still use x, y, and z. There is no saying in advance which constants, if any, a mathematician might want; a set theorist might want "∅" for the empty set, while a number theorist might want "0" for zero. So we offer a list

$$c_1, c_2,...$$

of countably many constants from which the mathematician may choose. There is also no saying in advance which simple predicates or function signs might be called for. But now we must also allow for polyadicity. So we offer a countable infinity of predicate letters for each polyadicity:

$$A_1^1, A_2^1, ... A_k^1, ...$$
$$A_1^2, A_2^2, ... A_k^2, ...$$
$$\vdots \quad \vdots \quad \quad \vdots$$
$$A_1^n, A_2^n, ... A_k^n, ...$$
$$\vdots \quad \vdots \quad \quad \vdots$$

The superscript gives the polyadicity, and the subscript tell us which predicate letter of that polyadicity we have; A_k^n is the kth n-ary predicate letter. Similarly, we have

$$f_1^1, f_2^1, ... f_k^1, ...$$
$$f_1^2, f_2^2, ... f_k^2, ...$$
$$\vdots \quad \vdots \quad \quad \vdots$$
$$f_1^n, f_2^n, ... f_k^n, ...$$
$$\vdots \quad \vdots \quad \quad \vdots$$

as our stock of function letters. Constants, predicate letters, and function letters are called extralogical signs, and a first-order language is fixed by the choice of its constants, predicate letters, and function letters.[12] Since identity is ubiquitous in mathematics, it would be natural to reserve A_1^2, the first dyadic predicate letter, for the double-bar used for identity.

---

[12] "First-order" means that we have only quantification binding individual variables in positions where singular terms but not predicates occur. Second-order quantification would bind another sort of variables occupying predicate positions.

We have seen how terms (of a language) are built up inductively from variables and constants (of that language) using function letters (of that language). Atomic formulae (of that language) are got by applying an n-adic predicate letter A_k^n (of the language) to n terms $t_1, \ldots, t_n$ (of the language) thus:

$$A_k^n(t_1, \ldots, t_n).$$

The specification of (the language's) atomic formulae is the basis step in an inductive specification of (its) formulae. The devices we use in building compound formulae are truth-functional connectives and quantification (which may be called logical operators). Two truth functions, say negation and conjunction, suffice; often "and" is shortened to "$\wedge$" and "not" to "$\neg$". So one inductive step is to say that if A and B are formulae, then so are

$$(\neg A)$$

and

$$(A \wedge B).$$

Then we need another one for quantification. In the presence of negation, we need take only one quantifier as basic; we pick universal quantification and shorten it to the upside-down "A." So if A is a formula and y is a variable, then $((\forall y)A)$ is a formula. The usual extremal clause says that's all, folks. Note that each introduction of an operator (connective or quantifier) comes with a pair of parentheses marking off the formula (for negation and universal quantifier) or pair of formulae (for conjunction) to which the operator applies. These formulae are called the operator's scope. In the case of quantification, occurrences of the variable y in the quantifier $\forall y$ and its scope A are called bound; all other occurrences are called free. For example, in

$$Ax \wedge (\forall x)Bx,$$

the first occurrence of x is free, but the last two are bound. A sentence is a formula in which no variable occurs free. We tend to suppress parentheses not needed to disambiguate.

During the twentieth century, a fairly stable consensus evolved that first-order languages are adequate for representing mathematical discourse and reasoning. As we saw in Chapter 2, Frege used second-order quantification, and as we saw in Chapter 3, Zermelo did too, but he limited the values of his second-order values to definite properties as a prophylactic against the paradoxes. We saw there too how Skolem finessed the problem of which properties are definite by trading in Zermelo's second-order axiom for first-order axiom schemata; instead of second-order variables with definite properties as values, we assume each axiom with a formula (built up from the membership and identity predicates using truth-functional connectives and first-order quantification) where that second-order variable would have been. In 1917, a year or two before Skolem, Hilbert presented logic as a first-order system.[13] First-order systems became the norm during the twentieth century, but second-order quantification enjoyed a revival later in the century.[14] The question of adequate representation of mathematical discourse is partly a matter of intellectual experiment. The massive tomes of Frege, Peano, and Russell show that one can develop recognizable versions of mathematics starting from slender means. The question of first- versus second-order logic is, as we shall see, somewhat more philosophical.

Philosophers have many theories of truth, but Alfred Tarski's has achieved preeminence among logicians.[15] We will consider only first-order languages. Along the way, we will glance at second-order languages, but we are not considering whole natural languages like English. That is partly because natural languages include devices like necessity and verbs of propositional attitude that we have no settled consensus on treating. Tarski also avoids natural languages for what he calls their universality.[16] This means that anything that can be said at all can be said in any natural language. Then, in particular, any natural language includes its own truth predicate. So we can write a sentence S in the language which says of itself that it is not true. But then, if S is true, it lacks the property it attributes to itself, and so is not true; while if S is not true, it has the property it attributes to itself, and so is true. This is an ancient paradox called the paradox of the liar. As a prophylactic against the paradox, Tarski looks only at languages not including their

[13] See Gregory H. Moore, "The Emergence of First-Order Logic," in *History and Philosophy of Modern Mathematics*, ed. William Asprey and Philip Kitcher (Minneapolis: University of Minnesota Press, 1988), 95–135.

[14] A seminal paper here is George Boolos's "On Second-Order Logic," reprinted in his *Logic, Logic, and Logic*, ed. Richard Jeffrey (Cambridge, Mass: Harvard University Press, 1998), 37–53.

[15] Alfred Tarski, "The Concept of Truth in Formalized Languages," reprinted in his *Logic, Semantics, Metamathematics: Papers from 1923 to 1938*, trans. J. H. Woodger (Oxford: Clarendon Press, 1956), 152–278.

[16] Ibid., 164.

own truth predicates. We could devise a first-order language that (in some sense) includes its own truth predicate, but Tarski is not looking at such languages. Instead, he wants to make mathematics out of truth. To that end, he wants precisely specified languages, and first-order languages have simple precise descriptions that natural languages lack. On the other hand, we can transfer Tarski's constructions from formalized languages to fragments of natural language built up from simple names, predicates, and function signs using truth-functional connectives and quantifiers.

Fix a first-order language L. Our aim is to define truth for sentences of L. We will state this definition in another language, English.[17] Tarski states a test that putative definitions of truth for L should pass in order to be what Tarski calls materially adequate.[18] To exposit this test, we make two assumptions. First, for each sentence of L there should be an English singular term that denotes the sentence; quotation marks are the usual device that, applied to a sentence (or any other expression), yield a singular term denoting the sentence (or expression). Second, each sentence of L should have a translation into English; in the simplest idealization, we suppose L is a fragment of English. Then the test is that for any sentence of L translated by English sentence A and denoted by English singular term t, the definition plus logic alone should suffice to deduce that

t is (a) true (sentence of L) if and only if A.

Such biconditionals are called T-sentences, and the standard example reads

"Snow is white" is true if and only if snow is white.

In a way, then, truth is inverse to, and undoes, quotation. Still, the example states a contingent *a posteriori* relation between an expression (denoted by the subject of the left-hand side) and a natural stuff (denoted by the subject of the right-hand side). In any first-order language, there are infinitely many T-sentences. Since definitions should be finite, the agglomeration of all the T-sentences is not a definition of truth.

---

[17] There has grown up a jargon in which the language *for* which we define truth is called the object language, while the language *in* which we define truth is called the meta-language. This jargon seems grandiose enough to be worth avoiding.

[18] Tarski, "Concept of Truth," 187–88. In the original 1931 version, the Polish word for "test" that Tarski used translates into English as "criterion." But Woodger instead translated it as "convention." Woodger's translation has stuck, but it is infelicitous.

A focus on material adequacy conditions marks a mode of the analytic style in philosophy. If those who differ over an interesting but contentious term like "true" can agree among themselves that an adequate account of the term should satisfy a condition articulated in advance, this may increase the chances of their being able to eliminate some pretenders and to certify some contenders by public and checkable accounts. Of course, those whose candidates get winnowed out by the condition of material adequacy may for that reason come to dissent from the condition, but there has always been more contention than consensus in philosophy. Testing philosophy against adequacy conditions is older than Tarski's terminology for the mode. When Frege gave his definition of "number," he argued for it by deriving the postulates for the natural numbers, thus treating those postulates as material adequacy conditions.[19]

One might wonder whether meeting a material adequacy condition suffices to settle a contentious term uniquely; perhaps different accounts will each satisfy such a condition. There is probably no uniform general way to rule this out. But Quine observes that if we come up with two predicates, "true 1" and "true 2," both of which meet Tarski's convention T for a first-order language L, then for any sentence A of L denoted by t we have

t is true 1 if and only if A

and

t is true 2 if and only if A,

from which it follows immediately that

t is true 1 if and only if t is true 2.

Thus the two truth predicates are coextensive. In that way convention T ensures a unique extension for the truth predicate, and for a philosopher like Quine who does not take intensions seriously, that is about the best to be had.[20] Another example is the ordered pair. One can get dizzy

---

[19] As we noted in Chapter 2, these postulates seem to be due to Grassmann, Peirce, Dedekind, and Peano. See note 7 in that chapter.

[20] W. V. Quine, "Notes on the Theory of Reference," reprinted in *From a Logical Point of View*, 2nd ed. rev. (Cambridge, Mass: Harvard University Press, 1961), 136. While we have no good reason to think there are absolutely indefinable terms (see the passage from Russell cited here in Chapter 2, note 18), identity is usually a wise and merciful choice among primitives, and seeking a definition of identity is

reading older discussions of order.[21] We write <a, b> for the ordered pair whose first member is a and whose second member is b. Without worrying about the nature or essence of order, of firstness and second-ness, we should be able to agree that

<a, b> = <c, d> if and only if a = c and b = d.

Intellectual experience shows that if we can define ordered pairs so as to satisfy this adequacy condition, we can get from them what we need. In 1914 Norbert Wiener showed (more or less) that if we set <a, b> equal to

$$\{\{a\}, \{b, \varnothing\}\},$$

the condition is met, while in 1921 Kazimierz Kuratowski showed that setting it equal to

$$\{\{a\}, \{a, b\}\}$$

also works. So the condition does not fix the extension. But no matter, Quine argues, since each works.[22]

   Tarski calls his definition of truth semantic.[23] This is a somewhat deviant but now entrenched use of "semantic." We usually say that semantics is about meaning. Frege argues that we should distinguish between sense and reference: the identity sentence "Clay is Ali" is true because the names have the same reference but informative because they have different senses.[24] But Tarski took meaning (sense, connotation,

---

probably a waste of time. But, as Quine also notes, there is a way the usual axioms for identity (reflexivity and substitutivity) fix its extension (in a model) uniquely, for two predicates in a single language both meeting these axioms are coextensive. In that way these axioms are like convention T. See W. V. Quine, "Reply to Professor Marcus," reprinted in his *The Ways of Paradox and Other Essays*, rev. and enl. ed. (Cambridge, Mass: Harvard University Press, 1976), 180.

[21] Try Bertrand Russell, *The Principles of Mathematics*, 2nd ed. (London: George Allen & Unwin, 1937), chaps. 24–25. This discussion was first published in 1903, before the Wiener and Kuratowski accounts.

[22] W. V. Quine, *Word and Object* (Cambridge, Mass: Technology Press of the Massachusetts Institute of Technology, 1960), sect. 53, "The Ordered Pair as Philosophical Paradigm," 257–62, and references to Kuratowski and Wiener given in the bibliography, pp. 280 and 284.

[23] Alfred Tarski, "The Semantic Conception of Truth," reprinted in *Semantics and the Philosophy of Language*, ed. Leonard Linsky (Urbana: University of Illinois Press, 1952), 13–47.

[24] Gottlob Frege, "On Sense and Reference," in *Translations from the Philosophical Writings of Gottlob Frege*, ed. Peter Geach and Max Black (Oxford: Basil Blackwell,

intension) no more seriously than did Quine.[25] For Tarski, semantics is about reference, denotation, extension, and truth. There has grown up among logicians and some philosophers a usage under which semantics is about relations between words and things that prescinds entirely from anything like meaning linking words to their references.

Under Tarski's semantic conception, truth is defined in semantic terms. We use a scheme of reference (or interpretation) for the extralogical expressions of the language for which we are defining truth. These expressions, we said, are the constants, predicate letters, and function letters whose choice fixed the language. To provide a scheme of reference for these expressions, we start with a nonempty set, the domain of the scheme.[26] Call our domain D. Our interpretation will assign the extralogical terms extensions in D. Call our interpretation I. For any constant c of the language L, all we require is that $I(c)$ be a member of D. (So if D were the set of people, I might assign to the name "Ali" the great American boxer and political activist born Cassius Clay.) For any n-ary predicate letter A_k^n of L, all we require is that $I(A_k^n)$ be an n-adic

---

1960), 56–62. John Stuart Mill distinguished between connotation and denotation, and Russell often talks of denotation where Frege talks of reference. Carnap distinguished between intension and extension. Sense, connotation, and intension go with meaning, even if the way Frege thought of sense was different from how we think of meaning. See Tyler Burge, "Frege on Sense and Linguistic Meaning," in his *Truth, Thought, Reason: Essays on Frege* (Oxford: Clarendon Press, 2005), 242–69.

[25] See Rudolf Carnap, "Carnap's Intellectual Autobiography," in *The Philosophy of Rudolf Carnap*, ed. Paul Arthur Schilpp (La Salle, Ill.: Open Court, 1963), 35–36.

[26] The laws of logic will be the sentences true under all schemes. It makes logical life convenient if both

$$(\forall x)Fx \rightarrow (\exists x)Fx$$

and

$$(\forall x)Fx \leftrightarrow \neg(\exists x)\neg Fx$$

are laws of logic. But at least one of these will fail in the empty domain: for if there is nothing, nothing fails to be F, so by the second, everything is F; and then by the first, something is F, which cannot be if there is nothing. So we assume for convenience that our domain is not empty. This is a matter of convenience; we are not saying it is analytic or known *a priori* that there is something. Those are not properties we are keen to attribute to the laws of logic.

It turns out that every sentence is equivalent to one in which every truth-functional connective lies in the scope of every quantifier; this is called prenex normal form. If we want to tell whether a sentence holds in the empty domain, we can put it in prenex form; if there are no existential quantifiers, it holds, while if there are, it fails.

relation on D, that is, a set of ordered n-tuples of members of D. (So I might assign to the dyadic predicate "beat" the set of pairs $\langle a, b \rangle$ of people such that a beat b in a boxing match.) For any n-ary function letter f_k^n of L, all we require is that $I(f_k^n)$ be a function whose value for each ordered n-tuple of members of D is a member of D. We have not explained reference or extension; we have just assumed a scheme of reference for the extralogical primitives.[27]

In addition to extensions for the extralogical signs of L, we also want values for the variables. We separate interpretation of the extralogical signs from values for the variables because, when we are considering whether for every object, let x be one, predicate P is true of x, we want to be able to hold the interpretation of predicate P fixed while the value of x is allowed to roam all over the domain D. Recall that (officially) the variables are

$$x_1, x_2, \ldots.$$

One way to make a single assignment of values from D to each of these variables is to drop "x" in favor of its positive integer subscript n, and assign to n a member of D. Tarski calls such assignments sequences. So a sequence is a function from positive integers (thought of as the distinguishing subscripts on the variables) to members of D. If s is such a sequence, then its value s(i) at positive integer i is often written s_i. As we just said, we want to be able to shift the value assigned by a sequence s to a variable x_i (treated for short as the number i). So if d is some

---

[27] It might seem we could avoid assuming reference in some cases. Suppose (for simplicity) that the language has no function signs. Suppose crucially that it has only finitely many constants and predicates. Say the constants are "MJ" (for Michael Jordan) and "SO" (for Shaquille O'Neal), and the only predicate is binary "T" (for "is taller than"). Then we could get the effect of a reference scheme by saying:

(1) A constant c refers to an object x if and only if either c is MJ and x is Michael Jordan or c is SO and x is Shaquille O'Neal.
(2) A pair $\langle a, b \rangle$ is in the extension of T if and only if a is taller than b.

We look to have defined reference and extension away rather than assumed them.

In the paper by Field cited in note 1 to this chapter, he observes that we could equally well define v as the valence of element e by saying either e is hydrogen and v is 1, or e is helium and v is 0, and so on. Field's point is that as this is not an adequate account of valence, neither is the account in the previous paragraph an adequate account of reference. This point is well taken quite apart from whether one says, as Field does, that the only adequate account of reference would be in purely physical terms.

member of the domain D, let s_i^d be the sequence just like s except that $s_i^d = d$; for $j \neq i$, s_i^d and s assign the same values to x_j, but s_i^d assigns d to x_i.[28]

Sequences give us values for the variables, and the interpretation gives us denotations for the constants. Next we want to join sequences and the interpretation to build up denotations for all the terms built up from variables and constants using function signs. We might write d(t, s, I) for the denotation of a term t as fixed by a sequence s and an interpretation I. But this notation is too cumbersome, so, since we are mostly interested in a shifting s while I is fixed, we will follow Elliot Mendelson and write s*(t) instead.[29] We define s*(t) by retracing the inductive specification of term t. In the basis case, t is either a variable or a constant. If it is a variable x_i, then s*(t) is s_i; but if it is a constant a, then s*(t) is I(a). In the induction step, t is $f_k(t_1,..., t_n)$. Here f_k is a function letter, so I assign it to a function g from n-tuples of members of D to members of D. Since $t_1,..., t_n$ are less-nested terms than t, we have already specified their denotations $s*(t_1),..., s*(t_n)$. So we set s*(t) = $g(s*(t_1),..., s*(t_n))$. (The notation here may be forbidding at first glance, but the idea is that if a denotes Hillary, b denotes Bill, and f denotes the eldest-child-of function, then f(a, b) should denote Chelsea.)

At last we return to atoms. But these are atomic formulae, rather than sentences, because any variables in them occur free. Suppose that in F(a, x), a denotes Eli Whitney and F denotes the invents relation, but x is a variable: as it were, Eli Whitney invented it. This is neither true period nor false period, but depends on the value of x. F(a, x) is like a predicate that is true *of* some values of x, the cotton gin, but not true *of* others, bifocals. Tarski puts "truth of" in the passive voice and calls it satisfaction: the cotton gin satisfies F(a, x), and the steam engine does not. But there is no upper bound on the number of distinct variables that may occur in an atomic formula (nor on how deeply nested in terms these variables may be). So rather than say this and such values of this and such variables satisfy an atomic formula, Tarski says a whole sequence satisfies (or does not) an atomic formula. To see how this is explained, let

$$F(x_2, f(x_5))$$

[28] In set theoretic terms

$$s_i^d = (s - \{<i, s_i>\}) \cup \{<i, d>\}.$$

Those who recall the Reagan administration sometimes call s_i^d the star wars construction.

[29] Elliott Mendelson, *Introduction to Mathematical Logic*, 4th ed. (New York: Chapman & Hall, 1997), 59. Having taught philosophers logic from Mendelson's text for many years, it is natural that I owe him a great deal.

be an atomic formula in which the interpretation of F is the teaching relation and that of f is the eldest-son function. Let s be any sequence whose second item is Aristotle and whose fifth is Philip of Macedon. The formula should be true of a pair a,b just in case a taught the eldest son of b. Equally, a sequence satisfies the formula when its second item taught the eldest son of its fifth, and our s is like this. In general, then, given an atomic formula,

$$A_k^n (t_1,\ldots, t_n)$$

and a sequence s, we have from I an extension (a set of ordered n-tuples of members of D) for A_k^n, and s and I give us denotations in D for $t_1,\ldots, t_n$. So we say that s satisfies $A_k^n (t_1,\ldots, t_n)$ just in case the denotations of $t_1,\ldots, t_n$ stand in the relation that is the extension of A_k^n, or for short

$$<s^*(t_1),\ldots, s^*(t_n)> \in I(A_k^n).$$

We alter our original inductive story about truth for negation and conjunction to allow for satisfaction and free variables. If A is the negation ¬B of a formula B, our inductive step says that a sequence s satisfies A just in case it does not satisfy B.[30] If A is the conjunction B ∧ C of formulae B and C, our inductive step says that a sequence s satisfies A just in case it satisfies B and it satisfies C. Turning to quantification, suppose A is $(\forall x_i)B(x_i)$.[31] To treat this inductively is to explain satisfaction conditions for $(\forall x_i)B(x_i)$ in terms of those for $B(x_i)$, where the variable x_i is free once we reduce complexity by stripping off the quantifier. Any one sequence s fixes a single value for the free variable x_i, but to make the quantifier *universal* we should consider *all* members of the domain D as alternative values for x_i. So given a sequence s, we consider all the sequences s_i^d, one for each member d of D. That is, s satisfies $(\forall x_i)B(x_i)$ just in case for all d in D, s_i^d satisfies $B(x_i)$. This completes our inductive specification of satisfaction.

We said that sentences are formulae in which no variable occurs free, and we explain truth for sentences in terms of satisfaction for formulae. The crux here is that for a sentence, either all sequences satisfy it or none do. Whereas for formulae, some sequences may satisfy it and others not, for sentences there is no such middle ground. While one can give a (hairy) general proof of this, the best way to see it is through

---

[30] We are explaining satisfaction, not negation. This clause coordinates "¬" with "not," and only someone who gets "not" will get this clause.

[31] In the interesting case, x_i is free in $B(x_i)$. If it is not, it turns out that s satisfies $(\forall x_i)B$ just in case it satisfies B.

an example. Consider existential quantification as in $(\exists x_i)B(x_i)$. This is short for $\neg(\forall x_i)\neg B(x_i)$, so we have

> s satisfies $(\exists x_i)B(x_i)$
> if and only if it is not true that s satisfies $(\forall x_i)\neg B(x_i)$
> iff not (for all d in D, s_i^d satisfies $\neg B(x_i)$)
> iff not (for all d in D, not s_i^d satisfies $B(x_i)$)
> iff for some d in D, s_i^d satisfies $B(x_i)$

just as one expects. Let the domain be the set D of natural numbers and let I of A_1^1 be the set of odd numbers. Then

$$(\exists x_1)A_1^1(x_1)$$

should say there is an odd natural number. Giving hostages to fortune, let s be a sequence whose first member is even, say 4. Then

> s satisfies $(\exists x_1) A_1^1 (x_1)$
> iff for some d in D, s_1^d satisfies $A_1^1 (x_1)$
> iff for some d in D, $(s_1^d)^*(x_1) \in I (A_1^1)$
> iff for some d in D, $(s_1^d)_1 \in I (A_1^1)$
> iff for some d in D, $d \in I (A_1^1)$
> iff for some d in D, d is odd

$((s_1^d)_1 = d$ because the first member of a sequence whose first member is d will be d; this is a who-is-buried-in-Grant's-Tomb point). Thus for *quantified* variables, the sequence drops out. Even if s has an even first member, what counts is whether it can be replaced by an odd member from D. So satisfaction is independent of the sequence when all the variables are quantified; either all satisfy it, or none do. (This example also illustrates how Tarski truth definitions meet convention T.)

We define truth for a sentence under an interpretation as satisfaction of the sentence by some (or equivalently every) sequence of members of the domain of the interpretation. Often we put this as the interpretation being a model for the sentence. After World War II there grew up a thriving branch of mathematical logic called model theory that investigates which set theoretic structures are models for which collections of sentences. But some of its most basic results are older. In 1915 Leopold Löwenheim argued that any first-order sentence having any model at all has a model whose domain is at most countably infinite.[32] Löwenheim's argument is at least difficult to follow, and Thoralf Skolem

---

[32] Löwenheim's original paper, "On Possibilities in the Calculus of Relatives," is translated with a commentary in Jean van Heijenoort, ed., *From Frege to Gödel: A Source*

gave two different proofs of Löwenheim's claim.[33] We can generalize truth of a sentence in a model to say that a structure is a model for a set of sentences if it is a model for every sentence in the set. What is now called the Löwenheim–Skolem theorem says that a set of first-order sentences that has any model at all has a model whose domain is at most countably infinite; we cannot insist first-order on uncountability. The Löwenheim–Skolem theorem was perhaps the first theorem of model theory, and it has some deep ramifications.

We can reconstruct the notion of a sentence following from, or being a logical consequence of, a set of sentences by saying that every model for the set is a model for the sentence.[34] Logical consequence turns on relations between signs and things, and is thus, in Tarski's sense, a semantical relation. But we have another, perhaps nonsemantical, picture of logical thinking. When people draw inferences, they look just to talk or write, not to inspect their subject matter. We can describe a conditional sentence purely grammatically as "if" followed by a sentence (called the antecedent) followed by a comma, "then," and finally another sentence (called the consequent). When we talk just about signs on their own and ignore any reference, extension, truth, and so on (semantics in Tarski's sense), and certainly any sense, connotation, intension, and so on (semantics in the popular sense), we are said to be talking syntax; the distinction between syntax and semantics is part of basic literacy in serious logic. We can construe the rule of inference modus ponens purely syntactically as a license, given a conditional and its antecedent, to inscribe its consequent. We can also do this for other traditional logical rules of inference. There then arises the question whether we can give a purely syntactical specification of logical rules R of inference such that for any set S of first-order sentences and any first-order

Book in Mathematical Logic, 1879–1931 (Cambridge, Mass: Harvard University Press, 1967), 228–51.

[33] See Skolem's "Logico-combinatorial Investigations in the Satisfiability or Provability of Mathematical Propositions: A Simplified Proof of a Theorem by L. Löwenheim and Generalizations of the Theorem," in van Heijenoort, *From Frege to Gödel*, 252–63, and Skolem's "Some Remarks on Axiomatized Set Theory," in ibid., 290–301. Geraldine Brady devotes the final chapters of her book *From Peirce to Skolem: A Neglected Chapter in the History of Logic* (Amsterdam and New York: North-Holland/Elsevier, 2000) to an examination of Löwenheim's argument and Skolem's response.

[34] See Alfred Tarski, "On the Concept of Logical Consequence," in his *Logic, Semantics, Metamathematics*, trans. J. H. Woodger (Oxford: Clarendon Press, 1956), 409–20.

sentence A, if A is a logical consequence of S, then we can derive A from S using just rules in R.[35] Kurt Gödel proved in 1929 that we can do so, a result now often called the completeness of first-order logic.[36] Because it involves syntax and deduction as well as semantics, completeness is perhaps not pure model theory, but for many philosophers, completeness is their first piece of adult logic. One of its consequences, called compactness, says that if a first-order sentence A follows from a set S of first-order sentences, then A follows from a finite subset of S.[37] Since it involves only consequence and not deduction, compactness is semantics, and like the Löwenheim–Skolem theorem, compactness also has some deep ramifications.

As we reconstructed "following from," so we can reconstruct "being a law of logic": a sentence is valid just in case it is true in all models.[38] Recall that we reserved the first binary predicate letter A_1^2 for the double-bar of identity. We might restrict the models we consider just to those in which A_1^2 is assigned the identity relation on members of the domain. Such models are sometimes called normal.[39] With this restriction,

$$(\forall x)(x = x)$$

is valid and a law of logic, but while this may look good, we should pause to make sure we get what it really says. It is valid because it is true in all models or interpretations. But we restricted models by insisting that the extension of the double-bar always be the identity relation on the domain. Thus, for this sentence, the only way models differ is

---

[35] In 1928 David Hilbert and his student Wilhelm Ackermann published a logic textbook, *Grundzüge der theoretischen Logik* (Berlin: Springer), in which they asked a (somewhat garbled) version of this question.

[36] Kurt Gödel, "On the Completeness of the Calculus of Logic," in *Collected Works*, vol. 1, *Publications 1929–1936*, ed. Solomon Feferman et al. (New York and Oxford: Oxford University Press and Clarendon Press, 1986), 61–101. On pp. 44–59 there is a fascinating introduction to Gödel's paper by Burton Dreben and Jean van Heijenoort in which they discuss how very close Skolem came in 1923 to Gödel's result (though Skolem perhaps would not have attached much significance to Hilbert and Ackermann's question).

[37] One can also prove compactness without first proving completeness. See Joseph R. Shoenfield, *Mathematical Logic* (Reading, Mass.: Addison-Wesley, 1967), 105. We will give another such proof in Chapter 9. Compactness in the logician's sense is an instance of compactness as topologists mean it. See Roger C. Lyndon, *Notes on Logic* (Princeton: Van Nostrand, 1966), 57.

[38] Validity is a special case of logical consequence, since a sentence is valid if it is a logical consequence of the empty set of sentences.

[39] See Mendelson, *Introduction to Mathematical Logic*, 100.

in their domains. A domain is any nonempty set. So the validity of this sentence boils down to the fact that every member of every nonempty set is identical with itself.

This will capture the universality of self-identity only if everything is a member of some nonempty set that can serve as the domain of an interpretation of our sentence. Set theory might seem to come to the rescue here, for if the theory includes absolutely everything in its subject matter, and if it guarantees everything a unit set, we get all the domains we need. This reasoning exhibits a sensitivity of set theory and the semantic conception of truth to one another, and we will probe that sensitivity.

Under any interpretation, our sentence says that every member of the domain of that interpretation is identical with itself. But a domain is any old nonempty set, and the prevailing set theory, ZFC, as well as the theory of types and NBG, denies that there is a set of which everything is a member. On that view there is no interpretation whose domain has everything in it. So the universal quantifier never gets to mean everything all at once; as it were, "all" does not mean all.

Validity is the usual dodge here. While there is no universe over which a universally quantified variable can range, sentences like ours are valid because they are true under every interpretation, and since everything has a unit set to serve as the domain of some interpretation, the self-identity of everything gets covered, perhaps a bit circuitously.

Note the "every" in "every interpretation" in the last paragraph. Each nonempty set is the domain of at least one interpretation. So the totality of interpretations is at least as large as the totality of nonempty sets, and by the lights of ZFC both are too big to exist. Hence, the set theory in which the semantic conception of truth is developed denies the existence of a domain in which the quantifiers deployed in that conception and in that theory can be interpreted.[40]

---

[40] Raúl Orayen was a philosopher-logician who devoted sustained thought to the problems of set theory and the semantic conception of truth, but who unfortunately died before being able to publish his work. See Alberto Moretti and Guillermo Hurtado, eds., *La Paradoja de Orayen* (Buenas Aires: Eudeba, 2003). Carlos Alchourrón called the difficulty we are considering Orayen's paradox in "On the Philosophical Adequacy of Set Theories," first published in *Theoria*, 2nd ser., year 2 (1986–87): 567–74; reprinted in Spanish in *La Paradoja de Orayen*, 68. See also Graham Priest, *In Contradiction* (Oxford: Clarendon Press, 2006), 36–37. I am grateful to Luis Estrada for pointing this reference out to me. Orayan always said that many others had noticed the paradox.

As we noted in Chapter 3, Russell's theory of types includes claims that are counterexamples to themselves, and something similar has happened here.[41] Suppose there were a theory T of theories that accounts aptly for all theories except T. T should be true of T too, but is not, and that failure to apply to itself seems a fault. In lecture, Burton S. Dreben used to call this sort of fault a failure (by a theory or whatever) to come back on itself. The set theory deployed in the semantic conception of truth seems unable to bring that conception back on itself.

We might try to assume our way out of trouble. Suppose there is an inaccessible cardinal c.[42] Then R_c, rank c, with membership and identity restricted on both sides to R_c, is a model for ZFC. Then we can take the set R_c to be the domain over which the variables in the quantifiers of the language of ZFC range, just as the semantic conception of truth prescribes. But now the missing domain question comes up again for ZFC plus the new assumption that there is an inaccessible cardinal.

An infinite progress of assumed domain plus missing domain for the assumption of a domain can be extended a long, long way, but it has no evident completion. As sometimes happens with ZFC, one can feel as if one is staring into the wild blue yonder wondering how seriously to take it. For one thing, these big cardinal numbers are just assumed, and, as Russell said, postulation has all the virtues of theft over honest toil.[43] For another, the progress merely punts our problem upward without ever solving it, since we never get to a set theory that provides a domain for itself, as the semantic conception of truth prescribes.

Assuming one's way out of trouble is a respectable mathematical ploy. At the beginning of *Introduction to Topology and Modern Analysis*, George F. Simmons writes:

> The study of sets and functions leads two ways. One path goes down, into the abysses of logic, philosophy, and the foundations of mathematics. The other way goes up onto the highlands of mathematics itself, where these concepts are indispensable in almost all pure mathematics as it is today. Needless to say, we follow the latter course.[44]

[41] Chapter 3, p. 62.
[42] Ibid., p. 83 nn34–35.
[43] Bertrand Russell, *Introduction to Mathematical Philosophy* (London: George Allen & Unwin, 1919), 71.
[44] George F. Simmons, *Introduction to Topology and Modern Analysis* (New York: McGraw-Hill, 1963), 3.

Having oriented us, Simmons continues: "There are certain logical difficulties which arise in the foundations of the theory of sets."[45] Parenthetically he refers to the first exercise in his book, where he rehearses Russell's paradox. Then he says, "We avoid these difficulties by assuming each discussion in which a number of sets are involved takes place in the context of a single fixed set. This set is called the *universal* set."[46] Simmons is assuming there is a set big enough to provide the examples he uses to introduce us to topology and modern analysis, but small enough to be relatively safe from paradox. The objects that mainstream mathematics studies are mostly much smaller than the big objects in which set theory exults, so if, as ZFC assumes, it is excessive size that is responsible for paradox, then Simmons's assumption is good expository strategy for mainstream mathematics.

But down in the abysses of logic and philosophy where we study quantification, we are having trouble getting "all" to mean all, which is as big as it gets. But all is not lost. Quine's theory New Foundations, NF, does provide the universe. Moreover, it provides identity, but we need to pause to see how. The distinctive idea of NF is stratification: a formula is stratified just in case we can replace the variables in it by numerals so that $\in$, the membership predicate, is always flanked by numerals such that the one on the right is the successor of the one on the left. Then for each stratified formula Fx, Quine's comprehension axiom schema says there is a set of all and only the objects x such that Fx. This covers sets, which are sort of extensional versions of properties, but we need to decide how to handle relations. They are, of course, sets of ordered pairs, but there is an extra wrinkle in which 2-place formulae have extensions. Such a formula F(x, y) must, of course, be stratified in the usual sense, but in addition, the same numeral should replace both "x" and "y."[47] This works for the identity predicate whether we take it as primitive or define it as

$$(\forall z)(x \in z \leftrightarrow y \in z).$$

So in NF we can say of everything all at once that it is self-identical.

But we should not get carried away by this success. The constraint on which 2-place predicates get extensions by comprehension in NF makes

[45] Ibid., 5.
[46] Ibid.
[47] J. Barkley Rosser, *Logic for Mathematicians* (New York: McGraw-Hill, 1953), 286–87.

it clear that the membership predicate will not get an extension in this way. But we do not really want it to. For if NF gave us both, its universe and its membership relation, it would provide the crucial elements of a model for NF, which would put it at serious risk on two fronts. As we shall see, when a theory provides us with the natural numbers and ways to present calculations on such numbers, both of which NF offers, then using techniques Gödel devised in 1931,[48] we can replace talk *about* the syntax of the language of NF with arithmetical talk *in* the language of NF. We could also use these techniques to imitate self-reference in the language of NF. The set theory used in defining truth of a sentence in a model is hardly beyond the means of NF. So if NF provided a model for NF, we should be able to define (an arithmetical replacement for) "is a true sentence of NF" in the language of NF itself. But then it would be only a short step to deriving the paradox of the liar in NF, thus proving NF inconsistent. That is the first risk. The second depends on the very basic observation that a theory with a model is consistent, that is, no contradictions are derivable in it. This is basic enough that it too has an arithmetical replacement in NF. But if we could prove in NF that NF has a model, we could then prove also in NF that NF is consistent. In 1931 Gödel proved that in any theory T that is consistent, in which we can do arithmetical calculations, and in which we can always recognize axioms of T as such, we cannot prove the consistency of T.[49] So if we could prove the consistency of NF in NF, it would follow that NF is again inconsistent. That is the second risk, and the two together should make us relieved that NF does not yield membership by its comprehension schema.

Raúl Orayen considers an approach to his paradox that starts from a linguistic notion of interpretation in Quine.[50] Try to forget model theory. A formula of a first-order language might look like

$$(\forall x)(\exists y)\, Fxy \rightarrow (\exists y)(\forall x)Fxy.$$

The basic idea is to interpret "F" in this formula (or schema, as Quine calls it) not by assigning a set as extension, but rather by replacing it

---

[48] Kurt Gödel, "On Formally Undecidable Propositions of *Principia Mathematica* and Related Systems I," trans. in van Heijenoort, *From Frege to Gödel*, 596–616. My next chapter contains a sketch of this material.

[49] Ibid.

[50] Raúl Orayen, "Una paradoja en la semántica de la teoría de conjuntos," in Moretti and Hurtado, *La Paradoja de Orayen*, 42–49.

with a predicate from a natural language like English. We get predicates by starting from sentences like

Jocasta is Oedippus's mother

and replacing singular terms with bracketed numerals, as in

(2) is (1)'s mother.

Alphabetically later variables go in for larger bracketed numerals, so we would get

$(\forall x)(\exists y)(y$ is x's mother$) \rightarrow (\exists y)(\forall x)(y$ is x's mother$)$.

For an analogue of a domain we could pick unary predicates like "(1) is a person" and "(2) is a person" and restrict each quantifier by them thus:

$(\forall x)(x$ is a person $\rightarrow (\exists y)(y$ is a person $\land$ y is x's mother$))$
$\rightarrow (\exists y)(y$ is a person $\land (\forall x)(x$ is a person $\rightarrow$ y is x's mother$))$.

Any constants in the formula should also be thus restricted if we use a unary predicate in lieu of a domain. (Describing interpretation is more succinct if we omit function signs. We can always get the net effect of an n-ary function sign using an (n+1)-ary predicate letter and a binary predicate letter always to be replaced by "is identical with.")[51]

Our interpretation of constants differs markedly from that of schematic predicate letters. To interpret a constant is to assign it an object, and if we are using a unary predicate in lieu of a domain, this predicate should be true of any object assigned as interpretation of a constant. We need to assume in general that the natural language predicates we use in interpretation are either definitely true or definitely false of objects we choose to interpret constants; similarly, a set that is the extension of a predicate has sharp boundaries only if the predicate is definitely true or definitely false of objects. Our assumption settles the truth values for atomic sentences under an interpretation, and we can extend through the truth functional connectives in the usual ways. For a formula A, a variable v, and a constant c not in A, let Av/c be the formula got from A by replacing all free occurrences of v with c. If I and J are interpretations in our present sense and c is a constant, then J is a c-variant of I just in case I and J differ at most in their assignments to c. Then $(\forall v)A$

---

[51] For more details, see W. V. Quine, *Methods of Logic*, rev. ed. (New York: Henry Holt, 1959), 127–46.

is true under I just in case Av/c is true under all c-variants of I, and (∃v) A is true under I just in case Av/c is true under some c-variant of I.[52]

Suppose we interpret the horizontal double-bar by the English predicate "is identical with" and just dispense with a unary predicate in lieu of a domain. Then our sentence

$$(\forall x)(x = x)$$

is true just in case everything is self-identical, and we have said of everything all at once that it is self-identical. In the case of ZFC we could use the predicate "is a set" in lieu of a domain and just not worry about whether this set has an extension. If the language, in our case English, from which we take our predicates includes enough elementary number theory, we can even prove soundness and completeness theorems for the Quinian linguistic notion of interpretation.[53]

On the other hand, because set theory has become a developed part of mathematics, model theory too is a developed part of mathematics (and perhaps even of set theory itself). But we have no settled and developed theory of English predicates. So we would have to be extra careful here about the liar paradox, and even if that works out, the relation between linguistic interpretation and model theory will be at least intriguing.

That we are not able to do everything in NF and that we should be wary of the liar under Quine's linguistic interpretations vindicate Tarski's distrust of universality. He blamed universality for semantic paradoxes like the liar. A prophylactic against such paradoxes associated with Tarski is a conception of levels of language. Suppose we start with a language L_0 with first-order sentences built up from constants, predicate letters, and function letters using truth functions and quantification. L_0 might have an interpretation in terms of, say, shoes and ships and cabbages and kings. But this scheme of reference is not mentioned in the interpretation of L_0, nor are satisfaction and truth for sentences of L_0. These do figure in another language, L_1, that includes L_0, a statement of a scheme of reference for extralogical signs of L_0, and singular terms (formed most naturally using quotation marks) denoting expressions of L_0. Assuming a little set theory, we can define "is a true sentence of L_0" in L_1. We might then iterate and have an infinite sequence L_0,

[52] See Benson Mates, *Elementary Logic*, 2nd ed. (New York: Oxford University Press, 1972), 77.
[53] W. V. Quine, *Philosophy of Logic* (Englewood Cliffs, N.J.: Prentice-Hall, 1970), 53–55.

$L_1, \ldots$ of languages such that in L_{n+1} we can define truth for sentences of L_n. Each language has a truth predicate (one level up), but none has its own truth predicate, so there is no evident way to produce the liar paradox.[54]

Levels of language á la Tarski were the received prophylactic against the liar until Saul Kripke published his "Outline of a Theory of Truth" in 1975.[55] Kripke aims to include a language's truth predicate in it. We start with a partially interpreted language L. It may include nonsemantic vocabulary fully interpreted in terms of, say, shoes and ships. So for sentences of L with nonsemantic subject matter, their truth or falsity is settled already in the usual way. But L also contains a predicate "$T(x)$" that is not interpreted to start with but which we aim to make into as much of a truth predicate for L as we can. L also contains singular terms denoting sentences of L, and to confront the liar, L should include singular terms that denote sentences in which they occur.[56] Because we start off with an uninterpreted predicate, we expect some sentences to be at first neither true nor false but unsettled, perhaps as "Frank is bald" is unsettled until the name is bestowed on someone. We think of this as having not two truth values but three: t, f, and u. There are several ways to do a logic with three truth values. We might do negations as usual except that it leaves u as u. Similarly, we might do conjunction

---

[54] There is a small irony here. As we saw in Chapter 3, Russell ramified his theory of types so as to deal with both his own paradox and the liar (and other paradoxes too). In 1925 Frank Ramsey argued that we should distinguish the logical (or, as we might now say, set theoretic) paradoxes like Russell's and Burali-Forti's from those couched in terms of thought or language (or, as we might say after Tarski, semantic terms) like the liar. (Ramsey, "The Foundations of Mathematics" in his *The Foundations of Mathematics and Other Logical Essays*, ed. R. B. Brathewaite [Paterson, N.J.: Littlefield, Adams, 1960], 20.) Without orders, we can picture types of sets in layers: type 0 has non-sets, type 1 has sets of things of type 0, type 2 has sets of things of type 1, and so on. But there is an evident similarity between Ramsey's simplified types and Tarski's levels of language; where in Ramsey things of type n can be members of those of type n + 1, in Tarski things of level n can be described by those of type n + 1. If the treatments of the set theoretic and semantic paradoxes are thus similar, perhaps Russell and Poincaré were right to put them together. See my "Russell and Ramsey," *Pacific Philosophical Quarterly* 64 (1984): 193–210.

[55] Saul Kripke, "Outline of a Theory of Truth," reprinted in Robert L. Martin, ed., *Recent Essays on Truth and the Liar Paradox* (Oxford: Clarendon Press, 1984), 53–81.

[56] Such terms are like "this very sentence." If L includes arithmetic calculation, the effective equivalent of such self-reference is inevitable. See Gödel, "On Formally Undecidable Propositions." A philosopher will refuse to give up the right to test whether a theory comes back on itself, so she will not surrender self-reference.

as usual except that f ∧ u goes to f while t ∧ u goes to u, as if were the u to become t, it would not make the first t, but it would the second. Thinking of universal quantification as like a big conjunction, $(\forall x)Fx$ will be u if it has a u case but only t ones otherwise, but f if it has any f cases.[57]

When a predicate is only partially interpreted, Kripke says it should have both an extension (the set of things of which it is determinately true) and an anti-extension (the set of things of which it is determinately false). These should be disjoint, but they need not exhaust the domain. We start off at stage 0 with the extension X_0^+ of T and its anti-extension X_0^- both empty. The sweet part of Kripke's construction is to use Tarski's convention to expand the extension and anti-extension of T in passing from stage α to stage $\alpha + 1$. So, for example, at stage 0 the sentence

No shoe is a ship

is already settled and is, of course, true. Then aiming for as much of Tarski's convention as we can get, we use

T("No shoe is a ship") ↔ no shoe is a ship

to put the sentence "No shoe is a ship" into the extension X_1^+ of T at stage 1 (and its negation into the anti-extension X_1^- of T at stage 1). Then another use of the convention will put

T("T("No shoe is a ship")")

into X_2^+. And so on. At limits λ, Kripke takes unions, so X_λ^+ is the union of X_α^+ for $\alpha < \lambda$, and similarly for X_λ^-. The stages are cumulative in the sense that when $\alpha < \beta$, $X_\alpha^+ \subseteq X_\beta^+$, and $X_\alpha^- \subseteq X_\beta^-$; nothing gets lost. But because there are only countably many sentences in L, we can make only countably many additions to the extensions of T and to its anti-extensions. So there is a least countable ordinal such that $X_\alpha^+ = X_{\alpha+1}^+$ and $X_\alpha^- = X_{\alpha+1}^-$. This is called a fixed point.[58] At a fixed point, for any sentence S of L denoted by singular term s, we have

$$T(s) \leftrightarrow S.$$

So we have met Tarski's convention, and we might take L with T interpreted by a fixed point as a language that includes its own truth

---

[57] This is Kleene's strong 3-valued logic. See Stephen Cole Kleene, *Introduction to Metamathematics* (Princeton: D. Van Nostrand, 1952), 332–40.

[58] There are many ways to start at stage 0, so there are many fixed points.

predicate. At that fixed point, both sides of the T-sentence for "$\neg T$(this sentence)" are u.[59]

Kripke inspired a great deal of philosophical work on the liar.[60] Two papers among many that reward study are Tyler Burge's "Semantical Paradox"[61] and Anil Gupta's "Remarks on Definitions and the Concept of Truth."[62] Burge and Gupta, like many others, shatter truth. Burge says elsewhere that the notion of truth cannot be adequately represented in terms of a truth predicate that lacks any sort of stratification.[63] We saw the hierarchy of languages L_0, L_1,... attributed to Tarski in which each language of positive subscript, say 5, includes a predicate we might index with 5 for being a true sentence of language L_4. Tarski's truth predicates are thus marked by positive integers for their level in the hierarchy. Kripke uses ordinals to mark the stages in building up to a fixed point at which to interpret the truth predicates in the languages he considers. In "Semantical Paradox" Burge marks occurrences of the truth predicate with names for the various contexts in which the predicate occurs. These names need not be numerals, nor need contexts be ordered as the less-than relation orders the natural numbers. The point is that the truth predicate we use in considering a sentence saying of itself in one context that it is not true comes from another different context. Gupta attaches numerals to sentences so that the numeral attached to an attribution of truth is the successor of that attached to the sentence to which truth is attributed; he thinks of these numerals as marking stages of revision.

Burge thinks of singular terms for contexts as present in the language and attached to occurrences of its truth predicate. Gupta thinks of numerals marking stages as present in the language and attached to

[59] Writers besides Kripke have approached the liar, allowing sentences, like the liar sentence, to be neither true nor false. One is Gilbert Harman, "Logical Form," *Foundations of Language* 9 (1972): 38–65, esp. 52. In note 11 to "The Liar Paradox" (reprinted in Martin, *Recent Essays*, 9–45), Charles Parsons remarks that when a liar sentence is treated as neither true nor false, it is natural for us to say that the sentence is not true. That being what the sentence says, it is true after all; but then, being true, it lacks the property it denies itself, and so is not true; in other words, the liar has returned. Kripke says in this connection that the ghost of the Tarski hierarchy is still with us. See his "Outline of a Theory of Truth" (cited in Martin's anthology), 80. Thus 3-valued logic might seem artificial.

[60] Martin, *Recent Essays*, gives a sample of such work.

[61] Reprinted in ibid., 83–117.

[62] *Proceedings of the Aristotelian Society* 89 (1988–89): 227–46.

[63] Tyler Burge, "Frege on Truth," reprinted in his *Truth, Thought, Reason*, 131.

its sentences. We have seen how natural it is to suppose the languages $L_1, L_2,\ldots$ in Tarski's hierarchy to include numerals to mark their respective truth predicates $T_1, T_2,\ldots$ for their levels in the hierarchy. Kripke's languages need not include ordinals, but it seems nearly as natural that anyone using such a language and building up to a fixed point for interpreting its truth predicate would introduce ordinal numerals to mark the stages along the way. How natural it seems is a measure of the power of the pressure toward what Tarski called semantic universality.

So far we have only marks associated with levels of language, or stages in building an interpretation, or contexts, or stages of revision. It is utterly natural to treat these marks as singular terms denoting levels, or stages of interpretation, or contexts, or stages of revision, for they mark out their associates, and we can use them elsewhere (for example, here) to talk about their associates.[64] Once we have an indefinitely extensible range of names or singular terms for an indefinitely extensible range of things, we ought to be able to introduce a predicate for things in that range, variables whose values are members of that range, and quantification over those things. Looking back at our earlier discussions of Tarski's hierarchy, Kripke, Burge, and Gupta, it is clear that we have already made much more use of such predicates, variables, and quantification than we did of any individual proper names for levels, stages, or contexts.

Let "$C(x)$" be a regimentation of our new predicate, say "is a context," and let "c" be a variable restricted to contexts.[65] Then, if "T" is the truth predicate to have contexts attached to its occurrences, let A be the sentence

$$(\forall c)((\neg T(A))^c).$$

A translates roughly as "This sentence is not true in any context." We recover the liar paradox from A. Suppose to begin with that

$$1. \quad T(A)^i$$

where i is any old context. Attributions of truth in a context, say i, are to attribute truth to a sentence in another context, say j (which, in the case of levels of language, stages of interpretation, or stages of revision, would be the predecessor of i). So by Tarski's convention

[64] See Peter Geach, *Mental Acts* (London: Routledge & Kegan Paul, 1957), 124.
[65] We often use "α" as a variable restricted to ordinals, so that if "$O(x)$" is short for "x is an ordinal," then "$(\forall\alpha)A(\alpha)$" is short for "$(\forall x)(O(x) \to A(x))$" and "$(\exists\alpha)A(\alpha)$" is short for "$(\exists x)(O(x) \wedge A(x))$."

$$2. \quad ((\forall c)((\neg T(A))^c))^i.$$

Then by ordinary logic (universal instantiation), which should hold in any context,

$$3. \quad (\neg T(A)^i)^i.$$

Nested marks for levels, stages, or contexts take us aback somewhat, but we tend to read them attached to sentences like prepositional phrases for location. Thus

$$B^i$$

is naturally pronounced as "B in context i." Confronted by nested prepositional phases for location, it is natural to take all but the inmost as superfluous. The idea is that "In England, people eat snails in France" comes to "People eat snails in France."[66] Then from 3 we get

$$4. \quad \neg T(A)^i.$$

Thus by ordinary logic (conditional proof in i) we get from 1 to 4

$$5. \quad (T(A)^i \rightarrow \neg T(A)^i)$$

and so by reductio ad absurdum in i

$$6. \quad \neg T(A)^i.$$

But then by universal generalization

$$7. \quad (\forall c)((\neg T(A)^c).$$

When, as here, we are entitled to an unqualified assertion not relativized to a context, we expect to be entitled to that assertion in any context; we might call a rule codifying such inference context introduction. Thus we get

$$8. \quad ((\forall c)((\neg T(A))^c))^i.$$

---

[66] With prepositional phrases for time ("at noon") as well as place, not all nesting need be redundant. But as yet, we have no story about different dimensions along which contexts are arrayed. Given such a story, we might restrict taking all but the inmost as superfluous only to contexts along a single dimension.

Dropping all but the outermost is reminiscent of our treatment of vacuous quantification under which "$(\forall x)(\exists x)(x$ is an even number)" amounts to "$(\exists x)(x$ is an even number)." In the first sentence no value for its "x" is relevant to satisfaction of the scope of its universal quantifier.

But then by Tarski's convention again (but now as it were the converse of the step from 1 to 2)

$$9. \quad T(A)^i.$$

Note that 6 and 9 are inconsistent. Our reasoning to them is a version of the liar paradox.[67]

In "New Paradoxes for Old," Hans Herzberger says, in effect, that machinery introduced to solve the liar can always be rejigged to yield another version of the liar.[68] It may be that explicit devices, like an indefinitely extensible range of names, make inevitable devices initially only implicit, like a predicate, variables, and quantification. But made explicit, these devices assemble into another liar. Since there is no surveying in advance all possible solutions to the liar that ingenuity might devise, one should not expect a conclusive proof of Herzberger's hypothesis. Its examination is more experimental than demonstrative, and we have just made one such experiment. Burge may be right that the notion of truth cannot be represented in terms of a truth predicate that lacks any sort of stratification, but we have just sketched a way to arrange the machinery implicit in such stratification into another version of the liar. This bears out the message in Herzberger's hypothesis: the liar paradox cannot be solved. Considering the evident centrality of the notion of truth in any understanding of understanding, one might be skeptical of the prospects for ultimate understanding.

[67] See my "For Anil Gupta," *Proceedings of the Aristotelian Society* 90 (1989–90): 161–64, and my "Invincible Ignorance," in Joseph Salerno, ed., *New Essays on the Knowability Paradox* (Oxford: Oxford University Press, 2008), 320–23.

[68] Hans G. Herzberger, "New Paradoxes for Old," *Proceedings of the Aristotelian Society* 81 (1980–81): 109–23.

FIVE

✦

Truth Eludes Proof

It is not true that Socrates was snub-nosed unless the flesh-and-blood nose of the flesh-and-blood man was stubby and perhaps a bit turned up. As we saw in the last chapter, whether a sentence is true depends on what the sentence is about and how it is with that subject matter. So, to take a justly famous example from Euclid, it is not *true* that there are infinitely many prime numbers unless there *are* infinitely many prime numbers, and thus unless there are numbers. This conclusion already makes some philosophers nervous, and their nerves tend to become more jangled when we add the natural reflection that numbers are neither mental nor physical but abstract objects. That reflection invites exploration and argument, but it is a view of early resort. On the other hand, we are happiest attributing knowledge to a person when we can make out how she interacted or otherwise had commerce with the subject matter of her belief so as to justify her belief. The only mode of such commerce that all parties grant is perception; sensible rationalists have an empiricist streak. H. P. Grice convinced us that perception is by its nature causal.[1] But it is pretty close to an axiom of metaphysics that very abstract objects like numbers are utterly inert. Hence, what makes mathematical truth possible makes mathematical knowledge impossible. This antinomy is known as Benacerraf's dilemma.[2]

[1] H. P. Grice, "The Causal Theory of Perception," reprinted in part in *Perceiving, Sensing, and Knowing*, ed. Robert J. Swartz (Garden City, N.Y.: Doubleday Anchor, 1965), 438–72.

[2] Paul Benacerraf, "Mathematical Truth," reprinted in the second edition of *Philosophy of Mathematics: Selected Readings*, ed. Paul Benacerraf and Hilary Putnam (Cambridge: Cambridge University Press, 1983), 403–20. It is also reprinted in W. D. Hart, ed., *The Philosophy of Mathematics* (Oxford: Oxford University Press, 1996), 14–30. For an exposition liberated from Goldman's causal theory of knowledge, see my "Benacerraf's Dilemma," *Crítica* 23 (1991): 87–103.

An escape from the antinomy that occurs to many people, especially mathematicians, is to say that truth in mathematics is neither correspondence to fact nor in need of reference to abstract objects but is rather just provability. Mathematicians neither perform experiments on primes in retorts nor make expeditions to examine exotic ones; instead they establish their claims by proving theorems, and that is just a mode of writing and talking. In the Middle Ages the doctrine that there are no abstracta, no Platonic forms like humanity but only predicates like "is a person," was called nominalism. Its twentieth-century incarnation that denies mathematics abstract subject matter and assimilates mathematical knowledge to empirical knowledge of expressions arrayed in proofs is called formalism. Formalism requires that all mathematical truths be provable (and proof should not smuggle in truth conceived semantically).

In 1931 Kurt Gödel proved a theorem that provides evidence against the formalist escape from Benacerraf's dilemma. This chapter is an experiment: the aim is to exposit enough of Gödel's seminal 1931 argument to give philosophers an appreciation of it, but to omit enough of its detail so that philosophers do not get bogged down; it is not plain such a middle course is possible, and the proof of the pudding is in the eating.

The simplest natural example to which Gödel's result applies is elementary number theory, the theory of the natural numbers 0, 1, and so on. Dedekind described the natural numbers in terms of an object a, a unary function f, and a set N. It is required that a be in N (as it were, 0 is a number), that f send N one-to-one into N (every number has a unique successor), that a not be a value of f (0 is the successor of no natural number), and that for any set A, if $a \in A$ and $f(x) \in A$ when $x \in A$, then $N \subseteq A$ (induction). This last clause, quantifying over sets of individuals as well as individuals, makes Dedekind's description second-order. It also guarantees that for any two models for Dedekind's description there is a one-to-one correspondence between their domains that sends the zero and successor function of one model into that of the other. So Dedekind's second-order description specifies the structure of natural numbers uniquely up to isomorphism.[3]

Because Dedekind's description is thus univocal, for any sentence in the language of number theory, either that sentence or its negation

---

[3] Dedekind actually started at 1, while we start at 0. But these structures are isomorphic.

follows from Dedekind's description. But it is demonstrable that in no reasonable sense of "logic" is there a logic that suffices to deduce from Dedekind's description anything that follows from it. We can, however, get a good notion of proof if we go first-order, and accordingly we do so.

We set up a first-order language as in the last chapter. We pick the constant a_1, which we will write as a little oval, and the first unary function sign f_1^1, which we will write as a stroke beside a term t as in t'. Second-order, Dedekind could define addition and multiplication, but first-order, we cannot. So we also take the first and second binary function signs, which we write + and × (or sometimes ·, or sometimes as juxtaposition as in a × b = ab). Our only predicate is the double-bar for identity.

Elliott Mendelson, whose exposition we are following, calls the system we are setting up S.[4] The axioms of S include 0 not being a successor and successor being one-to-one. We also include inductive definitions of addition

$$a + 0 = a$$
$$a + (b + 1) = (a + b) + 1$$

and multiplication

$$a \times 0 = 0$$
$$a \times (b + 1) = (a \times b) + a.$$

Where Dedekind has a second-order axiom of induction, we have a first-order axiom schema: for any formula $A(x)$ built up from 0, ', +, ×, and = using individual variables, truth-functional connectives, and quantifiers, the formula

$$(A(0) \wedge (\forall x)(A(x) \rightarrow A(x'))) \rightarrow (\forall x)A(x)$$

is an axiom of S. S is formed when these axioms are embedded in a logic (including identity) such that any sentence of the language of S that follows from them is deducible from them by the logic.[5] Deduction from these axioms by this logic is a purely syntactical sort of proof.

Gödel's argument at no point requires an interpretation of the language of S in the manner of the semantic conception of truth. In

---

[4] Elliott Mendelson, *Introduction to Mathematical Logic*, 4th ed. (New York: Chapman & Hall, 1997), chap. 3.
[5] See Chapter 4, pp. 109–10.

that way one might say that Gödel's argument does not involve reference, and thus, despite popular misdescriptions, does not involve self-reference. On the other hand, his argument does involve several different relations between the world of numbers and the notations of S together with descriptions of those notations. The most basic example of such a relation is an assignment to each natural number n of a term n̲ in the language of S got by applying n strokes to the little oval. This specification of n̲ invokes no notion of denotation or reference; we just count strokes. But it is true that if we *were* to interpret the language of S in the obvious way, then n̲ would denote n. Some of the assignments Gödel makes of numbers, relations on numbers, and functions on numbers to terms and formulae in the language of S are extensionally equivalent to a fragment of an interpretation of the language of S, but these assignments do not cover all the quantified formulae, and the conceptual resources used in making these assignments do not include denotation of a term, extension of a predicate of function sign, or satisfaction of a formula.

It may help to have a picture in which to place and keep track of the various devices Gödel deploys in his argument. In this picture, language is on the left and the world is on the right.

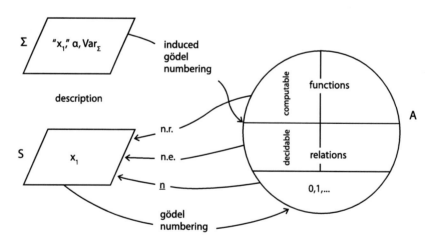

The lower language on the left is the uninterpreted formal system S we have already set up. It includes notations like the variable "x," and the numerals (as they are called) n̲. Σ is the language we are using right now to talk about S. We call it Σ because we will only ever talk about the syntax of S, and "syntax" begins with "s" and Σ is Greek for s; but also because Σ looks a bit like a capital English E, and we are discussing S in English. The world on the right is Plato's arithmetical heaven. On its first floor are the natural numbers. The second floor is inhabited by relations on numbers, and as we shall see, we will need to distinguish later between relations that are decidable and those that are not. The third floor is inhabited by functions from numbers to numbers, and we will similarly need to distinguish functions that are computable from those that are not.

The notation of S includes of course the first variable,

$$x_1,$$

but since S will not be interpreted and this variable will never have values, one might think of it as an empty mark. But it is denoted by the English singular term

$$``x_1"$$

since any expression put in quotation marks yields a singular term denoting that expression. We may also use in English small letters from early in the Greek alphabet as variables whose values are expressions of S. And we may shorten the English predicate "is a variable of S" to "Var_Σ," where the subscript shows we are talking syntax. So in a regimented English we may say

$$\mathrm{Var}_\Sigma(``x_1")$$

as short for

$$``x_1" \text{ is a variable of S.}$$

This is what is going on in the left-hand or language side of the picture.

We have three arrows leading from the arithmetic world A on the right to S. One, which sends the natural number n to n, the little oval with n strokes, we have already encountered. Even those whose metaphysical inclinations tend towards nominalism should be aware that it is hard to follow Gödel's argument unless one distinguishes, at least for purposes of argument, between numbers and numerals. Second, we have an arrow labeled "n.e." running from relations on numbers to S. The abbreviation "n.e." is short for "numeralwise expressible," which comes from Stephen Cole Kleene.[6] We say that a k-ary relation R on

[6] Stephen Cole Kleene, *Introduction to Metamathematics* (Princeton: D. Van Nostrand, 1952), 195.

natural numbers is n.e. by a formula $A(x_1,..., x_n)$ with n free variables in S if and only if for all natural numbers $n_1,..., n_k$

> (1) if $R(n_1,..., n_k)$, $A(\underline{n}_1,..., \underline{n}_k)$ is a theorem of S
> (2) if not-$R(n_1,..., n_k)$, $\neg A(\underline{n}_1,..., \underline{n}_k)$ is a theorem of S.

(The statement that a formula B is a theorem of a theory T is sometimes written $\vdash_T B$.) For example, let I be the identity relation on natural numbers. Then I is n.e. in S by the formula $x_1 = x_2$. For if n_1 and n_2 are the same number, then $\underline{n}_1$ and $\underline{n}_2$ are the same term, so $\underline{n}_1 = \underline{n}_2$ is a law of logic and so provable in S. But if n_1 and n_2 are different numbers, one of them, say n_1, is bigger. Then taking $\underline{n}_1 = \underline{n}_2$ as an hypothesis for reductio in S, we can strip $n_1 - n_2$ strokes off both sides (using the axiom that successor is one-to-one), which leaves us with $\underline{n_1 - n_2} = 0$, and since $n_1 > n_2$, there are strokes on the right contradicting the axiom that zero is not a successor. Thus, by reductio in S, $\vdash_s \underline{n}_1 \neq \underline{n}_2$. It will turn out that the decidable relations on numbers are n.e. in S, but it will take us a while to explain what it is for a relation to be decidable and to show that not all relations are decidable. If we were to interpret S in the obvious way in the domain of natural numbers, it would turn out that when a formula A n.e. a relation R in S, then R is the extension of A under this interpretation, but the converse fails. Note that n.e. is explained in arithmetic and syntactic terms without semantics.

The third arrow from A to S is labeled "n.r.," which is short for "numeralwise representable" and also comes from Kleene.[7] We say that k-ary function f from natural numbers to natural numbers is n.r. by a formula $A(x_1,..., x_n, x_{n+1})$ with (n+1)-free variables in S if and only if for all natural numbers $n_1,..., n_k, n_{k+1}$,

> (1) If $f(n_1,..., n_k) = n_{k+1}$, then $\vdash_s A(\underline{n}_1,..., \underline{n}_k, \underline{n}_{k+1})$
> (2) $\vdash_s (\exists!x)A(\underline{n}_1,..., \underline{n}_k, x)$.

(The backwards "E" with an exclamation mark is pronounced "E shriek" and is short for

$$(\exists x)(A(\underline{n}_1,..., \underline{n}_k, x) \wedge (\forall y)(A(n_1,..., n_k, y) \rightarrow y = x)),$$

which means that the named individuals bear the relation to one and only one thing. This is a version of Russell's theory of descriptions.)[8] We

---

[7] Ibid., 200.
[8] Alfred North Whitehead and Bertrand Russell, *Principia Mathematica*, 2nd ed., 3 vols. (Cambridge: Cambridge University Press, 1925), 1: 30–31.

use an extra variable because we are representing the relation between the arguments to a function and its values. If s is the successor function sending each number to the next, then s is n.r. in S by $x_2 = (x_1)'$. For if k is the number after n, then the numeral $\underline{k}$ is the numeral $\underline{n}$ with one more stroke, so $\vdash_s \underline{k} = (\underline{n})'$ by the logic of identity; while if $y = (\underline{n})'$, then $\underline{k} = y$ by the logic of identity too, so the value is unique as (2) requires. It will turn out that the computable functions are n.r. in S, but it will take us a while to explain what it is for a function to be computable and to show that not all functions are computable. Note that n.r. too is explained in arithmetic and syntactical terms without semantics.

We will not have to show separately which relations are n.e. in S and which relations are n.r. in S. Characteristic functions bridge the gap. Let R be a k-ary relation on natural numbers. Then the characteristic function c_R of R is the function such that for all $n_1, \ldots, n_k$

$$c_R(n_1, \ldots, n_k) = \begin{cases} 0 \text{ if } R(n_1, \ldots, n_k) \\ 1 \text{ if not } R(n_1, \ldots, n_k) \end{cases}$$

so zero plays the role of the truth-value truth, and 1, of falsity. Then if $A(x_1, \ldots, x_n)$ n.e. R in S,

$$(A(x_1, \ldots, x_n) \wedge x_{n+1} = 0) \vee (\neg A(x_1, \ldots, x_n) \wedge x_{n+1} = \underline{1})$$

will n.r. c_R in S, while if $A(x_1, \ldots, x_n, x_{n+1})$ n.r. c_R in S, then

$$A(x_1, \ldots, x_n, 0)$$

will n.e. R in S. (Try to show this.) It will turn out that the decidable relations are exactly those whose characteristic functions are computable, so we will be able to justify both the n.e. arrow and the n.r. arrow by justifying only one of them.

To say which relations are decidable, which functions are computable, and what gödel numbering, the arrow in the picture from S to the first floor of A, is, we need the idea of an algorithm. (The word "algorithm" is a corruption of an Arabic name. It has nothing to do with rhythm and is spelled with an "i.") An algorithm is always an algorithm for a class Q of questions (like "What is the sum of n and k?"). An algorithm for Q is a finite list of instructions that, given a question q from Q, yields the correct answer to q in finitely many mechanical steps. Note that it is assumed that q has a unique correct answer. Note too that finiteness is required twice, once in the length of the list of instructions, and once in the number of steps needed to answer q. These two requirements are independent. The table of sums of one-digit numbers and the rules of carrying are an algorithm for adding natural numbers.

The most interesting word in our description of algorithms is "mechanical." It is meant to rule out all use of intelligence, creativity, or insight. We have no articulate and settled body of doctrine saying just what intelligence, creativity, and insight are, and neither do we have such a body of doctrine saying just what a machine is. So we should not expect much cut-and-dried reasoning proceeding centrally from our description of algorithms without further ado, especially reasoning to show that there is no algorithm for a certain class of questions. (On the other hand, we can show that if Q is finite, there is an algorithm for it. If the members of Q are $q_1,..., q_n$ and their answers are $a_1,..., a_n$, then the list

$$\text{Asked } q_1, \text{ answer } a_1$$
$$\vdots$$
$$\text{Asked } q_n, \text{ answer } a_n$$

is an algorithm for Q. So since no one lives to age 150, there is an algorithm for the ages at which we will die. This example shows that the existence of an algorithm does not require our being able to recognize it as such.)

A k-ary relation R on natural numbers is decidable just in case there is an algorithm for the questions whether $R(n_1,..., n_k)$. A k-ary function f from natural numbers to natural numbers is computable just in case there is an algorithm for what $f(n_1,..., n_k)$ is. A gödel numbering (arithmetization, gödelization) of S is a function g that assigns natural numbers to notations of S so that, first, g is one-to-one, that is, g assigns different numbers to different notations; second, there is an algorithm that, given a notation of S, yields the number g assigns to it; and third, there are two algorithms, one that given a number says whether g assigns it to a notation, and another such that if g assigns a number to a notation, finds the notation. There are three levels of notation: primitive signs, like the variable "x_1"; finite sequences of primitive signs, like terms and formulae; and finite sequences of finite sequences, like proofs. Actually, lest some sentence we want S to prove is not a theorem because we overlooked an extralogical primitive, we assign gödel numbers to all the extralogical primitives. A language has a decidable vocabulary just in case there is an algorithm for whether an extralogical primitive is a primitive of that language. Since the language of S has five extralogical primitives, it has a decidable vocabulary.

In the 1930s and 1940s there were several attempts to characterize algorithms so as to enable precise reasoning about them, especially to show that there is no algorithm for thus and such a class of questions. Of these the most compelling is Alan Turing's.[9] His core idea is now called a Turing machine. Such a machine has a finite alphabet a_1,..., a_n of signs and a finite repertoire q_1,..., q_k of states. The machine has a scanner that is always focused on a single cell or square on a linear tape of cells that we may think of either as infinite or as indefinitely extensible in both directions. Only letters of the machine's alphabet are ever printed in cells on the tape; not more than one letter ever occupies a cell; and only finitely many cells ever have letters printed in them. The machine's program consists of finitely many quadruples or instructions. Those of the form

$$a_i q_j R q_m$$

tell the machine that when in state q_j scanning a square in which a_i is printed, it is to move one square right and go into state q_m. Those of the form

$$a_i q_j L q_m$$

say that when in q_j scanning a_i, move one square left and go into q_m. Those of the form

$$a_i q_j a_p q_m$$

tell the machine that when in state q_j scanning a square in which a_i is printed, erase a_i, print a_p, and go into state q_m. A program is consistent if no two quadruples begin with the same pair of letter and state. We require programs to be consistent. A consistent program has at most nk quadruples. We agree always to start the machine scanning the first cell (if any) to the left in which a letter is printed (and if there are none, any old cell will do). When the machine starts, what is then printed on its tape is called its input, and if, when the machine starts from a given input, it stops after finitely many steps, what is then on the tape is called the machine's output for the given input, and the machine is said to halt for that input. There is no guarantee that a machine will halt for a given input.

Suppose, for example, an alphabet consisting just of a blank B and a vertical stroke l. (With this alphabet we should revise our understanding

[9] Alan M. Turing, "On Computable Numbers with an Application to the Entscheidungsproblem," reprinted in Martin Davis, ed., *The Undecidable* (Hewlett, N.Y.: Raven Press, 1965), 116–54.

that only finitely many cells ever have letters printed in them, so that only finitely many cells ever have strokes printed in them.) Let us agree that a sequence of n + 1 consecutive strokes counts as notation for the natural number n. If we want to input n and k to the machine, we start it with n + 1 strokes, a blank, and k + 1 strokes. With the program

$$q_1 \mid R q_1$$
$$q_1 B \mid q_2$$
$$q_2 \mid R q_2$$
$$q_2 B \ L \ q_3$$
$$q_3 \mid B q_4$$
$$q_4 \mid B q_5$$

this machine finds the separating blank, replaces it with a stroke (making n + k + 3 strokes), and then erases the last two strokes and halts. So its output is n + k + 1 strokes, and thus this machine computes addition. If f is a k-ary function from natural numbers to natural numbers, then a Turing machine M computes f just in case for all $n_1,..., n_k$, when M starts with $n_1,..., n_k$ as input, its output is $f(n_1,..., n_k)$, and such an f is Turing recursive just in case there is an M that computes f. So addition is Turing recursive. A relation is Turing recursive just in case its characteristic function is.

A Turing machine can take only three sorts of steps: move a square left, move a square right, or put one letter for another. Each such step seems rudimentary enough to be mechanical and uncreative. So any function computed by a Turing machine seems clearly computable. Conversely, what a Turing machine does is to write mechanically, so one expects any algorithm for computing a function to be rewritable as a program for a Turing machine. This expectation is not some *a priori* insight, and since we have no settled, articulate doctrine about machines, one should not look for a proof that every algorithm can be written as the program of a Turing machine. Nonetheless, that claim rings true enough to make it plausible that any computable function is Turing recursive. The thesis that all and only the computable functions are Turing recursive might be called Turing's thesis. But Alonzo Church came up with a coextensive characterization of the Turing recursive functions at about the same time as Turing, so the thesis is called the Church–Turing thesis.[10] There is nearly unanimous agreement among

[10] Alonzo Church, "An Unsolvable Problem of Elementary Number Theory," reprinted in Davis, *Undecidable*, 89–107. Turing's paper was published in the 1936–37 volume

specialists about which functions are computable, and all have turned out to be Turing recursive. Moreover, any two of the several differently motivated precise characterizations of the computable functions turn out to be coextensive. The smart money bets that the Church–Turing thesis is true.

Kleene showed how to give a more internally mathematical description of the Turing recursive functions.[11] Let N be the successor function, such that $N(k) = k + 1$. (This name comes from Gödel, since the German for successor is *Nachfolger*.) Let Z be the zero function, such that $Z(k) = 0$. Let U_i^n, $i \leq n$, be the n-ary function that, given an n-tuple, gives back its ith member. (U_i^n is called the ith projection function because, given a point in n-dimensional space, it gives back its ith coordinate.) N, Z, and the U_i^n are called the initial functions. Suppose h is an m-ary function and $g_1, \ldots, g_m$ are n-ary functions. Then f comes from h, $g_1, \ldots, g_m$ by composition just in case for all numbers $k_1, \ldots, k_n$

$$f(k_1, \ldots, k_n) = h(g_1(k_1, \ldots, k_n), \ldots, g_m(k_1, \ldots, k_n)).$$

Suppose g is n-ary and h is (n+2)-ary. Then f comes from g and h by recursion just in case for all $k_1, \ldots, k_n$

$$f(k_1, \ldots, k_n, 0) = g(k_1, \ldots, k_n)$$
$$f(k_1, \ldots, k_n, y + 1) = h(k_1, \ldots, k_n, y, f(k_1, \ldots, k_n, y)).$$

Recursion is how functions are defined from others inductively. Suppose g is (n+1)-ary. Then g is regular just in case for all $k_1, \ldots, k_n$ there is a y such that $g(k_1, \ldots, k_n, y) = 0$. Write "$\mu y$" for "the least number y such that." The μ-operator is a kind of definite description operator. Then f comes from g by minimalization just in case g is regular and for all $k_1, \ldots, k_n$

$$f(k_1, \ldots, k_n) = \mu y(g(k_1, \ldots, k_n, y) = 0).$$

A function f is primitive recursive just in case there is a finite sequence $f_1, \ldots, f_n$ of functions that ends with f (so $f_n = f$) and begins with an initial function, and every function in the sequence is initial or comes from earlier functions in the sequence by composition or recursion. Let h come from N and U_3^3 by composition, so $h(x, y, z) = NU_3^3(x, y, z) = z + 1$. Then addition comes from U_1^1 and h by recursion, so addition is

of the *Proceedings of the London Mathematical Society*, and Church's in the 1935 volume of the *Bulletin of the American Mathematical Society*.

[11] Stephen Cole Kleene, "Recursive Predicates and Quantifiers," reprinted in Davis, *Undecidable*, 255–87.

primitive recursive. A function is general recursive (or μ-recursive) just in case there is such a finite sequence ending with f and beginning with an initial function, and every function in the sequence is either initial or comes from earlier functions in the sequence by composition, recursion, or minimalization. It is not immediate, but we can prove that all and only the Turing recursive functions are μ-recursive. It is also not immediate, but there are μ-recursive functions that are not primitive recursive. Nowadays, thinking extensionally, we call the Turing recursive functions the recursive functions.

We will not need the Church–Turing thesis to prove Gödel's 1931 theorem, but we have not been wasting our time, since we will need it later. Now let us return to the picture. The last thing there we described was gödelization, a one-to-one assignment of numbers (called gödel numbers) to notation that is algorithmic coming and going. The only bit of the picture left undescribed is the arrow going from Σ to the floor between computable functions and decidable relations, and labeled "induced gödelization." The word "induced" here is a useful bit of mathematical jargon. Suppose, for example, there is an assignment (marriage) of spouses to one another. There is then a natural or automatic – or, in the jargon, induced – assignment of families of in-laws to families of in-laws. Equally, once we have assigned a number to each notation of S, there is a natural or induced assignment of sets (and functions) of numbers to sets (and functions) of notation. Suppose, for example, to each variable x_i the gödel number assigned is $5 + 8i$. Then to the *set* of variables of S it is natural to assign the *set* of numbers of the form $5 + 8i$, that is, the set of all and only the numbers k such that for some i, $k = 5 + 8i$. Call this set Var_A, the subscript meaning the set lies in arithmetic heaven A. Then since the gödel number of "x_1" is 13, we may say $13 \in Var_A$, and for any notation α with gödel number $g(\alpha)$, $Var_\Sigma(\alpha)$ just in case $g(\alpha) \in Var_A$.

A small example of how these various parts work together might be in order. The set Var_A is n.e. in S by a formula we might write Var_S. Recall that this means that when $n \in Var_A$, $\vdash_S Var_S(\underline{n})$, but when $n \notin Var_A$, $\vdash_S \neg Var_S(\underline{n})$. So since $Var_\Sigma("x_1")$ and thus $13 \in Var_A$, $\vdash_S Var_S(\underline{13})$. More generally, if $Var_\Sigma(\alpha)$, $\vdash_S Var_S(g(\alpha))$, but if not-$Var_\Sigma(\alpha)$, $\vdash_S \neg Var_S(g(\alpha))$. Assuming no contradictions are provable in S,

$$Var_\Sigma(\alpha) \text{ if and only if } \vdash_S Var_S(g(\alpha)).$$

Gödel never interprets the language of S, but suppose we do so in the obvious way in the domain of natural numbers. This interpretation is called the standard model, and simple sentences like "$\text{Var}_S(\underline{g(\alpha)})$" are provable in S just in case they are true in the standard model. So

(1) $\text{Var}_\Sigma(\alpha)$ if and only if "$\text{Var}_S(\underline{g(\alpha)})$" is true in the standard model.

Some read the T-sentence

  Peter is tall if and only if "Pierre est grand" is true

as "Pierre est grand" says that Peter is tall, and some read (1) as "$\text{Var}_S(\underline{g(\alpha)})$" says that α is a variable of S. Such a reading is the origin of the idea that Gödel showed how to talk *about* S in S. But a few grains of salt are in order here. First, the name "Pierre" doubtless denotes the man Peter (if, as we usually don't, we translate names), but the term "$\underline{g(\alpha)}$" denotes the *number* $g(\alpha)$, not the notation α. Similarly, the extension of "est grand" is the set of tall people, but the extension under standard interpretation of "Var_S" is the set Var_A of *numbers*, not the set of *notations* Var_Σ is true of. So to get to the left-hand side of (1) we need to undo gödelization, as if the gödel number 13 of "x_1" gets bypassed in finding the denotation of $g(\underline{"x_1"})$. Hence, taking (1) as illustrating that Gödel showed how to talk about S in S uses a questionable notion of saying,[12] uses standard interpretation (which Gödel does not), and requires a circuitous version of reference based on undoing gödelization.

The number theoretic work in proving Gödel's 1931 theorem lies in showing that for many syntactical predicates and function signs used in Σ, the arithmetic sets and functions assigned to them under the induced gödelization are n.e. or n.r. in S. Some of this work is pretty, but we are going to omit it all here. But we mention one relation and two functions. The predicate $\text{Pf}_\Sigma(\alpha, \beta)$ holds just in case α is a proof in S of formula β. When $\varphi(\upsilon)$ is a formula of S, τ is a term of S and υ is a variable of S, $\text{sub}_\Sigma(\varphi, \tau, \upsilon)$ is the formula $\varphi(\tau)$. The gödelization of Pf_Σ is Pf_A, so $\text{Pf}_A(n, k)$ just in case n is the gödel number of a proof in S of the formula with gödel number k. The gödelization of sub_Σ is a function sub_A such that if n is the number of formula $\varphi(\upsilon)$, k is the number of term τ, and p is the number of variable υ, then $\text{sub}_A(n, k, p)$ is the number of $\varphi(\tau)$. Our third item is the arithmetical function num_A whose value at n is $g(\underline{n})$. (So num_A goes from A to S and back to A.) Then num_A, sub_A, and the characteristic function of Pf_A are primitive recursive.

---

[12] Saying that is close to meaning that, but without special and as yet unknown constraints, the proofs of T-sentences may well be too extensional for those sentences to bear so intensional a reading.

We need two more concepts before we can prove Gödel's 1931 theorem. Given a theory T fixed by its axioms embedded in our logic, T is consistent just in case for no formula A of its language are both A and its negation theorems of T. If the language for T includes the numerals, then T is ω-consistent just in case for no formula $A(x)$ of the language of T are all of

$$A(\underline{0}), A(\underline{1}),\ldots$$

and

$$(\exists x)\neg A(x)$$

theorems of T. In a theory like S designed to be about just the natural numbers, ω-consistency seems desirable. If T is inconsistent, then since

$$(A \wedge \neg A) \to B$$

holds by logic, everything is a theorem of T; and if T proves everything, it proves contradictions; so consistency is equivalent to the unprovability of something. If T is ω-consistent, something is unprovable, so T is consistent (but the converse fails).

Let $R_A(u, y)$ be the relation $Pf_A(y, \text{sub}_A(u, \text{num}_A(u), 13))$. Then $R_A(u, y)$ holds just in case u is the gödel number of a formula $A(x_1)$ and y is the gödel number of a proof in S of $A(\underline{u})$. The relation R_A is primitive recursive (that is, its characteristic function is) and n.e. in S by a formula $R_S(x_1, x_2)$; this we get from the number theoretic work we left out. Consider the formula

$$(\maltese) \ (\forall x_2)\neg R_S(x_1, x_2)$$

and let a be its gödel number. Now consider the sentence

$$(\maltese\ \maltese) \ (\forall x_2)\neg R_S(\underline{a}, x_2)$$

and let b be its gödel number. (The double-cross is an homage to Elliott Mendelson from whom this exposition descends.) Then $(\maltese\ \maltese)$ is the result of substituting in $(\maltese)$ the numeral for the gödel number a of $(\maltese)$ for x_1. Thus

$$b = \text{sub}_A(a, \text{num}_A(a), 13)$$

and hence

(P) $R_A(a, y)$ if and only if y is the gödel number of a proof in S of the formula with gödel number $\text{sub}_A(a, \text{num}_A(a), 13)$

iff y is the gödel number of a proof in S of the formula with gödel numbers b

iff y is the gödel number of a proof in S of (⌘ ⌘).

Now we are ready to prove Gödel's 1931 theorem, which is usually called Gödel's first incompleteness theorem: If S is ω-consistent, then neither double-cross nor its negation is provable in S.

Proof: First we show that if S is consistent, then (⌘ ⌘) is not provable in S. So suppose (⌘ ⌘) is provable. Then it has a proof, which has a gödel number m. Hence, by (P), $R_A(a, m)$, so since R_A is n.e. in S by R_S, $\vdash_S R_S(\underline{a}, \underline{m})$. But $\vdash_S$ (⌘ ⌘), that is, $\vdash_S (\forall x_2)\neg R_S(\underline{a}, x_2)$, so by logic, $\vdash_S \neg R_S(\underline{a}, \underline{m})$, and thus S is inconsistent. Second, we show that if S is ω-consistent, then $\neg$(⌘ ⌘) is not provable in S either. So suppose S is ω-consistent but $\vdash_S \neg$(⌘ ⌘), that is,

$$\vdash_S \neg(\forall x_2)\neg R_S(\underline{a}, x_2)$$

or equivalently, by logic,

$$\vdash_S (\exists x_2)\neg \neg R_S(\underline{a}, x_2).$$

(You will see in a bit why we left the double negation.) Since S is ω-consistent, it is consistent, and so by the first part of this proof, (⌘ ⌘) is not provable in S. Hence no number is the gödel number of a proof in S of (⌘ ⌘). Thus by (P) for all numbers n, not-$R_A(a, n)$. But R_A is n.e. in S by R_S, so for all n

$$\neg R_S(\underline{a}, \underline{n})$$

is provable in S. This and $\vdash_S (\exists x_2)\neg \neg R_S(\underline{a}, x_2)$ make S ω-inconsistent. Q.E.D.

Gödel's argument is an exercise in syntax and makes no use of truth. But it is a received property of truth that for any sentence, either it or its negation is true, so the first incompleteness theorem shows that a truth in the language of S is not provable in S; in this case, truth eludes proof. This observation makes it natural to wonder whether double-cross or its negation is the true one. Under standard interpretation, R_A is the extension in the standard model of R_S, so double-cross is true there just in case a is R_A to no y, and thus by (P) just in case no y is the gödel number of a proof in S of double-cross. Thus double-cross "says that" double-cross is not provable in S.[13] But

---

[13] It is natural for a mathematician to wonder just what claim about natural numbers double-cross makes (without undoing gödelization), and this is not easy to

by the first part of the first incompleteness theorem, if S is consistent, double-cross is not provable in S. So if S is consistent, double-cross is true in the standard model. Then it might occur to one that perhaps it was just an oversight not to have included double-cross when we axiomatized S; maybe every arithmetic truth is provable in this strengthening T of S. But no. We get a slightly different proof predicate Pf_T for T, but its arithmetization is still primitive recursive and so n.e. in T. Thus the original argument goes through pretty much unchanged, and we get an undecided sentence (neither it nor its negation provable) of T (and thus a new one of S). As we shall see, there is no easy escape from incompleteness.

But before we generalize the first incompleteness theorem, let us sketch the second. The first clause of the first theorem says that if S is consistent, double-cross is not a theorem of S. Suppose we want to translate this clause into the language of S. We have just seen that double-cross itself translates the consequent of the first clause. As for the antecedent, there is a syntactical relation Neg_Σ such that $Neg_\Sigma(\alpha, \beta)$ just in case formula α is the negation of formula β. Its gödelization, Neg_A, is primitive recursive and so n.e. in S by a formula Neg_S. So if Pf_S n.e. Pf_A in S, then

$$(\exists x_1, x_2, x_3, x_4)(Neg_S(x_1, x_2) \wedge Pf_S(x_3, x_1) \wedge Pf_S(x_2, x_4))$$

will say that S is inconsistent, and thus its negation, $Cons_S$, says that S is consistent. Hence

$$(*) \; Cons_S \rightarrow (⌘ ⌘)$$

translates the first clause of the first theorem into the language of S. But the reasoning we used to prove the first clause is elementary and combinatorial enough that (*) can be proved in S. This claim is where we (and Gödel) get sketchy. The claim is sensitive to the details of Pf_Σ, Pf_A, and Pf_S, but if we do them in the natural way, (*) is a theorem of S.[14] Hence if $\vdash_S Cons_S$, then double-cross is provable in S and S is

discern. Some then ask whether there are sentences of the language of S whose arithmetic content is discernable but such that neither the sentence nor its negation is provable in S. There are. For a discussion of some examples, see Daniel Isaacson, "Arithmetical Truth and Hidden Higher-Order Concepts," reprinted in Hart, *Philosophy of Mathematics*, 203–24.

[14] For more, see George Boolos, *The Unprovability of Consistency* (Cambridge: Cambridge University Press, 1979), chap. 2, and its fully rewritten and updated second edition, *The Logic of Provability*, 1993.

inconsistent. Hence we get Gödel's second incompleteness theorem: If S is consistent, then Con_S is not provable in S.

In the aftermath of the paradoxes, Hilbert proposed a program of formalizing theories, including eventually set theory, and proving them consistent. His idea was that even if the content intended for the theory is very abstract and powerful, consistency is concrete and combinatorial: it just requires that there be no finite sequence of formulae beginning with axioms of the theory, proceeding by the theory's logic, and ending with a formula of the shape $A \wedge \neg A$. Nevertheless, satisfactory consistency proofs for interesting theories were elusive. The message of the second incompleteness theorem seems to be that if we have a powerful set theory in which all conventional mathematics is formalized (like ZFC), then the consistency of the theory cannot be proved in the theory (i.e., using all mathematical methods) if the theory is consistent. So if the theory is consistent, its consistency can be proved only by using methods stronger than those of all mathematics. Gödel hesitated to draw this conclusion explicitly about his teacher's program.[15] Still, the second incompleteness theorem makes it wise to consider the significance of consistency proofs and, in particular, whether they justify one in being surer of the theory proved consistent.

We will use the Church–Turing thesis to generalize the first incompleteness theorem, and to do so we will prove two preliminary results. Let T be a theory whose language has a decidable vocabulary. Then T is decidable just in case there is an algorithm for theoremhood in T. Suppose T is a theory that is consistent and in which all recursive relations are n.e. and whose language has a decidable vocabulary and has the numerals. Then T is undecidable. For suppose not. Gödelize the language of T. Then $sub(x, num(x), 13)$ is recursive and so is the characteristic function c_T of gödel numbers of theorems of T. Let A be the set of all k such that $c_T(sub(k, num(k), 13)) = 0$. Then A is recursive, so it is n.e. in T by a formula $A_T(x_1)$. Let q be the gödel number of $\neg A_T(x_1)$, and let p be the gödel number of $\neg A_T(\underline{q})$. Then, as before, $p = sub(q, num(q), 13)$. If $c_T(p) = 0$, then $c_T(sub(q, num(q), 13)) = 0$, so $q \in A$, so $\vdash_T A_T(\underline{q})$ since A is n.e. by A_T; but since $c_T(p) = 0$, p is the gödel number of a theorem of T, and since p is the gödel number of $\neg A_T(\underline{q})$, $\vdash_T A_T(\underline{q})$, and T is inconsistent. But if $c_T(p) \neq 0$, $c_T(sub(q, num(q), 13)) \neq 0$, so

[15] Kurt Gödel, "On Formally Undecidable Propositions of *Principia Mathematica* and Related Systems I," reprinted in his *Collected Works*, vol. 1, ed. Soloman Feferman et al. (Oxford: Clarendon Press, 1986), 195.

$q \notin A$, so $\vdash_T A_T(\underline{q})$ since A is n.e. by A_T, and then $c_T(p) = 0$, which is impossible. Hence c_T is not recursive, and T is undecidable.

To make explicit something that has been implicit for a while, a theory is complete just in case for every sentence A in the language of the theory, either A is provable in the theory or ¬A is. (We restrict attention here to sentences because free variables are understood universally, as in "x + y = y + x."[16] But in number theory, we want neither "x is even" nor "x is not even" to be provable, since some numbers are not even but some are.) Next we use a feature called being axiomatic: A theory whose language has a decidable vocabulary is axiomatic just in case there is an algorithm for whether a formula of its language is an axiom. We will show that a complete, axiomatic theory is decidable. This will take several steps. First, a set is effectively enumerable just in case it is empty or there is a computable function that maps the natural numbers onto the set. If a is such a function for a set A, then the idea is that a(0), a(1),... is an enumeration of A that we can actually write out through any finite initial segment. For example,

$$<1, 1>, <1, 2>, <2, 1>,...$$

starts an effective enumeration of the ordered pairs of positive integers. Here $<n, k>$ precedes $<m, p>$ just in case $n + k < m + p$ or else both $n + k = m + p$ and $n < m$. A way to find the n assigned to $<m, p>$ is to list the pairs until $<m, p>$ crops up and then count up to it starting from 0. Using this enumeration of the ordered pairs of positive integers, we can effectively enumerate the whole stock of extralogical primitives from which those of a first-order language are selected thus:

$$a_1, f_1^1, A_1^1, a_2, f_2^1, f_1^2, A_2^1, A_2^2, a_3,...$$

We are considering an axiomatic theory T, so there is an algorithm for which extralogical primitives are primitives in the language of T. Using this algorithm to strike extralogical primitives not in the language of T from the effective enumeration of all extralogical primitives, we are left with an effective enumeration of the extralogical primitives of T. Weaving in the logical primitives (all but finitely many being variables), we get an effective enumeration of the primitive signs of the language of T. Using our inductive syntax for first-order languages, we can then get an effective enumeration of the formulae of the language of T. (There is a good deal to describing this enumeration, but we will slide over it. We

---

[16] Kleene, *Introduction to Metamathematics*, 149.

could also have got here by gödelizing the language and ordering its formulae by the size of their gödel numbers.) Since T is axiomatic, there is an algorithm for axioms of T, and using it to strike nonaxioms from our enumeration of the formulae of the language of T, we are left with an effective enumeration of the axioms of T. We use properties of our logic to extend this enumeration of axioms to an effective enumeration of theorems of T. We can present our logic so that it has only finitely many rules of inference and so that for each there is an algorithm that given the premises yields the conclusion (modus ponens yields the consequent from a conditional and its antecedent). Suppose for simplicity we have two rules, R_1 and R_2, where R_1 has one premiss and R_2 has two. We enumerate theorems of T in stages. To start, list the first axiom of T. At stage $n + 1$, add to the list axiom numbered $n + 1$ and then, in order, everything got from formulae on the list by one use of R_1, and everything got from pairs of formulae on the list ordered as we ordered the pairs of positive integers by one use of R_2.[17] (This technique is called dovetailing.[18] We would use it in enumerating formulae.) The result is an effective enumeration of the theorems of T.

We have just shown that the theorems of an axiomatic theory are effectively enumerable. Now we show that if T is axiomatic and complete, it is decidable. Suppose first that T is inconsistent. Then since everything is provable, an algorithm for whether a sentence is a theorem is "Say 'Yes.'" Now suppose T is consistent and let A be a sentence in the language of T. To test whether A is a theorem, start enumerating the theorems of T. If A is provable, it will crop up in finitely many steps; in this case, stop and say "Yes." Otherwise, since T is complete, ¬A will crop up in finitely many steps, and then since T is consistent, A will never crop up, so when ¬A crops up, stop and say "No."

Suppose T is a consistent axiomatic theory with numerals in which all recursive relations are n.e. Since T is consistent and all recursive relations are n.e. in T, T is undecidable. Then, since T is axiomatic and undecidable, T is incomplete. Hence any consistent axiomatic theory with numerals in which all recursive relations are n.e. is incomplete, that is, there is a sentence in the language of T such that neither the

---

[17] If R_1 is a rule like universal instantiation in which terms as well as formulae figure, we also need an effective enumeration of the terms. Then at stage $n + 1$ we add the finitely many formulae got by one application of R_1 to formulae on the list using the first n terms.

[18] Hartley Rogers Jr., *Theory of Recursive Functions and Effective Computability* (New York: McGraw-Hill, 1967), 60.

sentence nor its negation is a theorem of T. This is our generalization of Gödel's first incompleteness theorem.

We can use this result to drive undecidability and incompleteness down from S to weaker systems. Q has the same notation as S, but its numerical axioms are just that successor is one-to-one, zero is not a successor, any number not zero is a successor, and the inductive definitions of addition and multiplication.[19] Q is part of S but weaker, since in Q we cannot show that addition commutes, no number is its own successor, or zero times anything is zero.[20] But all recursive relations are n.e. in Q.[21] Q is certainly axiomatic, and the analogue Con_Q (saying Q is consistent) of Con_S for S is in fact a theorem of S. While S is stronger than Q, as the second theorem leads us to expect, the provability of Con_Q in S is pretty close to a flat-out proof that Q is consistent. Hence Q is both undecidable and incomplete.

Since there are infinitely many formulae in the language of S with a free variable, the axiom schema of induction produces an infinity of numerical axioms in S. (Moreover, there is no way to replace them with finitely many numerical axioms.)[22] But Q has only finitely many numerical axioms, in fact, just seven. Hence, for Q, unlike S, there exists a single sentence A_Q that is the conjunction of the numerical axioms of Q. Thus, for any sentence A in the language of Q, A is a theorem of Q just in case $A_Q \rightarrow A$ is a theorem of pure logic, or equivalently, by Gödel's completeness theorem for quantification theory,[23] just in case $A_Q \rightarrow A$ is quantificationally valid. So, if there were an algorithm for quantificational validity, we could apply it to $A_Q \rightarrow A$ to get an algorithm for the theoremhood in Q. So, since Q is undecidable, quantificational validity is too. This result is called Church's theorem.[24] It is well known that truth tables are an algorithm for truth-functional validity, so Church's theorem says that the quantifier is where undecidability comes from.

[19] Alfred Tarski in collaboration with Andrzej Mostowski and Raphael M. Robinson, *Undecidable Theories* (Amsterdam: North-Holland, 1953), 51. Q is known as Robinson's system.

[20] Ibid., 55.

[21] Ibid., 56.

[22] C. Ryll-Nardzewski, "The Role of the Axiom of Induction in Elementary Arithmetic," *Fundamental Mathematics* 39 (1952): 239–63.

[23] See Chapter 4, pp. 109–10.

[24] Alonzo Church, "An Unsolvable Problem of Elementary Number Theory" and "A Note on the Entscheidungsproblem," reprinted in Davis, *Undecidable*, 89–107 and 108–15.

Since quantification over infinite domains is infinitary while the truth functions are finitary, the contrast may not be entirely surprising.

We have shown that any consistent axiomatic theory in which all recursive relations are n.e. is incomplete.[25] So there is no way to make a theory in which all (mathematical) truths are provable by adding axioms to a powerful theory like ZFC, so long as the theory remains consistent and axiomatic. This looks like pretty strong evidence against the formalist doctrine that mathematical truth is provability, and insofar as formalism was motivated by a desire to avoid very abstract objects like numbers, evidence for platonism.

But our result applies only to theories that are consistent and axiomatic, and in which all recursive relations are n.e., so we should assess the reasonableness of these constraints. The leading formalist idea is that truth (in mathematics) is provability. But it is an elementary property of truth that no contradiction is true, so consistency seems a reasonable requirement on provability that is to constitute truth. That all recursive relations are n.e. and all recursive functions n.r. come down to being able to calculate algorithmically, and since equations like "2 + 2 = 4" and "7 + 5 = 12" are often cited as exemplars of mathematical truth, it seems reasonable to require that recursive relations be n.e. in a system of proof that is to constitute mathematical truth. That leaves axiomaticness and being formalized in a theory or system.

To take the second first, Gödel himself suggested that perhaps there is an absolute notion of provability that eludes capture in any formal system.[26] Let "Bp" be short for "It is absolutely provable that p." Two plausible assumptions are an axiom that anything absolutely provable is true, that is, $Bp \rightarrow p$, and a rule licensing inference from a theorem to its absolute provability, that is, having proved that p we may infer the Bp. By the axiom

$$B(p \land \neg p) \rightarrow (p \land \neg p),$$

so since no contradiction is true, by *modus tollens*

$$\neg B(p \land \neg p),$$

---

[25] We assume all recursive functions n.e., and we do not exhibit a sentence neither proved nor refuted. In his 1931 proof, Gödel needs only primitive recursive functions and relations to be n.e., and he exhibits a sentence neither proved nor refuted.

[26] Kurt Gödel, "An Interpretation of the Intuitionist Propositional Calculus," reprinted in *Collected Works*, 1: 301–03.

and having proved this, we infer by the rule that

$$B\neg B(p \wedge \neg p).$$

Hence B proves its own consistency, as it were, and thus, as Gödel puts it, B cannot be provability in any consistent, axiomatic system that contains arithmetic. One might wonder whether there is any such thing as absolute provability.

Logic is typically presented so that an algorithm for whether a formula is an axiom yields an algorithm for whether a finite sequence of formulae is a proof. Then whether it is reasonable to require axiomaticness turns into whether it is reasonable to require an algorithm for whether a finite stretch of discourse is a proof. Alonzo Church argues that it is the purpose of proof to settle mathematical questions decisively, once and for all, and without an algorithm for being a proof we cannot guarantee in advance to be able to tell whether putative proofs are indeed proofs, thus risking endless, indecisive wrangling.[27] For example, extend S to T by making all sentences in the language of S true under standard interpretation axioms of T. If T were axiomatic, it would be incomplete, which it is not (so arithmetic truth is undecidable).[28] Proof in T certainly smuggles in truth, and so is nominalistically unacceptable. But more important, no proof in T need be more than one line long, but any such proof begs, rather than settles, its question.

Mathematical induction is a way to establish truths about the infinity of natural numbers by a finite proof. A message of incompleteness is that induction does not suffice to establish all such truths. A way to cut the Gordian knot is to allow infinitely large proofs. Hilbert's rule, also known as the ω-rule, licenses inferences from all of A($\underline{n}$), one for each natural number n, to $(\forall x)A(x)$. There need be no pattern to how the numerical instances are proved. This time let T be S with Hilbert's rule. Then all sentences in the language of S true in the standard model are theorems of T, so T is complete. Every sentence is provably equivalent by logic to a sentence in prenex normal form, that is, in which every truth-functional connective lies in the scope of every quantifier. For any sentence in the language of S, let A be a prenex equivalent of the sentence. We show T complete by proving by induction on the

[27] Alonzo Church, *Introduction to Mathematical Logic*, vol. 1 (Princeton: Princeton University Press, 1956), 53–54.

[28] Hence, if S is consistent, theoremhood in S is undecidable. Truth for sentences of S is also undecidable. Truth is more undecidable than theoremhood, and how much more is a measure of how much truth eludes proof.

number of quantifiers in the prenex (initial string of quantifiers) of A that if A is true, then A is provable in T. As basis case, suppose A has no quantifiers. Then it is a truth-functional compound of atomic sentences. These atomic sentences are equations between terms built up from the little oval using the stroke, the addition sign, and the multiplication sign. Using the inductive definitions of addition and multiplication in the axioms of S, such equations are provably equivalent to equations between numerals. If the numerals on both sides are the same, the equation is true and provable in S, but if not, the equation is false and refutable in S. This settles the atoms, and the truth-functional logic of S suffices to deduce a true truth-functional compound of atoms from those atoms or their negations, according as the atoms are true (and provable) or false (and refutable). So any true quantifier-free sentence of S is provable in S, and so in T. As induction step, suppose there are n + 1 quantifiers in the prenex of A. Then A is $(\exists x)B(x)$ or $(\forall x)B(x)$ for some $B(x)$ with n quantifiers in its prenex. If A is $(\exists x)B(x)$ and true in the standard model, then for some n, $B(\underline{n})$ is true there, and so by the induction hypothesis is a theorem of T. Then $(\exists x)B(x)$, namely A, is deducible by one use of existential generalization in ordinary logic. (So all truths with one existential quantifier in the prenex are provable in S.) If A is $(\forall x)B(x)$ and true in the standard model, then for all n, $B(\underline{n})$ is true there, and so by the induction hypothesis is a theorem of T. Then $(\forall x)B(x)$, namely A, is deducible by Hilbert's rule.

The prospects for an algorithm that settles whether an arbitrary infinite patch of discourse is a proof seem pretty dim. Imagine the editor of a mathematics journal receiving an infinitely long submission (each page half as thick as its predecessor, perhaps). The prospect of checking it is daunting. But while all functions from natural numbers to natural numbers are infinitely large (sets of ordered pairs), some of them can be grasped by finite algorithms for computing them. Perhaps there might be a more limited sort of infinite proof where some sort of algorithmic grasp of its infinite stretches does not deprive the proof of epistemic significance. There is an interesting logical literature here that seems as yet not to have received the critical philosophical attention it deserves.[29] Lacking such criticism, infinitely large proofs seem like an epistemic illusion.

By the completeness of quantification theory, a sentence is a theorem of S just in case it is true in all models of S. Double-cross is not provable

[29] Jon Barwise, *Admissable Sets and Structures* (Berlin: Springer, 1975), and C.-T. Chong, *Techniques of Admissable Recursion Theory* (Berlin: Springer, 1984).

in S but is true in the standard model for S (assuming S is consistent). Hence there is a model for S where double-cross is false, and since isomorphic models agree on all sentences, this model is not isomorphic to the standard model. Such models are called nonstandard. We do not seem to have a direct description of a nonstandard model for S where double-cross fails. But we can get some idea of what some such nonstandard models are like. Add to the language of S a single new constant a, and this time let T be S together with $0 \neq a$, $\underline{1} \neq a$, and so on through all the natural numbers. We will use compactness to show that T is consistent.[30] If a contradiction were provable in T, it would be provable from finitely many axioms of T. These axioms can be split into two parts, those from S and finitely many of the new difference axioms. Those from S are true in the standard model for S, and if $0 \neq a$, $\underline{1} \neq a$,..., $\underline{n} \neq a$ is long enough to include all the difference axioms in the proof, then these too come out true in the standard model letting a denote n + 1. Hence T has a countable model M, and a denotes a member α of the domain of M.

The less-than relation of M is the extension in its domain of the formula $(\exists z)(x = y + z')$; the extension of this formula in the standard model is the ordinary less-than relation. We will look at less-than in M using the fact that T includes S, so all theorems of S are theorems of T and so true in M. S proves that zero is the least natural number, so M has a copy of zero that is M-least. S proves that every natural number has a successor and nothing comes between a number and its successor. So M has copies of all of 0, 1,... in order, but α is different from all of them, is not less than 0, and is never between n and n + 1. But S also proves that for any x and y, either $x < y$ or $x = y$ or $y < x$. So α must be greater than all of M's copies of 0, 1, and so on. M is nonstandard.

Nor is α alone out there beyond the standard natural numbers. By the laws of S, α has a successor $\alpha + 1$, which has a successor $\alpha + 2$, and so on. Similarly, since α is not zero, it has a predecessor $\alpha \dotminus 1$, which has a predecessor $\alpha \dotminus 2$, and so on.[31] None of these is standard; if, for example,

---

[30] On compactness, see Chapter 4, p. 110.

[31] Since 3 − 5 is negative and not a natural number, we cannot subtract in S. But if we set

$$d(0) = 0$$
$$d(y + 1) = y$$

and

$$x \dotminus 0 = x$$
$$x \dotminus (y + 1) = d(x - y),$$

$\alpha \dot- k$ were some standard n, then by the laws of arithmetic in S, α would be n + k and so standard. The numbers of the form $\alpha \dot- k$ and $\alpha + n$, k and n standard, constitute a sequence order-isomorphic to the integers, negative, zero, and positive, and are called the clump around α.

Nor is the clump around α alone out there beyond the standard naturals. By the laws of S, α has a double 2α. Were $2\alpha = \alpha + k$ for some standard k, then by arithmetic in S, $\alpha = k$, which is false. There is again a whole clump around 2α, all of it entirely above the clump around α. Since 5 is not even, we cannot divide 5 by 2 and stay in the natural numbers. But if we set $\left[\frac{n}{2}\right]$ equal to $\mu k(2(k + 1) > n)$, then $\left[\frac{n}{2}\right]$ is a recursive (in fact, primitive recursive) function whose value is the largest natural number less than or equal to $\left[\frac{n}{2}\right]$. The clump around $\left[\frac{\alpha}{2}\right]$ lies entirely below the one around α and above all the standard naturals. (To show this, consider cases according as α is even or odd.) Finally, if β and γ are non-standard and come from different clumps, the clump around $\left[\frac{\beta+\gamma}{2}\right]$ lies entirely between those around β and γ.

Recall that ω is the order-type of the standard natural numbers in their usual less-than order. Cantor called the reverse order-type, that of the negatives in less-than order, $^*\omega$. If β and γ are the types of linear orders, then $\beta + \gamma$ is the type of the order got by following an order of type β by one of type γ adjusted so that their fields are disjoint. So the order-type of any clump is $^*\omega + \omega$. Cantor called the type of a dense linear order without endpoints and a countable field η; he proved that any two are isomorphic. The leading example of an order of type η is the rational numbers ordered by less-than. If β and γ are the types of linear orders, then $\beta\gamma$ is the type of the order got by replacing each point in an order of type γ by an order of type β adjusted so that their fields are disjoint. We have seen that under its less-than relation, the domain of M begins with an order of type ω, and then there is a countable dense linear order without endpoints (of type η) of clumps, each ordered like the integers, and so of type $^*\omega + \omega$. Hence the order-type (under less-than) of the domain of M is $\omega + (^*\omega + \omega)\eta$.

The order-type (under less-than) of any countable model of S is either ω or else $\omega + (^*\omega + \omega)\eta$; there is no third option. But there are as many countable models for S no two of which are isomorphic as there are real numbers, that is, continuum many, and this is as many as there could be. Hence, the order-type of a countable model for S fails about

---

then $\dot-$ (pronounced monus) is a primitive recursive function whose value is x − y when we can subtract, but 0 otherwise.

as badly as possible to fix the rest of the structure of the model. (It is the multiplicative structure that varies.) Russell once toyed with the idea that there is nothing to being a natural number beyond occurring in a progression (fixed only by an object x, a unary function f, and a set A such that x is in A, f maps A one-to-one into A, x is not a value of f, and for any set X such that $x \in X$ and $f(y) \in X$ when $y \in X$, $A \subseteq X$).[32] Taken second-order, as Russell clearly intended, there is no logic such that both all logical consequences of these assumptions are derivable from them by the logic and there is an algorithm for whether a finite sequence of sentences is a derivation by the logic from the assumptions. Second-order we lose epistemic control. But first-order, where we have more epistemic control, the description of progressions is not univocal. So neither seems to nail down the natural numbers.

On first acquaintance, the nonstandard natural numbers may seem weird and undesirable, but they deserve a chance. Adding a to a theory of real numbers will vindicate the infinitesimals of Newton and Leibniz. Let R be the set of real numbers. Let M be a model whose domain is R, whose distinguished elements are all members of R, whose distinguished relations are all relations on R, and whose distinguished functions are all functions from R to R. Let L be a (larger than usual) first-order language with a constant for each distinguished element of M, a predicate sign for each distinguished relation of M, and a function sign for each distinguished function of M. Let T be the set of all sentences of L true in M. Add to L a new constant a and to T the sentences N(a), $a \neq 0$, $a \neq \underline{1}$, $a \neq \underline{2}$, and so on, where N is the predicate of L for the natural numbers in R. As before, this extension T' of T is consistent and has a model M' whose domain R' has the same cardinal number as R, and $\omega + (^*\omega + \omega)\eta$ is the order-type of the natural numbers of M'. So the integers of M' (negative, zero, and positive) have the order-type $(\omega^* + \omega)\eta$. Any of these integers is the numerator, and any nonzero one the denominator, of a ratio of M', and these ratios fix the rational numbers of M' according to the usual rule that $\frac{n}{m} = \frac{p}{q}$ if and only if nq = mp. The rationals of M' have the order-type η.

It is the reals of M' we are after, and we will think of reals in terms of decimals. A decimal like 3.14159... is a sequence of digits. Such sequences may be represented by functions from the integers to the set

[32] Bertrand Russell, *Introduction to Mathematical Philosophy* (London: George Allen & Unwin, 1919), 8. Similar ideas have often occurred to others.

of digits, that is, the set of natural numbers from 0 to 9. The integers in their usual array

$$\ldots, -2, -1, 0, 1, 2, \ldots$$

increase as we move to the right, but in decimal notation a step to the *left* is an increase in order of magnitude. This opposition produces irrelevant irritations. Let us picture the integers thus

$$\ldots, 2, 1, 0, -1, -2, \ldots$$

so that, as with decimals, advancement is toward the left (as seems progressive). It is required of any decimal d that there be an integer i such that for all $j > i$, $d(j) = 0$. Also, suppose d were a decimal such that for some i and all $j < i$, $d(j) = 9$. An example would be .2499..., which is notation for .25. Let i' be the greatest such i. Then we exclude d in favor of the d' such that

$$d'(j) = d(j) \text{ for all } j > i'$$
$$d'(j') = d(i) + 1$$
$$d'(j) = 0 \text{ for } j < i'.$$

Given these stipulations, for each non-negative (standard) real r there is a unique decimal d such that

$$r = \sum_i d(i) \cdot 10^i,$$

the sum being taken over all integers. Conversely, for each decimal d there is a unique non-negative (standard) real r obeying the same equations. For r negative, −r is positive, so we have a unique d such that

$$r = \sum_i -d(i) \cdot 10^i$$

and conversely. We made L rich enough to express these claims, so these claims are true in M, and thus members of T. (To avoid a second-order function quantifier on d, we use instead a single binary $D(r, i) = j$, saying that the ith digit of r is j.)

These claims are thus members of T′ and true in M′. But in M′, while the digits are as ever, the integers include the nonstandard integers. We have reached the long decimals. For each real r in R′ let d_r be its decimal. Then r is finite just in case there is a standard integer i such that $d_r(j) = 0$ for all $j > i$, and r is infinitesimal just in case $d_r(i) \neq 0$ at most for negative nonstandard integers i. If a denotes α in M′, then α is infinite. Moreover, since α is positive and greater than all of 1, 2, and so on, its reciprocal $\frac{1}{\alpha}$ is positive but less than all of 1, $\frac{1}{2}$, $\frac{1}{3}$, and so on, so $\frac{1}{\alpha}$ is a positive infinitesimal. With infinitesimals in hand we can develop the calculus, Berkeley notwithstanding, more in the manner of Newton and Leibniz.[33]

Infinitesimals thus open a mathematical avenue. But they may also open a geometrical avenue. Suppose it were in the nature of space that the standard real numbers are not of the right structure to serve as coordinate axes for space, but the nonstandard reals are. The standard and nonstandard reals differ in the infinite and the infinitesimal, and these differences could be either too big or too small to be obvious to middle-sized creatures like us. With nonstandard coordinates, space would divide into a countable infinity of shapes each with three clumps (now of nonstandard reals) *ω + ω units long as the axes of that shape. There does not seem to be a way to assign a specific shape (cube or sphere or whatnot) to these amorphous shapes. In any one shape all of Euclid's axioms for space hold except the parallels postulate. For within a shape consider the plane fixed by a line and a point not on the line, and drop a perpendicular from the point to the original line. Lines in the plane through the point whose angles with the perpendicular differ only infinitesimally from a right angle will not intersect the original line in the shape, but there are many of them. So the parallels postulate is independent of the rest of Euclid.

One of these shapes off to our left could be completely full of gold. One would expect this nugget to collapse under its own self-gravitation, and after collapsing enough it would no longer be gold, but its mass would still be infinite. The shapes between us and the nugget lie in a dense linear order without endpoints, but suppose the nugget is in

---

[33] For a taste of how this goes, see my "Long Decimals" in *Future Pasts: The Analytic Tradition in Twentieth-Century Philosophy*, ed. Juliet Floyd and Sanford Shieh (Oxford: Oxford University Press, 2001), 359–67. It was Abraham Robinson who first discovered how to vindicate infinitesimals. See his "Non-Standard Analysis," *Koninklijke Nederlandse Akademie van Wetenschappen* (Amsterdam), *Proceedings*, ser. A, vol. 64 (or *Indigationes mathematicae*, vol. 23) (1961): 432–40. My approach through compactness is like Robinson's. But mainstream mathematicians prefer to avoid languages and logic like compactness; they like a direct approach that never leaves the subject matter. There is a taste of that approach in my "Long Decimals" and for a feast, see Robert Goldblatt, *Lectures on the Hyperreals: An Introduction to Nonstandard Analysis* (New York: Springer, 1998).

the clump centered at α units to our left. Suppose the nugget filled not just one clump but an array of them α by α by β, β also infinite. Then if Newton were right and gravitational attraction occurred instantaneously between distant bodies, we would feel an infinite pull of order β to our left. The fact that we feel no such pull might then be evidence that there is no such nugget. On the other hand, if there were a similar nugget off to our right, they would balance each other out. But our best judgment is that Newton was wrong and that gravitational attraction propagates at a finite velocity, the speed of light c. In that case, the fact that we feel no such pull might be evidence that the nugget has been there no more than αc units of time. Infinitesimals can open new avenues in physics as well as mathematics and geometry.

SIX

✦

Accommodating Cantor

Cantor's key to paradise was his proof that every set is strictly smaller than its power set, the set of all its subsets. In von Neumann's theory of ordinals and cardinals, which is now the industry standard, the smallest infinite ordinal, ω, is the set of all finite ordinals, or natural numbers, and the smallest infinite cardinal, Cantor's $\aleph_0$. By Cantor's proof, the power set of ω, $P(\omega)$, has a cardinal number bigger than ω, and iterating opens the door to a paradise of different infinite numbers, as many as there are ordinals. In von Neumann's theory, the less-than relation between ordinals is just membership, a cardinal is an ordinal in one–one correspondence with none of its predecessors (or members), and by Cantor's proof for every cardinal there is a bigger one. So if we let $\omega(0)$ be ω, $\omega(\alpha + 1)$ be the least cardinal bigger than $\omega(\alpha)$, and, when λ is a limit, $\omega(\lambda)$ be the union of all the $\omega(\alpha)$ for α less than λ, we get as many infinite cardinals as there are ordinals. Our $\omega(\alpha)$ is our version of Cantor's $\aleph_\alpha$; both notations are still common.

$P(\omega)$ has exactly as many members as the set of real numbers. We have seen a natural one–one correspondence between $P(\omega)$ and the reals from zero up to, but not including, one.[1] Cartesian coordinates assume a one–one correspondence between the real numbers and the points on a line. Since lines are the basic example of continua, the cardinal of $P(\omega)$ is called the cardinal of the continuum. By our construction, $\omega(1)$ is the least cardinal bigger than $\omega(0) = \omega$, and by Cantor's theorem, the cardinal of $P(\omega)$ is bigger than ω, so the cardinal of the continuum is bigger than or equal to $\omega(1)$. But which, bigger or equal? Cantor conjectured that the cardinal of $P(\omega)$ is $\omega(1)$, and this is known as the continuum hypothesis. The generalized continuum hypothesis says that for all α,

---

[1] See Chapter 1, pp. 17–18.

the cardinal of $P(\omega(\alpha))$ is $\omega(\alpha + 1)$, which would make the power set function like the successor function on natural numbers.

David Hilbert's peers recognized him as one of the great mathematicians of their era. In 1900 he was invited to address the Second International Congress of Mathematicians. After some consultation, he decided to lay out an agenda for mathematicians in the twentieth century. In his talk, he had time only for the top ten problems, but there are twenty-three in the published version. Number one was the continuum hypothesis, which is evidence that it is a big mathematical deal.[2]

In 1940 Kurt Gödel published a monograph in which he proved that both the generalized continuum hypothesis and the axiom of choice are consistent with set theory.[3] The set theory with which Gödel proved the hypothesis and the axiom consistent is NBG, the theory named for John von Neumann, Paul Bernays, and Gödel himself. As we have seen, NBG proves just the same theorems about sets as ZF.[4] Since ZF is now the fashionable set theory, we will present Gödel's result for ZF. Note that since the axiom of choice is at issue, ZF does not include choice and is not ZFC. Remember too that because of Gödel's second incompleteness theorem, the consistency of a powerful theory like ZF is a delicate matter.[5] For that reason, Gödel's argument is a relative consistency proof: he shows that if ZF is consistent, then so is ZF plus the axiom of choice and the generalized continuum hypothesis.

To begin, we should review what ZF is and what its world is supposed to be. To do the second, recall the ranks. $R(0)$ is $\varnothing$, $R(\alpha + 1)$ is $P(R(\alpha))$, and when λ is a limit, $R(\lambda)$ is the union of the $R(\alpha)$ for $\alpha < \lambda$. We then define a predicate V of sets so $V(x)$ if and only if $x \in R(\alpha)$ for some ordinal α. The view of ZF is that the (pure) sets are all and only the sets satisfying the predicate V. (Pure sets are those in a world of nothing but sets, so there are no non-sets, or urelements, like shoes and ships and cabbages and kings.) In the view of ZF, there is no set

[2] For more on Hilbert's address and what became of his problems, see Benjamin H. Yandell, *The Honors Class: Hilbert's Problems and Their Solvers* (Natick, Mass.: A. K. Peters, 2002).

[3] Kurt Gödel, *The Consistency of the Axiom of Choice and of the Generalized Continuum Hypothesis with the Axioms of Set Theory* (Princeton: Princeton University Press, 1940). Reprinted in his *Collected Works*, vol. 2, *Publications 1938–1974*, ed. Solomon Feferman et al. (Oxford: Oxford University Press, 1990), 33–101.

[4] See Chapter 3, p. 82.

[5] See Chapter 5, pp. 138–39.

of all sets, so the predicate V has no extension. But informally we will sometimes pretend that this predicate does have an extension, and we will call it V too.

The axioms of ZF in decreasing order of strength and importance are:

I.   a. Power set: Every set has a power set.

     b. Replacement: Any collection the same size as a set is a set.

II. Closure axioms:

     a. Union, intersection, and difference: For any sets x and y, $x \cup y$, $x \cap y$, and x – y exist.

     b. Singletons: For any x there is a set whose only member is x.

     c. Big union: For any set A of sets, the union of all members of A exists.

III. Foundation: Membership is well-founded; there are no infinitely descending $\in$-chains.

IV. Infinity: There is an infinite set. (More explicitly, there is a set of which $\varnothing$ is a member and of which $x \cup \{x\}$ is a member when x is.)

V. Null set: There is a set with no members; $\varnothing$ exists.

VI. Extensionality: Sets with the same members are identical.

If α is a limit ordinal, it is pretty clear that all these assumptions except replacement hold in rank $R(\alpha)$. But there are huge sets in $R(\omega + n)$ for small n > 1, and a collection of ordinals as big as one of these sets will be a set by replacement. The union of that huge set of ordinals is a huge ordinal. It would take an ordinal bigger than any ZF proves to exist (if it is consistent) to get an α such that $R(\alpha)$ is a model for ZF.

To get used to the ranks and V, here are some propositions that can be proved using transfinite induction on ordinals. First, we have three equivalent versions of transfinite induction: any predicate true of α when it is true of all predecessors of α is true of all ordinals; any predicate true of 0, true of $\alpha + 1$ if true of α, and true of a limit λ when true of all predecessors of λ, is true of all ordinals; a predicate true of some ordinal is true of a least ordinal. Next, using transfinite induction, show that $R(\alpha) \subseteq R(\alpha + 1)$; and thus that $R(\beta) \subseteq R(\alpha)$ when $\beta < \alpha$; that $R(\alpha)$ is transitive, meaning that $y \in R(\alpha)$ when $x \in R(\alpha)$ and $y \in x$; that $x \in R(\alpha)$ when $y \in R(\alpha)$ and $x \subseteq y$; and that when $\{x\} \in R(\alpha)$, then $x \in R(\beta)$ for some $\beta < \alpha$. For any set x, let $\rho(x)$, the rank of x, be the least α such that $x \in R(\alpha + 1)$.[6] Finally, show that when $x \in y$, then $\rho(x) < \rho(y)$.

---

[6] A set is $\in$-connected if and only if for any y and z in x, $y \in z$ or $z \in y$ or y = z. An ordinal is a transitive set that is $\in$-connected. The smallest ordinal is $\varnothing$, and the first

Using these results one can formalize ZF first-order and prove that its axioms (except replacement) hold in V. (The serious reader does the homework.)

Gödel's result is a syntactical one about provability, but for quite a while our argument will be a semantical one about truth and satisfaction. Later we will see how this semantical argument yields a syntactical result. In the last chapter we used the notation $\vdash_T$ to mean that a formula A is a theorem of a theory T. The sign $\vdash$ is called the syntactical turnstile. There is also a semantical turnstile $\vDash$ with two sidebars. If M is an interpretation of a language and A is a sentence of that language, then M $\vDash$ A means that A is true in M. Next we introduce a slightly abusive notation that eliminates clutter and so improves readability. Our variables are the letter x with positive integer subscripts. Suppose that $A(x_{i_1},..., x_{i_n})$ is a formula of a language, that $x_{i_1},..., x_{i_n}$ are exactly the variables that occur free in this formula, that M is an interpretation, that $a_1,..., a_n$ are members of the domain of this interpretation, and that s is any sequence of members of the domain. Then we will write M $\vDash$ $A(a_1,..., a_n)$ to mean that $s^{a_1...a_1}_{i_1...i_n}$ satisfies A in M. We have cut out the variable middlemen. For the most part we will be looking at the language of ZF. We take identity to be part of the underlying logic; all our models will be normal in the sense that the extension of the double-bar predicate (for identity) will be the genuine identity relation on the domain of the model, and we will usually suppress mention of identity in specifying a model. The distinctive extralogical sign of the language of ZF is the $\in$ predicate for membership. So for the most part our models will be ordered pairs consisting of a domain and membership restricted on both sides to that domain. When we know thus what the relation is, it is the domain that distinguishes the model, so we will sometimes say that a sentence is true in a domain when we mean that the sentence is true in the model with that domain.

We now introduce first-order definability. A set x is first-order definable over (fodo) a set y if and only if there is a formula $A(x_1,..., x_n, x_{n+1})$ of the language of ZF with exactly the free variables exhibited and there are members $a_1,..., a_n$ of y such that

$$x = \{x_{n+1} \in y \mid y \vDash A(a_1,..., a_n, x_{n+1})\}.$$

rank it is in is R(1). The successor of α is $\alpha \cup \{\alpha\}$. The smallest limit is ω, and the first rank it is in is $R(\omega + 1)$. This is where the plus-one in the definition of ρ comes from.

For example, y fodo y since

$$y = \{z \in y \mid y \vDash z = z\},$$

and for a $\in$ y, {a} fodo y since

$$\{a\} = \{z \in y \mid y \vDash z = a\}.$$

If y is transitive and a $\in$ y, then a fodo y since

$$a = \{z \in y \mid y \vDash z \in a\}$$

because any member of a is in y since y is transitive.

Next we have the constructible sets.[7] First we let M(0) be $\varnothing$, M(α + 1) be {x | x fodo M(α)}, and M(λ) be the union of the M(α) for $\alpha < \lambda$. These are the orders. It is important to distinguish between the orders and the ranks. Suppose y is a countably infinite set. Then because there are countably many formulae in the language of ZF, {x | x fodo y} will be countable, but the power set P(y) of y is uncountable. Hence, while R(n) = M(n) for all finite n, and while R(ω) = M(ω), R(ω + 1) $\neq$ M(ω + 1) since the first is uncountable but the second is countable. A set x is constructible, L(x) for short, if and only if for some α, x $\in$ M(α). It will turn out that all ordinals are constructible, so the predicate L is true of too many things to have an extension by the lights of ZF. But as we did with V, we will sometimes pretend that the predicate L has an extension, and we will call it L too.

We will show that L is a part of V that is also a model for ZF; what exactly this means will call for some thought, since L is not a set. L is called an inner model. Next we sketch a proof that the axiom of choice holds in L because we can well-order L (and not just members of it). To do this, we want a function δ that is to L as ρ is to V, so we set δ(x) equal to the least α such that x $\in$ M(α + 1). Then we show that M(α) is always transitive, that $M_\alpha \subseteq M_\beta$ when $\alpha \leq \beta$, that $M_\alpha \in M_\beta$ when $\alpha < \beta$, that δ(x) < δ(y) when x $\in$ y, and that δ(α) = α for all ordinals α. For the last, note that α = {x $\in$ M(α) | M(α) $\vdash$ Ord(x)}. Next we take a well-ordering of the formulae of the language of ZF. For example, gödelize the language of ZF and order its formulae by the size of their gödel numbers. Now we well-order L. The basic idea is that a precedes b if and

<hr />

[7] Our definition comes from Gödel's "The Consistency of the Generalized Continuum Hypothesis" and "Consistency Proof for the Generalized Continuum Hypothesis," both in *Collected Works*, 2: 27; 2: 28–32, not from Gödel's 1940 monograph cited in note 3.

only if a is of a lower order than b, or they are of the same order but a is defined by an earlier formula than b, or they are of the same order and defined by the same formula but the parameters used to define a precede those used to define b, where the parameters are members of b, thus of lower order than a and b, and thus by induction already ordered by precedence. Suppose a and b are constructible. Then a precedes b if and only if $\delta(\alpha) < \delta(b)$, or $\delta(a) = \delta(b)$ and the alphabetically earliest formula defining a over $M(\delta(a))$ is alphabetically earlier than the alphabetically earliest formula defining b over $M(\delta(b)) = M(\delta(a))$, or $\delta(a) = \delta(b)$ and the same alphabetically earliest formula is used to define both over $M(\delta(a))$; in this third case, let n be the number of free variables in that formula, let $c(a, 1)$ be the precedence-least member of $M(\delta(a))$ used to define a with this formula and some $n-1$ other members of $M(\delta(a))$, let $c(a, 2)$ be the precedence-least member of $M(\delta(a))$ used to define a with $c(a, 1)$ and some $n-2$ other members of $M(\delta(a))$, and so on out to $c(a, n)$, let $c(b, 1), \ldots, c(b, n)$ be specified similarly, and for the least m such that $c(a, m) \neq c(b, m)$, $c(a, m)$ precedes $c(b, m)$. Later we will show how to formalize "fodo" in the language of ZF, so "preceded" would be definable in that language too, and we could prove in ZF that any set is well-ordered by precedence.

We will use several pieces to show in ZF that the generalized continuum hypothesis holds in the constructible sets, but pride of place goes to the Löwenheim–Skolem theorem. The version we will use is not the one that goes through the completeness of quantification theory and loses track of the original structure, but one that preserves much of the original structure. Let M be a structure with nonempty domain D. This means that in addition to D, M includes countably many relations on D, countably many functions from D to D, and countably many members of D; these relations, functions, and members are called the distinguished relations, functions, and members. As earlier, we assume that M is normal and that identity on D is distinguished. It will not hurt to picture M as having just a distinguished binary relation (for membership) on D. Let L be a first-order language with a predicate (of suitable polyadicity) for each distinguished relation, a function sign (of suitable polyadicity) for each distinguished function, and an individual constant for each distinguished member. A structure N is a substructure of M if and only if its domain E is a (nonempty) subset of D, its distinguished relations are those of M restricted (in all places) to E, the distinguished functions of M are closed on E and the distinguished functions of N are those of M restricted to E, and the distinguished members of M are in E and are the distinguished members of N. So if <S, R> is a structure with R a binary relation on S, a substructure is given by a subset T of S and a relation $Q = R \upharpoonright T$. N is an elementary substructure of M if and only if it is a substructure of M and for all formulae $A(x_1,..., x_n)$ with exactly the variables shown free and all members $a_1,..., a_n$ of the domain E of N, M $\vDash A(a_1,..., a_n)$ if and only if N $\vDash A(a_1,..., a_n)$. Our Löwenheim–Skolem theorem says that for any structure M and any nonempty subset A of its domain, there is an elementary substructure N of M such that A is a subset of the domain E of N and the cardinal of E is at most that of A plus ω. (As we shall soon see, the term ω is contributed by the size of the first-order language L.)

Our proof requires a well-ordering of the domain of M, so if we do not otherwise have one, we use the axiom of choice to ensure one. Pick any a in A. Skolem functions are what make our proof work. To see what these are, let

$$(\forall x)(\exists y)(\forall z)(\exists w)B(x, y, z, w, u)$$

go proxy for (a prenex equivalent of) any formula of L. Skolem functions evaluate existential quantifiers, and we specify them from the outside in. So for any x and u in D, the domain of M, let f(x, u) be the first (in terms of the well-order of D) member v of D such that

$$M \vDash (\forall x)(\exists w)B(x, v, z, w, u)$$

if there is one, but a otherwise. Then for any x, u, and z in D, let g(x, u, z) be the first member v of D such that

$$M \vDash B(x, f(x, u), z, v, u)$$

if there is one, but a otherwise. Then f and g are Skolem functions for our formula. Go through L to get Skolem functions for all the formulae of L. Each formula is of finite length, and so contributes only finitely many Skolem functions, so since there are only countably many formulae in L, there are only countably many Skolem functions in all.

Let C be the union of A with the set of all distinguished members of M and a. Let C_0 be C and for all n, let C_{n+1} be the union of C_n with the set of all values of Skolem functions and distinguished functions of M on members of C_n. Let E be the union of all the C_n. The distinguished members of M are in E, and E is closed under the distinguished functions of M and the Skolem functions. For each n, the cardinal of C_n is at most that of A plus ω, so the cardinal of E is no more than that of A plus ω. Form the structure of M by restricting the relations and functions of M to E, so that N is a substructure of M. Moreover, N is an elementary substructure of M. Consider a formula of L, say

$$(\forall x)(\exists y)(\forall z)(\exists w)B(x, y, z, w, u),$$

and let b be a member of E. If

$$M \vDash (\forall x)(\exists y)(\forall z)(\exists w)B(x, y, z, w, b),$$

then

$$M \vDash (\forall x)(\forall z)\ B(x, f(x, b), z, g(x, z, b), b).$$

Hence, since N is a substructure of M,

$$N \vDash (\forall x)(\forall z)B(x, f(x, b), z, g(x, z, b), b),$$

so

$$N \vDash (\forall x)(\exists y)(\forall z)(\exists w)B(x, y, z, w, b).$$

If, conversely,

$$M \nvDash (\forall x)(\exists y)(\forall z)(\exists w)B(x, y, z, w, b),$$

then

$$M \vDash (\exists x)(\forall y)(\exists z)(\forall w)\neg B(x, y, z, w, b).$$

Let h and j be the Skolem functions for the existential quantifiers on x and z. Then

$$M \vDash (\forall y)(\forall w)\neg B(h(b), y, j(y, b), w, b),$$

so as before

$$N \vDash (\forall y)(\forall w)\neg B(h(b), y, j(y, b), w, b),$$

and thus

$$N \vDash (\exists x)(\forall y)(\exists z)(\forall w)\neg B(x, y, z, w, b),$$

so

$$N \nvDash (\forall x)(\exists y)(\forall z)(\exists w)B(x, y, z, w, b).$$

This completes the proof of our Löwenheim–Skolem theorem. N preserves much of the structure of M because it is an elementary substructure of M. The domain E of N includes only as much of D as A and the countable language L forces into E (given a well-order of D). E, or sometimes N, is called the Skolem hull of M for L and A. The set theory of satisfaction is pretty basic, so replacing formulae with their gödel numbers, we can formalize the proof of our Löwenheim–Skolem theorem in ZF.

Our second piece comes from Shepherdson.[8] Let S be a set and let R be a binary relation on S. R is well-founded if and only if there is no function f mapping ω one–one into S so that for all n, $f(n + 1)Rf(n)$. S is extensional, or satisfies extensionality, if and only if for all x and y in S, $x = y$ if and only if for all z in S, zRx if and only if zRy. Shepherdson's result is that if S is extensional and R is well-founded, then there is a transitive set T and a function f mapping S one–one onto T so that for all x and y in S, xRy if and only if $f(x) \in f(y)$. To begin, if S is empty, it is transitive and we are done. So suppose S is not empty. Then there are R-least members of S, and since S is extensional, any two of them are identical. Hence S has a unique R-least member we might call $\varnothing_S$. Call a function f good if and only if $f(\varnothing) = \varnothing$, $Dom(f) \subseteq S$, $f(x) = \{f(y) \mid yRx\}$ for all $x \in Dom(f)$, and $y \in Dom(f)$ whenever $x \in Dom(f)$ and yRx. Then $\{< \varnothing_S, \varnothing >\}$ is good, so there are good functions. There is at most one good function whose domain is S, for if there were two, they would agree R-below the R-least member a of S on which they differ, and thus they would agree at a too. Similarly, any two good functions agree where both are defined.

Next we show that there is a good function whose domain is S. Let

$$F(x, y) \leftrightarrow (\exists f)(f \text{ is good} \wedge y = f(x)).$$

F is a formula of the language of ZF. Then

$$\vdash_{ZF} (\forall x \in S)(\exists! y)F(x, y).$$

Pick x in S. There is at most one y such that $F(x, y)$, for if there were two, there would be two good functions disagreeing on x, which we ruled out in the last paragraph. If there is no such y, let x' be the R-least member of S for which there is no such y. Then $x' \neq \varnothing_S$, so there are members z of such that zRx', and there is a unique good f such that these z are members of $Dom(f)$. Then $f' = f \cup \{<x', \{f(z) \mid zRx'\}>\}$ is good, $x' \in Dom(f')$ and $f'(x') = \{f(z) \mid zRx'\}$, so $F(x', \{f'(z) \mid zRx'\})$.

---

[8] J. C. Shepherdson, "Inner Models for Set Theory," *Journal of Symbolic Logic* 16 (1951): 161–90. There are sequels in 17 (1952): 225–37 and 18 (1953): 145–67. ZF has no comprehension axiom to provide for the existence of sets, and the proof of Shepherdson's result illustrates one way in which ZF uses replacement to prove existence.

By hypothesis, S is a set, so by replacement, there is a set T = {y | (∃x) (x ∈ S ∧ F(x, y)}. Then, by separation, f = {<x, y> | x ∈ S ∧ y ∈ T ∧ F(x, y)} is also a set. Clearly f is a good function and S is its domain. Then f is one–one, for if not, there are x and y in S such that f(x) = f(y), but x ≠ y, so since S is extensional, there is a z in S such that zRx but not (zRy), or not (zRx) but zRy. In the first case, since zRx, f(z) ∈ f(x) = f(y), so zRy after all, and similarly in the second case. T is transitive. For suppose x ∈ y and y ∈ T. Then y = f(v) for some v ∈ S. But f(v) ≠ ∅ since x ∈ y = f(v), so f(v) = {f(u) | uRv}. So since x ∈ y, x = f(u) for some uRv, and thus x ∈ T. For all x and y in S, xRy if and only if f(x) ∈ f(y). If xRy, y ≠ ∅$_s$, so f(y) is {f(u) | uRy}, and thus f(x) ∈ f(y). If f(x) ∈ f(y), then f(x) = f(u) for some uRy, so since f is one–one, x = uRy. This completes the proof of Shepherdson's result.

There are some related results we should mention here. First, it is clear that T and f are unique. Second, if T is transitive, R is a binary relation with field S, and f maps A one–one onto A so that for all x,y in A, xRy if and only if f(x) ∈ f(y), then f(x) = {f(y) | yRx} for all x in A. For if u ∈ f(x), then u = f(y) for some y ∈ A such that yRx, so f(x) ⊆ {f(y) | yRx}; and if yRx, then f(y) ∈ f(x), so {f(y) | yRx} ⊆ f(x). Call this T₁. Third, if A and B are both transitive and f maps A one–one onto B so that for all x,y in A, x ∈ y if and only if f(x) ∈ f(y), then f is the identity map restricted to A and A = B. By T₁, f(x) is {f(y) | y ∈ x}. If A or B is empty, both are, and we are done. When one is nonempty, both are, and ∅ is a member of both. Then f(∅) = ∅. If the claim fails, let x be the ∈-least member of A where it fails. Then for y ∈ x, f(y) = y, so f(x) = {f(y) | y ∈ x} = { y | y ∈ x} = x after all. Call this T₂. Fourth, if B and C are extensional, A is a transitive subset of B and f maps B one–one onto C so that for all x,y in B, x ∈ y if and only if f(x) ∈ f(y), then f is the identity on A and A ⊆ C. If A is empty, we are done. If A is not empty, then ∅ is the ∈-least member of A. If f(∅) = y and z ∈ y, then since z = f(u) for some u ∈ B, u ∈∅, which is impossible. So f(∅) = ∅. If f(a) ≠ a for some a ∈ A, let z be the ∈-least such member of a. If y ∈ z, then y ∈ A by transitivity, so f(y) = y. For y ∈ z, f(y) ∈ f(z), so y ∈ f(z), so z ⊆ f(z); and if y ∈ f(z), f(y) ∈ f(z), so y ∈ z, so f(z) ⊆ z. Hence f(z) = z, contradicting the choice of z. Call this P.[9]

[9] Our exposition of Gödel's argument follows Hilary Putnam's exposition of it in 1968, and notes by Putnam's student Leslie Tharp on an earlier exposition of the argument. T₁ and T₂ come from Tharp's notes, and P comes from Putnam.

Our third piece comes from Jech.[10] The product of cardinal numbers a and b is the cardinal a × b, the set of ordered pairs of members of a and b. We are going to show that for all α, $\omega(\alpha) \times \omega(\alpha)$ is $\omega(\alpha)$. We begin with a well-ordering of the ordered pairs of ordinals. Say that $<\alpha, \beta>$ precedes $<\gamma, \delta>$ if and only if the maximum of α and β is less than that of γ and δ, or these maxima are equal and $\alpha < \gamma$, or the maxima are equal and $\alpha = \gamma$ but $\beta < \delta$. The relationship of precedence is too big to be a set, but for all α and β, the collection of pairs $<\gamma, \delta>$ preceding $<\alpha, \beta>$ is a set well-ordered by precedence. For any α, $\alpha \times \alpha$ is the set of ordinals preceding $<0, \alpha>$. For any α and β, let $F(\alpha, \beta)$ be the ordinal of the set of pairs $<\gamma, \delta>$ preceding $<\alpha, \beta>$, and let $f(\alpha) = F(0, \alpha)$. For any α and β, if $\alpha > \beta$, then $f(\alpha) > f(\beta)$, since the predecessors of $<0, \beta>$ are a proper initial segment of the predecessors of $<0, \alpha>$. It follows that $f(\alpha) \geq \alpha$. (We deduce it by induction on α. It is clear for $\alpha = 0$. If $f(\alpha) \geq \alpha$, then $f(\alpha + 1) > f(\alpha) \geq \alpha$, so $f(\alpha + 1) \geq \alpha + 1$. Suppose $f(\alpha) \geq \alpha$ for all α less than a limit λ. Then $f(\lambda) > f(\alpha) \geq \alpha$ for all $\alpha < \lambda$, so since λ is the least ordinal greater than all $\alpha < \lambda$, $f(\lambda) \geq \lambda$.) Next we show that $f(\omega(\alpha)) = \omega(\alpha)$. This holds for $\alpha = 0$.[11] If the claim fails, let α be the least ordinal such that $f(\omega(\alpha)) \neq \omega(\alpha)$. Since $f(\omega(\alpha)) \geq \omega(\alpha)$, $f(\omega(\alpha)) > \omega(\alpha)$. So there are $\beta, \gamma < \omega(\alpha)$ such that $F(\beta, \gamma) = \omega(\alpha)$. Since $\omega(\alpha)$ is a limit, there is an ordinal δ such that $\beta, \gamma < \delta < \omega(\alpha)$. The set of pairs preceding $<0, \delta>$ is $\delta \times \delta$, and $<\beta, \gamma>$ is a member of this set, so $\omega(\alpha) = F(\beta, \gamma) < F(0, \gamma)$. Hence $\omega(\alpha) \subseteq F(0, \delta)$. The cardinal of $\delta \times \delta$ is that of $F(0, \delta)$, so the cardinal of $\delta \times \delta$ is greater than or equal to $\omega(\alpha)$. But the cardinal of $\delta \times \delta$ is the cardinal of δ times itself, and since the cardinal of δ is less than $\omega(\alpha)$, the cardinal of δ times itself is the cardinal of δ (by the leastness of α), which is less than $\omega(\alpha)$. This contradiction completes the proof.

We have just shown that for any infinite cardinal c, $c^2 = c$. It follows that if b is infinite and c is its cardinal, then the number of sets a such that a fodo b is at most c. There are no more a fodo b than there are formulae with n free variables and n-tuples of members of b to define such a. But the number of formulae is ω. So the number of formulae with n free variables evaluated by an n-tuple of members of b is $\omega \times c^n$. Since $c^2 = c$, $c^n = c$ for all n, so each of the terms $\omega \times c^n$ is c since $\omega \leq c$. The sum of c with itself ω times is $\omega \times c = c$, and we are done. For any ordinal α, let $c(\alpha)$ be the cardinal of α. We next show that for infinite α,

---

[10] Thomas Jech, *Set Theory*, 3rd ed., rev. and exp. (Berlin: Springer, 2003), 30–31. On p. 35, Jech says the result was first proved by Gerhard Hessenberg in 1906.

[11] See Chapter 1, pp. 13–14.

the cardinal of $M(\alpha)$ is $c(\alpha)$. We saw earlier that $\alpha \subseteq M(\alpha)$, so $c(\alpha) \leq$ the cardinal of $M(\alpha)$. Since $M(\alpha + 1)$ is the set of all a fodo $M(\alpha)$, the cardinal of $M(\alpha + 1)$ is less than or equal to that of $M(\alpha)$ by what we just proved. First, then, the cardinal of $M(\omega)$ is ω, since $M(\omega)$ is the union of ω finite sets. Second, $\alpha + 1 \subseteq M(\alpha + 1)$ so the cardinal of $M(\alpha + 1)$, is at most $c(\alpha + 1) = c(\alpha)$, since infinite cardinals are limits; and the cardinal of $M(\alpha + 1)$ is at most that of $M(\alpha) = c(\alpha) = c(\alpha + 1)$. Third, $M(\lambda)$ is the union of $c(\lambda)$ nested sets each with cardinality less than or equal to $c(\lambda)$, so the cardinal of $M(\lambda)$ is at most $c(\lambda)$, and since $\lambda \subseteq M(\lambda)$, the cardinal of $M(\lambda)$ is $c(\lambda)$. The cardinal of $R(\omega + 1)$ is 2^ω, but that of $M(\omega + 1)$ is ω. The first order with 2^ω members is $M(2^\omega)$. So V is fatter than L and spreads faster than L. We will see that it is consistent with ZF (if ZF is consistent) that all sets be constructible, but for the most part their orders would be much bigger than their ranks.

Our exposition of Gödel's argument follows lectures by Hilary Putnam. The heart of Putnam's presentation is a sentence σ in the language of ZF such that for any set S and any well-founded relation R on S, $<S, R> \vDash \sigma$ if and only if there is a limit ordinal λ and a function f mapping S one–one onto $M(\lambda)$ so that for all x and y in S, $x \in y$ if and only if $f(x) \in f(y)$. We could say that S is $\in$-isomorphic to some $M(\lambda)$, and we can almost say in the language of ZF that S is some $M(\lambda)$. Before we write σ down, let us see what it will do for us. Gödel's main technical lemma says that any constructible subset of $M(\omega(\alpha))$ is a member of $M(\omega(\alpha + 1))$. The sentence σ will enable us to prove this lemma. Suppose that S is a constructible subset of $M(\omega(\alpha))$. Then $S \in M(\lambda)$ for some limit λ, and since the orders are cumulative, we may take $\lambda > \omega(\alpha)$. Then $M(\omega(\alpha)) \cup \{S\} \subseteq M(\lambda)$. As we have seen, we may well-order $M(\lambda)$ without the axiom of choice. Let H be the Skolem hull of $< M(\lambda), \in \uparrow M(\lambda)>$ for σ and $M(\omega(\alpha)) \cup \{S\}$. Since $(\in \uparrow M(\lambda)) \uparrow H$ is $\in \uparrow H$, $<H, \in \uparrow H>$ is an elementary substructure of $<M(\lambda), \in \uparrow M(\lambda)>$. So since $M(\lambda) \vDash \sigma$, $H \vDash \sigma$. By the axiom of foundation, $\in$ is well-founded, and since $M(\lambda)$ satisfies extensionality, so does H. So by Shepherdson's result, H is $\in$-isomorphic to a transitive set H^*. Hence $H^* \vDash \sigma$ too. Then by T_2 and the character of σ, H^* is $M(\gamma)$ for some limit γ. $M(\omega(\alpha)) \cup \{S\} \subseteq H$, $M(\omega(\alpha)) \cup \{S\}$ is transitive, and both H and H^* are extensional, so by P, $M(\omega(\alpha)) \cup \{S\} \subseteq H^* = M(\gamma)$. Earlier we wrote $c(\alpha)$ for the cardinal of an ordinal α; from now on let us write $c(x)$ for the cardinal of any set x. Then

$$c(\gamma) = c(M(\gamma)) = c(H^*) = c(H) = \omega(\alpha),$$

so $\gamma < \omega(\alpha + 1)$. Hence $S \in M(\omega(\alpha + 1))$. This completes the proof of the lemma. The lemma shows that even if it looks as though one needs to go up to $M(\lambda)$ to first-order define a constructible subset S of $M(\omega(\alpha))$, one gets all one really needs for the definition of S in the Skolem hull H of $M(\lambda)$ for the language ZF and $M(\omega(\alpha)) \cup \{S\}$, where c(H) is $\omega(\alpha)$.

It follows from the lemma that the generalized continuum hypothesis is true of the constructible sets. We already know that $\omega(\alpha + 1) \le c(P(\omega(\alpha)))$. The constructible power set of $\omega(\alpha)$ is the set of all constructible subsets of $\omega(\alpha)$, and the lemma says these are all members of $M(\omega(\alpha + 1))$. So the constructible power set of $\omega(\alpha)$ is a subset of $M(\omega(\alpha + 1))$, and the cardinal of the constructible power set of $\omega(\alpha)$ is $\omega(\alpha + 1)$. So the generalized continuum hypothesis holds in the constructible sets.

It also follows from the lemma that the power set axiom holds in the constructible sets. If x is constructible, then $x \in M(\alpha)$ for some α, and then $x \in M(\omega(\alpha))$, since $\omega(\alpha) \ge \alpha$. So since $M(\omega(\alpha))$ is transitive, $x \subseteq M(\omega(\alpha))$. So if y is a constructible subset of x, $y \subseteq M(\omega(\alpha))$. By the lemma, $y \in M(\omega(\alpha + 1))$. But then the constructible power set of x is $\{y \in M(\omega(\alpha + 1)) \mid M(\omega(\alpha + 1)) \vDash y \subseteq x\}$, and thus is a member of $M(\omega(\alpha + 1) + 1)$. But we can also show without the lemma that the power set axiom is true of the constructible sets. Every set has a power set, so its constructible power set exists by separation; we have to show it constructible. But $\delta(x) = y$ is a functional relation in the sense that $\vdash_{ZF} (\forall x)(\exists ! y)(\delta(x) = y)$, so its range on the constructible power set of x is a set, and indeed a set of ordinals. Hence there is an ordinal $\beta > \delta(y)$ for all constructible subsets of x, so all constructible subsets of x are members of $M(\beta)$. Thus the constructible power set of x is $\{y \in M(\beta) \mid M(\beta) \vdash y \subseteq x\}$ and so a member of $M(\beta + 1)$.

Next we should write out σ. The first step is to formalize first-order definability in ZF. A set a is first-order definable over a set b if there is a formula $A(x_1, ..., x_n, v)$ of the language of ZF and members $a_1, ..., a_n$ of b such that a is the set of all v in b such that $A(a_1, ..., a_n, v)$ is true in b. The language of ZF makes no obvious allowance for talk of formulae or truth. But A is built up from "$\in$" and "=" using truth functions, variables, and quantifiers in finitely many steps. Our problem is to use the resources of the language of ZF to pick out of b the extension of $A(a_1, ..., a_n, v)$ as a combination of the extensions of the parts of A.

We want the extension of a conjunction to be the intersection of the extensions of the conjuncts. If we took the extensions of "$x_1 \in x_2$" and "$x_2 \in x_3$" both to be $\in \upharpoonright b$, then the extension of "$x_1 \in x_2 \wedge x_2 \in$

x_3" would also be $\in \uparrow$ b rather than the three-place relation we want. Tarski's sequences are real-world respecters of different occurrences of the same variables, but we do not need the whole of an infinitely long sequence Tarski would use. Instead we will use arbitrarily long finite sequences of members of b. So let i, j, k, m, and n be natural numbers. Then b^j is the set of all functions from j into b, our version of the set of all sequences of length j of members of b. E(b, j) is the set of all f from j + 2 into b such that $f(0) \in f(1)$. This would be our version of the extension of "$x_0 \in x_1$" if we had such a variable as "x_0." I(b, j) is the set of all $f : j + 2 \to b$ such that $f(0) = f(1)$, our version of the extension of "$x_0 = x_1$." It is a virtue of quantificational notation that we may substitute a term for, or quantificationally bind, any old variable anywhere in a formula anytime we wish. But keeping track of a particular place in a relation out in the world calls for a bit of thought, which fortunately Paul Bernays did for us. We will always plug an object into only the last place in a relation, and we will always bind (existentially) only the last place in a relation, but to ensure the last place is the one we want to plug or bind, we will allow ourselves all permutations of relations so that we can use one to shift a position to the end to plug or bind it and another to put it back. A j-ary relation for us is a set of functions $f : j \to b$, so a permutation will be given by a function h mapping j one–one onto j. Then if f is a j-tuple in a relation, the g such that $g(i) = f(h(i))$ for $i < j$ will be a j-tuple in a permutation of the relation. In such a case g is the composition of f on h, and we write $g = f \cdot h$. Perm(r_1, h, r_2) holds if and only if for some b and j, $r_2 \subseteq b^j$ and h maps j one–one onto j and for all x, x is in r_1 if and only if for some y in r_2, $x = y \cdot h$. This means that relation r_1 comes from relation r_2 by a permutation. Exist(r_1, r_2) if and only if for some b and j, $r_2 \subseteq b^{j+1}$ and for all x, $x \in r_1$ if and only if $x : j \to b$ and for some u, $x \cup \{<j, u>\} \in r_2$. This means that r_1 is the j-ary relation got by existentially quantifying the last place in the (j+1)-ary relation r_2. Sub(r_1, u, r_2) if and only if for some b and j, $r_2 \subseteq b^{j+1}$ and for all x, $x \in r_1$ if and only if $x : j \to b$ and $x \cup \{<j, u>\} \in r_2$. This means that r_1 is the j-ary relation got by plugging u into the last place of the (j+1)-ary relation r_2.

Now we assemble these pieces into a definition in the language of ZF of first-order definability. We say that a fodo$_{ZF}$ b if and only if there is a function g and a natural number n such that the domain of g is n + 1, and for some j, $g(0) = E(b, j)$ and $g(1) = I(b, j)$, and for $i > 1$, either for some j, $k < i$ and some m, $g(j), g(k) \subseteq b^m$ and $g(i) = g(j) \cup g(k)$, or for some j, $k < i$ and some m, $g(j), g(k) \subseteq b^m$ and $g(i) = g(j) - g(k)$, or for some j, $g(i) = b^j$, or for some $k < i$ and some h, $Perm(g(i), h, g(k))$, or for some $k < i$, $Exist(g(i), g(k))$, or for some $k < i$ and some $u \in b$, $Sub(g(i), u, g(k))$, and $g(n) \subseteq b^1$ and $a = \{v \mid \{<o, v>\} \in g(n)\}$. The next-to-last clause requires that $g(n)$ be a set of unary functions whose only argument is thus 0, and the last clause, that a be the set of values of these functions on 0. It should be pretty clear that if "fodo" is our original predicate not in the language of ZF and "$fodo_{ZF}$" is the predicate in the language of ZF just defined, then for any sets a and b, a fodo b if and only if a $fodo_{ZF}$ b is true in V. One could prove this by induction on the length of the shortest formula A such that a is fodo b using A, since each step in how A is built up is mirrored by a clause in $fodo_{ZF}$. (In effect, the logical primitives have been taken as disjunction, negation, and existential quantification.)

We just said, slightly abusively, that a fodo b if and only if $V \vDash$ a $fodo_{ZF}$ b. The abuse is that V is too big to be a set, so no interpretations have V as their domains.[12] Now we want to figure out a condition on a *set* t such that a fodo b if and only if $t \vDash$ a $fodo_{ZF}$ b. This is an example of what is called invariance: a formula $A(x_1,..., x_n)$ of the language of ZF is invariant for sets meeting a condition C if and only if for all t meeting C and all $a_1,..., a_n$ in t, $A(a_1,..., a_n)$ if and only if $t \vDash A(a_1,..., a_n)$. Invariance is, on the face of it, semantic, but sometimes we can make syntax of it. Suppose condition C can be expressed by a formula F(x) in the language of ZF and $t \vDash A(a_1,..., a_n)$ is equivalent to $A(a_1,..., a_n)$ relativized to t. This means replacing the clauses $(\forall x)(B(x))$ and $(\exists x)(B(x))$ in $A(a_1,..., a_n)$ with $(\forall x)(x \in t \rightarrow B(x))$ and $(\exists x)(x \in t \land B(x))$. Call the result $(A(a_1,..., a_n))_t$. Then we can prove invariance in ZF by proving $F(t) \rightarrow (A(a_1,..., a_n) \leftrightarrow (A(a_1,..., a_n)_t))$. Let C be transitivity, which is expressed by $(\forall u)(u \in t \rightarrow (\forall v)(v \in u \rightarrow v \in t))$, and let A(x) be "x is transitive." Then we can show in ZF that A(x) is invariant for transitive sets. In this way we can also show that $\in$-connectedness is invariant for transitive sets. Equally, the formulae for being an ordinal, a successor, a limit, a finite ordinal, or a function are invariant for transitive sets. It is around cardinality that invariance gets dicey.

For $fodo_{ZF}$ to be invariant for a set, the set should include all the apparatus mentioned in $fodo_{ZF}$, and this in turn means that t should meet a number of closure conditions. We say that Closed(t) if and only if t is transitive, $t \neq \emptyset$, and for $x, y \in t$ and $j \in \omega$, (1) $\{x, y\} \in t$, (2) $x \cup y \in t$, (3) $x - y \in t$, (4) $\{v \mid (\exists u)(\exists z)(\{<u, v>\} \in z \land z \in x)\}$, (5) $x^j \in t$, (6)

12 This is Orayen's paradox in Chapter 4.

$E(x, j) \in t$, (7) $I(x, j) \in t$, (8) for any $y \subseteq x^{i+1}$, any permutation of y is in t, (9) for any $y \subseteq x^{i+1}$, any existential quantification of y is in t, and (10) for any $y \in x^{i+1}$ and $u \in x$, the substitution of u in y is in t. Note that if t is transitive and nonempty, $\emptyset \in t$, so by (1) and (2), $\omega \subseteq t$; and if $f : j \rightarrow b$ and $b \in t$, $f \in t$. Observe that when λ is a limit, Closed$(M(\lambda))$, since it suffices to go only a few orders above the maximum of those of x and y to define the sets clauses (1) to (10) required to be in $M(\lambda)$. Closed(L) too. Moreover, if Closed(t), then fodo$_{ZF}$ is invariant for t, since clauses (1) to (10) ensure that t has in it what fodo$_{ZF}$ calls for. If Closed(t), a fodo$_{ZF}$ b, and $b \in t$, then $a \in t$; for if g and n are as in the definition of fodo$_{ZF}$, then for $i = 0, 1, \ldots, n$, $g(i) \in t$, so $a = g(n) \in t$.

Let Close be the sentence of the language of ZF that is the conjunction of the ten clauses $C_1, \ldots, C_{10}$ stating that objects required by (1) to (10) exist. For example, C_1 is $(\forall x, y)(\exists z)(\forall u)(u \in z \leftrightarrow u = x \vee u = y)$, C_2 is $(\forall x, y)(\exists z)(\forall u)(u \in z \leftrightarrow u \in x \vee u \in y)$, and C_5 is $(\forall x, u)(u \in \omega \rightarrow (\exists y)(\forall z)(z \in y \leftrightarrow (z$ is a function $\wedge$ u is the domain of z $\wedge$ the range of z is a subset of x)))$, and similarly for the other seven clauses. Then if t is transitive and nonempty, Closed(t) $\leftrightarrow t \vDash$ Close. Going right to left, since $t \vDash$ Close, it is closed under unordered pairs and unions by C_1 and C_2, and thus meets (1) and (2). Thus, as noted, $\omega \subseteq t$ and if $x \in t$ and $f : j \rightarrow x$, then $f \in t$ for any $j \in \omega$. So if by C_5, $(\forall y)(y \in z \leftrightarrow y$ is a function $\wedge$ j is the domain of y $\wedge$ the range of y is a subset of x) is true in t, then since all such y are in t, $z = x^j$. The rest is similar.

Let M be the function whose value at any ordinal α is the order $M(\alpha)$. M is too big to be a set. But we can say in the language of ZF that a function is an initial segment of M. We say that Cond(f) if and only if f is a function and for some ordinal α, the domain of f is α, $f(0) = \emptyset$, for all β such that $\beta + 1 < \alpha$, $f(\beta + 1)$ is the set of all z such that a fodo$_{ZF}$ $f(v)$, and for all limits $\lambda < \alpha$, $f(\lambda)$ is the union of $f(\beta)$ for $\beta < \lambda$. Then we can show that if Closed(t) and $f \in t$, then $t \vDash$ Cond(f) if and only if f is $M \restriction \alpha$ for some ordinal α. Suppose, for example, that $t \vDash f(\beta + 1) = \{z \mid z$ fodo$_{ZF}$ $f(\beta)\}$. If $t \vDash$ a fodo$_{ZF}$ b for a, $b \in t$, then a fodo b, so $f(\beta + 1) \subseteq \{z \mid z$ fodo $f(\beta)\}$. If z fodo $f(\beta)$, then $z \in t$ and $t \vDash z$ fodo$_{ZF}$ $f(\beta)$, so $\{z \mid z$ fodo $f(\beta)\} \subseteq f(\beta + 1)$. Hence $f(\beta + 1) = \{z \mid z$ fodo $f(\beta)\}$.

$M \restriction \alpha$ is constructible and is a member of $M(\alpha + 3)$. At the basis, $M \restriction 0 = \emptyset \in M(0) \in M(3)$. For the induction step, suppose $M \restriction \beta \in M(\beta + 3)$. $M \restriction (\beta + 1) = M(\beta) \cup \{<\beta, M(\beta)>\}$. Orders are like ranks (or types) in that if the order of x is γ, then that of $\{x\}$ is $\gamma + 1$. So since $\beta \in M(\beta + 1)$ and $M(\beta) \in M(\beta + 1)$, $<\beta, M(\beta)> \in M(\beta + 3)$, so $\{<\beta, M(\beta)>\} \in M(\beta + 4)$. Hence $M \restriction (\beta + 1) \in M(\beta + 4)$. If λ is a limit, then $M \restriction \lambda = \{u \in$

$M(\lambda) \mid M(\lambda) \vDash (\exists f)(\text{Cond}(f) \wedge u \in f)\}$, so $M \uparrow \lambda$ fodo $M(\lambda)$ and thus $M \uparrow \lambda \in M(\lambda + 1) \subseteq M(\lambda + 3)$.

At last we can write σ down and show that it has the desired properties. The sentence σ is

$$\text{Ext} \wedge \text{Close} \wedge (\forall x)(\exists f)(\text{Cond}(f) \wedge (\exists y)(x \in f(y))),$$

where Ext is the axiom of extensionality. Let S be a set and let R be a well-founded relation on S. We must show that $<S, R> \vDash \sigma$ if and only if there is a limit λ and a function f mapping S one–one onto $M(\lambda)$ so that for all $x, y \in S$, $x \in y$ if and only if $f(x) \in f(y)$. Suppose first that there is a limit λ and an f that is an $\in$-isomorphism from S to $M(\lambda)$. $M(\lambda)$ is extensional, transitive, closed, and since $M \uparrow \beta \in M(\lambda)$ for all $\beta < \lambda$, satisfies $(\forall x)(\exists f)(\text{Cond}(f) \wedge (\exists y)(x = f(y)))$. Hence $<M(\lambda), \in \uparrow M(\lambda)> \vDash \sigma$, so since S is $\in$-isomorphic to $M(\lambda)$, $<S, R> \vDash \sigma$. Now suppose, conversely, that $<S, R> \vDash \sigma$, where R is well-founded. $S \vDash \text{Ext}$, so S is extensional, so by Shepherdson's result there is a transitive set t such that S is $\in$-isomorphic to t. Then $t \vDash \text{Close}$, so Closed(t). Also, $t \vDash (\forall x) (\exists f)(\text{Cond}(f) \wedge (\exists y)(x \in f(y)))$, so each such f is $M \uparrow \alpha$ for some ordinal α. So if β is the least ordinal $< \alpha$ such that $x \in f(b)$, then $x \in f(b) = M(\beta)$ and $M(\beta) \in t$. Then $M(\beta) \subseteq t$ since t is transitive. Since t is a set and the relation $y = f(x)$ is functional, the collection of all ordinals β such that $\beta = f(x)$ for some $x \in t$ is a set. Let λ be the least ordinal greater than all these β. Then λ is a limit. (For $0 = \varnothing \in t$ since t is transitive and non-empty, and if $\alpha \in t$, then since $\{\alpha\} \in t$ because t is closed, $\alpha + 1 = \alpha \cup \{\alpha\} \in t$, again because t is closed.) Hence every x in t is in $M(\beta)$ for some $\beta < \lambda$, so $t \subseteq M(\lambda)$. And if $x \in M(\lambda)$, $x \in M(\beta)$ for some $\beta < \lambda$. But by the leastness of λ, there is a γ such that $\beta \leq \gamma < \lambda$ and $M(\gamma) \in t$, so x $\in$ t since t is transitive. Hence S is $\in$-isomorphic to $M(\lambda)$. Therefore σ is as desired.

We have shown that the axiom of choice and the generalized continuum hypothesis are true of the constructible sets. But we can also show that the axioms of ZF are true of the constructible sets. Of course, by the lights of ZF there is no model whose domain is the constructible sets, so this will not give us a consistency proof. But be patient; we can eventually get syntax from it. All constructible sets are sets, so extensionality holds of the constructible sets. The null set is in $M(1)$, so null set holds. $\omega \in M(\omega + 1)$, so the axiom of infinity holds. If there were an infinitely descending chain of constructible sets, there would be one of sets, so foundation holds. It is not difficult to show that the closure axioms hold. For example, let A be a constructible set of sets. Then A

$\in M(\alpha)$ for some α. Since $M(\alpha)$ is transitive, the union of the members of A is $\{x \in M(\alpha) \mid M(\alpha) \vDash (\exists y)(y \in A \wedge x \in y)\}$, so it is fodo $M(\alpha)$ and thus in $M(\alpha + 1)$. We have shown that the axiom of power sets holds in the constructible sets. These arguments are all arguments in ZF, and so assume the axioms of ZF.

What remain are the replacement axioms. So suppose a formula $A(x, y)$ is functional on a constructible set a, that is, that

$$(\forall x)(L(x) \wedge x \in a \rightarrow (\exists! y)(L(y) \wedge A(x, y))),$$

where the clause "$L(x)$" is superfluous since $L(a)$, and L is transitive, and where the quantifiers in A are also relativized to L. We have to deduce in ZF that

$$(\exists b)(L(b) \wedge b = \{y \mid L(y) \wedge (\exists x)(x \in a \wedge A(x, y))\}).$$

To do this we prove what is called a reflection principle.[13] Suppose for perspicuity that $A(x, y)$ is

$$(\forall z)(L(z) \rightarrow (\exists w)(L(w) \wedge (\forall u)(L(u) \rightarrow (\exists v)(L(v) \wedge B(z, w, u, v, x, y))))),$$

where B is quantifier-free. This is a bit too long for perspicuity, so abbreviate it as

$$(\forall z)_L (\exists w)_L (\forall u)_L (\exists v)_L B(z, w, u, v, x, y).$$

We will show that for any constructible a there are ordinals α, β, γ, and δ such that if $x \in a$, then

$$(\forall z)_L (\exists w)_L (\forall u)_L (\exists v)_L B(z, w, u, v, x, y)$$

---

[13] Richard Montague and R. K. Vaught in "Natural Models of Set Theory," *Fundamenta Mathematica* 47 (1959): 219–42, prove a reflection principle for V that they use to show that the least α such that $R(\alpha)$ is a model for ZF is less than the least strongly inaccessible cardinal. Let Z be ZF minus replacement. We saw (Chapter 3, pp. 75–76) that $R(\omega \times 2)$ is a model for Z; it is replacement that raises the rank of a model for ZF. Let ZF1 be first-order ZF, and ZF2, second. The language of each is countable, so let r be an enumeration of the replacement axioms of ZF1. By reflection, for each n there is a least ordinal $\alpha(r(n))$ such that $r(n)$ is true in $R(\alpha(r(n)))$. By replacement in ZF2, there is a set of these $\alpha(r(n))$; let α be their least upper bound, and let λ be the least limit greater than or equal to α. Then $R(\lambda)$ is a model for ZF1. This is a proof in ZF2, so λ is less than the least strongly inaccessible cardinal β, since $R(\beta)$ is a model for ZF2. There is a nonvacuous instance of second-order replacement for each functional relation, and for each collection, identity restricted to it is functional, so there are more instances of second-order replacement than there are sets.

is equivalent to

$$(\forall z)_{M(\alpha)}(\exists w)_{M(\beta)}(\forall u)_{M(\gamma)}(\exists v)_{M(\delta)}B(z, w, u, v, x, y).$$

First, by replacement in ZF, $\{y \mid L(y) \wedge (\exists x)(x \in a \wedge A(x, y))\}$ is a set, since a is a set and A is functional. Hence, again by replacement, the set of ordinals that are the orders of the y such that $L(y) \wedge (\exists x)(x \in a \wedge A(x, y))$ is also a set. Let η be the least upper bound of this set of ordinals. Then for all these y, $y \in M(\eta)$. Going perhaps a bit higher, we may arrange that $a \in M(\eta)$ also.

Now consider

$$(\exists z)_L(\forall w)_L(\exists u)_L(\forall v)_L \neg B(z, w, u, v, x, y).$$

The relation

$$(\exists z)_L(\theta = \delta(z) \wedge (\forall w)_L(\exists u)_L(\forall v)_L \neg B(z, w, u, v, x, y) \wedge (\forall z')_L(\delta(z')$$
$$< \delta(z) \rightarrow \neg(\forall w)_L(\exists u)_L(\forall v)_L \neg B(z', w, u, v, x, y)))$$

is functional for $x \in a$ and $y \in M(\eta)$ since for each such x and y, it picks the least order of a constructible z such that $(\forall w)_L(\exists u)_L(\forall v)_L \neg B(z, w, u, v, x, y)$; there is one if

$$(\exists z)_L(\forall w)_L(\exists u)_L(\forall v)_L \neg B(z, w, u, v, x, y),$$

and it is unique by leastness. So since $a \times M(\eta)$ is a set, there is a set of these θ by replacement in ZF. Let α be an upper bound for the set of these θ. Then for $x \in a$ and $y \in M(\eta)$,

$$(\exists z)_L(\forall w)_L(\exists u)_L(\forall v)_L \neg B(z, w, u, v, x, y),$$

is equivalent to

$$(\exists z)_{M(\alpha)}(\forall w)_L(\exists u)_L(\forall v)_L \neg B(z, w, u, v, x, y),$$

and thus

$$(\forall z)_L(\exists w)_L(\forall u)_L(\exists v)_L B(z, w, u, v, x, y)$$

is equivalent to

$$(\forall z)_{M(\alpha)}(\exists w)_L(\forall u)_L(\exists v)_L B(z, w, u, v, x, y).$$

Again, the relation

$$(\exists w)_L(\theta = \delta(w) \wedge (\forall u)_L(\exists v)_L B(z, w, u, v, x, y)$$
$$\wedge (\forall w')_L(\delta(w') < \delta(w) \rightarrow \neg(\forall u)_L(\exists v)_L B(z, w', u, v, x, y)))$$

is functional for $x \in a$, $y \in M(\eta)$, and $z \in M(\alpha)$ since for each such x, y, and z it picks the least order of a constructible w such that $(\forall u)_L(\exists v)_L$

B(z, w, u, v, x, y); there is one if $(\exists w)_L(\forall u)_L(\exists v)_L B(z, w, u, v, x, y)$ and it is unique by leastness. So since a × M(η) × M$_{(\alpha)}$ is a set, there is a set of these ordinals θ. Let β be an upper bound for the set of them. Then for x ∈ a and y ∈ M(η),

$$(\forall z)_{M(\alpha)}(\exists w)_L(\forall u)_L(\exists v)_L B(z, w, u, v, x, y)$$

is equivalent to

$$(\forall z)_{M(\alpha)}(\exists w)_{M(\beta)}(\forall u)_L(\exists v)_L B(z, w, u, v, x, y).$$

Continuing in this way, we get ordinals γ and δ to complete the proof of the reflection principle.

Returning to replacement in L, we have to show that {y | L(y) ∧ (∃x) (x ∈ a ∧ A(x, y))} is in L. This set is

$$\{y \mid L(y) \wedge (\exists x)(x \in a \wedge (\forall z)_L(\exists w)_L(\forall u)_L(\exists v)_L B(z, w, u, v, x, y))\}.$$

By the reflection principle, this set is

$$\{y \in M(\eta) \mid (\exists x)_{M(\eta)}(x \in a \wedge (\forall z)_{M(\alpha)}(\exists w)_{M(\beta)}(\forall u)_{M(\gamma)}(\exists v)_{M(\delta)}$$
$$B(z, w, u, v, x, y))\}.$$

Call this set b. Then for any ordinal θ > η, α, β, γ, δ, b fodo M(θ), so b ∈ M(θ + 1). This completes the proof.

Let us wring some syntax out of our semantics. Gödel's result says that if ZF is consistent, then so is ZF together with the axiom of choice, the generalized continuum hypothesis, and the statement that all sets are constructible. Let AC be the axiom of choice and let GCH be the generalized continuum hypothesis. The statement that all sets are constructible is usually put as V = L. We have deduced AC and GCH from V = L in ZF, so it suffices to show that if ZF is consistent, so is ZF plus V = L. Let L(x) be the predicate $(\exists f)(\exists \alpha)(\text{Cond}(f) \wedge x \in f(\alpha))$ of the language of ZF; Cond is the predicate defined above in terms of fodo$_{ZF}$. For any formula A in the language of ZF, let A$_L$ be the formula got by replacing every clause $(\forall x)B(x)$ or $(\exists x)B(x)$ in A by $(\forall x)(L(x) \rightarrow B(x))$ or $(\exists x)(L(x) \wedge B(x))$, respectively. Proving, as we have, in ZF that L is a model for ZF amounts to showing for each axiom A of ZF, $\vdash_{ZF} A_L$. It follows that for any theorem T of ZF, $\vdash_{ZF} T_L$. Suppose we could show that $\vdash_{ZF} (V = L)_L$. Then if ZF plus V = L were inconsistent, so that V = L $\vdash_{ZF} 0 \neq 0$, then clearly, $\vdash_{ZF} (V = L) \rightarrow (0 \neq 0)$, so relativizing $\vdash_{ZF} (V = L)_L \rightarrow (0 \neq 0)$. But $\vdash_{ZF} (V = L)_L$, so $\vdash_{ZF} 0 \neq 0$ and ZF is inconsistent. Hence it will suffice to show that $\vdash_{ZF} (V = L)_L$.

Let us get clear on what $(V = L)_L$ looks like. There are no singular terms in the language of ZF denoting V or L, so the best way to put

V = L in the language of ZF is $(\forall x)L(x)$. When we relativize this, we get $(\forall x)L(x) \to (L(x))_L)$, where $(L(x))_L$ is $L(x)$ with all its quantifiers restricted as above by $L(x)$. This sentence is emphatically not quantificationally valid. So we have to show that $\vdash_{ZF} L(x) \to (L(x))_L$. This is a bit intricate, but it is mostly a matter of invariance, and we have mostly done the work already. Let us review.

We said that a formula $A(x_1,..., x_n)$ of the language of ZF is invariant for sets meeting a condition C if and only if for all t meeting C and all $a_1,..., a_n$ in t, $A(a_1,..., a_n)$ if and only if $t \vDash A(a_1,..., a_n)$; truth in t is equivalent to truth (in the real world, mostly V). This is a semantical concept, but for some conditions C, we can turn it into provability in ZF. Suppose C can be expressed by a formula F(t) in the language of ZF and $t \vDash A(a_1,..., a_n)$ is equivalent to $A(a_1,..., a_n)$ relativized to (membership in) t. Then we can prove invariance in ZF by proving $F(t) \to (A(a_1,..., a_n) \leftrightarrow (A(a_1,..., a_n))_t)$. For example, let C be transitivity, which is expressed by $(\forall u)(u \in t \to (\forall v)(v \in u \to v \in t))$, and let A(x) be "x is transitive." Then showing A(x) invariant for C comes to proving in ZF that if t is transitive and $a \in t$, then

$$(\forall y)(\forall z)(y \in z \wedge z \in a \to y \in a)$$
$$\leftrightarrow (\forall y)(y \in t \to (\forall z)(z \in t \to (y \in z \wedge z \in a \to y \in a)).$$

Going left to right is just logic. To go right to left, assume the right and suppose $y \in z \wedge z \in a$. Since t is transitive and $a \in t$, $z \in t$ and so $y \in t$ too, whence by the right $y \in a$ as required.

In the same way we can show in ZF that being $\in$-connected, being an ordinal, being a limit ordinal, being a successor ordinal, and being a function are invariant for transitive sets. We defined Closed(x) by requiring in part that x be transitive, so anything invariant for transitive sets is also invariant for closed sets. We showed above that fodo$_{ZF}$ is invariance for closed sets. All the ordinals are in L and L is closed. These are about all the pieces we need to show in ZF that $L(x) \leftrightarrow (L(x))_L$. $(L(x))_L$ is

$$(\exists \alpha)_L(\exists f)_L(Function(f) \wedge Dom(f) = \alpha \wedge Ordinal(\alpha)$$
$$\wedge f(0) = \varnothing \wedge (\forall \beta)_L(\beta+1 \in \alpha \to ((\forall y)_L(y \in f(\beta+1)$$
$$\leftrightarrow y \text{ fodo}_{ZF} f(\beta)))) \wedge (\forall \beta)_L(\beta \in \alpha \wedge \lim(\beta)$$
$$\to (\forall y)_L(y \in f(\beta) \leftrightarrow (\exists \gamma)_L(\gamma \in \beta \wedge y \in f(\gamma))))$$
$$\wedge (\exists \beta)_L(x \in f(\beta))),$$

while L(x) is this without the subscripts. We skim through a proof in ZF that $L(x) \leftrightarrow (L(x))_L$. If α is an ordinal as provided by L(x), then $L(\alpha)$ and the requirement for $(L(x))_L$ that there be an appropriate ordinal in L is thus far met. Conversely, if α is an object in L such that $L \vDash \text{Ordinal}(\alpha)$, then since Ordinal is invariant for L because L is transitive, the requirement for $L(x)$ that there be an appropriate ordinal is thus far met too. Suppose f is a function provided by $L(x)$. Then f is $M \uparrow \alpha$. $M \uparrow \alpha \in M(\alpha + 3)$, so the requirement for $(L(x))_L$ that such an f be in L is thus far met. Conversely, if f is an object in L such that $L \vDash \text{Cond}(f)$, then since L is closed and Cond is invariant for closed sets, the requirement for $L(x)$ that there be an appropriate function is thus far met. Ordinals are invariant for transitive sets and L is transitive, so the last clause works too. This completes the relative consistency proof.[14]

One feature of this argument is confronting the failure by the lights of the prevailing set theory, ZF, of V and L to exist, and thus to provide models for ZF. This is the salient instance of Orayen's paradox.[15] The way we got around it here looks very like a linguistic version of interpretation.[16] There is no L to be a model of ZF, but there is a predicate $L(x)$, defined as $(\exists f)(\exists \alpha)(\text{Cond}(f) \land x \in f(\alpha))$, and we can prove in ZF the relativization of each axiom of ZF to $L(x)$. Asked from what domain the variables f and α take their values, we may reply that when $(\exists f)(\exists \alpha)(\text{Cond}(f) \land x \in f(\alpha))$, then $(\exists f)(\exists \alpha)(L(f) \land L(\alpha) \land (\text{Cond}(f) \land x \in f(\alpha))$, so the predicate $L(x)$ will serve as the domain, in the linguistic sense. In the case of V, we could similarly appeal to the predicate $V(x)$, defined as $(\exists \alpha)(x \in R(\alpha))$.[17]

This chapter has followed lectures Hilary Putnam gave at Harvard in the spring of 1968. He gave a persuasive argument for believing that V is not L. For ease in imagining, suppose space is Euclidean and give it rectangular Cartesian coordinates where the unit distance is one mile. There is a rational number in each unit side of a cube and there are only countably many rationals, so we have split space up into a countable

[14] Our argument is for ZF, and Gödel's 1940 monograph is an argument for NBG. It does not seem to have been done for NF or ML, but in "The Relative Strength of Zermelo's Set Theory and Quine's New Foundations," in *Proceedings of the International Congress of Mathematicians 1954, Amsterdam, September 2–September 9*, vol. 3 (Groningen and Amsterdam: Erven P. Noordhoff N.V. and North-Holland, 1956), 289–94, J. Barkley Rosser presents some information on constructible sets in NF.

[15] See Chapter 4, pp. 110–16.

[16] Ibid., 114–16.

[17] See Petr Hájek and Pavel Pudlák, *Metamathematics of First-Order Arithmetic* (Berlin: Springer, 1993), 148–50.

infinity of cubes. Let f be a one–one correspondence between the cubes and the natural numbers. Let P be an empirical property with more than a zero chance, but less than a unit chance, of being instantiated by a cube; if one believes in randomness, let the distribution of P across cubes be random. (Maybe an example would be containing more than a ton of red stuff.) Then {n ∈ ω | (∃x)(P(x) ∧ f(x) = n)} is a set of natural numbers. Hence, if V = L, this set is first-order definable. This would require that there be a predicate F in the language of ZF, and thus built up from just ∈ and = using only variables, truth-functional connectives, and quantifiers, such that P and F are coextensive. It overstrains credulity that an empirical property like P be definable in purely set theoretic terms.

SEVEN

✦

Or Not

After Gödel proved the consistency of the continuum hypothesis with set theory, many people expected him also to prove its independence, but it was Paul Cohen who did so.[1] There is a story, perhaps apocryphal, as such stories sometimes are, that Cohen passed by Georg Kreisel's office at Stanford in the spring and asked for a problem to work on. To get rid of Cohen, Kreisel gave him the independence of the continuum hypothesis, and by the next fall Cohen had solved it. There is another story, certainly apocryphal, that after Gödel heard of Cohen's success, Gödel feared that the Institute for Advanced Studies would fire him and he would starve to death as an old man. This story may be a garbled version of Gödel's decline after the death of his wife, who had looked after him well.

We will show that if ZF is consistent, it remains so even with the addition of a sentence saying there is a nonconstructible set of natural numbers, so V = L is independent. We will show that if ZF is consistent, it remains so with the addition of a sentence saying there is a set of sets of natural numbers that is not well-ordered, so the axiom of choice is independent. We will show that if ZF is consistent, it remains so with the addition of the denial of the continuum hypothesis, so the generalized continuum hypothesis is independent. We will make constant use of the constructible sets from the last chapter, and, as there, our exposition will follow lectures given by Hilary Putnam at Harvard in the spring of 1968.

---

[1] Paul J. Cohen, *Set Theory and the Continuum Hypothesis* (New York: W. A. Benjamin, 1966). Akihiro Kanamori, "Cohen and Set Theory," *Bulletin of Symbolic Logic* 14 (September 2008): 351–78, is instructive.

As in the last chapter too, for much of this chapter our argument will be semantic, but we will show how to squeeze syntax out of it. Our semantics will look at a stronger theory than ZF. This theory is ZF plus the assumption that there is a *set* that is a model for ZF. Given a set x that is a model for ZF, by Shepherdson's result in the last chapter there is a transitive set that is a model for ZF and is $\in$-isomorphic to x, so we will confine our attention to transitive models for ZF. We will do some preliminary thinking about how to get such a model with a nonconstructible set of natural numbers.

Given a transitive model x for ZF, say that y is x-constructible if and only if $x \vDash L(y)$. Then

$$x \vDash L(y)$$
$$\text{iff } x \vDash (\exists f, \beta)(\text{Cond}(f) \wedge y \in f(\beta))$$
$$\text{iff } (\exists f, \beta)(f, \beta \in x \wedge \text{Cond}(f) \wedge y \in f(\beta))$$

(since Cond is invariant for closed sets, and x is closed because it is a model for ZF)

$$\text{iff } (\exists f, \beta)(f, \beta \in x \wedge (\exists \alpha)(f = M \restriction \alpha) \wedge y \in f(\beta))$$
$$\text{iff } (\exists f, \alpha, \beta)(\beta < \alpha \wedge f = M \restriction \alpha \wedge f, \beta \in x \wedge y \in f(\beta))$$
$$\text{iff } (\exists \alpha, \beta)(\alpha \in x \wedge \beta \in \alpha \wedge y \in M(\beta))$$

(since $M \restriction \alpha \in x$ and x satisfies replacement, the set of first members of pairs in $M \restriction \alpha$ is in x, and this set is α)

$$\text{iff } (\exists \alpha)(\alpha \in x \wedge y \in M(\alpha))$$

(if $\alpha \in x$, then since $x \vDash ZF$, $\alpha + 1 \in x$, so $\beta = \alpha$ is an ordinal such that $\alpha + 1 \in x$, $\beta \in \alpha + 1$, and $y \in M(\beta)$). So y is x-constructible if and only if $y \in M(\alpha)$ for some $\alpha \in x$.

Let $\alpha(x)$ be the least ordinal not in x. Then $\alpha(x)$ exists because the ordinals in x form a set since x is a set, so because no set exhausts the ordinals, there is an ordinal not in x. Since x is a model for ZF, it satisfies the axioms of null set, singleton, and union; thus $0 \in x$, and if $\beta \in x$, then $\beta + 1 \in x$, while if $\beta + 1$, then $\beta \in x$ too, because x is transitive. Hence $\alpha(x)$ is a limit. For $\beta < \alpha(x)$, $\beta \in x$, for if not, then by the leastness of $\alpha(x)$, there is a γ such that $\beta < \gamma \in x$, and then $\beta \in x$ since x is transitive.

Let x^* be the set of all y such that y is x-constructible. Then $x^* = M(\alpha(x))$. For if $y \in M(\alpha(x))$, then since $\alpha(x)$ is a limit, $y \in M(\beta)$ for some $\beta < \alpha(x)$, so $\beta \in x$. Thus $y \in M(\beta)$ for some $\beta \in x$, so y is x-constructible, and then $y \in x^*$. If, conversely, $y \in x^*$, then y is x-constructible, so y ∈ M(β) for some β ∈ x. Thus β < α(x), so y ∈ M(β) ⊆ M(α(x)). Since α(x) is a limit, x* ⊨ σ, where σ is the sentence featured in the last chapter. Also, x* ⊨ (∀y)L(y). For if y ∈ x*, y ∈ M(β) for some β < α(x). Then β + 1, β + 4 < α(x). So M ↑ (β + 1) ∈ M(β + 4) ∈ M(α(x)), and thus for some f, γ, we have f, γ ∈ x*. Cond(f) and y ∈ f(γ). Hence x ⊨ L(y). Next M(β) ∈ x when β ∈ x. If β = 0, then M(β) = ∅ ∈ x since x satisfies the axiom of null set. If β = γ + 1 and M(γ) ∈ x, then P(M(γ)) ∈ x since x satisfies the axiom of power sets, and since M(γ + 1) ⊆ P(M(γ)), M(γ + 1) ∈ x since x satisfies the axiom of separation. If β is a limit, M(γ) ∈ x for γ < β and β ∈ x, then {M(γ) | γ < β} ∈ x since x satisfies replacement, so M(β) ∈ x since x satisfies the axiom of big unions. It follows that x* ⊆ x. For if y ∈ x*, y ∈ M(β) for some β ∈ x, whence M(β) ∈ x, and then y ∈ x since x is transitive. The sense of this is that x* is to x as L is to V. Indeed, x* ⊨ ZF. The proof is pretty much the proof that ZF is true in the constructible sets.

We have shown that α(x) is an ordinal α such that M(α) is a model for ZF. Let α′ be the least such ordinal. For any transitive model y of ZF, construct α(y) and y* as before. As before, y* = M(α(y)) and y* ⊆ y. By the leastness of α′, α′ ≤ α(y) and so M(α′) ⊆ M(α(y)) = y* ⊆ y and so ∈ ↑ M(α′) = (∈ ↑ y) ↑ M(α′). Thus M(α′) is a submodel of y for ZF. In this sense M(α′) is the minimal transitive model for ZF.

We show that α′ is countable. Recall that M(α(x)) can be well-ordered without the axiom of choice. Let H be the Skolem hull of M(α(x)) for the language of ZF and {∅}. H is a countable elementary substructure of M(α(x)), and since M(α(x)) ⊨ σ, H ⊨ σ. Let H′ be the transitive image of H by Shepherdson's result. Then H′ = M(γ) for some limit γ, and since H′ is countable because H is, γ is countable. Since M(α(x)) ⊨ ZF, H ⊨ ZF, so H′ ⊨ ZF. Thus α′ ≤ γ, so since γ is countable, α′ is countable too. As before, M(α′) ⊨ (∀y)L(y). By the minimality of M(α′), no member of M(α′) is a model for ZF, so there is no hope of deducing that ZF has a model from ZF plus V = L.

It is obvious that x* ⊆ x ∩ L. But one should not expect that x ∩ L ⊆ x*. For y might be in x, so ρ(y) is some α < α(x) since regularity holds in x, and y might also be constructible but with δ(y) > α(x), so y ∉ x*. Thus, even if L(y) and y ∈ x, it need not be that x ⊨ L(y). That is, L is not invariant for models of ZF. Let us sharpen up this rather casual reasoning. Suppose a is a constructible set of natural numbers not in M(ω × 2). There are such sets. For we can prove in ZF that M(ω × 2) has ω members and that P(ω) has more than ω members. But we saw that the relativization of a theorem of ZF to L is a theorem of ZF. So we can show in ZF that the cardinal in the sense of L of M($\omega \times 2$) is ω, while that of the constructible power set of ω is bigger in the sense of L than ω. It follows that there is a constructible set a of natural numbers not in M($\omega \times 2$). Now let

$$M_\alpha(a) = M(\alpha) \text{ for } \alpha \leq \omega$$
$$M_{\omega+1}(a) = M(\omega + 1) \cup \{a\}$$
$$M_{\alpha+1}(a) = \{x \mid x \text{ fodo } M_\alpha(a)\} \text{ for } \alpha > \omega$$
$$M_\lambda(a) = \cup \,\beta_<\lambda \; M_\beta(a).$$

It is as if a were fodo M(ω). Then $a \in M_{\omega+1}(a)$ and, as before, $M_{\omega+1}(a) \subseteq M_{\omega \times 2}(a)$. But L(a) is not true in $M_{\omega \times 2}(a)$. For suppose it were. Then for some ordinal $\alpha \in M_{\omega \times 2}(a)$, $a \in M(\alpha)$. But $M_\beta(a)$ and M(β) contain the same ordinals; the argument is basically the proof that $\delta(\beta) = \beta$. Hence for some α in M($\omega \times 2$), a is in M(α) and then since $\alpha \in M(\omega \times 2)$, $\alpha < \omega \times 2$ contrary to the choice of a. Hence L(a) but $M_{\omega \times 2}(a) \nvDash L(a)$, so L is not invariant.

The ordinal α' of the minimal model is countable, so there is also a set a of natural numbers not in M(α'). As in the last paragraph,

$$M_{\alpha'}(a) \vDash \neg L(a) \wedge a \subseteq \omega$$

(since $\alpha \subseteq \omega$ is invariant). If we also had

$$M_{\alpha'}(a) \vDash ZF$$

we would have shown in ZF plus "ZF has a model" that there is a model for ZF plus "there is a nonconstructible set of natural numbers," and this would be a strong independence argument. But, alas, it is not true that

$$M_{\alpha'}(a) \vDash ZF$$

for all constructible $a \subseteq \omega$ not in M(α'). Let p be a pairing function on natural numbers, that is, p maps pairs n,k to natural numbers so that p(n, k) = p(i, j) if and only if n = i and k = j; p(n, k) = $2^n \times 3^k$ is a pairing function. Say $a \subseteq \omega$ is well-ordered if and only if {<n, k> | p(n, k) $\in$ a} well-orders its field. Let a be a well-ordered set such that the type of {<n, k> | p(n, k) $\in$ a} is α'; there is one because α' is countable. Then replacement fails in $M_{\alpha'}(a)$. For $a \in M_{\alpha'}(a)$, so {<n, k> | p(n, k) $\in$ a} $\in M_{\alpha'}(a)$, so if replacement held in $M_{\alpha'}(a)$, then $\alpha' = \{\alpha \mid \alpha < \alpha'\} \in M_{\alpha'}(a)$, and then since M($\alpha'$) and $M_{\alpha'}(a)$ agree on ordinals, $\alpha' \in M(\alpha')$, which is impossible. But there may nonetheless be sets a such that $a \subseteq \omega$, $a \notin M(\alpha')$, and $M_{\alpha'}(a) \vDash ZF$. Paul Cohen called them *generic*, and our task is to find some.

Forcing is Cohen's method of finding generic sets. Forcing is a variation on the theme of truth, but of a particular arrangement of truth.
When we defined truth, we never said that $(\forall x)F(x)$ is true if and only
if for all terms t, $F(t)$ is true. That was because many things are not
denoted by any singular term. But in the special case of L, we can
arrange for a (vast) class of terms, enough to denote constructible sets.
These terms will be part of a language, the L-language, that we will
associate with L.

The L-language includes the following primitive signs:

$$(,), x, \, ', \in, \neg, =, \rightarrow, \forall.$$

The prime sign is to distinguish variables: x, x', and so on. To these nine
signs we could assign the digits thus:

(	)	x	'	$\in$	$\neg$	=	$\rightarrow$	$\forall$
1	2	3	4	5	6	7	8	9.

Our primitive signs suffice for the usual language of set theory, and
following Quine we could gödelize the formulae of that language by
concatenation.[2] To illustrate how this works, consider the empty set
axiom. This says that $(\exists y)(\forall x)(x \notin y)$, and put into primitive notation
this reads:

$$\neg(\forall x)\neg(\forall x')\neg(x' \in x).$$

Reading off the gödel numbers of these primitives in order

$$619326193426134532$$

and, concatenating, we have the gödel number of the empty set axiom.

But the L-language is bigger than this. In addition to the usual quantifiers, we also have the bounded quantifiers. These are

$$(\forall x)_\alpha F(x),$$

which means that

$$(\forall x)(x \in M(\alpha) \rightarrow F(x)),$$

and

$$(\exists x)_\alpha F(x),$$

---

[2] W. V. Quine, *Mathematical Logic*, rev. ed. (New York: Harper Torchbooks, 1962),
313.

which means that

$$(\exists x)(x \in M(\alpha) \wedge F(x)).$$

Thus the L-language has as many signs as there are ordinals, so there is no set of all the formulae of the L-language. We call a formula limited if and only if all its quantifiers are bounded.

We have in effect added all the ordinals to our notation. To avoid this mixture of signs and numbers, we use our gödelization of our original primitives to replace them with their gödel numbers, and we take each ordinal as its own gödel number. Then a formula like

$$\neg(\forall x)_\theta \neg(\forall x')_\beta \neg(x \in x')$$

goes to the finite sequence

$$6, 1, 9, 3, 2, \theta, 6, 1, 9, 3, 4, 2, \beta, 6, 1, 3, 5, 3, 4, 2$$

of ordinals. This sequence can be taken as a function from the ordinal 20 into a finite set of ordinals. We may thus take the formulae we have so far to be finite sequences of ordinals. This enables us to talk about these formulae in the L-language.

We now suppose the L-language extended using implicit definition by bounded set abstracts written $\{x_\alpha \mid F(x)\}$ that mean $\{x \in M(\alpha) \mid F(x)\}$. Abstracts must meet four conditions: (i) the variable x must be bounded as indicated by an ordinal α; (ii) every quantifier in F(x) must be bounded by an ordinal no bigger than α; (iii) x must be the only variable free in F(x); and (iv) no abstracts may occur in F(x). Bounded set abstracts can always be eliminated in context; this is why they are implicitly defined. Abstracts are terms, and there are only two predicates ($\in$ and =) in the L-language, which form the contexts in which abstracts may occur. There are three rules for eliminating abstracts in context.

(1) Replace $y \in \{x_\alpha \mid F(x)\}$ with

$$F(y) \wedge (\exists z)_\alpha(z = y).$$

(2) Replace $y = \{x_\alpha \mid F(x)\}$ with

$$(\forall x)(x \in y \leftrightarrow (F(x) \wedge (\exists z)_\alpha(x = z))).$$

(Given $\{x_\alpha \mid F(x)\} = \{x_\beta \mid G(x)\}$, go to

$$(\forall y)_\alpha(F(y) \leftrightarrow y \in \{x_\beta \mid G(x)\})$$

and then use (1).)

(3) Replace $\{x_\alpha \mid F(x)\} \in y$ with

$(\exists z)_{\alpha+1}(z = \{x_\alpha \mid F(x)\} \wedge z \in y)$,

and replace $\{x_\alpha \mid F(x)\} \in \{x_\beta \mid G(x)\}$ with

$(\exists z)_{\alpha+1}(z = \{x_\alpha \mid F(x)\} \wedge z \in \{x_\beta \mid G(x)\})$.

When introducing new variables, pick ones that are not bound by quantifiers already present. The universal quantifier for x in (2) is the only unbound quantifier in the implicit definition. But if the clause in (2) occurs in a limited sentence, then the ordinal bounding y will bound x too. So the result of eliminating abstracts from a limited sentence is a limited sentence.

Let a be a constructible set and let α be the order of a. Then there is an abstract $\{x_\alpha \mid F(x)\}$ in which the quantifiers are bound by ordinals no bigger than α that denotes a. Suppose as induction hypothesis that the claim holds for all constructible sets of order less than α. Since a fodo $M(\alpha)$, there are members $a_1, \ldots, a_n$ of $M(\alpha)$ and a formula $F(x_1, \ldots, x_n, x)$ of the language of ZF such that a is $\{x \in M(\alpha) \mid M(\alpha) \vDash F(a_1, \ldots, a_n, x)\}$. We may assume F in prenex normal form, say $(Q_1y_1) \ldots (Q_ky_k)G(y_1, \ldots, y_k, x_1, \ldots, x_n, x)$ where Q_i is $\forall$ or $\exists$ as the case may be. Hence a is $\{x_\alpha \mid (Q_1y_1)_\alpha \ldots (Q_ky_k)_\alpha G(y_1, \ldots, y_k, a_1, \ldots, a_n, x)\}$. This last term fails to be an abstract only because of the constants $a_1, \ldots, a_n$, but by the induction hypothesis each is denoted by an abstract of the required sort. We use those abstracts to transform $G(y_1, \ldots, y_k, a_1, \ldots, a_n, x)$. For any terms t_1 and t_2, replace $t_1 = t_2$ with $(\forall x)_\alpha(x \in t_1 \leftrightarrow x \in t_2)$. The remaining atomic formulae with constants are of one of the three forms $b \in c, c \in v$, or $v \in c$, where v is a variable and b and c are constants. Suppose $\{x_\beta \mid H(x)\}$ denotes b and $\{x_\gamma \mid J(x)\}$ denotes c, where β is the order of b, γ is the order of c, and $\beta, \gamma < \alpha$. Replace $b \in c$ with

$$(\exists x)_{\beta+1}((\forall y)_\beta(y \in x \leftrightarrow H(y)) \wedge (\exists z)_\gamma(x = z \wedge J(z))).$$

Replace $c \in v$ with

$$(\exists x)_\gamma(v = x \wedge J(x)),$$

and $v \in c$ with

$$(\exists x)_{\gamma+1}((\forall y)_\gamma(y \in x \leftrightarrow J(y) \wedge x \in v)).$$

This transformation is equivalent to G, so putting it in for G we have an abstract of the required form that denotes a. Since every constructible set is denoted by a term of the L-language, a way is open to a different explanation of truth for quantified sentences of the L-language.

With bounds on quantifiers our earlier gödelization of the L-languages ceases to be one–one. For example, the ordinal 9 is both a bound on quantifiers and the gödel number of the universal quantifier. This equivocation is ill-advised. But it arises only for finite ordinals. So we will introduce another notation for the hereditary finite sets, which include the finite ordinals. The hereditary finite sets are those sets that are finite, and so are their members, and so on; the set of all of them is $R(\omega)$, which is the same as $M(\omega)$. We can write list terms for the hereditary finite sets using just $\{$, $\}$, $\varnothing$, and the comma, so we add these four signs and the vertical stroke for abstracts to the primitives of the L-language. Their gödel numbers are 10, 11, 12, 13, and 14. Then the formula $(\forall x)_2 F(x)$ is $(\forall x)_{\{\varnothing, \{\varnothing\}\}} F(x)$ whose gödel sequence begins 1, 9, 3, 2, 10, 12, 13, 10, 12, 11, 11, and similarly we write out a bound on a quantifier or a variable in an abstract in von Neumann terms when it is finite; infinite ordinals still occur in L-formulae.

We can effectively enumerate the hereditary finite sets.[3] Let h be such an enumeration and let n(i) be the list term for h(i), the one that lists the members of h(i) in order, and so also for their members, and so on. The limited sentences of the L-language are the sentences built up from atomic sentences of the form $n(i) \in n(j)$ using truth-functional connectives ($\neg$ and $\rightarrow$), bounded quantification and formation of abstracts. The level of an abstract $\{x_\alpha \mid F(x)\}$ is α; it is the maximum of the ordinals in the abstract. Tracing the specification of limited sentences, we define truth for limited sentences thus:

(1) $n(i) \in n(j)$ is true iff $h(i) \in h(j)$.
(2) $n(i) = n(j)$ is true iff $h(i) = h(j)$.

---

[3] Here is a way to do so. First, $\varnothing$ is the only hereditary finite set of order 0; if $a_1,\ldots,$ a_k are hereditary finite sets of order at most n, and at least one of them is of order n, then $\{a_1,\ldots, a_k\}$ is a hereditary finite set of order n + 1; a set a is a hereditary finite set if and only if it is a hereditary finite set of some finite order. Second, let P be the relation on hereditary finite sets such that aPb if and only if either the order of a is less than the order of b, or their orders are equal but a has fewer members than b, or their orders and cardinals are equal, n is that cardinal, a is $\{a_1,\ldots, a_n\}$ where $a_1 P$ $\ldots$ Pa_n, b is $\{b_1,\ldots, b_n\}$ where $b_1 P$ $\ldots$ Pb_n, and for the least m such that $a_m \neq b_m$, $a_m P b_m$. Third, assign to each such set the number of such sets that precede it in P order; the enumeration of the hereditary finite sets is the inverse of this assignment. Fourth, n(0) is $\varnothing$, and if the members of h(k + 1) are $h(k_1),\ldots, h(k_m)$ where $k_1 < \ldots < k_m$, then n(k + 1) is $\{n(k_1),\ldots, n(k_m)\}$.

(3) ¬A is true iff A is not true.

(4) A → B is true iff A is not true or B is true.

(5) $(\forall x)_\alpha F(x)$ is true iff for every abstract a of level less than α, F(a) is true.

(6) For $\alpha < \beta$, $\{x_\alpha \mid F(x)\} \in \{x_\beta \mid G(x)\}$ is true iff $G(\{x_\alpha \mid F(x)\})$ is true.

(7) For $\alpha \geq \beta$, $\{x_\alpha \mid F(x)\} \in \{x_\beta \mid G(x)\}$ is true iff $(\exists y)_\beta((\forall x)_\alpha(x \in y \leftrightarrow F(x)) \wedge G(y))$ is true.

(8) For $\alpha \leq \beta$, $\{x_\alpha \mid F(x)\} = \{x_\beta \mid G(x)\}$ is true iff $(\forall x)_\beta(G(x) \leftrightarrow (F(x) \wedge (\exists y)_\alpha(x = y)))$ is true, and similarly if $\alpha \geq \beta$.

(9) If α is infinite, $n(i) \in \{x_\alpha \mid F(x)\}$ is true iff F(n(i)) is true, but if α is finite, say h(j) for some j, then $n(i) \in \{x_\alpha \mid F(x)\}$ is true iff $F(n(i)) \wedge (n(i) \in n(j) \vee n(i) = n(j))$ is true.

(10) If i = 0, $n(i) = \{x_\alpha \mid F(x)\}$ is true iff $(\forall x)_\alpha \neg F(x)$ is true, but if i = k + 1 and n(i) is $\{n(q_1),..., n(q_m)\}$, then $n(i) = \{x_\alpha \mid F(x)\}$ is true iff $(\forall x)_\alpha F(x) \leftrightarrow x = n(q_1) \vee ... \vee x = n(q_m))$ is true.

(11) Consider $\{x_\alpha \mid F(x)\} \in n(i)$. If i = 0, this sentence is not true. Suppose i = k + 1 and n(i) is $\{n(q_1),..., n(q_m)\}$. Replace the sentence with $\{x_\alpha \mid F(x)\} = n(q_1) \vee ... \vee \{x_\alpha \mid F(x)\} = n(q_m)$. Let $D_1 \vee ... \vee D_m$ be the result of replacing each disjunct according to (10). Then $\{x_\alpha \mid F(x)\} \in n(i)$ is true iff $D_1 \vee ... \vee D_m$ is true.

This completes the definition of "true limited sentence of the L-language."

We next formalize this inductive definition as an explicit definition in the L-language. We replace limited sentences with their gödel sequences, each of which is constructible and so denoted by an abstract in the L-language. This enables us to replace mention in English of limited sentences with mention in the L-language of their gödel sequences. We assume that we have codified the syntax of the L-language we will need in the L-language by Gödel's methods. The level of a limited sentence is the maximum of the levels of the abstracts in the sentence and the bounds of the quantifiers in the sentence (or if the sentence is a truth-functional compound of atomic sentences and only list terms occur in the atoms, then the level is the maximum of the orders of the hereditary finite sets mentioned in it, which is the maximum of the number of close-curly-brackets at the end of the list terms for such sets). Let λ be a limit ordinal. Then the gödel sequence of a limited sentence of level less than λ is a member of $M(\lambda)$, for such a gödel sequence is a finite set of ordered pairs of ordinals less than λ. Let β be the maximum of these ordinals. All ordered pairs of ordinals with maximum β are members of $M(\beta + 2)$, so the gödel sequence of a limited sentence of level β is a member of $M(\beta + 3)$. Consider, for example, the sentence "$\emptyset \in \emptyset$." Its gödel sequence is the function f such that $f(0) = 12$, $f(1) = 5$, and $f(2) = 12$. The pairs $<0, 12>$, $<1, 5>$, and $<2, 12>$ are in $M(14)$, so since $f = \{x \in M(14) \mid M(14) \vDash x = <0, 12> \vee x = <1, 5> \text{ or } x = <2, 12>\}$, $f \in M(15)$. Thus, if D is the set of all gödel sequences of limited sentences of level less than λ, then

D = $\{x \in M(\lambda) \mid M(\lambda) \vDash x$ is the gödel sequence of a limited sentence of level less than $\lambda\}$,

where the membership of x in $M(\lambda)$ makes the phrase "of level less than λ" redundant. So $D \in M(\lambda + 1)$. In the following definition, G(x) is short for "x is the gödel sequence of a limited sentence," and A(x, i, j) is short for "x is the gödel sequence of $n(i) \in n(j)$," I(x, i, j) is short for "x is the gödel sequence of $n(i) = n(j)$," C(x, y, z) is short for "x is the gödel sequence of the conditional of the limited sentences with gödel sequences y and z," and so on through the ellipsis. We define

u is a true limited sentence of level less than λ iff $(\exists f)_{\lambda+4}$ (f is a function $\wedge$ the domain of $f = \{x_\lambda \mid x$ is the gödel sequence of a limited sentence$\} \wedge$ the range of $f = n(2) \wedge (\forall x)_\lambda (G(x) \rightarrow ((\forall i, j)_\omega (A(x, i, j) \rightarrow (f(x) = 0 \leftrightarrow n(i) \in n(j))) \wedge (\forall i, j)_\omega (I(x, i, j) \rightarrow (f(x) = 0 \leftrightarrow n(i) = n(j))) \wedge (\forall y, z)_\lambda (C(x, y, z) \rightarrow (f(x) = 0 \leftrightarrow (f(y) = 1 \vee f(z) = 0)))) \wedge \ldots)) \wedge f(u) = 0)$

where the ellipsis is to be filled by conjuncts for each of the other eight clauses of our earlier inductive definition of truth.

We have to ensure that for each limited sentence (with gödel sequence) u the function f required for truth exists. This is an existence proof like the one in the argument for Shepherdson's result.[4] Uniqueness comes before existence, and for uniqueness we need an ordering. First, let u be a limited sentence, let $a_1, \ldots, a_k$ be the abstracts in u, let $\alpha_1, \ldots, \alpha_k$ be the levels of $a_1, \ldots, a_k$, respectively, let u' be the result of replacing each of $a_1, \ldots, a_k$ throughout u with by a new and distinct variable not in u, and let $\beta_1, \ldots, \beta_n$ be the bounds on the quantifiers in u'. Let the ordinal of u be the maximum of $\beta_1, \ldots, \beta_n$, $\alpha_1 + 1, \ldots, \alpha_k + 1$. For limited sentences u and v, we say that vBu (pronounced v is below u) if and only if the ordinal of v is less than the ordinal of u or else these ordinals are equal but the number of occurrences of truth-functional connectives and

---

[4] See Chapter 6, pp. 160–61.

quantifiers in v is less than that of u. Then B is a partial ordering of the limited sentences such that there are no infinitely descending B-chains, and for any nonatomic limited sentence u (that is, not of the form n(i) ∈ n(j) or n(i) = n(j)), whether u is true depends only on whether certain limited sentences below u are true. Now suppose that for some limited sentence (with gödel sequence) u of level less than λ, there were two functions f and g as required by truth. Then f and g would have a point of first B-difference. But then the clauses of our definition would by agreement below this point require agreement at this point. So there is at most one such function. We can then complete the proof of the existence of f as we did in Shepherdson's result. Then we can define "u is a true limited sentence" to mean that for some limit λ, u is a true limited sentence of level less than λ. The point of this definition is that it foreshadows forcing.

It will make life easier if we drop identity in favor of coextensiveness, so we treat a = b as an abbreviation for $(\forall x)(x \in a \leftrightarrow x \in b)$. To explain forcing, we next replace L with M, which is M(α'). The M-language is like the L-language except that instead of all ordinals, we now use only the ordinals less than α'. A limited sentence of the M-language is one limited by ordinals less than α'. But an unlimited sentence of the M-language is a limited sentence of the L-language, the limit being α'. We want a set a ⊆ ω such that for N = $M_{\alpha'}$(a) we have a ∉ M and N ⊨ ZF, since then N ⊨ ZF ∧ ¬L(a), which will show V = L independent of ZF. To do this, we pick a new constant τ; let its gödel number be 15. Let the N-language be the M-language plus τ. The idea is that τ will come to name an a of the sort we want. Note that both the M-language and the N-language are countable, and that since the gödel number of τ is the ordinary ordinal 15, the syntax of the N-language is specifiable independently of the a we are after.

Forcing is a relation between conditions, which are members of M, and (for now) limited sentences of the N-language, which are also members of M. A condition C is a function whose domain is a natural number and whose range is 2 = {0, 1}, the set of truth values. The idea is that C will be a description of a finite initial segment of a, so that n ∈ a if C(n) = 0. It will turn out that the forcing relation between conditions and limited sentences of the N-language is definable in the M-language even though forcing resembles truth and truth for limited sentences of the N-language is definable only in the N-language, not the M-language. This is because we get a from forcing, but truth from a.

The idea of forcing is that we focus on what we can say about a set given a *finite* amount of information about it. Logical consequence has this property because of compactness, but the trouble with logical consequence is that no finite amount of information need decide between a sentence and its negation. Forcing differs from logical consequence in that for every limited sentence, some finite amount of information will force either it or its negation. Indeed, it will turn out that for every condition C and every limited s of the N-language, some condition extending C forces s or its negation.

There are a few preliminaries before we define forcing. Recall that we eliminated identity. We replace $\forall$ with $\exists$, and $\to$ with $\vee$. That understood, the definition of forcing looks rather like the inductive definition of truth for limited sentences. A condition, as we said, is a function C from some natural number j into $2 = \{0, 1\}$.

(1) C forces $n(i) \in n(k)$ iff $h(i) \in h(k)$.
(2) C forces $n(i) \in \tau$ iff $h(i)$ is a natural number in the domain of C and $C(h(i)) = 0$. No condition forces $\tau \in n(i)$.
(3) C forces $\neg A$ iff no extension of C forces A.
(4) C forces $A \vee B$ iff C forces A or C forces B.
(5) C forces $(\exists x)_\alpha F(x)$ iff for some abstract a of level less than α, C forces $F(a)$, or $\alpha \geq \omega + 1$ and C forces $F(\tau)$.
(6) C forces $\{x_\alpha \mid F(x)\} \in \{x_\beta \mid G(x)\}$ iff C forces the appropriate transform of $\{x_\alpha \mid F(x)\} \in \{x_\beta \mid G(x)\}$ depending on whether $\alpha < \beta$ as in clauses 6 and 7 of the definition of truth. Similarly for list terms, abstracts, and clauses 9 and 11.
(7) C forces $\{x_\alpha \mid F(x)\} \in \tau$ iff for some $i \in \omega$, $h(i)$ is a natural number, C forces $(\forall x)_\alpha (F(x) \leftrightarrow x \in n(i))$, and $C(h(i)) = 0$.
(8) C forces $\tau \in \{x_\alpha \mid F(x)\}$ iff $\alpha \geq \omega + 1$ and C forces $F(\tau)$.

It is in clause (3) that forcing differs most from truth. Much as for truth, we can define "x is the gödel sequence of a limited sentence of the N-language that condition y forces" explicitly in the M-language.

An unlimited sentence of the N-language is one in which some quantifier is unbounded. A condition C forces $(\exists x)F(x)$ if for some term a of the N-language that is an abstract or τ, C forces $F(a)$. For any unlimited sentence s of the N-language, there is a definition in the M-language of C forces s. (Note that in this last sentence, the existential quantifier lies in the scope of the universal; it is like everyone has a mother, not someone is the mother of us all.) The proof is by induction on the number of quantifiers in the prenex of s.[5] In the basis case, there are no unbounded quantifiers, so s is limited, and then we have seen how to define forcing for s in the M-language. In the interesting induction step where s is $(\forall x)$ F(x), we have

C forces $\neg(\exists x)\neg F(x)$

iff it is false that some extension C′ of C forces $(\exists x)\neg F(x)$;

iff it is false that for some C′ such that $C \subseteq C'$ and some a (abstract or τ) C′ forces $\neg F(a)$;

iff it is false that for some C′ such that $C \subseteq C'$ and some a, it is false that some C″ such that $C' \subseteq C''$, C″ forces F(a);

iff for all C′ such that $C \subseteq C'$ and all a, there is a C″ such that $C' \subseteq C''$, and C″ forces F(a).

By the induction hypothesis, C″ forces F(a) is definable in the M-language, so since we can quantify over conditions and abstracts in the M-language, we can build a definition in the M-language of C forces $(\forall x)F(x)$.

Forcing is complete: For every condition C and every limited s, there is an extension of C that forces s or its negation. For if no extension of C forces s, then by (3) C is an extension of C that forces ¬s. Forcing is monotonic: If C forces s and C′ extends C, then C′ forces s. The proof is by induction on the definition of forcing. We do the negation case. If C forces ¬s, no extension of C forces s; but any extension of C′ is an extension of C, so no extension of C′ forces s; so C′ forces ¬s. Forcing is consistent: If C forces s, it does not force ¬s. For if C forces ¬s, no extension of C forces s, and then since C is an extension of C, C does not force s.

An unlimited sentence of the N-language is one in which some quantifiers are unbounded. We extend forcing to unlimited sentences by saying that C forces $(\exists x)F(x)$ if and only if for some abstract a, C forces F(a), or C forces F(τ). The ordinal α' is countable, so there is an enumeration $s_0, s_1, \ldots$ of the sentences, limited and unlimited, of the N-language. We next define a sequence $C_0, C_1, \ldots$ of conditions. The empty set $\varnothing$ is

---

[5] To form this prenex, we need to be able to pull unbounded quantifiers out in front of bounded quantifiers. Suppose that $(\forall x)_\alpha (\exists y)F(x, y)$. The range of δ on $M_\alpha(a)$ is a set, so for some β, $(\forall x)_\alpha (\exists y)_\beta F(x, y)$. We can extend the well-ordering of $M(\beta)$ to $M_\beta(a)$ by putting a first among the members of $M_{\omega+2}(a)$. So without using the axiom of choice, $(\exists f)(\forall x)_\alpha F(x, f(x))$. To deal with $(\exists x)_\alpha (\forall y)F(x, y)$, negate, precede as before, and negate again.

a condition, so there is a condition C extending $\varnothing$ that forces s_0 or $\neg s_0$, and if 0 is not in the domain of C, there is an extension C_0 of C that has 0 in its domain and forces s_0 or $\neg s_0$. Then there is an extension of C_0 that forces s_1 or $\neg s_1$, and if 1 is not in its domain, it has an extension C_1 that has 1 in its domain and forces s_1 or $\neg s_1$. Since C_1 extends C_0, C_1 agrees with C_0 on s_0. Continuing in this way we get a sequence $C_0, C_1,...$ of conditions such that for all n, the numbers 0, 1,..., n are in the domain of C_n, C_n forces s_n or $\neg s_n$, and for $k < n$, C_n agrees with C_k on $s_0,..., s_k$. This is called a complete sequence of conditions. For any complete sequence $C_0, C_1,...$, let a = {n | $C_n(n) = 0$}. Such a set is called generic. Let N = $M_{\alpha'}(a)$ for a generic a. We will show that $N \vDash s$ if and only if for some i, C_i forces s, that $N \vDash ZF$, and that $N \vDash \neg L(a)$.

We prove that $N \vDash s$ if and only if for some i, C_i forces s by induction along the partial order by belowness. If s is $n(i) \in n(j)$, then C_k forces it if and only if it is true, and so, by invariance, true in N; and if it is true in N, it is true and so forced by C_k. Suppose s is $n(j) \in \tau$. If C_i forces s, then $C_i(h(j)) = 0$, so if $h(j) = n$, $C_n(n) = 0$ by monotonicity. Thus $n \in a$, so $N \vDash s$. If $N \vDash s$, $n \in a$, so $C_n(n) = 0$ and C_i forces s. If C_i forces $\neg s$, no extension of C_i forces s. By the induction hypothesis, if $N \vDash s$, some c_j forces s, and any such C_j has an extension that is an extension of C_i. Hence s is not true in N, so $N \vDash \neg s$. If, conversely, $N \vDash \neg s$, s is not true in N, so no C_i forces s. Hence, since $C_0, C_1,...$ is a complete sequence, some C_i forces $\neg s$. The other cases in which s is limited are straightforward. When s is unlimited, we use induction on the number of quantifiers in the prenex.[6]

A condition C weakly forces a sentence s if and only if C forces $\neg \neg s$. Sentences s and t are wf-equivalent if and only if for all $a \subseteq \omega$, $M_{\alpha'}(a) \vDash s$ if and only if $M_{\alpha'}(a) \vDash t$, and t wf-follows from s if and only if for all $a \subseteq \omega$, if $M_{\alpha'}(a) \vDash s$, then $M_{\alpha'}(a) \vDash t$. First we show that if C weakly

[6] The interesting case for unlimited sentences is the induction step when s is $(\forall x)F(x)$. We argue

$N \nvDash (\forall x)F(x)$ iff $N \vDash (\exists x)\neg F(x)$
    iff for some term a that is an abstract or τ, $N \vDash \neg F(a)$
    iff for some a, $N \nvDash F(a)$
    iff for some a, no C_i forces $F(a)$
    iff for some a, some C_i forces $\neg F(a)$
    iff some C_i forces $\neg F(a)$ for some a
    iff some C_i forces $(\exists x)\neg F(x)$.

So $N \vDash (\forall x)F(x)$ iff no C_i forces $(\exists x)\neg F(x)$ iff some C_i forces $\neg(\exists x)\neg F(x)$, which is short for C_i forces $(\forall x)F(x)$.

forces s and t wf-follows from s, then C weakly forces t. So suppose C forces ¬¬s but not ¬¬t. Then some extension C' of C forces ¬t. But for any condition C there is a complete sequence C_0, C_1,... such that $C_0 = C$. So let C_0, C_1,... be a complete sequence such that $C_0 = C'$ and let a = {n | $C_n(n) = 0$}. By the result in the last paragraph, $M_{\alpha'}(a) \vDash \neg t$. But since C forces ¬ ¬s and C_0 extends C, C_0 forces ¬¬s, so by the last paragraph again, $M_{\alpha'}(a) \vDash \neg\neg s$, and thus $M_{\alpha'}(a) \vDash s$. This is impossible, since t wf-follows from s. Hence, second, $N \vDash s$ if and only if for some i, C_i weakly forces s. For if $N \vDash s$, then some C_i forces s, so C_i forces ¬ ¬s by consistency, so C_i weakly forces s, and if C_i weakly forces s, C_i forces ¬¬s, so $N \vDash \neg\neg s$ and thus $N \vDash s$. The second shows that weak forcing has a key property of forcing, and so could be used in its stead. The first shows that weak forcing is sometimes more convenient.

Any generic set contains infinitely many primes. Consider the sentence

$$\neg(\exists x)(x \in \omega \wedge \tau \text{ contains exactly x primes}).$$

This sentence is invariant for N. We show it is true in N. Otherwise $N \vDash (\tau$ contains n(i) primes exactly) for some h(i) ∈ ω. Then for some j, C_j forces (τ contains n(i) primes exactly). Let p_0, p_1,..., p_n be n + 1 = h(i) + 1 distinct primes not in the domain of C_j, pick k bigger than all of p_0, p_1,..., p_n, and let C be a condition extending C_j with domain k such that $C(p_0)$,..., $C(p_n)$ are all 0. Since C extends C_j, C forces (τ contains n(i) primes exactly), so C weakly forces this sentence. But ¬(p_0, p_1,..., $p_n \in \tau$) wf-follows from this sentence, so C weakly forces ¬(p_0, p_1,..., $p_n \in \tau$). But by the choice of C, C forces $p_0 \in \tau$,..., $p_n \in \tau$, so C weakly forces them, and this violates consistency. So a contains infinitely many primes. In the same way we can show that a contains infinitely many composite numbers. We will use a related argument to show that $N \vDash \neg L(\tau)$.

To show that $N \vDash \neg L(\tau)$, we need five preliminary pieces. The first is that for any b ⊆ ω and any limit λ > ω, {x | $M_\lambda(b) \vDash L(x)$} = M(λ). For if $M_\lambda(b) \vDash L(x)$, then x ∈ M(α) for some α ∈ $M_\lambda(b)$. But $M_\lambda(b)$ and M_λ agree on ordinals, so α ∈ M(λ). Hence α < λ, so M(α) ∈ M(λ), and thus x ∈ M(λ). If, conversely, x ∈ M(λ), then since λ is a limit, x ∈ M(α) for some α < λ, and since M(λ) and $M_\lambda(b)$ agree on ordinals, α ∈ $M_\lambda(b)$, so $M_\lambda(b) \vDash L(x)$. The next four pieces are about abstracts. To show that $N \vDash \neg L(\tau)$, we want to compare a with constructible sets. But in the abstract {x_α | F(x)} in the N-language, x is confined not to M(α) but to $M_\alpha(a)$, and the quantifiers in F(x) are bounded not by M(β) for some β

$\le \alpha$ but by $M_\beta(a)$. So we want to shrink abstracts back to constructible sets, and we will do so in two ways. For the first, we use the fact that we can say in the $M_\lambda(b)$-language that $x \in M(\alpha)$. The required predicate is

$$(\exists f)_{\alpha+4}(\exists y)_{\alpha+1}(\text{Cond}(f) \wedge \text{Ordinal}(y)$$
$$\wedge \ y + 1 = \text{the domain of } f \wedge x \in f(y)).$$

Consider an abstract $\{x_\alpha \mid F(x)\}$ of the $M_\lambda(b)$-language. In the first shrinkage, replace any clause $(\forall y)_\beta F(y)$ in the abstract with $(\forall y)(y \in M(\beta) \to F(y))$, replace $(\exists y)_\beta F(y)$ with $(\exists y)(y \in M(\beta) \wedge F(y))$, and replace $\{x_\alpha \mid F(x)\}$ with $\{x_\alpha \mid x \in M(\alpha) \wedge F(x)\}$. The result is still an abstract in the $M_\lambda(b)$-language. Write the transformed abstract as $\{x_\alpha \mid F(x)\}'$. For the second shrinkage, replace each bound $M_\beta(b)$, $\beta \le \alpha$, in a quantifier in $F(x)$ or on x with the bound $M(\beta)$. The result is an abstract in the $M(\lambda)$-language. Write the transformed abstract as $\{x_\alpha \mid F(x)\}''$. Our second piece is that for any $b \subseteq \omega$ and any $\lambda > \omega$,

$$\{x \mid M_\lambda(b) \vDash x \in \{x_\alpha \mid F(x)\}\}' = \{x_\alpha \mid F(x)\}''.$$

This holds because the bounds in $\{x_\alpha \mid F(x)\}'$ and $\{x_\alpha \mid F(x)\}''$ are really the same. The point of this second piece is that any set in $M(\lambda)$ is denoted by some abstract $\{x_\alpha \mid F(x)\}''$ in the $M(\lambda)$-language and is also denoted by the abstract $\{x_\alpha \mid F(x)\}'$ in the $M_\lambda(b)$-language independently of b.[7]

    From the first two pieces we get our third: for any $b \subseteq \omega$, and any limit $\lambda > \omega$ and any abstract $\{x_\alpha \mid F(x)\}$ in the $M_\lambda(b)$-language, $M_\lambda(b) \vDash L(\{x_\alpha \mid F(x)\}')$. For consider any set $\{x_\alpha \mid F(x)\}$ in $M_\lambda(b)$. By our second piece, $\{x_\alpha \mid F(x)\}'$ is $\{x_\alpha \mid F(x)\}''$. But $\{x_\alpha \mid F(x)\}'' \in M(\lambda)$, so $\{x_\alpha \mid F(x)\}' \in M(\lambda)$. Hence by our first piece, $M_\lambda(b) \vDash L(\{x_\alpha \mid F(x)\}')$. Our fourth piece is implicit in what we have already said: for any limit $\lambda > \omega$ and any y, y $\in M(\lambda)$ if and only if for any $b \subseteq \omega$ there is an abstract $\{x_\alpha \mid F(x)\}$ in the $M_\lambda(b)$-language such that $M_\lambda(b) \vDash y = \{x_\alpha \mid F(x)\}'$. For our fifth piece we specialize to $\lambda = \alpha'$ and b, a generic a. Then M is $M(\alpha')$ and N is $M_{\alpha'}(a)$, as before. Let $\{x_\alpha \mid F(x)\}$ be an abstract in the N-language. Then for any natural number h(i), if $h(i) \in \{x_\alpha \mid F(x)\}''$, then $n(i) \in \tau$ wf-follows from $\tau = \{x_\alpha \mid F(x)\}'$, and if $h(i) \notin \{x_\alpha \mid F(x)\}''$, then $n(i) \notin \tau$ wf-follows from $\tau = \{x_\alpha \mid F(x)\}'$.

---

[7] We want two transforms of $\{x_\alpha \mid F(x)\}$, one in the $M_\lambda(b)$-language and one in the $M(\lambda)$-language. The second is a plain way of mentioning the constructible sets. But the first interpreted in $M(\lambda)$ would misread the bound $M_\alpha(b)$ as $M(\alpha)$, and the second interpreted in $M_\lambda(b)$ would misread the bound $M(\alpha)$ as $M_\alpha(b)$.

These five pieces in place, assume for reductio that $N \vDash L(\tau)$. Then by our first piece, $a \in M$. Thus $a = \{x_\alpha \mid F(x)\}''$ for some abstract $\{x_\alpha \mid F(x)\}''$ in the M-language. So by our fourth piece, $N \vDash \tau = \{x_\alpha \mid F(x)\}'$, and thus for some i, C_i weakly forces $\tau = \{x_\alpha \mid F(x)\}'$. Either $\{x_\alpha \mid F(x)\}''$ is infinite or $\omega - \{x_\alpha \mid F(x)\}''$ is infinite. Suppose first that $\tau = \{x_\alpha \mid F(x)\}''$ is infinite. Then there is a natural number $h(j) \in \tau$ but not in the domain of C_i. By the first part of our fifth piece, $n(j) \notin \tau$ wf-follows from $\tau = \{x_\alpha \mid F(x)\}'$, so C_i weakly forces $n(j) \in \tau$. But this cannot be, for since $h(j)$ is not in the domain of C_i, C_i has an extension C such that $C(h(j)) = 1$, so C forces $n(j) \notin \tau$. Suppose second that $\omega - \{x_\alpha \mid F(x)\}''$ is infinite. Then there is a natural number $h(j) \notin \{x_\alpha \mid F(x)\}''$ and not in the domain of C_i. By the second part of our fifth piece, $n(j) \notin \tau$ wf-follows from $\tau = \{x_\alpha \mid F(x)\}'$, so C_i weakly forces $n(j) \in \tau$. But since $n(j)$ is not in the domain of C_i, there is an extension C of C_i such that $C(h(j)) = 0$, and then C forces $n(j) \in \tau$. Hence $N \vDash \neg L(\tau)$.

We have yet to show that $N \vDash ZF$. As with L, it is all but immediate that the axioms of extensionality, null set, infinity, foundation, and closure are true in N. The remaining cases are power set and the replacement axioms. We will look at power sets first. Our aim is to show that for any x in N, the set y of all the subsets of x in N is in N. Any member x of N is denoted by an abstract $\{x_\alpha \mid F(x)\}$ of the N-language. (This includes a, which is denoted by $\{x_\omega \mid x \in \tau\}$.) So we aim to show that for any abstract $\{x_\alpha \mid F(x)\}$, $N \vDash (\exists y)(\forall z)(z \in y \leftrightarrow z \subseteq \{x_\alpha \mid F(x)\})$. The clause $z \subseteq \{x_\alpha \mid F(x)\}$ expands to $(\forall u)(u \in z \rightarrow u \in \{x_\alpha \mid F(x)\})$. Any member of a subset of $\{x_\alpha \mid F(x)\}$ is a member of $\{x_\alpha \mid F(x)\}$, and so in $M_\alpha(a)$. Hence the expansion is equivalent to $(\forall u)_\alpha(u \in z \rightarrow u \in \{x_\alpha \mid F(x)\})$, which is equivalent to $(\forall u)_\alpha(u \in z \rightarrow F(u)\}$. So we aim to show that $N \vDash (\exists y)(\forall z)$ $(z \in y \leftrightarrow (\forall u)_\alpha(u \in z \rightarrow F(u)))$. It suffices for there to be an abstract $\{z_\beta \mid G(z)\}$ such that $N \vDash (\forall v)_\beta(\{v \in \{z_\beta \mid G(z)\} \leftrightarrow (\forall u)_\alpha(u \in z \rightarrow F(u)))$. The obvious choice for $G(z)$ is $z \subseteq \{x_\alpha \mid F(x)\}$, or, expanded, $(\forall w)_\alpha(w \in z \rightarrow F(w)\}$. The problem is the ordinal β.

We will show that β can be specified in M independently of the generic set a used in forming N from M. This is important because it enables us to use the fact that M is a model for ZF. We could call this generic uniformity. We will hold the ordinal α and (the gödel sequence of) the formula $F(x)$ fixed throughout our argument; remember that no ordinal in the gödel sequence of $F(x)$ is greater than α. For each ordinal γ in N and for the gödel sequence of each formula $H(x)$ of the N-language such that $\{x_\gamma \mid H(x)\}$ is well-formed, let $R^{\gamma,H}$ (C, β, G)

be the relation C forces $\{x_\beta \mid G(x)\} \in \{x_\gamma \mid H(x)\} \wedge \beta \leq \alpha$. Here C is a condition, and thus a hereditary finite set in $M(\omega)$, and thus in M. The ordinal β is no bigger than $\alpha < \alpha'$, so $\alpha + 1$, the set of all such β, is in M too. The ordinal sequence of the formula $G(x)$ of the N-language is a finite function whose domain is a natural number and whose range is the set of ordinals no bigger than α, which is the set $\alpha + 1$. So the set of all such gödel sequences is a subset of $M_{\alpha+\omega}$, assuming we are in the interesting case in which α is infinite. (We go up to ω because there is no finite bound on the length of a formula.) Therefore, because forcing for limited sentences of the N-language is definable in the M-language and because M is a model for ZF, for each γ and H, the relation $R^{\gamma,H}$ is first-order definable over $M(\alpha+\omega+5)$ and thus a member of $M(\alpha+\omega+6)$. So each $R^{\gamma,H}$ is a member of M.

For each α, let CR_α be the collection of all the relations $R^{\gamma,H}$ for $\gamma < \alpha'$ and H in the N-language such that $\{x_\gamma \mid H(x)\}$ is well-formed, so the bounds in H are no bigger than γ. Then $CR_\alpha \in M$. One might wonder about this because we have not restricted γ. But for each γ and H, $R^{\gamma,H} \in M(\alpha + \omega + 6)$. Since $M(\alpha + \omega + 6) \in M$ and the axiom of power sets is true in M, $P(M(\alpha + \omega + 6)) \in M(\theta)$ for some $\theta < \alpha'$. But $CR_\alpha \subseteq P(M(\alpha + \omega + 6))$, so CR_α is first-order definable over $M(\theta)$, and $CR_\alpha \in M(\theta + 1)$. For each x in CR_α, let $\gamma^*(x)$ be the least ordinal γ such that x is $R^{\gamma,H}$ for some H, and let $H^*(x)$ be the earliest H in M such that x is $R^{\gamma^*(x),H}$. (Remember that M is well-ordered without choice.) Then for each $x \in CR_\alpha$ there are a unique γ^* and H^* such that x is R^{γ^*,H^*}. So since $CR_\alpha \in M$ and M verifies the replacement axioms, the range of γ^*, H^* on CR_α is a set $D \in M$. $D = \{\gamma \mid (\exists x)(x \in CR_\alpha \wedge (\exists H)(\gamma = \gamma^*(x) \wedge x = R^{\gamma^*,H^*}))\}$. Since D is a set of ordinals in M and M is a model for ZF, there is an upper bound δ in M for D. Observe that we found δ entirely within M; we did not need anything special about a, N, or the complete sequence of conditions used to get a.

The ordinal δ is what we wanted. Suppose $z \in N$ is a subset of a set $\{x_\alpha \mid F(x)\}$ in N. Then for some γ and H, z is $\{x_\gamma \mid H(x)\}$ and

(1) $N \vDash \{x_\gamma \mid H(x)\} \subseteq \{x_\alpha \mid F(x)\}$.

Consider any $y \in N$ such that

(2) $N \vDash y \in \{x_\gamma \mid H(x)\}$.

Then

(3) $N \vDash y \in \{x_\alpha \mid F(x)\}$

and y is denoted by an abstract $\{x_\beta \mid G(x)\}$ in the N-language, where $\beta < \alpha$. Hence

(4) $N \vDash \{x_\beta \mid G(x)\} \in \{x_\gamma \mid H(x)\}$,

so for some $i \in \omega$

(5) C_i forces $\{x_\beta \mid G(x)\} \in \{x_\gamma \mid H(x)\} \wedge \beta \leq \alpha$.

Thus

(6) $R^{\gamma,H}(C_i, \beta, G)$.

Hence

(7) $R^{\gamma^*,H^*}(C_i, \beta, G)$.

Thus

(8) C_i forces $\{x_\beta \mid G(x)\} \in \{x_{\gamma^*} \mid H^*(x)\} \wedge \beta \leq \alpha$,

so

(9) $N \vDash \{x_\beta \mid G(x)\} \in \{x_{\gamma^*} \mid H^*(x)\}$,

that is,

(10) $N \vDash y \in \{x_{\gamma^*} \mid H^*(x)\}$.

Having deduced 10 from 2, we have

(11) $N \vDash \{x_{\gamma^*} \mid H^*(x)\} \subseteq \{x_\gamma \mid H(x)\}$.

Then from 1 and 11 we have

(12) $N \vDash \{x_\gamma \mid H(x)\} \subseteq \{x_{\gamma^*} \mid H^*(x)\} \cap \{x_\alpha \mid F(x)\}$.

The inferences from 4 to 10 are reversible, so we can infer

(13) $N \vDash \{x_{\gamma^*} \mid H^*(x)\} \cap \{x_\alpha \mid F(x)\} \subseteq \{x_\gamma \mid H(x)\}$.

Thus

(14) $N \vDash \{x_\gamma \mid H(x)\} = \{x_{\gamma^*} \mid H^*(x)\} \cap \{x_\alpha \mid F(x)\}$.

But $\gamma^* < \delta$, and we can ensure that $\alpha < \delta$, so

(15) $N \vDash (\exists x)_\delta(x = \{x_{\gamma^*} \mid H^*(x)\} \cap \{x_\alpha \mid F(x)\})$.

So

(16) $N \vDash (\exists x)_\delta(x = \{x_\gamma \mid H(x)\})$.

But z = $\{x_\gamma \mid H(x)\}$ was any subset of $\{x_\alpha \mid F(x)\}$ in N, so all subsets of $\{x_\alpha \mid F(x)\}$ in N are members of $M_\delta(a)$.

Putnam credits this argument to Leslie Tharp. It depends on forcing for limited sentences of the N-language being definable in the M-language and on the totality of conditions being small enough to be a set in M.

Replacement remains. Replacement says that for any formula F(x, y) it is an axiom of ZF that for any set z, if for every x in z there is a unique y such that F(x, y), then there is a set of all those y such that F(x, y) for some x in z. Interpreted in N, the quantifiers in F(x, y) need not be bounded. As we did for L, suppose F(x, y) is

$$(\forall z)(\exists w)(\forall u)(\exists v)G(z, w, u, v, x, y),$$

where there are no quantifiers in G and where any abstracts in it have been eliminated by their implicit definitions (though τ will remain). Suppose that for any member x of a set s, there is a unique y such that F(x, y). But s is denoted by an abstract $\{x_\alpha \mid H(x)\}$, so our supposition is that $(\forall x)_\alpha(H(x) \to (\exists! y)F(x, y))$. Our aim is to show that there is a t in N such that t is $\{y \mid (\exists x)_\alpha(H(x) \wedge F(x, y))\}$. If this last expression were an abstract of the N-language, we would be home and dry, but it is not because neither the y nor the quantifiers in F are bounded. To bound y we use techniques like those we used to show that the axiom of power sets holds in N, and once we have bounded x we will prove a reflection principle to bound the quantifiers in F, as we did for L.

To bound x, we want an ordinal β depending on α, H, and F such that for all y in N, if $(\exists x)_\alpha(H(x) \wedge F(x, y))$, then $y \in M_\beta(a)$. Fix α, H, and F for this argument. For each ordinal γ in N and each formula J(x) of the N-language such that $\{x_\gamma \mid J(x)\}$ is well-formed, let $R^{\gamma, J}(C, \delta, K)$ be the relation

C forces $\{x_\delta \mid K(x)\} \in \{x_\alpha \mid H(x)\} \wedge \delta \le \alpha \wedge F(\{x_\delta \mid K(x)\}, \{x_\delta \mid J(x)\})$
   $\wedge (\forall y)(F(\{x_\delta \mid K(x)\}, y) \to y = \{x_\delta \mid J(x)\}).$

Because F is fixed, this relation is definable in the M-language. As with power sets, all the conditions are in $M(\omega)$, the ordinals δ not bigger than α form $\alpha + 1$, and the gödel sequences of the formulae J(x) are all in $M(\alpha + \omega)$. (Assuming $\alpha \ge \omega$, the interesting case.) Then, as before, for each γ, J, and F, the relation $R^{\gamma, J}$ is first-order definable over an $M_\theta(a)$ of which $M(\omega) \times (\alpha + 1) \times M(\alpha + \omega)$ is a subset, and there is such a θ, since $M \vDash ZF$. Next, for each F, let $CR_{\alpha, F}$ be the collection of all $R^{\gamma,K}$ for $\gamma < \alpha'$ and K in the N-language such that $\{x_\gamma \mid K(x)\}$ is well-formed. Since $R^{\gamma,J}$ is fodo $M_0(a)$, $CR_{\alpha,F}$ is first-order definable over an $M_\pi(a)$ of which $P(M(\omega) \times (\alpha + 1) \times M(\alpha + \omega))$ is a subset, and there is such a π, since $M \vDash ZF$. For each x in $CR_{\alpha,F}$, let $\gamma^*(x)$ and K^* be the least γ,K such that x is $R^{\gamma,K}$. Then γ^* is functional on $CR_{\alpha,F}$, $CR_{\alpha,F}$ is a set in M, and replacement holds in M, so the range of γ^* on $CR_{\alpha,F}$ is a set in M. This set $D = \{\gamma \mid (\exists x)(x \in CR_{\alpha,F} \wedge \gamma = \gamma^*(x))\}$ is a set of ordinals, so there is an upper bound β for D in M. This β is the ordinal we wanted.

To show this, suppose that $y \in N$ and

(1) $N \vDash (\exists z)(z \in \{x_\alpha \mid H(x)\} \wedge F(z, y))$.

Then for some $\delta \leq \alpha$ and some K

(2) $N \vDash \{x_\delta \mid K(x)\} \in \{x_\alpha \mid H(x)\} \wedge F(\{x_\delta \mid K(x)\}, y)$,

and for some γ and J

(3) $N \vDash \{x_\delta \mid K(x)\} \in \{x_\alpha \mid H(x)\} \wedge F(\{x_\delta \mid K(x)\}, \{x_\gamma \mid J(x)\})$.

By hypothesis

(4) $N \vDash (\forall x)(x \in \{x_\alpha \mid H(x)\} \rightarrow (\exists!y)F(x, y))$

and $\delta \leq \alpha$, so

(5) $N \vDash \{x_\delta \mid K(x)\} \in \{x_\alpha \mid H(x)\} \wedge \delta \leq \alpha \wedge F(\{x_\delta \mid K(x)\}, \{x_\gamma \mid J(x)\})$
     $\wedge (\forall y)(F(\{x_\delta \mid K(x)\}, y) \rightarrow y = \{x_\gamma \mid J(x)\})$.

Hence for some $i \in \omega$

(6) C_i forces $\{x_\delta \mid K(x)\} \in \{x_\alpha \mid H(x)\} \wedge \delta \leq \alpha \wedge F(\{x_\delta \mid K(x)\}, \{x_\gamma \mid J(x)\})$
     $\wedge (\forall y)(F(\{x_\delta \mid K(x)\}, y) \rightarrow y = \{x_\gamma \mid J(x)\})$,

so

(7) $R^{\gamma,J}(C_i, \delta, K)$,

and thus

(8) $R^{\gamma^*,J^*}(C_i, \delta, K)$.

Hence

(9) C_i forces $\{x_\delta \mid K(x)\} \in \{x_\alpha \mid H(x)\} \wedge \delta \leq \alpha \wedge F(\{x_\alpha \mid K(x)\}, \{x_{\gamma^*} \mid J^*(x)\})$
     $\wedge (\forall y)(F(\{x_\delta \mid K(x)\}, y) \rightarrow y - \{x_{\gamma^*} \mid J^*(x)\})$,

so

(10) $N \vDash \{x_\delta \mid K(x)\} \in \{x_\alpha \mid H(x)\} \wedge \delta \leq \alpha \wedge F(\{x_\alpha \mid K(x)\}, \{x_{\gamma^*} \mid J^*(x)\})$
$\wedge (\forall y)(F(\{x_\delta \mid K(x)\}, y) \rightarrow y = \{x_{\gamma^*} \mid J^*(x)\})$.

From the last conjunct of 5

(11) $N \vDash (\forall y)(F(\{x_\delta \mid K(x)\}, y) \rightarrow y = \{x_\gamma \mid J(x)\})$

and from the third of 10

(12) $N \vDash F(\{x_\delta \mid K(x)\}, \{x_{\gamma^*} \mid J^*(x)\})$,

so

(13) $N \vDash \{x_{\gamma^*} \mid J^*(x)\} = \{x_\gamma \mid J(x)\}$.

But $\gamma^* < \beta < \alpha'$, so $\{x_{\gamma^*} \mid J^*(x)\} \in M_\beta(a)$. Since $\{x_\gamma \mid J(x)\}$ denotes y, so does $\{x_{\gamma^*} \mid J^*(x)\}$. So all the members of the range of f on $\{x_\alpha \mid H(x)\}$ are in $M_\beta(a)$.

With β in hand, we next bound the quantifiers in $F(x, y)$, and for this purpose we use a reflection principle. To sketch an argument for this principle briefly, suppose $F(x, y)$ is $(\forall z)(\exists u)G(z, u, x, y)$, where G contains neither abstracts nor quantifiers, $x \in \{x_\alpha \mid H(x)\}$, and $y \in \{x_\beta \mid P(x)\}$. If for some $\{x_\gamma \mid J(x)\}$

$$N \vDash (\forall u)\neg G(\{x_\gamma \mid J(x)\}, u, x, y),$$

then for some $i \in \omega$

$$C_i \text{ forces } (\forall u)\neg G(\{x_\gamma \mid J(x)\}, u, x, y).$$

For fixed G and depending on α and β we define sets $S^{\gamma, J}$ of conditions as we defined $R^{\gamma, J}$ earlier. The totality of these sets is again a set in M. We next define the *-operations as before, apply replacement in M, and again take an upper bound δ. Reasoning as before, we show that when there is a z in N such that $N \vDash (\forall u)\neg G(z, u, x, y)$, then there is one in $M_\delta(a)$. Hence

$$N \vDash (\exists z)(\forall u)\neg G(z, u, x, y)$$

if and only if

$$N \vDash (\exists z)_\delta(\forall u)\neg G(z, u, x, y),$$

and so

$$N \vDash (\forall z)(\exists u)G(z, u, x, y)$$

if and only if

$$N \vDash (\forall z)_\delta (\exists u) G(z, u, x, y).$$

Continuing in this way, we establish the reflection principle. Replacement for F follows as it did in L. So N is a model for ZF.

Next we squeeze some syntax out of our semantics. Let Models be a sentence saying that there is a set that is a model for ZF. We have deduced from ZF plus Models that there is a set that is a model for ZF plus $(\exists y)(y \subseteq \omega \wedge \neg L(y))$. From this we aim to show that if ZF is consistent, then so is ZF plus $(\exists y)(y \subseteq \omega \wedge \neg L(\tau))$. To do this we look again at our deduction from ZF plus Models that N is a model for ZF plus $(\tau \subseteq \omega \wedge \neg L(\tau))$. When we showed that the axiom of power sets holds in N, we proved that for all α and all F in the N-language, $N \vDash (\exists y)(P(\{x_\alpha \mid F(x)\}) = y)$. To prove this we used replacement in M. But we did not use infinitely many replacement axioms. Instead we used just one replacement axiom with two free variables, one for α and one for F. Similarly, when we prove that any single replacement axiom (from the N-language) holds in N, we use only finitely many replacement axioms that hold in M.[8]

Let ZF_n be the first n axioms of ZF (in some reasonable enumeration). In showing that $N \vDash \tau \subseteq \omega \wedge \neg L(t)$, we did not use the fact that $M \vDash ZF$ at all. For any single replacement axiom A (in the N-language), in order to show that $N \vDash A$ we do not need $M \vDash ZF$ but only $M \vDash ZF_n$ for some n computable from the sentence A. More generally, let Models (ZF_n) be a sentence saying that there is a set that is a model for ZF_n. Then there is a primitive recursive function f such that from ZF plus Models $(ZF_{f(n)})$ we can deduce that N is a model for ZF_n plus $(\exists y)$ $(y \subseteq \omega \wedge \neg L(y))$. But, as we shall see, for any $n \in \omega$, we can in ZF prove Models (ZF_n). (This says that for any n there is a proof of Models (ZF_n) in ZF; different n call for different proofs, and these quantifiers do not commute.) Hence, for every n we can prove in ZF that there is a set that is a model for ZF_n plus $(\exists y)(y \subseteq \omega \wedge \neg L(y))$. From this last we can squeeze out the proof theoretic syntax we want. For if ZF plus $(\exists y)(y \subseteq \omega \wedge \neg L(y))$ is inconsistent, then by the finiteness of proof, there is an n such that ZF_n plus $(\exists y)(y \subseteq \omega \wedge \neg L(y))$ is inconsistent. We can formalize this proof in ZF, and we can show in ZF that any theory with a model

---

[8] That we can use replacement axioms with parameters depends on our being able to specify the ordinals in M we need uniformly from what we are given, like α and the ordinal sequence of F.

is consistent. Hence we could prove in ZF that no set is a model for ZF_n plus $(\exists y)(y \subseteq \omega \wedge \neg L(y))$. Then, since we can prove in ZF that some set is a model for ZF_n plus $(\exists y)(y \subseteq \omega \wedge \neg L(y))$, ZF would be inconsistent. (This argument depends on the fact that ZF has infinitely many axioms; other arguments work for systems like NBG that can be presented with only finitely many nonlogical axioms.)

Fix $n \in \omega$. We want to prove in ZF that there is a set that is a model for ZF_n. L is of course not a set. But there is a primitive recursive function g such that we need only $g(n)$ axioms of ZF to show that L is a model for ZF_n. We can well-order L without using the axiom of choice. Hence we can in ZF define Skolem functions for the existential quantifiers in the prenexes of the $g(n)$ axioms of ZF we use in showing that L is a model for ZF_n. Using these finitely many Skolem functions, we can define in ZF a countable Skolem hull H of L for ZF_n. Then H is a set that is a model for ZF_n.

Now we turn to the axiom of choice. We will show that if ZF is consistent, it remains consistent if we add that there is a set of sets of natural numbers that is not well-ordered. We again start from $M = M(\alpha')$, and we form the N-language by adding to the M-language countably many new individual constants $\tau_1, \tau_2, \ldots$ and one more new individual constant τ. The constants $\tau_1, \ldots$ will denote generic sets of natural numbers, and τ will denote the set of these generic sets. We earlier took conditions to be functions from a natural number j into 2. For $k < j$, $C(k) = 0$ meant that k is to go in the generic set, and $C(k) = 1$, that k is to stay out. But now we have an infinity of generic sets to work out, and we have to keep track of which of them a condition puts a natural number into. So this time we will take a condition to be a consistent finite set of atomic sentences of the form $n(j) \in \tau_i$ where $n(j)$ is a numeral, or the negation of such a sentence.[9] Such a set is consistent if and only if for no j and i are both $n(j) \in \tau_i$ and its negation in the set. In the old sense, when a condition settled whether k is in a generic set, it also settled the question for all numbers less than k, but this may fail for conditions in the new sense. But now they can address all of $\tau_1, \tau_2, \ldots$. For each i let the gödel number of τ_i be 17^i and let that of τ be 19. Then the set of gödel sequences of members of a condition is a member of $M(\omega)$, and the set of all of them is fodo $M(\omega)$.

<hr/>

[9] The terms $\emptyset$ and $\{\emptyset\}$ for hereditary finite sets are numerals, and if $\{n(k_1), \ldots, n(k_m)\}$ is a numeral, then so is $\{n(k_1), \ldots, n(k_m), \{n(k_1), \ldots, n(k_m)\}\}$. Extending a usage of Quine's, atomic sentences and their negations could be called literals. See his *Methods of Logic*, rev. ed. (New York: Henry Holt, 1959), 56.

We define forcing as before with two exceptions. First, a condition C forces $n(j) \in \tau_i$ where $n(j)$ is a numeral if and only if the sentence $n(j) \in \tau_i$ is a member of C. Second, for any abstract $\{x_\alpha \mid F(x)\}$ of the N-language, C forces $\{x_\alpha \mid F(x)\} \in \tau$ if and only if for some i, C forces $\tau_i \in \{x_\alpha \mid F(x)\}$, namely, $(\forall x)_\alpha (x \in \tau_i \leftrightarrow F(x))$. Since we added only countably many constants to the M-language to form the N-language, the set of sentences of the N-language is still countable. Thus, as before, there is a complete sequence of conditions, that is, a sequence of $C_1, C_2,\ldots$ of conditions such that $C_n \subseteq C_{n+1}$ and every sentence in the N-language is settled by some condition in the sequence. For each i, let a_i be the set of all natural numbers $h(j)$ such that the sentence $n(j) \in \tau_i$ is in some condition in the complete sequence, and let a be the set of all the a_i. For $\alpha < \omega$, we let $N(\alpha)$ be $M(\alpha)$, let $N(\omega + 1)$ be $M(\omega + 1) \cup \{a_1, a_2,\ldots\}$, and let $N(\omega + 2)$ be $\{x \mid x$ fodo $N(\omega + 1) \cup \{a\}$; for $\alpha \geq \omega + 2$, let $N(\alpha + 1)$ be $\{x \mid x$ fodo $N(\alpha + 1)$; for limits $\lambda \leq \alpha'$, let $N(\lambda)$ be the union of the $N(\alpha)$ for $\alpha < \lambda$, and let N be $N(\alpha')$. As before, for any sentence (limited or unlimited) s of the N-language, s is true in N if and only if some condition in the complete sequence forces s, and the same goes again for weak forcing.

Note first that for different numbers i and j, the empty condition weakly forces $\tau_i \neq \tau_j$.[10] For suppose some condition weakly forces $\tau_i = \tau_j$. Pick a natural number $h(m)$ not mentioned in C and let C′ be C together with $n(m) \in \tau_i$ and $n(m) \notin \tau_j$. Then C′ weakly forces $n(m) \in \tau_i \wedge n(m) \notin \tau_j$, so since $\tau_i \neq \tau_j$ wf-follows from this conjunction, C′ weakly forces $\tau_i \neq \tau_j$. But since C′ extends C, C′ weakly forces $\tau_i = \tau_j$, and this violates the consistency of weak forcing. (Similarly, $a_i \cap a_j$ is always infinite.)

Note second that if t is an abstract in the N-language in which τ_i does not occur, then $\tau_i \neq t$ is true in N. Suppose for reductio that $\tau_i = t$ is true in N for some abstract t without τ_i. Then $\tau_i = t$ is weakly forced by some condition C in the complete sequence. Let τ_j occur in neither C nor t, and let s be the syntactical operation of swapping τ_i for τ_j and vice versa. Then, by induction, s(C) weakly forces $s(\tau_i = t)$. But $s(\tau_i = t)$ is $\tau_j = t$, so s(C) weakly forces $\tau_j = t$. C and s(C) differ only on τ_i and τ_j, C does not mention τ_j, and s(C) does not mention τ_i, so $C \cup s(C)$ is a consistent condition. Hence $C \cup s(C)$ weakly forces $\tau_i = t \wedge \tau_j = t$, so $C \cup s(C)$ weakly forces $\tau_i = \tau_j$, contrary to the previous paragraph. (This argument is due to Christopher Hill.)

Now we can show that $(\exists x)(x$ well-orders a) is not true in N. Suppose for reductio that for some abstract t in the N-language, "t well-orders a"

---

[10] $\tau_i \neq \tau_j$ is short for $\neg(\forall x)_\omega (x \in \tau_i \leftrightarrow x \in \tau_j)$.

The Evolution of Logic

is true in N. Let $\tau_1, \tau_2, ..., \tau_n$ include all the new constants for generic sets in the N-language that occur in t. Let τ be an abstract of the N-language for the t-least member of a other than $\tau_1, ..., \tau_n$.[11] Since a is infinite, τ denotes a member a_i of a, and the term τ_i does not occur in τ. Then by the supposition for reductio, $\tau_i = \tau$ is true in N, but by the previous paragraph this sentence is not true in N. The argument that $N \vDash ZF$ is as before, as is squeezing syntax from the semantics. The shape of this argument for the independence of the axiom of choice is by Hilary Putnam and Solomon Feferman.

Now we turn to the continuum hypothesis. Our aim is to show that if ZF is consistent, then so is ZF plus the axiom of choice and the denial of the continuum hypothesis. Let $\omega(1)^M$, $\omega(2)^M, ...$ be the uncountable cardinals of M. These are ordinals of M, and so less than α', which means they are really countable ordinals. But when we cut back to the minimal model M, we lost the functions that map $\omega(1)^M$ one–one into $\omega(0)$, those that map $\omega(2)^M$ one–one into $\omega(1)^M$, and those mapping it one–one into $\omega(0)$, and so on; uncountable cardinals are not invariant. Our plan is to add a sequence a_β of generic sets to M, one for each $\beta < \omega(2)^M$. Any two of them will be different, so the continuum hypothesis will fail in the model N we build. Since we also want the axiom of choice to hold in N, we will also add the relation $\{< a_\beta, a_\gamma > \mid \beta < \gamma\}$.

As before, we begin with the M-language. For each $\beta < \omega(2)^M$, we add a distinct new constant τ_β, and we add yet one more new constant τ. Since $\omega(2)^M$ is countable, the N-language is still countable. Conditions are defined as for the independence of the axiom of choice. Forcing is defined as before except that now we say that for any abstract a, a condition C forces $a \in \tau$ if and only if there are ordinals β and γ such that $\beta < \gamma$ and C forces $a = <\tau_\beta, \tau_\gamma>$. Because the N-language is countable, there is a complete sequence of conditions. For each β, let a_β be the set of natural numbers h(j) such that the sentence $n(j) \in \tau_\beta$ is a member of some condition in the complete sequence, and let a be $\{< a_\beta, a_\gamma > \mid \beta < \gamma\}$. For $\alpha \leq \omega$, N(α) is M(α), N($\omega + 1$) = M($\omega + 1$) $\cup$ $\{a_\beta \mid \beta < \omega(2)^M\}$, and N($\omega + 2$) = $\{x \mid x$ fodo N($\omega + 1$)$\} \cup \{a\}$; for $\alpha \geq \omega + 2$, N($\alpha + 1$) = $\{x \mid x$ fodo N(α)$\}$; for limits $\lambda \leq \alpha'$, N(λ) is the union of the N(α) for $\alpha < \lambda$, and N = N(α'). As before,

---

[11] τ could be $\{x_{\omega+1} \mid (\exists y)_{\omega+1}(y \in a \land x \in y \land y \neq t_1 \land ... \land y \neq t_n \land (\forall z)_{\omega+1}(z \in a \land z$ is t-earlier than $y \rightarrow z = t_1 \lor ... \lor z = t_n))\}$, but the bound on x may need to be raised so as not to be surpassed by bounds in t.

for any sentence s of the N-language, s is true in N if and only if some condition in the complete sequence forces (or weakly forces) s. The argument that N is a model for ZF is as before.[12] We can well-order N by inserting the a_β in a-order at the beginning of the M-order of $N(\omega + 1)$, and by inserting a at the beginning of the M-order of $N(\omega + 2)$, so the axiom of choice is true in N.

We can show as before that for $\beta \neq \gamma$, $\tau_\beta \neq \tau_\gamma$ is true in N. For each β, $\tau_\beta \subseteq \omega$ is true in N. Moreover, it is also true in N that a is a well-ordering of the a_β of order-type $\omega(2)^M$. But this does not quite show that the continuum hypothesis fails in N. For we do not yet know that $\omega(2)^M$ is a cardinal in N, and is $\omega(2)^N$ in particular. Perhaps our additions have allowed a function mapping $\omega(2)^M$ one–one into $\omega(1)^N$ or even $\omega(0)$ to slip back into N. We need to show that the cardinals of M are preserved in N. We show this in several steps.

Our first step is called the countable chain lemma: in any set there are at most ω conditions any two of which are inconsistent with each other. We will use an infinitary pigeonhole principle. The finitary pigeonhole principle says that if there are more pigeons than coops in which they roost, then more than one pigeon roosts in some coop. Our infinitary version says that if uncountably many things are distributed into at most countably many sets, then at least one of these sets contains uncountably many things. Now suppose for reductio that S is an uncountable set of conditions any two of which are inconsistent with each other. For each $n \in \omega$ let S_n be the set of conditions in S of cardinality n. Then by our infinitary pigeonhole principle, there is an n such that S_n is uncountable. Let k be the least such n; obviously $k > 0$. Pick C from S_k and let $a_1, \ldots, a_k$ be the members of C. For each $i = 1, \ldots, k$, let a_i^* be the negation of a_i if a_i is not negated, but a_i without its negation if a_i is negated; a_i^* contradicts a_i. For each $i = 1, \ldots, k$, let T_i be the set of all conditions C such that $a_i^* \in C$ and $C \in S_k$. Then $\{C\} \cup T_1 \cup \ldots \cup T_k$ is S_k, so by our infinitary pigeonhole principle, some T_i is uncountable. Let T be the set of conditions C of cardinal $k - 1$ such that $C \cup \{a_i^*\} \in T_i$. For any two conditions C_1 and C_2 in T, $C_1 \cup \{a_i^*\}$ and $C_2 \cup \{a_i^*\}$ are in T_i, and thus in S, so they are inconsistent. But they agree on a_i, so C_1 and C_2 are inconsistent. Hence T is an uncountable set of conditions

---

12 The totality of conditions is a set in M, since it has $\omega(2)^M$ members, but it is not countable in M. Still, all we need to show that N is a model for ZF is that the conditions form a *set* in M. The positive powers of 17 well-ordered in type $\omega(2)^M$ will do as gödel numbers for the generic terms τ_β.

all of cardinal $k - 1$, and any two of them inconsistent, contrary to the choice of k. Hence S is at most countable. (Our pigeonhole principle is proved in ZF using the axiom of choice too. Thus, since M and N are models for ZFC, the lemma holds in M and N.)

Let us show first that $\omega(1)^M = \omega(1)^N$. It is clear that if $\alpha < \omega(1)^M$, then $\alpha < \omega(1)^N$, since any enumeration of α in M is still available in N. The difficulty is to show that there is still no enumeration of $\omega(1)^M$ in N. For this it suffices to show that for any abstract t in the M-language, the sentence

$$(t \text{ is a function} \wedge \text{Dom}(t) \subseteq \omega \wedge \text{Range}(t) \subseteq \omega(1)^M)$$
$$\rightarrow (\exists \alpha)(\alpha < \omega(1)^M \wedge \text{Range}(t) \subseteq \alpha$$

is true in N, for this shows that no function with domain ω can have range all of $\omega(1)^M$, and thus that $\omega(1)^M$ is still uncountable in N. (We may only mention t in reasoning about M, but we may use it in reasoning about N.) So suppose the sentence

$$t \text{ is a function} \wedge \text{Dom}(t) \subseteq \omega \wedge \text{Range}(t) \subseteq \omega(1)^M$$

is true in N. Then some condition C_i in the complete sequence weakly forces this sentence. We can define in M a well-ordering of the conditions. For each $n \in \omega$, let

$$F(n) = \{C \mid C_i \subseteq C \wedge (\exists \alpha)(C \text{ weakly forces } <n, \alpha> \in t$$
$$\wedge \, C \text{ is the first condition extending } C \text{ that weakly forces}$$
$$<n, \alpha> \in t)\}.$$

For each n, $F(n)$ is a set in M (by separating it from the set of conditions). Since F is functional on its domain $\omega \in M$ and replacement holds in M, the range of F is in M too. Since F is separable from the cross product of ω and the range of F, F is also in M.

Next we show that the sentence $(\forall n)(F(n) \text{ is countable})$ is true in M. Let C_1 and C_2 be different conditions in $F(n)$. Then C_1 weakly forces $<n, \alpha_1> \in t$ for some α_1, and C_2 weakly forces $<n, \alpha_2> \in t$ for some α_2, and C_1 and C_2 are the first conditions to weakly force these sentences. If $\alpha_1 = \alpha_2$, C_1 and C_2 weakly force $<n, \alpha_1> \in t$, but since $C_1 \neq C_2$, one of them is earlier in the well-order of conditions, so the other is not in $F(n)$. Thus $\alpha_1 \neq \alpha_2$. If C_1 and C_2 were compatible, $C_1 \cup C_2$ would be a condition extending both. Then since each weakly forces t is a function, $C_1 \cup C_2$ would weakly force t is a function $\wedge <n, \alpha_1> \in t \wedge <n, \alpha_2> \in t$, so $C_1 \cup C_2$ would weakly force $\alpha_1 = \alpha_2$. This is impossible, for since $\alpha_1 \neq \alpha_2$ is true in N, no extension of C_i can weakly force $\neg(\alpha_1 \neq \alpha_2)$. Hence C_1 and C_2 are inconsistent, and so, by the countable chain lemma, F(n) is countable.

Now we show that the sentence

$$(\exists\alpha)(\alpha < \omega(1)^M \wedge (\forall n, C, \beta)((n \in \omega \wedge C \in F(n) \wedge C$$
$$\text{weakly forces } <n, \beta> \in t) \rightarrow \beta < \alpha)$$

is true in M. By the previous paragraph, $\{\beta \mid (\exists C)(C \in F(n) \wedge C$ weakly forces $<n, \beta> \in t)\}$ is a countable (in M) set of countable (in M) ordinals. So if $F^*(n)$ is its least upper bound, then for all n, $F^*(n)$ is countable (in M). Thus $F^*(0)$, $F^*(1)$,... is a countable (in M) sequence of countable (in M) ordinals, and hence has a countable (in M) limit α. Thus $\alpha < \omega(1)^M$.

To return to the preservation of $\omega(1)^M$ in N, recall our supposition that the sentence

$$\text{t is a function} \wedge \text{Dom(t)} \subseteq \omega \wedge \text{Range(t)} \subseteq \omega(1)^M$$

is true in N. Suppose that for some β greater than the α of the previous paragraph, the sentence $<n, \beta> \in t$ is true in N. Then for some j, C_j weakly forces $<n, \beta> \in t$, and by picking j large enough, we may arrange that $C_i \subseteq C_j$. So there is a first (in the well-ordering of conditions) condition C that extends C_i and weakly forces $<n, \beta> \in t$. But then $C \in$ F(n), so $\beta < \alpha$. This is impossible. Hence the sentence $(\exists\alpha)(\alpha < \omega(1)^M \wedge$ Range(t) $\subseteq \alpha)$ is true in N. Thus $\omega(1)^M = \omega(1)^N$.

To show that $\omega(2)^M = \omega(1)^N$, it is enough to show that for any abstract t of the N-language, the sentence

$$(\text{t is a function} \wedge \text{Dom(t)} \subseteq \omega(1) \wedge \text{Range(t)} \subseteq \omega(2)^M)$$
$$\rightarrow (\exists\alpha)(\alpha < \omega(2)^M \wedge \text{Range(t)} \subseteq \alpha)$$

is true in N. So we suppose the antecedent true in N. Then it is weakly forced by some condition C_i. For each γ in $\omega(1)^M$ (which is $\omega(1)^N$), we let $F(\gamma)$ be the set of first extensions of C_i that weakly force $<\gamma, \alpha> \in t$ for some α. As before, for each γ in $\omega(1)^M$, $F(\gamma)$ is countable in M. So again the sequence $F^*(0)$, $F^*(1)$,... is a sequence of length $\omega(1)^M$ of ordinals less than $\omega(2)^M$, so its limit is less than $\omega(2)^M$. Hence it is true in N that the range of t is included in an ordinal less than $\omega(2)^M$, so $\omega(2)^M = \omega(2)^N$.

A sentence saying ω has at least $\omega(2)$ subsets is true in N, so the continuum hypothesis fails in N, and thus is independent of ZFC. Cantor's hypothesis made the continuum as small as possible. Putnam once said that if the cardinal of the continuum were weakly inaccessible, it would perhaps be as big as possible. There seems to be a popular opinion that the continuum hypothesis is false.[13] But there is no guarantee that we will ever know.

[13] In "Recent Progress on the Continuum Hypothesis (after Woodin)," www.math. unicaen.fr/~dehornoy/Surveys/DgtUS.pdf, Patrick Dehornoy describes some of W. Hugh Woodin's work aimed at refuting the continuum hypothesis in plausible extensions of ZFC. Robert M. Solovay wrote the Introductory Note to Gödel's work in volume 2 of his *Collected Works, Publications 1938–1974*, ed. Solomon Feferman et al. (Oxford: Oxford University Press, 1990), 1–25, and part 4 of Solovay's note is a survey of some work on constructible sets after Gödel and on forcing after Cohen. An approach to whether $V = L$ comes from large cardinals (those too big for ZF to prove to exist). In 1961 Dana Scott showed that if there is a measurable cardinal, then $V \neq L$. There is a readable exposition of this in Joseph R. Shoenfield, "Measurable Cardinals," in *Logic Colloquium '69*, ed. R. O. Gandy and C. E. M. Yates (Amsterdam: North-Holland, 1971), 19–49.

EIGHT

✦

The Critique of Pure Reason

In Chapter 5 we looked at a theory about natural numbers. Since all recursive relations are n.e. in Q, and the consistency of Q is provable in elementary number theory, we concluded that Q is undecidable. But Q has only finitely many axioms specific to natural numbers, so there is a conjunction A of these axioms. So if we let P be the logic fixed by the language of Q, then a sentence B of that language is a theorem of Q if and only if $A \to B$ is a law of logic according to P. By the completeness theorem for first-order logic we mentioned in Chapter 4, being a law of logic according to P may be read equivalently either as being deducible from logical axioms of P by logical rules of inference of P or as being true in all interpretations of the language of P (which is that of Q). So if being a law of logic according to P were decidable, we could apply an algorithm for it to $A \to B$ to decide whether B is a theorem of Q, so Q would be decidable. Hence being a law of logic according to P is undecidable.

Suppose, conversely, there were an algorithm α for being a theorem of Q. The property F_{Σ} of being a proof in Q in which only logical axioms and rules of P are used is a decidable property; just look at the proof to see which axioms and rules are used. So its gödelization F_A is recursive, as is the predicate $L_A(x, y)$, which holds if and only if x is the gödel number of a proof in Q whose last line is the formula with gödel number y. Let B be any sentence in the language of Q and let b be its gödel number. Then B is a law of logic according to P if and only if $(\exists x)$ $(F(x) \wedge L(x, \underline{b}))$ is a theorem of Q (where F and L n.e. F_A and L_A), so by applying α to the second we could effectively decide whether B is a law of logic according to P.

Hence not only are the problem of being a theorem of Q and the problem of being a law of logic according to P both unsolvable, but they are also of equal difficulty. We have effective means of converting a solution of either into a solution to the other. By 1944 many axiomatic theories had been shown to be undecidable (if consistent). Emil Post noted that any two of them are, in the sense just observed, of equal difficulty, and he asked whether all undecidable axiomatic theories are equally difficult.[1] This question is Post's problem.

So far the only tools we have with which to approach this problem are the recursive functions, but our grip on these is not as firm as we would wish. There is an enumeration of these functions. To see why, recall that they are built up in finitely many steps from the initial functions (the successor function N, the zero function Z, and the projection functions U_i^n) using composition, recursion, and minimalization of regular functions. We can effectively enumerate the initial functions. First list N, then Z, and then put U_i^n before U_j^m if and only if n < m or else n = m but i < j. Then we can describe an enumeration of the recursive function in stages. At stage n + 1, add the $(n+1)^{th}$ initial function to the list and then in some order the finitely many functions that come from functions on the list up to the $(n+1)^{th}$ initial function by one use of composition, recursion, and minimalization of a regular function. This list is an enumeration that eventually includes all and only the recursive functions.

But there is no effective enumeration of the recursive functions. For suppose to the contrary that f_0, f_1,... were such an effective enumeration. Let g be the function whose value at n is the successor of the value of f_n with n put in all its argument places. Then g is computable. To compute g at any n, generate our effective enumeration out to f_n, compute f_n with n in all its argument places and add one. Since g is computable, it is recursive by the Church–Turing thesis, so for some k, g is f_k. But then $f_k(k) = f_k(k) + 1$, which is not possible. If all the f_n were unary, the numbers $f_n(n)$ would lie along the diagonal of the infinite square of all the numbers $f_n(k)$, so this mode of argument is called diagonalizing out. (It follows that there is no algorithm for whether a function is regular, for if there were, it could be used to avoid minimalizing functions that are not regular, thus making our enumeration of the recursive functions effective.)

We would have a better grip on our basic building blocks if we had an effective enumeration of them, and if it is to be an enumeration

---

[1] Emil Post, "Recursively Enumerable Sets of Positive Integers and Their Decision Problems," reprinted in Martin Davis, ed., *The Undecidable* (Hewlett, N.Y.: Raven, 1965), 304–37. This is a seminal paper that philosophers can read with pleasure.

of all of them, we should not be able to diagonalize out. It was Alan Turing who saw how to do so using partial functions.[2] Fix the set ω of natural numbers. An n-ary partial function from n-tuples of natural numbers to natural numbers is a set of ordered (n+1)-tuples of natural numbers such that for all $k_1,..., k_n$ in ω there is at most one k in ω such that $<k_1,..., k_n, k>$ is in it. A partial function is total if and only if for every $k_1,..., k_n$ there is a k such that $<k_1,..., k_n, k>$ is in it. So far we have looked mostly at total functions, but the eldest-sibling function is partial on the domain of people. We say that this function is undefined or diverges at only children, and if σ is this function and a is an only child, we write $\sigma(a)\uparrow$ if σ diverges at a. But if a has brothers or sisters, we say σ is defined or converges at a, and we write $\sigma(a)\downarrow$. We tend to use Greek letters like φ and ψ for functions that, for all we know so far, are partial.

Partiality comes into play with minimalization. Suppose ψ is a binary partial function on natural numbers. Fix a number m and suppose that for all numbers $k < n$, $\psi(m, k)$ converges to a positive number, but $\psi(m, n)$ is defined and equal to 0. Then we say that n is the least number such that $\psi(m, n)$ is defined and equal to 0, written $\mu k(\psi(m, n) = k)$. Using partial functions allows us to minimalize any old functions regular or not; $\mu y(\psi(x_1,..., x_n, y) = 0)$ is the partial function whose value at $x_1,..., x_n$ is the least y such that $\psi(x_1,..., x_n, y)$ is defined and equal to zero, if there is one, and for all z less than this least y is defined and positive, but the function diverges otherwise. The minimalization of a total regular function is total, but the minimalization of a function that is not regular is partial. If $\varphi(x)$ is $\mu y(x + y + 1 = 0)$, then φ converges nowhere and is thus utterly partial.

Permitting partiality requires broadening some of our basic notions. A partial algorithm for a class Q of questions is a finite list of instructions that, applied to any question q from Q, issues in at most one answer to q, and if it issues in an answer, it does so in finitely many mechanical steps, and that answer is correct. An n-ary partial function φ is partial computable if and only if there is a partial algorithm for the questions what $\varphi(k_1,..., k_n)$ is, and that answers if and only if $\varphi(k_1,..., k_n)\downarrow$. A function φ is partial recursive if and only if there is a finite sequence of partial functions that begins with an initial function, ends with φ, and in which every function is either initial or comes from

[2] Alan M. Turing, "On Computable Numbers, with an Application to the Entscheidungsproblem," reprinted in Davis, *Undecidable*, 116–54.

earlier functions in the sequence by composition, recursion, or minimalization. We now redefine a recursive function as a partial recursive
function that is total.

We can effectively enumerate the partial recursive functions because
our earlier enumeration of the recursive functions becomes effective
once we no longer have to worry about regularity. (It follows that there
is no algorithm for being total, for if there were we could strike the
nontotal functions, leaving an effective enumeration of the recursive
functions.) Assign to each partial recursive function in this list the number of its predecessors; this number is an r.e. index of the partial recursive function. For each n we also assign to n the history or derivation D_n
of how φ_n was derived from which initial functions. It comes to pretty
much the same thing, but for emphasis we also assign to each n a partial algorithm α_n for partial computing φ_n according to D_n.

Algorithms are sensitive to notation. The successor function is computable, but we compute the successor of n one way if we are given n in
decimal notation, and another if we are given n as the little oval with n
strokes, and who knows how if we are given n as Plato's favorite number. Let us settle on the little oval with n strokes as our notation for n.
Our algorithm for N is the instruction: given n, add another stroke. Our
algorithm for Z is: given n, yield 0. Our algorithm for U_i^m is: given $k_1,\ldots,$
k_n, yield k_i. Suppose φ comes from ψ and $\theta_1,\ldots,\theta_m$ by composition and $\alpha,$
$\alpha_1,\ldots,\alpha_m$ are partial algorithms for $\psi, \theta_1,\ldots,\theta_m$. Then an algorithm for φ
is: given $k_1,\ldots,k_n$, use $\alpha_1,\ldots,\alpha_n$ to compute $\theta_1(k_1,\ldots,k_n),\ldots,\theta_m(k_1,\ldots,k_n),$
and if they converge use α to compute $\psi(\theta_1(k_1,\ldots,k_n),\ldots,\theta_m(k_1,\ldots,k_n));$
if it converges it is $\theta(k_1,\ldots,k_n)$. (Let us assume we have also attached to
each n a record of the polyadicity of φ_n.) Suppose φ comes from ψ and
θ by recursion and we have partial algorithms α and β for ψ and θ. (If φ
is unary, we can take θ to be the constant function whose value at any
x is $\varphi(0)$. The constant function whose value is n is the n-fold composition of N on Z, and thus primitive recursive.) Then a partial algorithm
for φ is: given $k_1,\ldots,k_n$, k, use β to compute $\theta_1(k_1,\ldots,k_n)$; if it converges
use α successively to compute $\psi(k_1,\ldots,k_n, 1, \theta(k_1,\ldots,k_n)),\ldots,\psi(k_1,\ldots,$
$k_n, p, \psi(k_1,\ldots,k_n, p))$ where p + 1 = k. If the last converges, it is $\varphi(k_1,\ldots,$
$k_n, k)$. Suppose φ comes from ψ by minimalization and α is a partial
algorithm for ψ. Then a partial algorithm for φ is: given $k_1,\ldots,k_n$, use α
to compute $\psi(k_1,\ldots,k_n, 0)$; if it converges to 0, stop and yield 0, but if it
converges to something positive, go on; and so forth. (Note that we go
on only if all the earlier computations converge to something positive.
That is why we specified $\mu y(\varphi(x_1,\ldots,x_n, y) = 0)$ by requiring not only

that $\varphi(x_1,\ldots, x_n, y)$ converge to 0 but also that for $z < y$, $\varphi(x_1,\ldots, x_n, z)$ converge to something positive. For if $\varphi(x, 1)$ converges to 0 but the computation for $\varphi(x, 0)$ never stops, we will never recognize $\mu y(\varphi(x, y) = 0)$ as such.) Any partial recursive function recurs infinitely often in our enumeration, and it may recur with very different derivations and thus partial algorithms for computing it; a trivial example is $2x = x + x$.[3]

We have a broader Church–Turing thesis saying that a function is partial computable if and only if it is partial recursive. Let ψ be the partial function whose value at n, if any, is the successor of the value, if any, of φ_n with n in all its argument places. Then ψ is partial computable and so, by the Church–Turing thesis, partial recursive. So ψ is φ_k for some k. The impossibility that $\varphi_k(k)$ be defined and equal to $\varphi_k(k) + 1$ shows that φ_k is not defined at k. So instead of diagonalizing out, we get partiality. This turn impressed Gödel.[4]

Dimension is mostly just a nuisance in recursion theory, but we should confront it briefly somewhere. Let the ordered pair <n, k> precede <i, j> if and only if $n < i$ or else $n = i$ and $k < j$. We can effectively enumerate the pairs in this order since the $n + 1$ pairs whose first component is n come in a block ordered by the size of their second components. Let $\tau(n, k)$ be the number of pairs preceding <n, k> in this order. Then τ maps the pairs one–one onto ω. Moreover τ is computable and thus recursive. Conversely, given p, list the first $p + 1$ pairs to get the <n, k> such that $\tau(n, k) = p$ and let $\pi_1(p) = n$ and $\pi_2(p) = k$. These instructions are algorithms for π_1 and π_2, so they are computable and hence recursive. Now we generalize. Let τ^1 and π_1^1 both be U_1^1. Let τ^2 be τ, π_1^2 be π_1, and π_2^2 be π_2. Given τ^n let $\tau^{n+1}(x_1,\ldots, x_n, x_{n+1}) = \tau^2(\tau^n(x_1,\ldots, x_n), x_{n+1})$. Then τ^n is a recursive function mapping ω^n one–one onto ω. Conversely, suppose we have $\pi_1^n,\ldots, \pi_n^n$. For $k \le n$, let $\pi_k^{n+1}(p) = \pi_k^n(\pi_1^2(p))$ and $\pi_{n+1}^{n+1}(p) = \pi_2^2(p)$. For any n, we can pass effectively back and forth between ordered n-tuples of natural numbers and natural number codes for them.

A relation R on natural numbers is recursive if and only if its characteristic function c_R is recursive. So by the Church–Turing thesis, a set A is decidable if and only if it is recursive. We said in Chapter 5 that a

---

[3] Indexing can be done in a sophisticated way so that we can recover a partial algorithm for a partial recursive function just from an r.e. index for it, without, as we have done, attaching partial algorithms. See Peter G. Hinman, *Fundamentals of Mathematical Logic* (Wellesley, Mass.: A. K. Peters, 2005), sect. 5.2.

[4] Kurt Gödel, "Remarks Before the Princeton Bicentennial Conference on Problems in Mathematics," reprinted in Davis, *Undecidable*, 84.

theory is decidable if and only if the set of gödel numbers of its theorems is decidable. An n-ary relation R on natural numbers is recursively enumerable (r.e. for short) if and only if it is empty or the set of code numbers of the n-tuples of numbers in R is the range of a recursive function. A set of numbers is effectively enumerable if and only if it is r.e. We saw in Chapter 5 that a theory is axiomatic if and only if the set of gödel numbers of its theorems is r.e. A set of numbers that is r.e. and recursive is an abstract form of a decidable axiomatic theory, and an r.e. set that is not recursive is an abstract form of an undecidable axiomatic theory.

A set is r.e. if and only if it is the domain of a unary partial recursive function. Suppose first that A is r.e. If A is empty, let ψ be the partial function nowhere defined. The instruction "Given n, stop" is a partial algorithm for ψ, so ψ is partial computable and thus partial recursive, and A is the domain of ψ. Otherwise A is the range of a recursive function. The instruction:

Given n, go through the following stages:
Stage k: Compute f(k); if it is n, yield 0 and stop; otherwise go on to the next stage

is a partial algorithm. So it determines a partial computable, and thus partial recursive, function ψ. For each n, $\psi(n)$ converges if and only if n is in the range of f, so A is the domain of ψ. Suppose second that A is the domain of a unary partial recursive ψ. We will show that if A is not empty, it is the range of a recursive function. Consider the following instructions, given in stages, for listing A:

Stage 1: Do one step in the computation of $\psi(0)$; if it converges thereby, put 0 on the list.
Stage n + 1: Do as many of the n + 1 steps in the computations of $\psi(0),\dots, \psi(n)$ as possible, and if any converge thereby, add their arguments in order of size to the list.

Since ψ is partial computable, we can execute any finite number of these steps. Let $\varphi(0)$ be the first number put on the list; there is one because A is not empty. Let $\varphi(n + 1)$ be the least number on the list at stage n + 1 and different from $\varphi(0),\dots, \varphi(n)$ if there is one, but $\varphi(0)$ if there is not. Then φ is partial computable and thus partial recursive; and since $\varphi(0)$ converges, $\varphi(n + 1)$ converges for all n, so φ is total and thus recursive. Moreover, A is the range of φ. (Note that we do not first compute $\psi(0)$, for if this computation never halts, we will never get to $\psi(1)$. Instead we dovetail our computations, which guarantees that for each n on which ψ converges, we will eventually recognize it as such.)[5]

A set A is r.e. if and only if for some binary recursive B, A is $\{n \mid (\exists k)B(n, k)\}$. If A is r.e., it is the domain of a partial recursive ψ. The instruction

> Given n and p, take no more than p steps in the computation of $\psi(n)$;
>   if it converges, yield 0, but if it does not, yield 1

is an algorithm for the characteristic function of a binary relation B, so B is recursive. But

$$A = \{n \mid \psi(n)\!\downarrow\}$$
$$= \{n \mid (\exists p)B(n, p)\}.$$

Now suppose, conversely, that $A = \{n \mid (\exists k)B(n, k)\}$ for some recursive B. Consider the instruction:

> Given n, go through the following stages:
> Stage k: Compute $c_B(n, k)$; if it is 0, stop and yield 0; otherwise go
>   on to the next stage.

This is a partial algorithm, so it determines a partial computable, and thus partial recursive, function ψ. A is the domain of ψ.

Any recursive set is r.e. If A is recursive, so is c_A. Let $B(n, k)$ be the relation $c_A(n) = 0 \wedge k = k$. This relation is decidable and thus recursive. But $A = \{n \mid (\exists k)B(n, k)\}$. We can then show that A is recursive if and only if A and $\omega - A$ are r.e. Suppose first that A is recursive. Then A is r.e. Also, if $f(n) = 1$ when $c_A(n) = 0$ but $f(n) = 0$ when $c_A(n) = 1$, then f is the characteristic function of $\omega - A$, and since f is computable, it is recursive. Hence $\omega - A$ is recursive and thus r.e. Suppose, conversely, that A and $\omega - A$ are both r.e. To decide whether $n \in A$, list A and $\omega - A$ until n turns up, as it must, in one of these lists; $n \in A$ if and only if n is on the A-list.

For any n, let $d(n)$ be the polyadicity of φ_n. We attached a record of the value of $d(n)$ to φ_n in the effective enumeration of partial recursive functions, so d is computable, and thus recursive; the d is for dimension. Suppose $d(n) = p$ and that $\pi_1^p(k) = k_1, \ldots, \pi_p^p(k) = k_p$. For each n and k, let $q_{n,k}$ be the question whether $\varphi_n(k_1, \ldots, k_p)$ converges. The set of all the $q_{n,k}$ is the halting problem. Suppose there were an algorithm α for

5 Hartley Rogers, Jr., *Theory of Recursive Functions and Effective Computability* (New York: McGraw-Hill, 1967), 60.

the halting problem. Then the function f whose value at n and k is 0 if the answer to $q_{n,k}$ is yes, but 1 if the answer is no, would be computable and thus recursive. Let ψ be the unary partial function whose value at k is 1 if f(k, k) = 1 but which diverges otherwise. Then ψ is partial computable, and thus partial recursive. So $\psi = \varphi_n$ for some n. But

$$\varphi_n(n) = 1 \text{ iff } \psi(n) = 1$$
$$\text{iff } f(n, n) = 1$$
$$\text{iff the answer to } q(n, n) \text{ is no}$$
$$\text{iff } \varphi_n(n) \text{ diverges,}$$

which is impossible. Hence there is no algorithm for the halting problem. It should be pretty clear that we can recursively enumerate those $\tau(n, k)$ for which the answer to $q_{n,k}$ is yes. So since the set of $\tau(n, k)$ such that $q_{n,k}$ is in the halting problem is not recursive, the set of $\tau(n, k)$ for which the answer to $q_{n,k}$ is no is not r.e. The halting problem is thus an abstract version of an undecidable axiomatic theory.

The r.e. indices are natural numbers, so there are recursive functions of them, some of which are useful in recursion theory. We will sketch two, but because we have only described the indices informally, we will only sketch these functions. When we showed that if A is r.e., then it is {n | (∃k)B(n, k)} for some recursive B, we truncated computations of a partial recursive ψ of which A is the domain at a maximum of p steps. There is a binary recursive function t such that for all n and p, t(n, p) is an r.e. index for a d(n)-ary partial recursive function $\varphi_{t(n,p)}$ such that for all $x_1,...,x_{d(n)}$, the computation of $\varphi_{t(n,p)}$ at $x_1,...,$ $x_{d(n)}$ according to $\alpha_{t(n,p)}$ copies the computation of φ_n at $x_1,..., x_{d(n)}$ according to α_n except that the first computation never goes beyond p steps. $\varphi_{t(n,p)}$ is the p-truncation of φ_n. To specify it, we have to settle exactly what a step in a computation is and then uniformly for all n,p and $x_1,..., x_{d(n)}$ add to α_n an instruction to keep count of the steps in the computation of $\varphi_n(x_1,..., x_{d(n)})$ and an instruction to stop before p + 1 steps are taken.[6]

---

[6] The Turing machine whose quadruples are $q_1 \mid Rq_1$ and $q_1B \mid q_2$ computes the successor function. The machine whose quadruples are

$$q_1 \mid Rq_3$$
$$q_3 \mid Rq_4$$
$$q_3B \mid q_2$$
$$\vdots$$
$$q_{p+1} \mid Rq_2$$
$$q_{p+1}B \mid q_2$$

For any n, let W_n be the domain of $\varphi_{u(n)}$. Then W_0, W_1,... is an effective enumeration of the r.e. sets. Let $K = \{n \mid n \in W_n\}$. The instruction

Given n, stop and yield 0 only if $\varphi_{u(n)}(n)\downarrow$

is a partial algorithm, so it determines a partial computable, and thus partial recursive, function ψ. K is the domain of ψ, so K is r.e. If K were recursive, $\omega - K$ would be r.e. and thus W_n for some n. Then $n \in K$ if and only if $n \in W_n$, and $n \in (\omega - K)$ if and only if $n \in W_n$, so $n \in K$ if and only if $n \in (\omega - K)$, which is impossible. Hence K, like HP, is an abstract form of an undecidable axiomatic theory.

The s-m-n theorem is named for a way to calculate an r.e. index for the function got by substituting <u>m</u> numbers for the first m arguments of a partial recursive function φ_x of $\underline{n} = d(x)$ arguments. We form the required function by composing φ_x with m constant functions whose values are the required numbers and U_1^1 in the last n – m places (because our description of composition requires that we compose on functions all of the same polyadicity). The constant function C^k whose value is always k can be got by composing N on Z k times. Let $y_1,..., y_m$ be the numbers we want to plug into the first m places of φ_x. Let $x_1,..., x_m$ be the r.e. indices for $C^{y_1},..., C^{y_m}$ and let i be an r.e. index for U_1^1. If p is the maximum of x, $x_1,..., x_m$ and i, then we can find an r.e. index for $\varphi_x(y_1,..., y_m, z_1,..., z_{n-m})$ at stage $p + 1$ in the effective enumeration of the partial recursive functions. So there is a recursive function s of m + 1 arguments such that for all x and $y_1,..., y_m$, $\varphi_{s(x,y_1,...,y_m)}$ is the (n–m)-ary partial recursive function $\varphi_x(y_1,..., y_m, z_1,..., z_{n-m})$. We also want to be able to pass effectively back and forth between polyadic functions and what we will call their unifications. Suppose φ_n has $p = d(n)$ argument places. Let $i_1,..., i_p$ be r.e. indices for $\pi_1^p,..., \pi_p^p$ and let m be the maximum of n, $i_1,..., i_p$. We can find an r.e. index for $\varphi_n(\pi_1^p(x),..., \pi_p^p(x))$ at

computes the p-truncation of the successor function. There is an algorithm that given the derivation D_n of the partial recursive function φ_n yields a Turing machine M_n that halts on exactly those inputs on which φ_n converges and yields then the same output as φ_n. (Elliott Mendelson, *Introduction to Mathematical Logic*, 4th ed. [New York: Chapman & Hall, 1997], cor. 5.3, p. 321.) There is an algorithm that given M_n and p yields a Turing machine that computes the p-truncation of φ_n. (Expand the quadruples of M_n using new states as we did those of our machine for N.) There is an algorithm that, given this machine that computes the p-truncation of φ_n, yields a derivation $D_{t(n,p)}$ of the p-truncation $\varphi_{t(n,p)}$ of φ_n. (Mendelson, cor. 5.6, p. 325.) Joining up these algorithms, t is computable and thus recursive. The point of the detour through Turing machines is that there is a natural way to individuate steps taken by a Turing machine.

stage $m + 1$, so there is a recursive function u such that for all n, $\varphi_{u(n)}(x)$ $= \varphi_n(\pi_1^p(x),\ldots, \pi_p^p(x))$. Suppose, conversely, that φ_n is unary. Let i_p be an r.e. index for τ^p. If m is the maximum of n and i_p, we can find an r.e. index for $\varphi_n(\tau^p(x_1,\ldots, x_p))$ at stage $m + 1$, so there is a recursive function $f(n, p)$ such that $\varphi_{f(n,p)}(x_1,\ldots, x_p) = \varphi_n(\tau^p(x_1,\ldots, x_p))$; we call $\varphi_{f(n,p)}$ a p-dilation of φ_n.

We began this chapter by observing that theoremhood in Q and validity in its quantification theory P are unsolvable problems of equal difficulty; if we could solve either, we could solve the other. Now we want to make mathematics out of this subjunctive, and as is usual we do so by evaluating the existential quantifier under the subjunctive.[7] Let c_q and c_p be the characteristic functions of gödel numbers of theorems of Q and P, respectively. The basic idea is that there is one finite sequence of partial functions starting with c_q, built up using initial function, composition, recursion, and minimalization, and ending with c_p, and another going from c_p to c_q. We set about codifying this basic idea.

Let P be the set of all partial unary functions from ω to ω. By a functional we mean a unary function whose arguments and values are members of P. (Our use of "functional" is not the usual one; usually, a functional has functions and numbers as arguments and numbers as values. But what is usually said can be said our way.) We will be working with things arrayed in four levels: natural numbers, unary partial functions from numbers to numbers, unary functionals from and to such partial functions, and operations (like composition, recursion, and minimalization) on functionals. The unifications of our familiar partial recursive functions will reappear as the values of certain constant functionals. It is plain that composition, recursion, and minimalization are sensitive to the polyadicities of the functions on which they operate, so we will use dilation to recover polyadic functions. To illustrate, we will use a binary operation Rec_1 such that for all functionals H and G, $Rec_1(H, G)$ is the functional whose value at any α in P is the β such that

$$(\beta)_2(x, 0) = G(\alpha)(x)$$
$$(\beta)_2(x, y + 1) = (H(\alpha))_3(x, y, (\beta)_2(x, y))$$

where $(\beta)_n$ is the n-dilation of β. We want two initial functionals whose values at any α are our old N and Z, respectively. For $n > 1$, the projection functions U_i^n are hopelessly polyadic, so instead we want initial

[7] W. V. Quine, "Necessary Truth," reprinted in his *The Ways of Paradox*, rev. and enl. ed. (Cambridge, Mass.: Harvard University Press, 1976), 68–76.

functionals whose values at any α are π_i^n. These initial functionals all lose α, and we want to be able to keep and use it, so we want an initial functional I whose value at any α is α.

We now raise composition, recursion, and minimalization to operations on functionals. First, for any n and m both positive and functionals H, $G_1,\ldots, G_m$, let $\text{Comp}_{n,m}(H, G_1,\ldots, G_m)$ be the functional whose value at any α is the β such that for all $x_1,\ldots, x_n \in \omega$

$$(\beta)_n(x_1,\ldots, x_n) = (H(\alpha))_m((G_2(\alpha))_n(x_1,\ldots, x_n),\ldots, (G_m(\alpha))_n(x_1,\ldots, x_n)).$$

Second, for any positive n and functionals H and G, $\text{Rec}_n(H, G)$ is the functional whose value at α is the β such that for all $x_1,\ldots, x_n, y \in \omega$,

$$(\beta)_{n+1}(x_1,\ldots, x_n, 0) = (G(\alpha))_n(x_1,\ldots, x_n)$$
$$(\beta)_{n+1}(x_1,\ldots, x_n, y + 1) = (H(\alpha))_{n+2}(x_1,\ldots, x_n, y, (\beta)_{n+1}(x_1,\ldots, x_n, y)),$$

but when n = 0, then for any functional H and number k, $\text{Rec}_0(H, k)$ is the functional whose value at α is the β such that $\beta(0) = k$ and for all y, $\beta(y + 1) = (H(\alpha))_2(y, \beta(y))$. Third, for any k > 0 and any H, $\text{Min}_k(H)$ is the functional whose value at any α is the β such that for all $x_1,\ldots, x_k \in \omega$,

$$(\beta)_k(x_1,\ldots, x_k) = \mu y((H(\alpha))_{n+1}(x_1,\ldots, x_k, y) = 0).$$

A functional F is a relative recursion scheme if and only if there is a finite sequence of functionals that begins with an initial functional, ends with F, and in which every functional is either initial or the value of some operation $\text{Comp}_{k,m}$, Rec_k (k > 0), or Min_k for functionals earlier in the sequence, or the value of Rec_0 for a functional earlier in the sequence and a number. Such a finite sequence with, for each initial function, a statement of which initial function it is, and, for any others in the sequence, a statement of what it comes from earlier in the sequence and how, is a derivation of F. A relative recursion scheme is called an r.r.s. for short.

For any φ and α in P, φ is partial α-recursive if and only if $\varphi = H(\alpha)$ for some r.r.s. H. There is the existential quantifier that evaluates the subjunctive; there are r.r.s. H and G such that $c_Q = H(c_p)$ and $c_p = G(c_q)$. When A is a set, φ is partial A-recursive if it is partial c_A-recursive. A unary f is α-recursive if and only if it is partial α-recursive and total. Then f is A-recursive if and only if it is c_A-recursive.[8]

---

[8] To give some examples, let N,Z and U_i^n denote the constant functionals whose values are the functions N,Z and π_i^n. Then the sequence

To relativize the Church–Turing thesis, we regiment some auxiliary notions. For α in P, Turing imagines an oracle. We have no idea how an oracle works, or even whether in any recognizable sense it works at all. But we can ask it questions and, at least sometimes, it answers. An α-step in the application of a finite list A of instructions to a number n consists in asking the oracle for the value of α at n and, if n is in the domain of α, being told the value of α at n, but, if n is not in the domain of α, not being told anything and stopping the application of A to n without yielding an output. A is a partial α-algorithm if and only if A is a finite list of instructions such that for any n, A applied to n either goes on through steps that are mechanical or α-steps forever without yielding an output, or stops after finitely many such steps without yielding an output, or stops and yields a unique output after finitely many such steps. For any α, any partial α-algorithm A determines the partial function ψ such that for all n and k, $\psi(n)$ is defined and equal to k if and only if A applied to n yields k. Then ψ is partial α-computable if and only if there is a partial α-algorithm A that determines ψ. The *weak* relativized Church–Turing thesis says that ψ is partial α-computable if and only if it is partial α-recursive. A relative algorithm scheme is an algorithm that, given an oracle for an α in P, yields a partial α-algorithm. The *strong* relativized Church–Turing thesis says that for any relative algorithm scheme G, there is a relative recursion scheme H such that for all α in P, $H(\alpha)$ is the partial function determined by $G(\alpha)$.[9] The strong

$F_1 = U_1^1$	x
$F_2 = U_3^3$	$\pi_3^3(x)$
$F_3 = N$	$x + 1$
$F_4 = \text{Comp}_{3,1}(F_3, F_2)$	$\pi_3^3(x) + 1$
$F_5 = \text{Rec}_1(F_4, F_1)$	$\pi_1^2(x) + \pi_2^2(x)$
$F_6 = Z_3$	0
$F_7 = U_1^3$	π_1^3
$F_8 = \text{Comp}_{3,2}(F_5, F_7, F_2)$	$\pi_1^3(x) + \pi_3^3(x)$
$F_9 = \text{Rec}_1(F_8, F_6)$	$\pi_1^2(x) \cdot \pi_2^2(x)$
$F_{10} = \text{Comp}_{1,2}(F_9, F_1, F_1)$	x^2
$F_{11} = I$	$\alpha(x)$
$F_{12} = \text{Comp}_{1,1}(F_{11}, F_{10})$	$\alpha(x^2)$
$F_{13} = \text{Comp}_{1,2}(F_5, F_1, F_1)$	$2x$
$F_{14} = \text{Comp}_{1,1}(F_{13}, F_{12})$	$2\alpha(x^2)$

shows that $2\alpha(x^2)$ is partial α-recursive. Let $f(0) = 0$ and $f(n + 1) = \alpha(f(n))$. Then $f = \text{Rec}_0(\text{Comp}_{1,1}(I, U_2^2), 0)(\alpha)$, so f is partial α-recursive.

[9] Conversely, given an r.r.s. H, we can read off a derivation of H a relative algorithm scheme G such that for $\alpha \in P$, $G(\alpha)$ is the partial function determined by $H(\alpha)$. So we can prove the converse of the strong thesis, and from it we can deduce that for all α, $H(\alpha)$ is partial α-computable, which is half the weak thesis.

thesis articulates the idea that any machinery in which we imbed an oracle must, in order to be machinery, work uniformly for whatever, if anything, happens inside the oracle.[10]

For any r.r.s. H, any α in P, and any x and y in ω, if $H(\alpha)(x)$ is defined and equal to y, then only finitely many values of α are used in showing that $H(\alpha)(x) = y$. This is called the use principle, and establishing it is mostly a matter of understanding the predicate:

> The values of α on the members of A are used in showing that $H(\alpha)(x) = y$ by derivation D of H.

We mention D because the computation of the value (if any) of $H(\alpha)$ at x will vary with D. The predicate presupposes that $H(\alpha)(x)$ converges to y. For the rest we proceed by induction on D. If H is a constant initial functional, $A = \emptyset$. If $H = I$, $A = \{x\}$. Note that in either case, A is a unique finite set. Suppose $H = \text{Comp}_{n,m}(F, G_1,\ldots, G_m)$. Then there are unique $y_1,\ldots, y_m$, $A_1,\ldots, A_m$, and B such that for $i = 1,\ldots, m$, the values of α on the members of A_i are used in showing that $(G_i)(\alpha)(x) = y_i$ by D, and the values of α on B are used in showing that $(F(\alpha))_m(y_1,\ldots, y_m) = y$ by D. Then A is $A_1 \cup \ldots \cup A_m \cup B$. Suppose $H = \text{Rec}_n(F, G)$ for some $n > 0$. There are unique $x_1,\ldots, x_n, x_{n+1}$ such that $\tau^{n+1}(x_1,\ldots, x_n, x_{n+1}) = x$. There are also unique $y_0,\ldots, y_{x_{n+1}}, A_0,\ldots, A_{x_{n+1}}$ such that the values of α on A_0 are used in showing that $(G(\alpha))_n(x_1,\ldots, x_n) = y_0$, and if $0 \leq i < x_{n+1}$, the values of α on A_{i+1} are used in showing that $(F(\alpha))_{n+2}(x_1,\ldots, x_n, i, y_i) = y_{i+1}$ by D where $y_{x_{n+1}} = y$. Then A is the union of the A_i for $i \leq x_{n+1}$. If $H = \text{Rec}_0(F, k)$, there are unique $y_0,\ldots, y_x, A_0,\ldots, A_{x-1}$ such that $y_0 = k$, $y_x = y$, and for $i < x$, the values of α on A_i are used in showing that $(F(\alpha))_2(i, y_i) = y_{i+1}$ by D. Then A is the union of the A_i for $i < x$. Suppose H is $\text{Min}_k(F)$. There are unique $x_1,\ldots, x_k$ such that $\tau^k(x_1,\ldots, x_k) = x$. There are also unique $z_0,\ldots, z_y, A_0,\ldots, A_y$ such that for $i = 0,\ldots, y$, the values of α on A_i are used in showing that $(F(\alpha))_{k+1}(x_1,\ldots, x_k, i) = z$; by D, where $z_i > 0$ if $i < y$, but $z_y = 0$. Then A is the union of the A_i for $i \leq y$. Tracing thus along derivation D of H, we specify a unique set A such that the values of α on A are used in showing that $H(\alpha)(x) = y$. Since the union of finitely many finite sets is finite, the use principle follows by induction. Note too the following uniformity: if the values of α on A are used in showing that $H(\alpha)(x) = y$ by D and β agrees with α on A, then $H(\beta)(x) = y$ and the values of β on A are used in showing that $H(\beta)(x) = y$.

---

[10] We can extend our constructions to polyadic functions. If ψ and α are polyadic, ψ is partial α-computable if and only if the unification of ψ is partial computable from the unification of α.

We can index the relative recursion schemes effectively in just about the same way we indexed the partial recursive functions effectively. First enumerate the initial functionals effectively. We might start with I, Z, N in that order and then add the projection functions so that U_i^n precedes U_j^k if and only if $\tau(n, i) < \tau(k, j)$. Remember that now I is the functional whose value at any α is α, Z and N are the functionals whose values at any α are the zero function and the successor function, and U_i^n is the functional whose value at α is π_i^n. Next enumerate most of the operations effectively, say on the pattern:

$$\text{Comp}_{1,1}, \text{Rec}_1, \text{Min}_1, \text{Comp}_{1,2}, \text{Rec}_2,\ldots$$

where $\text{Comp}_{n,k}$ precedes $\text{Comp}_{i,j}$ if and only if $\tau(n, k) < \tau(i, j)$. Our list of the r.r.s. will assign each $n \in \omega$ an r.r.s. H_n and a derivation D_n of H_n. The list is drawn up in stages.

Stage 1: Let H_0 be the first initial functional and let D_0 be a statement of which initial functional H_0 is.

Stage 2: There are only two functionals that come from H_0 by one use of the first operation or of $\text{Rec}_0(-, 0))$. Let these be H_1 and H_2 in some order. Let D_1 and D_2 be D_0 with H_1 and H_2 tacked on, respectively, plus a statement of how it comes from H_0.

Stage $2k + 1$: Let p be the least number so far assigned to no r.r.s., and let H_p be the earliest initial functional so far assigned no number. Let D_p be H_p plus a statement of which initial functional H_p is.

Stage $2k + 2$: There are only finitely many functionals that come from $H_0,\ldots, H_p$ by exactly one use of the first k operations or of $\text{Rec}_0(-, 0),\ldots, \text{Rec}_0(-, k))$. Let them be $H_{p+1},\ldots, H_{p+m}$ in some order. For $i = 1,\ldots, m$, let D_{p+1} be got by amalgamating the derivations of the functional from which H_{p+i} comes, and then tacking on H_{p+i} plus a statement of which functionals it comes from and how.

A functional G is an r.r.s. if and only if for some n, G is H_n; n is an r.r.s. index for G.

The instruction:

> Given an oracle for α, write down the instruction:
> Given x and y, yield $H_x(\alpha)(y)$

is a relative algorithm scheme. It is a single finite effective way of writing down for any α in P a partial α-algorithm G. The instruction constituting G, which is there before your very eyes, has this character even if for most or all α in P, we never will, or even could, be given an oracle for

α; similarly, an ordinary algorithm that given a number yields another, is an algorithm even if for most numbers x we never will, or even could, be given a numeral for x. By the *strong* Church–Turing thesis, there is an r.r.s. H such that for all α, $H(\alpha)$ is the partial function determined by $G(\alpha)$. H has an r.r.s. index z. Hence there is a z such that for all α in P and all x and y in ω, $H_z(\alpha)(\tau(x, y)) = H_x(\alpha)(y)$. This is called an enumeration theorem; its strength is the independence of z not only from x and y but also from α.[11]

When A and B are sets (of natural numbers), we say that A is Turing-reducible to B if and only if there is an r.r.s. H such that $c_A = H(c_B)$. This is sometimes written $A \leq_T B$. Since c_A can be built up from c_B, membership in A is no harder to decide than membership in B. Since $c_A = I(c_A)$, $A \leq_T A$, so $\leq_T$ is reflexive. Given derivations D_G of G and D_F of F, we can show by induction on D_F how, for each F_i in D_F, to extend D_G to a derivation of the composition of F_i on G. It follows that if F and G are r.r.s., so is the composition of F on G, and thus that $\leq_T$ is transitive. It is false that for all A and B, $A \leq_T B$ or $B \leq_T A$; there are Turing incomparable sets.[12] But the relation $A \leq_T B \land B \leq_T A$ is reflexive, symmetric, and transitive, that is, it is an equivalence relation. So it partitions the sets of natural numbers into sets any two members of which are of equal degree of Turing difficulty. When A and B are of the same Turing degree, we write $A \equiv_T B$. We use letters like a and b for degrees, the equivalence classes of $\equiv_T$. Because $\leq_T$ is transitive, if there are $A \in a$ and $B \in b$ such that $A \leq_T B$, then the same goes for all A in a and all B in b, so we may say $a \leq_T b$ (usually written $a \leq b$) if and only if there are $A \in a$ and $B \in b$ such that $A \leq_T B$.

If φ is partial recursive with r.e. index n, there is an r.r.s. such that for all α in P, $H(\alpha) = \varphi_{u(n)}$; H is got by raising the partial recursive functions in a derivation of φ to the corresponding constant schemes. So if B is recursive, there is a scheme H such that $H(\alpha) = c_B$ for all α, and thus $H(c_A) = c_B$, so $A \leq_T B$. If ,conversely, $A \leq_T B$ and B is recursive, then $c_A = H(c_B)$ for some scheme H; so we can build c_A by extending a derivation of c_B using initial functions, composition, recursion, and minimalization, so c_A is recursive. Hence, if A and B are recursive, $A \equiv_T B$, so

---

[11] There are more constructive proofs of this relativized enumeration theorem that make no appeal to any form of the Church–Turing thesis. See J. L. Bell and M. Machover, *A Course in Mathematical Logic* (Amsterdam: North-Holland, 1977), 266–67. For an unrelativized enumeration theorem, see Martin Davis, *Computability and Unsolvability* (New York: McGraw-Hill, 1958), chap. 4.

[12] Rogers, *Theory of Recursive Functions*, 260.

there is a single degree of all and only the recursive sets. This degree is called 0. (It is the only solvable degree of unsolvability.) If $A \in 0$, c_A is recursive, so there is an H such that $H(\alpha) = c_A$ for all α. Hence for any $B \in a$, $H(c_B) = c_A$, and $A \leq_T B$; thus $0 \leq_T a$ for all degrees of a. The sets $\varnothing$ and K are both r.e. sets. A degree is r.e. if and only if it has an r.e. member. Asking whether there is an r.e. degree besides 0 and the degree of K is another way of posing Post's problem.

Earlier we proved that a set is r.e. if and only if it is the domain of a unary partial recursive function; that a set A is r.e. if and only if for some binary recursive B, $A = \{n \mid (\exists k)B(n, k)\}$; that a recursive set is r.e., and that A is recursive if and only if A and $\omega - A$ are r.e. These results have relativized forms. To prove the relativization of the first, we want to be able to truncate computations of $H_n(\alpha)(x)$ according to D_n at p or fewer steps. There is in fact a recursive function t such that the computation of $H_{t(n,p)}(\alpha)(x)$ according to $D_{t(n,p)}$ agrees with that of $H_n(\alpha)(x)$ according to D_n except for going through no more than p steps. Note that t is recursive, not just α-recursive; this is because we can count steps, even α-steps, without having to ask for values of α. Note too that, while computing $H_{t(n,p)}(\alpha)(x)$ may omit asking for values of α requested after step p in the computation of $H_n(\alpha)(x)$, truncation never swaps use. A set A is r.e. in α if and only if A is empty or the range of an α-recursive function. Then, sprinkling α around our earlier proof, we can prove that A is r.e. in α if and only if A is the domain of a partial α-recursive function. For any n and α, let W_n^α be the domain of $H_n(\alpha)$, so A is r.e. in α if and only if for some n, A is W_n^α. When B is a set, A is r.e. in B if and only if A is r.e. in c_B. We write W_n^B for $W_n^{c_B}$. Sprinkling around some more αs, we can prove that A is r.e. in D if and only if there is a B recursive in D such that $A = \{n \mid (\exists k)B(n, k)\}$; that a set recursive in A is r.e. in A; and that B is recursive in A if and only if B and $\omega - B$ are r.e. in A.

There are versions of reducibility narrower than Turing reducibility. For example, A is reducible to B via f if and only if f is recursive and for all n, $n \in A$ if and only if $f(n) \in B$. If A is reducible to B via f, then $A \leq_T B$. For if $c_A(n) = c_B(f(x))$, then $c_A = \text{Comp}_{1,1}(c_B, f)$. But it is false that if $A \leq_T B$, then A is reducible to B via some recursive f. We show this in stages. First, let $\delta(0) = 1$ and $\delta(y + 1) = 0$. Then δ is (primitive) recursive. Second, for any A, $c_{\omega-A}(x) = \delta(c_A(x))$, so $(\omega - A) \leq_T A$. Third, if A is reducible to B via f and B is r.e., then A is r.e. For then B is $\{n \mid (\exists k) R(n, k)\}$ for some recursive R. But then A is $\{n \mid (\exists k)R(f(n), k)\}$, where $R(f(n), k)$ is recursive, so A is r.e. Fourth, K is r.e. but not recursive, so $\omega - K$ is not r.e., and thus $\omega - K$ is not reducible to K, but $(\omega - K) \leq_T K$.

Reducibility via f is simpler than Turing reducibility, but Turing reducibility is the right version of reducibility.

Let HP be $\{\tau(n, k) \mid \varphi_{u(n)}(k) \text{ converges}\}$. HP is the set of codes of pairs <n, k> such that the answer is yes to the question $q_{n,k}$ in the halting problem. Then HP is r.e., a point we slighted earlier. For if $\pi_1(m) = n$ and $\pi_2(m) = k$, then

$$m \in \text{HP iff } \varphi_{u(n)}(k)\downarrow$$
$$\text{iff } (\exists p)(\varphi_{t(u(n),p)}(k)\downarrow).$$

It takes at most p mechanical steps to decide whether $\varphi_{t(u(n),p)}(k)$ converges, so the relation $\varphi_{t(u(n),p)}(k)\downarrow$ is decidable, and thus recursive. So HP is r.e. A set is complete-r.e. if and only if it is r.e. and every r.e. set is reducible to it. HP is complete-r.e. Let W_n be any r.e. set and let $f(x) = \tau(n, x)$. Then f is recursive and $x \in W_n$ if and only if $f(x) \in \text{HP}$, so W_n is reducible to HP via f. Thus for every r.e. A, $A \leq_T \text{HP}$. Turing made the halting problem central in recursion theory, and we want to relativize it.

Let $\varnothing'$ be $\{n \mid H_n(c_\varnothing)(n) \text{ converges}\}$. We will show that HP and $\varnothing'$ are of the same Turing degree. First we show that $\varnothing'$ is r.e.; then, since HP is complete-r.e., $\varnothing' \leq_T \text{HP}$. Showing that $\varnothing'$ is r.e. is mostly a matter of linking r.r.s. and r.e. indices. We saw earlier how for any unary φ_x to find a scheme H such that for all α, $H(\alpha) = \varphi_x$; indeed, there is a recursive g such that for all x and α, $H_{g(x)}(\alpha) = \varphi_x$ (independently of α). We saw earlier how, given schemes F and G, to find a scheme H that is the composition of F on G; indeed, there is a recursive f such that for all x, y, and α, $H_{f(x,y)}(\varphi) = H_x(H_y(\alpha))$ independently of α. When $H_x(\alpha)$ is constant independently of α, a derivation of H_x can be lowered to a derivation of a partial recursive function; indeed, there is a recursive j such that for all x, if $H_x(\alpha)$ is constant independently of α, then $H_x(\alpha) = \varphi_{j(x)}$. Let a be an r.e. index for $c_\varnothing$; $c_\varnothing$ is the constant function whose value is always 1, and is the composition of N on Z. Then for all x

$$x \in \varnothing' \text{ iff } H_x(c_\varnothing)(x) \text{ converges}$$
$$\text{iff } H_x(\varphi_a)(x)\downarrow$$
$$\text{iff } H_x(H_{g(a)}(\alpha)(x)\downarrow$$
$$\text{iff } H_{f(x,g(a))}(\alpha)(x)\downarrow$$
$$\text{iff } \varphi_{j(f(x,g(a)))}(x)\downarrow$$
$$\text{iff } (\exists p)(\varphi_{t(j(f(x,g(a))),p)}(x)\downarrow),$$

so since the scope of the existential quantifier is recursive, $\varnothing'$ is r.e.

Next we show that $\text{HP} \leq_T \varnothing'$. The instruction

Given x, start computing $\varphi_{u(\pi_1(x))}(\pi_2(x))$ and yield its output if and when it converges

is a partial algorithm. So it determines a partial computable, and thus partial recursive, function that has an r.e. index z. Similarly, there is a w such that $\varphi_w(x, y) = \varphi_z(U_1^2(x, y))$. By the s-1-1 case of the s-m-n theorem, there is a recursive s such that for all x, $\varphi_{s(w,x)}(y) = \varphi_w(x, y)$. Let $f(x) = s(w, x)$. Then f is recursive and for all x and y,

$$\begin{aligned}
\varphi_{f(x)}(y) &= \varphi_{s(w,x)}(y) \\
&= \varphi_w(x, y) \\
&= \varphi_z(U_1^2(x, y)) \\
&= \varphi_z(x) \\
&= \varphi_{u(\pi_1(x))}(\pi_2(x)).
\end{aligned}$$

Thus $W_{f(x)}$ is ω if $\varphi_{u(\pi_1(x))}(\pi_2(x))$ converges, but $\varnothing$ if not. Note that we calculate an r.e. index for $W_{f(x)}$ *without* deciding which case applies. Recall the function g from the last paragraph and let $j(x) = g(f(x))$. Then

$$\begin{aligned}
H_{j(x)}(\alpha)(y) &= H_{g(f(x))}(\alpha)(y) \\
&= \varphi_{f(x)}(y),
\end{aligned}$$

so $W_{j(x)}^\alpha = \mathrm{Dom}H_{j(x)}(\alpha) = W_{f(x)}$, which is ω if $x \in$ HP but $\varnothing$ if $x \notin$ HP. Hence

$$\begin{aligned}
x \in \text{HP iff } j(x) &\in W_{j(x)}^\varnothing \\
\text{iff } H_{j(x)}(c_\varnothing)&(j(x))\downarrow \\
\text{iff } j(x) &\in \varnothing',
\end{aligned}$$

so HP is reducible to $\varnothing'$ via j.

$\varnothing'$ is thus in the same degree as HP, and we use $\varnothing'$ to generalize HP, since we can do for any set what $\varnothing'$ does for $\varnothing$. For any set A, let $A' = \{n \mid H_n(c_A)(n) \text{ converges}\}$. A' is the jump of A. To generalize, we should have A' r.e. in A but not recursive in A. The relation $H_{t(x,p)}(c_A)(x) = y$ is recursive in A, for if we could decide A we could decide the relation. But $x \in A'$ if and only if $(\exists p, y)(H_{t(x,p)}(c_A)(x) = y)$, so A' is r.e. in A. If A' were recursive in A, $\omega - A'$ would be r.e. in A, so $\omega - A'$ would be W_z^A for some z. But then $z \in (\omega - A')$ if and only if $z \in W_z^A$ if and only if $z \in A'$, which is impossible.

Let $A^* = \{\tau(n, k) \mid H_n(c_A)(k) \text{ converges}\}$. A is reducible to A^* via $f(x) = \tau(x, x)$. Conversely, raise the s-m-n theorem and so forth to show there is a recursive m such that for all x, α, and y, $H_{m(x)}(\alpha)(y) = H_{\pi_1(x)}(\alpha)(\pi_2(x))$. Then for all α and n, $W_{m(x)}^\alpha$ is ω if $\pi_2(n) \in W_{\pi_1(n)}^\alpha$ but $\varnothing$ if not.

Then, as before, A* is reducible to A' via m. This result enables us to show that B is r.e. in A if and only if B is reducible to A'. (So A' generalizes the fact that HP is complete-r.e.) If B is r.e. in A, B is the domain of $H_n(c_A)$ for some n. Then

$$x \in B \text{ iff } H_n(c_A)(x) \text{ converges}$$
$$\text{iff } \tau(n, x) \in A^*$$
$$\text{iff } m(\tau(n, x)) \in A',$$

so because for each n, $m(\tau(n, x))$ is a (unary) recursive function, B is reducible to A'. Conversely, for any α and any recursive h, the set R_h = $\{\tau(x, p) \mid H_{t(h(x),p)}(\alpha)(h(x)) \text{ converges}\}$ is recursive in α. Suppose B is reducible to A' via f. Then

$$x \in B \text{ iff } f(x) \in A'$$
$$\text{iff } H_{f(x)}(c_A)(f(x))\downarrow$$
$$\text{iff } (\exists p)(H_{t(f(x),p)}(c_A)(f(x))\downarrow$$
$$\text{iff } (\exists p)(\tau(x, p) \in R_f),$$

so B is r.e. in A.

Next we show that $A \leq_T B$ if and only if A' is reducible to B'. A' is not recursive in A, so A' is not recursive, and thus $A' \neq \varnothing$. But A' is r.e. in A. So A' is the range of an A-recursive f. Then $f = H(c_A)$ for some scheme H. If $A \leq_T B$, $c_A = G(c_B)$ for some scheme G. So $f = H(c_A) = H(G(c_B))$. But the schemes are closed under composition, so A' is the range of the B-recursive function f, and then A' is r.e. in B. So by the last paragraph, A' is reducible to B'. Conversely, A and $\omega - A$ are recursive in A, so both are r.e. in A. Then both are reducible to A' and thus to B'. So both are r.e. in B, and hence A is recursive in B. It follows that if $A \equiv_T B$, then $A' \equiv_T B'$. (As we shall see, the converse is false.)[13] So if for any degree a, we pick $A \in a$ and set a' equal to the degree of A', then the jump is well-defined on degrees. Post's problem is equivalent to whether there is an r.e. degree a such that $0 <_T a$ and a $<_T 0'$.

S is the first-order theory of natural numbers we examined in Chapter 5. We saw that the relation $Pf_A(n, k)$ is recursive (k is the gödel number of a proof in S of the formula with gödel number n), and thus numeralwise expressed by a formula $Pf_s(x, y)$ in the language of S. Let Thm_s be $\{n \mid (\exists k)Pf_A(n, k)\}$. Then Thm_s is r.e. Consider any r.e. set A. Then $A = \{n \mid (\exists k)B(n, k)\}$ for some recursive B. Since B is recursive, it

[13] Ibid., 266.

is n.e. in S by a formula $B_s(x, y)$. If $(\exists k)B(n, k)$, then $B(n, k)$ for some $k \in \omega$, so $\vdash_s B_s(\underline{n}, \underline{k})$, and then $\vdash_s (\exists y)B_s(\underline{n}, y)$; and conversely, if $\vdash_s (\exists y)$ $B_s(\underline{n}, y)$, then this sentence is true in the standard model for S where $\underline{n}$ denotes n and B is the extension of B_s, so $(\exists k)B(n, k)$. Hence $(\exists k)B(n, k)$ if and only if $\vdash_s (\exists y)B_s(\underline{n}, y)$. Let $f(n)$ be the gödel number of the sentence $(\exists y)B_s(\underline{n}, y)$. Then $n \in A$ if and only if $f(n) \in Thm_s$, so A is reducible to Thm_s via f. Hence Thm_s is complete-r.e., and so $HP \equiv_T Thm_s$.

Let $\emptyset^{(0)}$ be $\emptyset$, $\emptyset^{(n+1)}$ be the jump of $\emptyset^{(n)}$ and let $\emptyset^{(\omega)}$ be $\{\tau(n, k) \mid n \in \emptyset^{(k)}\}$. For $n \in \omega$, let 0^n be the degree of $\emptyset^{(n)}$, and let 0^ω be the degree of $\emptyset^{(\omega)}$. Then $0, 0^1, 0^2,\ldots$ is a Turing increasing sequence of degrees, and 0^ω tops them all. We have just seen that Thm_s is in 0^1. A sequence of adjacent like quantifiers in a formula of S can always be replaced equivalently by a single quantifier of that type; this is because $(\exists x_1) \ldots (\exists x_n)$ $R(x_1,\ldots, x_n)$ is equivalent to $(\exists x)R(\pi_1^n(x),\ldots, \pi_n^n(x))$. So as far as quantification goes, all that really matters in a prenex equivalent of a formula of S is alternations of quantifiers. A formula in the language of S is both Σ_0 and Π_0 if and only if it is equivalent to a quantifier-free formula. It is Σ_{n+1} if and only if it is equivalent to $(\exists x)P(x)$ where $P(x)$ is Π_n, and it is Π_{n+1} if and only if it is equivalent to $(\forall x)P(x)$ where $P(x)$ is Σ_n. Let T_n be the set of all gödel numbers of Σ_n sentences of the language of S true in the standard model for S, and let T_s be the set of all gödel numbers of sentences in the language of S true in the standard model. Then for each n, T_n is in 0^n, and T_s is in 0^ω.[14] We said in Chapter 5 that truth eludes proof, and here we see a measure of how much T_s eludes Thm_s.[15]

Post had a program for addressing his problem, and we will describe the first two stages of that program. A set A is productive with productive partial recursive function ψ if and only if whenever $W_x \subseteq A$, then $\psi(x)$ converges and $\psi(x) \in A - W_x$. The partial computability of ψ makes A non-r.e. in a constructive way. A set A is creative if and only if it is r.e. and $\omega - A$ is productive. The set $K = \{x \mid \varphi_{u(n)}(x) \text{ converges}\}$ is creative. We have seen that K is r.e. Suppose $W_x \subseteq (\omega - K)$. If $x \in W_x$,

---

[14] Ibid., 318–19.

[15] In second-order ZFC we have second-order axioms rather than first-order schemata. So there is a single sentence A that is the conjunction of the set theoretic axioms of second-order ZFC. Then for any formula B in the language of second-order ZFC, B is a logical consequence of A if and only if $A \to B$ is a valid formula of second-order logic. So if we had an algorithm for second-order validity, we could use it to test whether a set theoretic claim follows from second-order ZFC. Let a be the degree of second-order ZFC and let b be the degree of second-order logic; then $a \leq_T b$. Clearly $0^\omega \leq_T a$, so second-order logic is much more undecidable than first.

then $x \notin K$, so $\varphi_{u(x)}(x)$ diverges, and thus $x \notin W_x$. Hence $x \notin W_x$, and so $x \in (\omega - K)$. Hence $x \in (\omega - K) - W_x$, so $\omega - K$ is productive with U_1^1. (The term "creative" is Post's. Dekker later introduced "productive.") Let $R(x, p)$ hold if and only if $\varphi_{t(u(x),p)}(x)$ converges. Then R is recursive, so some formula $B(x, y)$ n.e. R in S. Let $A_s(x)$ be the formula $(\exists y)B(x, y)$. K is $\{x \mid (\exists p)R(x, p)\}$. When e is an expression in the language of S, let 'e' be its gödel number. Let A be $\{'A_s(\underline{n})' \mid n \in (\omega - K)\}$. There is a recursive g such that for all x, if $W_x \subseteq A$, then $W_{g(x)} = \{n \mid 'A_s(\underline{n})' \in W_x\}$; in effect, g just reads off n as '$A_s(\underline{n})$' ticks by in an effective enumeration of W_x. We can show that A is productive with the f such that $f(x)$ = '$A_s(g(x))$'.[16] For any r.e. B there is a recursive h such that for all x, $W_{h(x)} = W_x \cap B$. Let U be $\{'F' \mid F \text{ is a sentence of the language of } S \wedge \vdash_s F\}$, and let B be $\{'A_s(\underline{n})' \mid n \in \omega\}$. U is productive with fh. Let W be $\{'F' \mid \vdash_s \neg F\}$. W is r.e., so $W = W_x$ for some x. If S is consistent, $W \subseteq U$, and then $fh(x) \in U - W$. Hence $A_s(g(h(x)))$ is not provable in S, because its gödel number is in U, and because its gödel number is not in W, neither is $\neg A_s(g(h(x)))$ provable in S. So S is incomplete. Creativity is thus an abstract form of undecidability and incompleteness. We saw a recursive j such that for all x, if $x \in HP$, then $W_{j(x)} = \omega$, but if $x \notin HP$, then $W_{j(x)} = \varnothing$. Then

$$x \in HP \text{ iff } W_{j(x)} = \omega$$
$$\text{iff } j(x) \in W_{j(x)}$$
$$\text{iff } j(x) \in K.$$

So HP is reducible to K via j. Hence $HP \leq_T K$, so $K \in 0'$. Thus a creative set does not automatically solve Post's problem.

Post's idea was to make an r.e. set A less recursive by weeding out r.e. subsets of $\omega - A$. But if B is productive with ψ, it has an infinite r.e. subset. For if a is an r.e. index for $\varnothing$, $W_a \subseteq B$, so $\psi(a) \in B - W_a$; let $f(0) = \psi(a)$. Assume $f(0),\ldots, f(n)$ defined, and let b be an r.e. index for $\{f(0),\ldots, f(n)\}$. Then $W_b \subseteq B$, so $\psi(b) \in B - W_b$. Let $f(n + 1) = \psi(b)$. Then f is a one–one recursive function, so its range is an infinite r.e. subset of B. Post called a set A simple if and only if it is r.e., but $\omega - A$ is infinite and has no infinite r.e. subsets. (So no creative set is simple.) The first order of business is to prove the existence of a simple set, and to do so we use some tools. A binary relation R is r.e. if and only

---

[16] Suppose $W_x \subseteq A$. Then $W_{g(x)} \subseteq (\omega - K)$. Since $\omega - K$ is productive with U_1^1, $g(x) \in (\omega - K) - W_{g(x)}$. Since $g(x) \in (\omega - K)$, '$A_s(g(x))$' $\in A$. If '$A_s(g(x))$' $\in W_x$, then since $W_x \subseteq A$, $g(x) \in W_{g(x)}$, which is impossible since $g(x) \in (\omega - K)$. Hence '$A_s(g(x))$' $\in A - W_x$, so A is productive with f.

if $\{\tau(x, y) \mid R(x, y)\}$ is r.e. If R is r.e., then there is a partial recursive ψ such that $\psi(x)$ converges if and only if $(\exists y)R(x, y)$, and if $(\exists y)R(x, y)$, then $R(x, \psi(x))$. Since R is r.e., there is a recursive Q such that $R(x, y)$ if and only if $(\exists z)Q(x, y, z)$. Let $\theta(x) = \mu y(Q(x, \pi_1(y), \pi_2(y)))$. Then θ is partial recursive, and setting $\psi(x) = \pi_1(\theta(x))$, ψ has the required properties. ψ is a selector for R. Next, A is r.e. if and only if it is the range of a partial recursive function. For if A is $\varnothing$, it is the range of the empty function, which is partial recursive, and if $a \neq \varnothing$, it is the range of a recursive f, which is partial recursive. Conversely, if A is the range of a partial recursive ψ, let n be an r.e. index for ψ. Then $A = \{x \mid (\exists y)(\varphi_{t(n,\pi_1(y))}(\pi_2(y)) = x)\}$ where the scope of the existential quantifier is recursive, so A is r.e.

There is a simple set. Let $R(n, x)$ hold if and only if $x \in W_n$ and $x > 2u(n)$. Then $R(n, x)$ if and only if

$$(\exists y)(\varphi_{t(u(n),\pi_1(y))}(x) = \pi_2(y) \wedge x > 2u(n)),$$

so since the scope of the existential quantifier is recursive, R is r.e. Let ψ be a partial recursive selector for R, and let S be the range of ψ. Then S is r.e. So to show S simple, we need to show that $\omega - S$ is infinite but has no infinite r.e. subsets. The distinctive property of ψ is that for all n, if $\psi(n)$ converges, then $\psi(n) > 2u(n) \geq n$. So for any n and all $k \geq n$, if $\psi(k)$ converges, then $\psi(k) > 2k \geq 2n$. Thus $\psi(k)$ converges and is in $\{0, 1,\ldots, 2n\}$ only if $k < n$. Hence at most n members of $\{0, 1,\ldots, 2n\}$ are in the range of ψ, that is, in S. But $\{0, 1,\ldots, 2n\}$ has $2n + 1$ members, so at least $n + 1$ of its members lie outside S, that is, in $\omega - S$. Since this holds for all n, $\omega - S$ is infinite. Let W_n be any infinite r.e. set. Since W_n is infinite, there is an $x \in W_n$ such that $x > 2u(n)$. Thus $(\exists x)R(n, x)$, so since ψ is a selector for R, $\psi(n)$ converges and $R(n, \psi(n))$. Thus $\psi(n) \in W_n$. So since S is the range of ψ, $\psi(n) \in S$. So S meets W_n, and thus W_n is not a subset of $\omega - S$.

But we have not yet solved Post's problem, for perhaps S is in $0'$. Post was aware of this, and in fact proved in 1944 that there is a simple set in $0'$. As for S, suppose W_n is an r.e. subset of $\omega - S$, and that there is a k in W_n bigger than $2u(n)$, so $R(n, k)$. R is r.e., so there is a recursive Q such that $R(n, k)$ if and only if $(\exists z)Q(n, k, z)$. Then there is a least y such that $Q(n, \pi_1(y), \pi_2(y))$, so $R(n, \pi_1(y))$, and thus $\pi_1(y) \in W_n$ and $\pi_1(y) > 2u(n)$. Then $\psi(n) = \pi_1(y)$, so $\pi_1(y) \in S$. But since $\pi_1(y) \in W_n \subseteq (\omega - S)$, this is impossible. So it follows that when $W_n \subseteq (\omega - S)$, then $W_n \subseteq \{0, 1,\ldots, 2u(n)\}$. Thus $f(n) = 2u(n) + 1$ is a recursive function such that when $W_n \subseteq (\omega - S)$, W_n has at most $f(n)$ members. A set A is effectively simple if

and only if it is simple and there is a recursive f such that W_n has at most
f(n) members when $W_n \subseteq (\omega - S)$. In 1966 D. A. Martin proved that
effectively simple sets are complete-r.e.[17] It follows that S is in $0'$.

A nonempty r.e. set is the range of a recursive function f. The idea is
that f ticks off members of the set one by one. But in some constructions
we build up an r.e. set by adding finite sets in stages. To see how such
recursive enumerations work, we begin with canonical indices. These
indices are a way of taking binary numerals. For every positive integer
n, there is a unique sequence, $k_0, k_1,..., k_p$ of natural numbers such that
$n = 2^{k_p} + ... + 2^{k_1} + 2^{k_0}$ where $k_p > ... > k_0$.[18] This can be taken as the
existence and uniqueness of binary numerals for positive integers. For

---

[17] D. A. Martin, "Completeness, the Recursion Theorem, and Effectively Simple Sets,"
Proceedings of the American Mathematical Society 17 (1966): 838–42. When S is
simple, ω – S is poor in r.e. subsets. Since the union of two r.e. sets is r.e., this can
also be put by saying a simple set is poor in r.e. supersets. At one extreme, an r.e.
set is maximal when its only r.e. supersets are those it must have, namely, when its
complement (ω – A) is infinite but when $A \subseteq B \subseteq \omega$ and B is r.e., then B – A or ω – B
is finite. John Myhill asked whether there are any in "The Lattice of Recursively
Enumerable Sets," *Journal of Symbolic Logic* 21 (1956): 215, 220 (abstract). Richard
M. Friedberg named them and proved that there is one in "Three Theorems on
Recursive Enumeration: I. Decomposition; II. Maximal Set; III. Enumeration without Duplication," *Journal of Symbolic Logic* 23 (1958): 309–16. Georg Kreisel and
Gerald E. Sacks called Friedberg's construction of a maximal set "one of the deepest
results in the theory of recursively enumerable sets" in "Metarecursive Sets," *Journal
of Symbolic Logic* 30 (1965): 318–38. C. E. M. Yates simplified Friedberg's construction and showed that there is a maximal set in $0'$ in "Three Theorems on the Degree
of Recursively Enumerable Sets," *Duke Mathematical Journal* 32 (1965): 461–68. If
Post's program were taken as a search for a property P of nonrecursive r.e. sets poor
in r.e. supersets such that there is a set with P and every set with P is in neither 0 nor
$0'$, then Post's program could be said to have failed. But it does not have to be taken
that way, and it has produced ideas of lasting importance.

[18] This is proved by induction on n. For n = 1, $1 = 2^0$ and any other sum of powers of 2
is greater than 1, so that claim holds at 1. Suppose $k_0,..., k_p$ are the only numbers such
that $n = 2^{k_p} + ... + 2^{k_0}$ and $k_p > ... > k_0$. Let k be the least number not among $k_0,..., k_p$.
Strike from $k_0,..., k_p$ those $k_i < k$, insert k, and let $m_0,..., m_q$ be the resulting numbers
in order of size. Then $n + 1 = 2^{m_q} + ... + 2^{m_0}$ and $m_q > ... > m_0$. If $2^{a_r} + ... + 2^{a_0}$ is a
different representation of n + 1, then

$$2^{a_r} + ... + 2^{a_0} = 2^{m_q} + ... + 2^{m_0}.$$

If 2 divides one side of this equation, it divides both, and the quotient will be a number less than n + 1 with two representations, contrary to the induction hypothesis.
Thus, 2 divides neither side, so $2^0 = 1$ occurs on both sides. Then subtracting 1 from
both sides, we have different representations of n, again contrary to the induction
hypothesis. This proof includes an algorithm that given n, yields $k_p,..., k_0$.

where $n = 2^{k_p},\ldots, 2^{k_0}$ and $k_p > \ldots > k_0$, let $c_n(k) = 1$ if 2^k is a term in the sum representing n, but let $c_n(k) = 0$ if not. Then n is the sum as k goes from 0 to k_p of $c_n(k)2^k$, and the coefficients $c_n(k_p) \ldots c_n(k_0)$ in that order constitute the binary numeral for n. For example, "11111" is the binary numeral for 31, and "100000" for 32. We can pass effectively back and forth between n and the $k_0,\ldots, k_p$ such that $n = 2^{k_p} + \ldots + 2^{k_1}$ and $k_p > \ldots > k_0$.

Let A be a finite set of natural numbers. We assign A a unique natural number called its canonical index. The canonical index of $\varnothing$ is 0. Otherwise let $k_p,\ldots, k_0$ be a list without repetitions of the members of A (in decreasing order of size), and let the canonical index of A be $2^{k_p} + \ldots + 2^{k_0}$. If we set $c_n(k) = 0$ for the $k > k_p$, then c_n is the characteristic function of $\omega - \{k_p,\ldots, k_0\}$. In effect we index A by the binary numeral fixed by the values of its characteristic function. This assignment is an effective one–one map of the finite sets of natural numbers onto ω. For each $k \in \omega$, let E_k be the unique finite set of natural numbers whose canonical index is k. This is an effective one–one map of ω onto its finite subsets.

A recursive enumeration of a set A is a recursive function f such that for all n, $E_{f(n)} \subseteq E_{f(n+1)}$ and $A = \bigcup_n E_{f(n)}$. We will often write A_s for $E_{f(s)}$ and $\{A_s\}$ for f. The sequence $\{A_s\}$ is a way of building A up effectively in cumulative finite stages. A is r.e. if and only if there is a recursive enumeration of A. For if $\{A_s\}$ is a recursive enumeration of A, the relation $n \in A_s$ is recursive and $n \in A$ if and only if $(\exists s)(n \in A_s)$, so A is r.e. If, conversely, A is r.e. and empty, $Z(n) = 0$ is a recursive enumeration of A. Otherwise A is the range of a recursive g. For each s, let A_s be (the canonical index of) $\{g(0),\ldots, g(s)\}$. Then $\{A_s\}$ is a recursive enumeration of A. For any n and s, let

$$W_{n,s} = \{x \leq s \mid \varphi_{t(u(n),s)}(x) \text{ converges}\}.$$

Then $W_{n,s}$ is a recursive enumeration of W_n. So we have a standard recursive enumeration of each r.e. set.

A sequence $\{f_s\}$ of total unary functions converges to a function f if and only if for every x there is a t such that for all $s \geq t$, $f(x) = f_s(x)$. In other words, for each x, the sequence $f_0(x), f_1(x),\ldots$ is eventually constant, and f(x) is this constant. This is written $f = \lim_s f_s$. The sequence $\{f_s\}$ is recursive if and only if the binary function $g(x, s) = f_s(x)$ is recursive. A modulus for $\{f_s\}$ is a function m such that for all x and all $s \geq m(x)$, $f_s(x) = f(x)$. If $m(x)$ is $\mu t((\forall_s \geq t)(f_t(x) = f(x)))$, then m is the least modulus for $\{f_s\}$. We will show that if $f = \lim_s f_s$ for some recursive $\{f_s\}$, then $f \leq_T \varnothing'$. For each x, let

$$A_x = \{s \mid (\exists t)(s \le t \land f_t(x) \ne f_{t+1}(x)\}.$$

And let

$$B = \{\tau(s, x) \mid s \in A_x\}.$$

(A_x is the set of stages at which $f(x)$ is still unsettled.) Draw up a list in the following stages:

At stage n, compute $f_s(x)$ for all pairs $<s, x>$ such that $s + x \le n$, and when $s = t + 1$ and $f_s(x) = f_t(x)$, put all of $\tau(0, x),..., \tau(t, x)$ on the list.

At none of these stages are we guaranteed to have finished listing A_x. But all and only the members of B are eventually listed. So B is r.e. Because HP is reducible to $\varnothing'$, $\varnothing$ is complete-r.e., so $B \le_T \varnothing'$. Let

$$m(x) = \mu s(\tau(s, x) \notin B)$$
$$= \mu s(s \notin A_x)$$
$$= \mu s((\forall t \ge s)(f_t(x) = f_{t+1}(x))).$$

Because $\{f_s\}$ converges to f, m is total; m is the least modulus for $\{f_s\}$, and if we could decide membership in B, we could complete m. But $f(x) = f_{m(x)}(x)$, so if we could compute m, we could compute f. Thus $f \le_T m \le_T B \le_T \varnothing'$. This is called a limit lemma.[19]

Post's problem was solved by two people independently in the mid-1950s. One, A. A. Muchnik, was a Russian; the other, Richard M. Friedberg, an American, and both were very young at the time.[20] Although they worked independently, each discovered the same new method by which they solved the problem. We will use that method to show there is a low simple set.[21] Our exposition follows Robert I.

---

[19] Joseph R. Shoenfield, *Degrees of Unsolvability* (Amsterdam: North-Holland, 1971), 29.

[20] A. A. Muchnik, "On the Unsolvability of the Problem of Reducibility in the Theory of Algorithms," *Doklady Akademii Nauk SSSR*, n.s. 108 (1956): 194–97. Richard M. Friedberg, "Two Recursively Enumerable Sets of Incomparable Degrees of Unsolvability (Solution of Post's Problem 1944)," *Proceedings of the National Academy of Sciences* 43 (1957): 236–38. They showed that there are A and B such that neither $A \le_T B$ nor $B \le_T A$, so $\varnothing <_T A <_T \varnothing'$ and $\varnothing <_T B < \varnothing'$. Friedberg later wrote *An Adventurer's Guide to Number Theory* (New York: Dover, 1994), an historical guidebook by someone at home among the natural numbers.

[21] It turned out later that Post's problem could be solved without this new method. A. Kučera, "An Alternative Priority-Free Solution to Post's Problem," in *Twelfth Symposium Held in Bratislava, Czechoslovakia, August 25–29, 1968*, Lecture Notes

Soare.[22] A set A is low if and only if $A' \leq_T \varnothing'$. Because A is low, $A <_T A' \leq_T \varnothing'$. Because A is simple, A is r.e. but not recursive, so $\varnothing <_T A$. So A is an r.e. set such that $\varnothing <_T A$ and $A <_T \varnothing'$, which solves Post's problem.[23] We will construct A by giving a recursive enumeration $\{A_s\}$ of finite sets in stages and setting $A = \bigcup_s A_s$. This will guarantee that A is r.e.

To make A simple, we must guarantee that $\omega - A$ is infinite but has no infinite r.e. subsets. For the last we must ensure that

$$(\forall n)(W_n \text{ is infinite} \rightarrow W_n \cap A \neq \varnothing).$$

Here we will use Post's strategy. For each n such that W_n has a member greater than $2u(n)$, we will put exactly one such member in A. Just as in Post's construction, this will ensure both that $\omega - A$ is infinite and that W_n meets A, so since A is r.e., A is simple. The universal quantification splits into an infinity of instances, and for each n, A must meet the requirement P_n that

$$W_n \text{ is infinite} \rightarrow W_n \cap A \neq \varnothing.$$

These are called positive requirements because to meet them we put numbers into A.

Making A low is another matter. Let us write $(\exists Is)Q(s)$ to mean that there are infinitely many s such that $Q(s)$. Suppose that for each n, A meets the requirement N_n that

$$(\exists Is)(H_{t(n,s)}(c_{A_s})(n) \text{ converges}) \rightarrow H_n(c_A)(n) \text{ converges}.$$

Then A will be low. To show this, let $g(n, s)$ be 0 if $H_{t(n,s)}(c_{A_s})(n)$ converges, but 1 if not. The set A_s is always finite, so c_{A_s} is recursive. So we will always be able to decide in finitely many mechanical steps whether $H_{t(n,s)}(c_{A_s})(n)$ converges. The number of steps is finite because the computation is truncated at no more than s steps, and each step is mechanical because our "oracle" c_{A_s} is recursive. Hence g is recursive.

in Computer Science No. 233, Proceedings, Mathematical Foundations of Computer Science '86, ed. J. Gruska et al. (Heidelberg: Springer, 1986). By the 1980s the new method had acquired a life of its own.

[22] Robert I. Soare, *Recursively Enumerable Sets and Degrees* (Berlin: Springer, 1987), 110–13.

[23] For every degree a there is a deductive theory T such that the set of gödel numbers of theorems of T is in a, and if a is r.e., T is axiomatic. Solomon Feferman, "Degrees of Unsolvability Associated with Classes of Formalized Theories," *Journal of Symbolic Logic* 22 (1957): 161–75.

We show that for all n, $\lim_s g(n, s) = c_{A'}(n)$. For each n, either $n \in A'$ or $n \notin A'$. Suppose first that $n \in A' = \{k \mid H_k(c_A)(k)$ converges$\}$. Then $H_n(c_A)(n)$ converges. So there is a unique finite set U such that the values of c_A on the members of U are used to show that $H_n(c_A)(n)$ converges. Let $U_{pos} = \{k \in U \mid c_A(k) = 0\}$ and $U_{neg} = \{k \in U \mid c_A(k) = 1\}$. Then $U_{neg} \cap A = \varnothing$ and $A_s \subseteq U_s A_s = A$, so for all s, $U_{neg} \cap A_s = \varnothing$. U_{pos} is a finite subset of A and $A = U_s A_s$, so there is a least t such that $U_{pos} \subseteq A_t$, and then since the stages A_s are cumulative, $U_{pos} \subseteq A_s$ for all $s \geq t$. So for all $s \geq t$, c_A agrees with c_{A_s} on U. Since $H_n(c_A)(n)$ converges, there is a least p such that $H_{t(n,p)}(c_A)(n)$ converges, and then for $q \geq p$, $H_{t(q,n)}(c_A)(n)$ converges. So if m is the maximum of t and p, then for $r \geq m$, $H_{t(r,n)}(c_{A_s})(n)$ is defined and equal to $H_n(c_A)(n)$. For all $s \geq n$, c_{A_s} agrees with c_A on U, so the information an oracle for c_A provides for the computation of $H_{t(n,s)}(c_{A_s})$ (n) is the same as the information the recursive function c_{A_s} provides for the computation of $H_{t(n,s)}(c_{A_s})(n)$. So these computations coincide, and since the first stops and yields an output within m steps, the second also stops and yields the same output. So for all $s \geq m$, $H_{t(n,s)}(c_{A_s})(n)$ is defined and equal to $H_n(c_{A_s})(n)$. So for all $s \geq m$, $H_{t(n,s)}(c_{A_s})(n)$ converges, and thus $g(n, s) = 0 = c_{A'}(n)$. (In this case we do not need the fact that A meets N_n.) Now suppose $n \notin A'$. Then $H_n(c_{A_s})(n)$ diverges. So by N_n, there are at most finitely many s such that $H_{t(n,s)}(c_{A_s})(n)$ converges. Then for some least m, $H_{t(n,s)}(c_{A_s})(n)$ diverges for $s \geq m$. Thus $g(n, s) = 1 = c_{A'}(n)$. But g is recursive. So by the limit lemma, $A' <_T \varnothing'$. Thus A will be low if it meets all the requirements N_n.

We need a way to meet the requirements of N_n. Suppose that at stage s, $H_{t(n,s)}(c_{A_s})(n)$ converges. If we can somehow preserve this computation forever after s, then by the use principle N_n will be met. But there is a problem about preserving the computation. Since $H_{t(n,s)}(c_{A_s})$ (n) converges, there is a unique finite set U such that the values of c_{A_s} on U are used to show convergence. As earlier, U is the disjoint union of $U_{pos} = \{k \in U \mid c_{A_s}(k) = 0\}$ and $U_{neg} = \{k \in U \mid c_{A_s}(k) = 1\}$. Clearly $U_{pos} \subseteq A_s \subseteq A_t$ for $t \geq s$. So the *positive* information used at s to show convergence is preserved after s. But for all we know, meeting one of the positive requirements P_k may later push us to put some number in U_{neg} into A, that is, into A_t for $t > s$. That would damage the information used negatively to show convergence at stage s, and maybe cause divergence at t. Suppose that for infinitely many s, $H_{t(n,s)}(c_{A_s})(n)$ converges, but that for every s there comes a $v > s$ and a k such that to meet P_k we put into A_v a number used negatively to show that $H_{t(n,s)}(c_{A_s})(n)$ converges, and thereby bring it about that $H_{t(n,v)}(c_{A_v})(n)$ diverges. If so, then by the use principle, $H_n(c_A)(n)$ diverges and A does not meet N_n.

Each P_k is a positive requirement because to meet it we will in general put numbers into A. We have just seen that to meet N_n we must in general keep numbers out of A, the ones used negatively. For that reason the requirements N_n are called negative. Our problem is a clash between the positive and the negative requirements on A. It was to solve this that Muchnik and Friedberg, independently, devised the priority method. We order our requirements thus:

$$N_0, P_0, N_1, P_1, \dots.$$

The idea is that N_i has priority over P_j if and only if $i \le j$, and P_j has priority over N_i if and only if $j < i$. Then we will be allowed to injure, as we will say, N_i for the sake of meeting P_j but only if P_j has priority over N_i. It is *not* supposed to be immediately obvious how to do this or that it will work.

We start by defining the use function. Let $\{B_s\}$ be a recursive enumeration. For each s, B_s is finite and thus recursive. For any n and x such that $H_{t(n,s)}(c_{B_s})(x)$ converges, there is a unique finite set U such that the values of c_{B_s} on U are used to show that $H_{t(n,s)}(c_{B_s})(x)$ converges. Moreover, because c_{B_s} is recursive, we can effectively list the members of U. If, on the other hand, $H_{t(n,s)}(c_{B_s})(x)$ diverges, then because c_{B_s} is recursive and we truncate computations by s steps, we can effectively determine that $H_{t(n,s)}(c_{B_s})(x)$ diverges. In the first case, let $v(B_s; n, x, s)$ be the successor of the largest member of U (or 1 if $U = \varnothing$), but 0 in the second case. We have just seen that v is computable.

As we enumerate the stage A_s, we will define the restraint function r thus: $r(n, s) = v(A_s; n, n, s)$. Then r is a recursive function. We use r to give P_j priority over N_i for $j < i$ as follows. Suppose at stage s we find numbers j and x such that $A_s \cap W_j = \varnothing$ but $x \in W_j$ and $x > 2u(j)$. Then to meet P_j we want to put x into A_{s+1}. (If we do so, $A_t \cap W_j \ne \varnothing$ for all t $> s$, so we need never worry about P_j again.) We allow ourselves to put x into A_{s+1} only if $x \ge r(i, s)$ for all $i \le j$. Then if $H_{t(i,s)}(c_{A_s})(i)$ converges for any $i \le j$, the information used (negatively) to establish this at stage s is preserved at stage s + 1. That is how N_i has priority over P_j for $i \le j$. But of course it may be that $x \le r(i, s)$ for some i > j, and in that case it may be that for this i, $H_{t(i,s)}(c_{A_s})(i)$ converges in part because $x \notin A_s$, yet $H_{t(i,s+1)}(c_{A_{s+1}})(i)$ diverges because $x \in A_{s+1}$. Then N_i has been injured for the sake of meeting P_j, but we have permitted this possibility only when j < i. That is how P_j has priority over N_i for j < i.

Now we give the recursive enumeration $\{A_s\}$. To do so we use $W_{i,s} = \{x \le s \mid \varphi_{r(u(i),s)}(x)$ converges$\}$; for each i, $\{W_{i,s}\}$ is a recursive enumeration of W_i. At stage 0, $A_0 = \varnothing$. At stage s + 1, we have A_s, so r(i, s) is defined for all i. We can decide whether there is an i ≤ s such that

$$(1) \quad W_{i,s} \cap A_s = \varnothing$$

and

$$(\exists x)(x \in W_{i,s} \wedge x > 2u(i) \wedge (\forall j \le i)(r(j, s) < x)).$$

If there is no such i, set $A_{s+1} = A_s$ and go on to the next stage. If there is such an i, let i^* be the least. Then we can find the least x such that $x \in W_{i^*,s} \wedge x > 2u(i^*) \wedge (\forall j \le i^*)(r(j, s) < x)$; call it x^*. Let $A_{s+1} = A_s \cup \{x^*\}$, and say that P_{i^*} receives attention. Since $W_{i^*,s} \cap A_{s+1} \ne \varnothing$, P_{i^*} is met; (1) will now fail for i = i^* and stages after this, so P_{i^*} will never again receive attention. Let $A = \cup_s A_s$, so A is r.e.

This construction works. A number x injures a requirement N_i at stage s + 1 if and only if $x \in A_{s+1} - A_s$ and x ≤ r(i, s). Here injury is meant only potentially. It need not be that $H_{t(i,s)}(c_{A_s})(i)$ converges and $H_{t(i,s+1)}(c_{A_{s+1}})(i)$ diverges, but it may be so. The injury set I_i for N_i is the set of those x that injure N_i at some stage s + 1. Our first result is that for each i, I_i is finite. Suppose x injures N_i at s + 1. Then $x \in A_{s+1} - A_s$ and x ≤ r(i, s). Since $x \in A_{s+1} - A_s$, there is a j such that $x \in W_{j,s}$, x > 2u(j), and for all e ≤ j, r(e, s) < x. So P_j receives attention at s + 1. Since x ≤ r(i, s) but x > r(e, s) for all e ≤ j, i > j. Thus x injures N_i only when P_j receives attention for some j < i. Each P_j receives attention at most once. So N_i is injured by at most one x for each j < i. Hence I_i has at most i members. The fact that I_i is finite is the hallmark of the original priority method.

Our next result is that for each i, N_i is met and $r(i) = \lim_s r(i, s)$ exists. Fix i. By our first result, there is a stage s_i such that N_i is injured at no stage beyond s_i. Suppose that for some s > s_i, $H_{t(i,s)}(c_{A_s})(i)$ converges. Then for all p ≥ s, $H_{t(i,p)}(c_{A_p})(i)$ is defined and equal to $H_{t(i,s)}(c_{A_s})(i)$ by the same computation. For otherwise let p be the earliest stage at which this fails. Then p > s, so p = m + 1 for some m ≥ s. The only way the failure could happen at p is that some x used negatively from s through m is added to A at m + 1 = p. But then $x \in A_{m+1} - A_m$ and x ≤ r(i, s) = r(i, m). So N_i is injured at m + 1 > s > s_i, contrary to the choice of s_i. But then N_i is met. For if $H_{t(i,s)}(c_{A_s})(i)$ converges infinitely often, it converges at an s > s_i. Then for all p ≥ s, r(i, s) = r(i, p). So from s onward, no number less than or equal to r(i, s) is added to A. Hence c_A agrees with c_{A_s} at and below r(i, s). Then since $H_{t(i,s)}(c_{A_s})(i)$ converges, $H_i(c_A)(i)$ converges by the use principle. Thus N_i is met. If, on the other hand, $H_{r(i,s)}(c_{A_s})(i)$ diverges for all $s > s_i$, then $r(i, s) = 0$ for all $s > s_i$. So in either case, $r(i, s)$ converges to some number $r(i)$.

Our third result is that for each i, P_i is met. Fix i. By our last result, there is an s such that for all $t \geq s$ and all $j \leq i$, $r(j, t) = r(j)$). Each positive requirement receives attention at most once, so there is an $s' \geq s$ such that for all $j < i$, P_j does not receive attention after s'. Suppose W_i is infinite. Then there is a $t > s'$ such that for some x, $x \in W_{i,t}$ and $x > 2u(i)$ and $r(e) < x$ for all $e \leq i$. Either $W_{i,t} \cap A_t \neq \varnothing$ or else P_i receives attention at $t + 1$. In either case $W_{i,t+1} \cap A_{t+1} \neq \varnothing$, so P_i is met by stage $t + 1$. Since A is simple and low, it solves Post's problem.

Because the injury sets are always finite in the method just used, that method is called the priority method with finite injury. There is also a priority method with infinite injury in which the injury sets may be infinite but will always be recursive. G. E. Sacks used it in 1964 to show that the r.e. sets are dense, that is, if A and B are r.e. and $A <_T B$, then there is an r.e. C such that $A <_T C$ and $C <_T B$.[24]

A person interested in the extinction of dinosaurs 65 million years ago would be quixotic to think that 32.5 million years ago a mirror on a planet circling a star then 32.5 million light-years from the Earth reflected their demise to where we are now, so we can see what killed them. A person interested in the curvature of spacetime does not expect to pick up a chunk of spacetime and see how bent it is. Many interesting phenomena are studied not directly but by what we think are their effects that are accessible to us. It is like that with reason. There is little hope of laying hands on the reason of a genius and dissecting it. The accessible products of reason are reasoning as in arguments and explanations, and of these, deductive theories are among the richest samples. So a critique of reason should include an examination of deductive theories. From a less empirical perspective one might hope to examine a structure into which all possible deductive theories fall. So a critique of pure reason should examine the structure of the r.e. degrees.[25]

---

[24] Soare, *Recursively Enumerable Sets*, 142–45. There are yet more sophisticated versions of the priority method. Soare's book is a masterpiece of exposition from which ordinary mortals can learn about them. Earlier masterpieces of exposition are Rogers, *Theory of Recursive Functions*, and Davis, *Computability and Unsolvability*.

[25] No one knows why the theories we devise naturally always lie at the extremes, 0 or $0'$. Feferman's examples are pretty artificial. But perhaps we, or other rational beings, will one day have more intermediate natural theories in which problems we now find hard will be easier.

NINE

✦

The Ways of the World

There are at least three ways a theory might nail down its subject matter. The theory might be decidable, so there is an algorithm for whether a sentence in the language of the theory is a theorem of it. The theory might be complete, so any sentence in the language of the theory is either proved or refuted. Both these properties concern the deductive structure of the theory, but the third does not. The theory might be categorical, so any two models for it are isomorphic. Let M and N be models for a theory T. Let the domain of M be $D(M)$, and the domain of N be $D(N)$. For each constant c in the language of T, let c^M and c^N be its denotations in M and N; for each predicate F, let F^M and F^N be its extensions in M and N; and for each function sign f, let f^M and f^N be its extensions in M and N. An isomorphism between M and N is a function g that maps $D(M)$ one–one onto $D(N)$, so that (1) $g(c^M) = c^N$, (2) if F is n-ary, then for all $x_1,..., x_n$ in $D(M)$, $F^M(x_1,..., x_n)$ if and only if $F^N(g(x_1),..., g(x_n))$, and (3) if f is n-ary, then for all $x_1,..., x_n$ in $D(M)$, $g(f^M(x_1,..., x_n)) = f^N(g(x_1),..., g(x_n))$. An isomorphism is a one–one correspondence that preserves structure. M and N are isomorphic if and only if there is an isomorphism between them. A categorical theory individuates the structure of its subject matter.[1]

Let A be the second-order sentence

$$(\forall x)(f(x) \neq c) \wedge (\forall x, y)(f(x) = f(y) \to x = y)$$
$$\wedge (\forall F)((F(c) \wedge (\forall x)(F(x) \to F(f(x)))) \to (\forall x)F(x)).$$

A model M for A has a domain $D(M)$ and extensions c^M and f^M for c and f; the second-order variable "F" has all subsets of $D(M)$ as values.

---

[1] The notion of categoricity comes from Oswald Veblen, "A System of Axioms for Geometry," *Transactions of the American Mathematical Society* 5 (1904): 343–84.

The structure M whose domain is ω, in which c^M is 0 and f^M is the successor function, is a model for A and is indeed the standard model. Suppose N is a model for A. We can show in set theory that there is a $g : \omega \to D(N)$ such that $g(0) = c^N$ and for all $n \in \omega$, $g(n') = f^N(g(n))$, so g preserves the structure of M. So if g maps ω one–one onto D(N), then g is an isomorphism. If g is not one–one, let m be the least number such that for some $n > m$, $g(m) = g(n)$. Then n is a successor, so $n = p'$ for some p, and then $g(n) = f^N(g(p))$. Also $m \neq 0$, for otherwise, $f^N(g(p)) = g(n) = g(m) = g(o) = c^N$, which would make c^N an N-successor, which A forbids. Thus $m = q'$ for some q. Then $f^N(g(p)) = g(n) = g(m) = g(q') = f^N(g(q))$, so since f^N is one–one, $g(p) = g(q)$. But $p' = n > m = q'$, so since successor is one–one, $p > q$, but $g(p) = g(q)$ contrary to the leastness of m, since $q < m$ because $q' = m$. If g is not onto, let a be the N-least member of D(N) not in the range of g. Since $g(o) = c^N$, $a \neq c^N$, so $a = f^N(b)$ for some $b \in D(N)$. Then $g(n) = b$ for some $n \in \omega$, whence $g(n') = f^N(g(n)) = f^N(b) = a$. Hence g maps ω one–one onto D(N). So A is categorical. We saw in Chapter 5 that S, the first-order version of A, is not categorical. The difference is that A allows us to do induction on sets, values of "F," that we specify in terms of M, N, and both, while S allows us induction only for formulae built up from 0, ', +, ×, and = using truth-functional connectives and first-order quantification, thus confining us to one model of S at a time.

There is no developed mathematics of models for second-order theories, so for the most part, model theory is about models for first-order theories. The theory that says there are exactly three things and stops there is categorical. But most theories have infinite models, and those with countable languages that do, have models of all infinite cardinalities. There is no one–one correspondence between domains of different cardinalities, so no such theories are categorical. For first-order theories, categoricity shatters into categoricity in power.[2] Let κ be an infinite cardinal. Then a first-order theory is κ-categorical if and only if it has a model of cardinality κ and any two models of it of cardinal κ are isomorphic. We saw in Chapter 5 that S is not ω-categorical.

[2] The rational numbers with their less-than relation are a dense linear order without endpoints. In 1895 Cantor published a proof that any two countable dense linear orders without endpoints are isomorphic; see Georg Cantor, *Contributions to the Founding of the Theory of Transfinite Numbers*, trans. Philip E. B. Jourdain (New York: Dover, [1952]), 124–27. So the theory of dense linear orders without endpoints is ω-categorical. In a way, Cantor isolated categoricity in power before Veblen defined categoricity.

Let T_1 be the theory with no extralogical signs, that is, the pure theory of identity. For any two models of T_1 with the same cardinality, any one–one correspondence between their domains preserves differences, and thus structure, according to T_1. So T_1 is κ-categorical for all κ. Let T_2 be the theory with a single unary predicate F as its only extralogical sign, and no axioms peculiar to F. For any κ, T_2 has two models of cardinal κ, in one of which nothing satisfies F and in the other, everything does. So T_2 is κ-categorical for no κ. Let T_3 be the theory with the unary predicate G as its only extralogical constants, and axioms saying for each natural number n that at least n things satisfy G and at least n things do not. Let M and N be countable models for T_3. Let $m_0^+, m_1^+, \ldots$ be the members of D(M) satisfying G, let $m_0^-, m_1^-, \ldots$ be the members of D(M) not satisfying G, let $n_0^+, n_1^+, \ldots$ be the members of D(N) satisfying G, and let $n_0^-, n_1^-, \ldots$ be the members of D(N) not satisfying G. Let $g(m_i^+) = n_i^+$ and $g(m_i^-) = n_i^-$. Then g is an isomorphism between M and N. So T_3 is ω-categorical. If κ is uncountable, T_3 has a model M of cardinal κ in which ω things in D(M) satisfy G, so κ things do not, and a model N of cardinal κ in which ω things in D(N) do not satisfy G, so κ things do. So T_3 is κ-categorical for no uncountable κ. Let T_4 be the theory with a countable infinity $c_0, c_1, \ldots$ of constants and the axioms $c_i \neq c_j$ for $i \neq j$. T_4 has two countable models, M and N, such that every member of D(M) is denoted by a constant but some members of D(N) are not. If $n \in D(N)$ is unnamed and g maps D(M) one–one onto D(N), then for some $m \in D(M)$, $g(m) = n$, so if $c_i^M = m$, then $g(c_i^M) \neq c_i^N$. Thus T_4 is not ω-categorical. If M and N are models of T_4 of uncountable cardinal κ, let f map D(M) one–one onto D(N). We define a sequence of maps. Let f_0 be f. If f_n is an isomorphism between M and N, let $f_{n+1} = f_n$. Otherwise let i be the least number such that $f_n(c_i^M) \neq c_i^N$. There is an $m \in D(M)$ and a $p \in D(N)$ such that $f_n(c_i^M) = p$ and $f_n(m) = c_i^N$. Let f_{n+1} be f_n with the pairs $<c_i^M, p>$ and $<m, c_i^N>$ replaced with $<c_i^M, c_i^N>$ and $<m, p>$. For all i and all $k > i$, $f_k(c_i^M) = c_i^N$. For each $m \in D(M)$, let g(m) be $f_k(m)$ for the least k such that $f_k(m)$ becomes constant. Then g is an isomorphism between M and N, so T_4 is κ-categorical.

We have exemplified four varieties of categoricity in power for infinite cardinals: categorical in all, categorical in none, ω-categorical but categorical in no uncountable cardinal, and not ω-categorical but categorical in all uncountable cardinals. Suppose that any complete theory with a countable language is categorical in all uncountable cardinals if it is categorical in any.[3] Equivalently, the theory is categorical in no

---

[3] An incomplete theory in a countable language that has an infinite model is categorical in no infinite cardinal. For if A is not decided in the theory, then for all infinite

uncountable cardinal or in all. Combining these two possibilities with being either ω-categorical or not, we get the four varieties exemplified in the previous paragraph. In 1954 Jerzy Łoś conjectured that a complete theory in a countable language categorical in one uncountable cardinal is categorical in all.[4] Łoś's conjecture was proved by Michael Morley in his Ph.D. thesis in 1962.[5] David Marker says, "Morley's proof was the beginning of modern model theory."[6] Wilfrid Hodges says, "The statement of the theorem is no big deal; the value lies in two other things. There are, first, the techniques one develops in order to prove the theorem, and, second, the elegant structure theory which emerges from the proof."[7] Our proof of Morley's theorem will follow the simplification of Morley's argument by John Baldwin and A. H. Lachlan.[8] This omits some of Morley's techniques but is a good beginning and exhibits some of the varieties of models, ways the world might be from a first-order point of view.

We want two monuments of earlier model theory, the Löwenheim–Skolem theorem the compactness. We proved the first in Chapter 6, but while we mentioned the second in Chapter 4, we did not prove it. So we are out to show that if every finite subset of a set of first-order sentences has a model, then so does the set. A set of sentences is finitely satisfiable if and only if all its finite subsets have models. A set

κ, the theory has two models of cardinal κ, one in which A holds, and another in which it fails. Isomorphic models agree on all sentences, so these models are not isomorphic. In thinking about categoricity we focus on complete theories.

4   Jerzy Łoś, "On the Categoricity in Power of Elementary Deductive Systems and Some Related Problems," *Colloquium Mathematicum* 3 (1954): 58–62. It seems to have been in the mid-1950s that Łoś and Robert Vaught focused attention on categoricity in power. See Evert W. Beth, *The Foundations of Mathematics*, rev. ed. (New York: Harper Torchbooks, 1964), 238, but it is difficult to make out what Beth means by Vaught's 1953 paper.

5   Michael Morley, "Categoricity in Power," *Transactions of the American Mathematical Society* 114 (1965): 514–38. Wilfrid Hodges says, "The paper which gave us Morley's theorem is a jewel of the logical literature. Almost every line in it contains a new idea which later model theorists have worked out in the more general setting of stability theory; and yet it is beautifully readable." *A Shorter Model Theory* (Cambridge: Cambridge University Press, 1997), 296. Morley finished his thesis under Vaught.

6   David Marker, *Model Theory: An Introduction* (New York: Springer, 2002), 207.

7   Hodges, *Shorter Model Theory*, 250.

8   J. T. Baldwin and A. H. Lachlan, "On Strongly Minimal Sets," *Journal of Symbolic Logic* 36 (1971): 71–96. Marker's book is an excellent place to learn Baldwin and Lachlan's argument.

of sentences has witnesses if and only if for every formula $F(x)$ in its language with only x free there is a constant c such that $(\exists x)F(x) \rightarrow F(c)$ is in the set.[9] A set of sentences is maximal if and only if for every sentence in its language, either that sentence or its negation is in the set. For theories without deductive structure, completeness is maximality. Suppose T is maximal and finitely satisfiable; then if a sentence A follows from a finite subset S of T, A is in T. For if not, $\neg A \in T$, and then S $\cup \{\neg A\}$ is a finite subset of T with no model.

Suppose that T is finitely satisfiable. We will show that T has a finitely satisfiable extension with witnesses. Let C_1, C_2,... be a countable sequence of pairwise disjoint countable sets of constants not in the language of T.[10] Enumerate the formulae $F_i(x_{i_n})$ of the language of T with at most the variable x_{i_n} free. Enumerate the constants in C_1. Let A_i be $(\exists x_{i_n})F_i(x_{i_n}) \rightarrow F_i(c_i)$, and let T_1 be T together with all the A_i. Then T_1 is finitely satisfiable. For let S be a finite subset of T_1. S is the disjoint union of a finite subset S^* of T and a finite set of the new A_i. Since T is finitely satisfiable, S^* has a model M. For any A_i in S, if $(\exists x_{i_n})F_i(x_{i_n})$ is not true in M, A_i is true in M, but if $(\exists x_{i_n})F_i(x_{i_n})$ is true in M, we can expand M to a model for A_i by choosing from $D(M)$ a denotation for c_i that satisfies $F_i(x_{i_n})$. Now repeat the construction of T_1 through all the natural numbers using the constants in C_n at stage n to witness existential sentences in T_n. At each stage the language is expanded by a set of new constants. For all n, T_n is finitely satisfiable. Let T' be the union of all the T_n. Then T' is finitely satisfiable, because any finite subset of it is a subset of some T_n and so has a model. Moreover, T' has witnesses, because any existential sentence in T' is in some T_n and received a witness in T_{n+1}.

Next we show that T' has finitely satisfiable extension that is maximal and has witnesses. Let A_1, A_2,... be an enumeration of the sentences of T'. Let V_0 be T'. If $V_n \cup \{A_n\}$ is finitely satisfiable, let V_{n+1} be $V_n \cup \{A_n\}$, but otherwise let it be $V_n \cup \{\neg A_n\}$. For all n, V_n is finitely

---

[9] The term "witness" comes from C. C. Chang and H. Jerome Keisler, *Model Theory* (Amsterdam: North-Holland, 1973), 61. The idea is that because $F(c)$ when $(\exists x)$ $F(x)$, c is a witness to the existence of Fs.

[10] The language of T is countably infinite. Were it bigger, we would need a longer sequence of bigger sets of constants. The union of C_1, C_2,... is countable. If all the constants in our original stock were used in T, we could replace a_n there with a_{2n}, and get C_1, C_2,... by splitting the constants of odd subscript into countably many disjoint parts. C_q could be the constants whose subscripts are the positive powers of $p(q + 1)$, where $p(i)$ is the $(i+1)^{th}$ prime in order of size. So the members of C_1 would be $c_3, c_9, c_{27}, \ldots$.

satisfiable. V_0 is because it is T'. Suppose V_n is finitely satisfiable. If $V_n \cup \{A_n\}$ is not finitely satisfiable, then there is a finite $W \subseteq V_n$ such that $\neg A_n$ follows from W. Then $V_n \cup \{\neg A_n\}$ is finitely satisfiable. Let U be a finite subset of V_n. Then $W \cup U$ is a finite subset of V_n, so it has a model M, and since $\neg A_n$ follows from $W \cup U$, M is a model for $U \cup \{\neg A_n\}$. Hence, V_{n+1} is finitely satisfiable. Let T'' be the union of all the V_n. Any finite subset of T'' is a subset of some V_n, and so has a model; so T'' is finitely satisfiable. T'' has the same language as T', so since T' has witnesses, T'' does too. Any sentence A in the language of T'' is A_n for some n, and either A_n is in V_{n+1} or $\neg A_n$ is, so T'' is maximal.

Let C be the union of the sets C_1, C_2,... of constants. We will build a model for T'' from the constants in C, and since T is part of T'', this will also be a model for T.[11] For constants c and d in C, write $c \sim d$ if and only if the sentence $c = d$ is in T''. Then $\sim$ is an equivalence relation. It is reflexive. For $c = c$ is valid, and so follows from T'', and then since T'' is maximal and finitely satisfiable, $c = c$ is in T''. Symmetry and transitivity are similar. For each c in C, let [c] be its equivalence class under $\sim$, and let D be the set of all these equivalence classes. D will be the domain of our model for T''. For any constant a in the language of T'' (whether a is in C or not), $(\exists x)(x = a)$ is valid, and so follows from T'', and thus is in T''. Then since T'' has witnesses, there is a constant c in C such that $c = a$ is in T''. Let a^M be [c]. Were there two such, say c and d, then $c = a$ and $d = a$ are in T'', so $c = d$ is in T'', and then [c] = [d]; thus a^M is well-defined. Let f be an n-ary function sign in the language of T'' and let $[c_1],...,[c_n]$ be members of D. Since $(\exists x)(f(c_1,...,c_n) = x)$ is valid, there is a c in C such that $f(c_1,...,c_n) = c$ is in T''. Let f^M be the function whose value at $[c_1],...,[c_n]$ is [c]. Then f^M is also well-defined. Now let A be an n-ary predicate letter in the language of T''. Then let A^M be the set of all $<[c_1],...,[c_n]>$ such that $A(c_1,...,c_n)$ is in T''; A^M is also well-defined. This completes the specification of M. A closed term is a term in which no variables occur. Note that for each closed term t in the language of T'' there is a constant c(t) in C such that t^M, the denotation of t in M, is [c(t)]. (We can make c(t) unique using the enumeration of the sets C_1, C_2,....)

Next we show that M is a model for T''. We prove by induction on the complexity of a sentence A in the language of T'' that A is true in M

---

[11] The idea of using constants to interpret a language in which they occur comes from Leon Henkin. See his "The Completeness of the First-Order Functional Calculus," *Journal of Symbolic Logic* 14 (1949): 159–66. Model theorists call this building models from constants.

if and only if A is a member of T″. In the basis case, A is atomic. Suppose A is not an identity sentence, and for simplicity that its predicate is unary. Then A is F(t) for some closed term t. So

$$F(t) \text{ is true in M iff } t^M \in F^M$$
$$\text{iff } [c(t)] \in F^M$$
$$\text{iff } F(c(t)) \in T''$$
$$\text{iff } F(t) \in T''$$

where the last step holds because the sentence c(t) = t is in T″. If A is an identity sentence t = s, then

$$t = s \text{ is true in M iff } t^M = s^M$$
$$\text{iff } [c(t)] = [c(s)]$$
$$\text{iff } c(t) \sim c(s)$$
$$\text{iff } c(t) = c(s) \in T''$$
$$\text{iff } t = s \in T''$$

since c(t) = t and c(s) = s are in T″. If A is ¬B, then if ¬B is true in M, B is not true in M, so B is not in T″, so ¬B is in T″ because T″ is maximal; conversely, if ¬B is in T″, B is not in T″ because T″ is finitely satisfiable, so B is not true in M, so ¬B is. The conjunction case is easy. Suppose A is $(\forall x_i)B(x_i)$. If A is true in M but not in T″, then $(\exists x_i)\neg B(x_i)$ is in T″ because T″ is maximal. Since T″ has witnesses, ¬B(c) is in T″ for some constant c. Since T″ is finitely satisfiable, B(c) is not in T″, so by the induction hypothesis, B(c) is not true in M. But since $(\forall x_i)B(x_i)$ is true in M and B(c) follows from $(\forall x_i)B(x_i)$, B(c) is true in M. Hence by reductio, when the universal quantification is true in M, it is a member of T″. Now suppose, conversely, that A is in T″ but not true in M. Then $(\exists x_i)\neg B(x_i)$ is true in M, so some member d of D does not satisfy B(x_i). This d is [c] for some constant c, so B(c) is not true in M. Hence B(c) is not in T″ by the induction hypothesis. But B(c) follows from A, which is in T″, so B(c) is in T″. Thus by reductio when the universal quantification is in T″, it is true in M. This completes the induction. Thus M is a model for T″. Since T is a subset of T″, M is a model for T. This completes the proof of compactness.[12]

This argument gives us a countable model. From now on we will assume there are as many constants as we might need; say that for every

---

[12] This proof of compactness does not go through completeness (and makes no use of ultraproducts). It comes from Marker, *Model Theory*, 35–38, and deserves to be well known among philosophers.

infinite cardinal κ, there are at least κ constants. Adjusting our argument here and there we could have added κ constants instead of just ω. Then we get a model of at most cardinality κ. Suppose T has an infinite model. Then we can add another κ constants plus the sentences $c_\alpha \neq c_\beta$ for any distinct ordinals α, β less than κ. This preserves finite satisfiability, so we get a model of cardinality κ. Now suppose T is an incomplete theory with an infinite model. By the Löwenheim–Skolem theorem and the last paragraph, T is κ-categorical for no infinite κ. Hence, for purposes of proving Morley's theorem, we confine our attention to complete theories (usually with countable languages).

Suppose M and N are interpretations of a single language L. Recall that M is a substructure of N (and N is an extension of M) if and only if the domain of M is a subset of that of N, for every constant a of L, $a^M = a^N$, and for every predicate letter A and function letter f of L, A^M and f^M are the restrictions of A^N and f^N to the domain of M. Suppose $t(x_1,..., x_n)$ is a term of L whose variables are among $x_1,..., x_n$, and $m_1,..., m_n$ are members of D(M). We define $t^M(m_1,..., m_n)$ inductively: if t is x_i, $t^M(m_1,..., m_n)$ is m_i; if t is a constant a, $t^M(m_1,..., m_n)$ is a^M; and if t is $f(t_1,..., t_k)$, $t^M(m_1,..., m_n)$ is $f^M(t_1^M(m_1,..., m_n),..., t_k^M(m_1,..., m_n))$. (This is a rethinking of s*(t) in Chapter 5.) It is an easy induction to show that for any term $t(x_1,..., x_n)$ of L and $m_1,..., m_k$ in D(M), if M is a substructure of N, then $t^M(m_1,..., m_k) = t^N(m_1,..., m_k)$. It is then an easy induction to show that for any formula $A(x_1,..., x_n)$ of L without quantifiers and any $m_1,..., m_k$ in D(M),

$A(m_1,..., m_k)$ is true in M iff $A(m_1,..., m_k)$ is true in N.

If this equivalence holds for all formulae of L, then M is an elementary substructure of N (and N is an elementary extension of M). The equivalence includes the case k = 0, and so requires that M and N agree on all sentences of L (such equivalence on sentences is called elementary equivalence). The rationals are a substructure of the reals, but since the sentence

$$(\forall x)(x \geq 0 \rightarrow (\exists y)(x = y \cdot y))$$

holds in the reals but fails in the rationals, the reals are not an elementary extension of the rationals. A condition on quantification necessary and sufficient for a substructure M of N to be elementary is that for any formula $A(x, y_1,..., y_p)$ of L and any $m_1,..., m_p$ in D(M), if there is a b in D(N) such that $A(b, m_1,..., m_p)$ is true in N, then there is a c in D(M) such that $A(c, m_1,..., m_p)$ is true in N. For then if $(\exists x)A(x, m_1,..., m_p)$ is true in N, then there is a c in $D(M)$ such that $A(c, m_1,..., m_p)$ is true in N, so by induction $A(c, m_1,..., m_p)$ is true in M, and then so too is $(\exists x)A(x, m_1,..., m_p)$. (The converse does not need the condition.) This condition is called the Tarski–Vaught test.

It is tiresome to write out tuples of variables and objects, especially when we do not care how long those tuples are. So we will start using underlining instead to mean multiplicity. Thus $\underline{x}$ will be short for a tuple of variables, and $\underline{m}$, for a tuple of objects.

Let $<$ be a linear order with field I. Suppose that for each i in I, M_i is an interpretation of a language L. If for $i < j$, M_i is a substructure of M_j, then $\{M_i \mid i \in I\}$ is called a chain, and it is elementary if M_i is an elementary substructure of M_j. Let $\{M_i \mid i \in I\}$ be a chain. Let $D(M)$ be the union of the $D(M_i)$ for i in I. For a constant a of L, let a^M be a^{M_i} for any i. Let f be an n-ary function sign of L, and let $\underline{m}$ be an n-tuple of members of M. Since $<$ is linear, there is an i in I such that each member of $\underline{m}$ is in $D(M_i)$. Let f^M be the function whose value at $\underline{m}$ is $f^{M_i}(\underline{m})$. Similarly, if A is an n-ary predicate letter of L, let A^M hold on $\underline{m}$ if and only if A^{M_i} holds on $\underline{m}$. This M is called the union of the chain $\{M_i \mid i \in I\}$, and each M_i is a substructure of M. Moreover, if the chain is elementary, each M_i is an elementary substructure of its union. We prove this by induction but give only the Tarski–Vaught case. So suppose for some $A(x, \underline{z})$ of L and $\underline{m}$ in M_i there is a $b \in D(M)$ such that $A(b, \underline{m})$ is true in M. Since $b \in D(M)$, b is in some $D(M_j)$, so there is a $p \geq i$ such that $b \in D(M_p)$. By induction, $A(b, \underline{m})$ is true in M_p, so $(\exists x)A(x, \underline{m})$ is true in M_p, and then since M_i is an elementary substructure of M_p, $(\exists x)A(x, m)$ is true in M_i.

Types are basic to modern model theory. Let M be an interpretation of a language L and let A be a subset of $D(M)$. Let L_A be L together with a constant for each member of A. $Th_A(M)$ is the set of sentences of L_A true in M. Let p be a set of formulae of L_A such that for any F in p, the variables free in F occur among $x_1,..., x_n$. If we wish we may make the variables explicit by writing p as $p(x_1,..., x_n)$. Then p is an n-type over A if and only if $Th_A(M) \cup p$ has a model. We say p is complete if and only if for each F with variables among $\underline{x}$, F or $\neg F$ is in p. $S_n^M(A)$ is the set of all complete n-types over A. Let $\underline{m}$ be an n-tuple of members of $D(M)$. Then $tp^M(\underline{m} \mid A)$ is the set of formulae F of L_A with free variables among $x_1,..., x_n$ such that $F(\underline{m})$ is true in M. We call $tp^M(\underline{m} \mid A)$ the type of $\underline{m}$ over A; it is always complete. We write $tp^M(\underline{m})$ for $tp^M(\underline{m} \mid \varnothing)$. A tuple $\underline{m}$ realizes a type p if and only if $F(\underline{m})$ is true in M for all $F(\underline{x})$ in p; and if no tuple realizes p in M, we say M omits p.[13]

Any type of M over A is realized in an elementary extension of M. Let p be an n-type of M over A. Form L_M by adding to L_A a constant c(m) for each $m \in D(M)$. The elementary diagram of M is the set of all sentences of L_M true in M. Let ED be the elementary diagram of M. Add to L_M n new constants $c_1,\ldots, c_n$. Let Γ be the union of ED and $p(\underline{c})$, and let Δ be a finite subset of Γ. Let $B(\underline{c}, \underline{a}_1)$ be the conjunction of the members of $p(\underline{c})$ in Δ, and let $F(\underline{a}_2, \underline{m})$ be the conjunction of the members of ED in Δ, where $\underline{a}_1, \underline{a}_2 \in A$ and $\underline{m} \in D(M) - A$. Since p is an n-type, there is a model for $p(\underline{c}) \cup Th_A(M)$, and since $(\exists x)F(\underline{a}_2, x)$ is in $Th_A(M)$, this model is a model for $B(\underline{c}, \underline{a}_1) \cup (\exists x)F(\underline{a}_2, x)$. Letting $\underline{m}$ be the values of $\underline{x}$, this model is a model for Δ. This Δ is satisfiable, so Γ is finitely satisfiable. Hence by compactness, Γ has a model N. Next we show M isomorphic to a submodel of N. For $m \in D(M)$, let g(m) = $c(m)^N$. Let D(M') be the range of g on D(M). For any constant c of L, let $c^{M'}$ be $g(c^M)$; for any predicate letter F of L, let $F^{M'}$ be $g(F^M)$; and for any p-ary function letter f of L and any $n_1,\ldots, n_p$ in D(M'), let $m_1,\ldots, m_p$ be the unique members D(M) such that $g(m_1) = n_1,\ldots, g(m_p) = n_p$, and let $f^{M'}(n_1,\ldots, n_p) = g(f^M(m_1,\ldots, m_p))$. Then M' is a substructure of N, and g is an isomorphism from M to M'. M' is an elementary substructure of N. If $n_1,\ldots, n_p$ are in D(M'), there are unique $m_1,\ldots, m_p$ in M such that $g(m_1) = n_1,\ldots, g(m_p) = n_p$. Then for any formula $F(\underline{x})$ of L

$$F(\underline{n}) \text{ is true in M' iff } F(\underline{c(m)}) \text{ is true in M}$$
$$\text{iff } F(\underline{c(m)}) \text{ is true in N}$$
$$\text{iff } F(\underline{n}) \text{ is true in N}$$

where the first equivalence holds by isomorphism, the second because N is a model for ED, and the third because each n_i is $c(m_i)^N$. Form N' by replacing g(m) in D(M') by m. Then M is an elementary submodel of N', and if the members of $\underline{b}$ are the denotations of $\underline{c}$ in N', $\underline{b}$ realizes p in N'. (In fact, $p \in S_n^M(A)$ if and only if there is an elementary extension N of M and an n-tuple $\underline{a}$ in D(M) such that $p = tp^N(\underline{a} \mid A)$.)

A kind of mathematical serendipity happens when a pattern native to one part of mathematics recurs in another part. The calculus Newton

---

[13] Bruno Poizat says that types were worked out in the 1950s and that the first systematic exposition of types (and saturated models) is in Michael Morley and Robert Vaught, "Homogeneous Universal Models," *Mathematica Scandinavica* 11 (1962): 37–57. See Poizat, *A Course in Model Theory*, trans. Moses Klein (New York: Springer, 2000), 63.

and Leibniz discovered matured into analysis in the nineteenth century, and toward the end of that century topology, an abstract theory of continuity, emerged from analysis. A topological space is given by a nonempty set S together with a collection T of subsets of S called open sets that is closed under arbitrary unions and finite intersections.[14] But though continuity is about preserving contiguity, and types do not come with an evident measure of separation, $S_n^M(A)$ is a topological space. One way to construct a topology of open sets is to start with basic open sets, take open sets as arbitrary unions of basic open sets, and check that these open sets are closed under finite intersections. Let F be a formula of L_A with free variables among $x_1, \ldots, x_n$. Then [F] is the set of types p in $S_n^M(A)$ such that F is a member of p. Since types in $S_n^M(A)$ are complete, $[F] \cup [G] = [F \vee G]$. We take the sets [F] as basic open sets, so we have to check that arbitrary unions of them are closed under finite intersections. If B and C are open, the members of B $\cap$ C are all intersections of basic open sets unioned to make B and C, and if [F] and [G] are basic open sets for B and C, $[F] \cap [G] = [F \wedge G]$, a basic open set. So $S_n^M(A)$ is a topological space.

An open cover of a topological space S is a class of open subsets of S such that S is a subset of the union of the class. The space S is compact if and only if every open cover of S has a finite subcover.[15] We can show that if every cover by basic open sets has a finite subcover, then the space is compact. Let C be an open cover and let B be the set of

[14] A function f from one topological space S_1 to another S_2 is continuous if and only if for any subset X of S_1, if f(X) is an open subset of S_2, X is an open subset of S_1. The function f is open if and only if when X is an open subset of S_1, f(X) is an open subset of S_2. Then f is a homeomorphism if and only if it is continuous, open, and maps S_1 one–one onto S_2. The topological properties are those, like not being torn in two, preserved under homeomorphisms.

[15] For a survey of compactness, see Edwin Hewitt, "The Rôle of Compactness in Classical Analysis," *American Mathematical Monthly* 67 (1960): 499–516. Compactness in the logician's sense of satisfiable if finitely satisfiable is compactness in the topologist's sense. A subset of a topological space is closed if and only if its complement is open. We may give a topology in terms of closed sets by requiring that any intersection of closed sets be closed and any finite union of closed sets be closed. As we shall see, compactness in terms of closed sets says that if no finite set of closed sets has empty intersection, then neither does the intersection of all closed sets. For a countable language of L, we may take the space S to be the set of all interpretations of S whose domains are sets of natural numbers. A subset X of S is closed if and only if for some set F of formulae of L, X is the set of models for F. Then compactness in the logician's sense is equivalent to the compactness of S under this topology. See Roger C. Lyndon, *Notes on Logic* (Princeton: Van Nostrand, 1966), 57.

basic open sets. Each set D in C is the union of a subset B_D of B. The union of all the B_D is a basic open cover, so by the hypothesis it has a finite subcover $\{X_1,..., X_n\}$. But for each X_i there is a D_i in C such that $X_i \subseteq D_i$. Then $\{D_1,..., D_n\}$ is a finite subcover of the space. We use this to show that $S_n^M(A)$ is compact. Suppose for reductio that I is some set of indices and that

$$C = \{[F_i] \mid i \in I\}$$

is a basic open cover of $S_n^M(A)$ with no finite subcover. Let

$$\Gamma = \{\neg F_i \mid i \in I\}.$$

We show that $\Gamma \cup \text{Th}_A(M)$ has a model. Let I_0 be a finite subset of I. There is a type p not in the union of the $[F_i]$ for $i \in I_0$; this is because C has no finite subcover. Let N be an elementary extension of M with a realization $\underline{a}$ of p. Then N is a model of $\text{Th}_A(M)$ plus the conjunction of the $\neg F_i(\underline{a})$ for $i \in I_0$; that is because $\neg F_i \in$ p since $p \notin [F_i]$. Thus Γ is finitely satisfiable, so by compactness, it is satisfiable. That is, Γ is an n-type of M. So there is an elementary extension N of M with a realization $\underline{a}$ of Γ. But then $\text{tp}^N(\underline{a} \mid A)$ is in $S_n^M(A)$ but not in the union of the $[F_i]$ for $i \in I$, and this is impossible, since C is a basic open cover.

A map f from one topological space S_1 to another S_2 is continuous if and only if for any subset X of S_1, if $f(X)$ is an open subset of S_2, then X is an open subset of S_1. Similarly, f is open if and only if $f(X)$ is an open subset of S_2 when X is an open subset of S_1. Then f is a homeomorphism if and only if it maps S_1 one–one onto S_2 and is both open and continuous. Topology is the study of properties, like compactness, preserved under homeomorphisms. Suppose M and N are interpretations of a language L and X is a subset of D(M). Then a map f from X to D(N) is partial elementary if and only if for all formulae G of L and all finite sequences $\underline{b}$ of members of X, $G(\underline{b})$ is true in M if and only if $G(f(\underline{b}))$ is true in N. We are going to show that if f is a partial elementary map from A to D(N), then $S_n^M(A)$ is homeomorphic to $S_n^N(f(A))$. First we extend f from A to $S_n^M(A)$. For any type p in $S_n^M(A)$, let $f(p)$ be the set of those formulae $B(\underline{x}, f(\underline{a}))$ for $L_{f(A)}$ for all the formulae $B(\underline{x}, \underline{a})$ of L_A in p. We must show that $f(p)$ is a type of N over $f(A)$. This requires that $\text{Th}_{f(A)}(N) \cup f(p)$ have a model. Let S be a finite subset of $\text{Th}_{f(A)}(N) \cup f(p)$. Let $C(\underline{x}, f(\underline{a}))$ be the conjunction of the members of S from $f(p)$. Then $C(\underline{x}, \underline{a})$ is in p. Since p is a type of M over A, $\text{Th}_{f(A)}(N) \cup f(p)$ has a model that is an elementary extension of M. So $(\exists \underline{x})C(\underline{x}, \underline{a})$ is true in M. Since f is partial elementary, $(\exists x)C(\underline{x}, f(\underline{a}))$ is true in N. Hence any model for $Th_{f(A)}(N)$ is a model for S too. Thus by compactness $Th_{f(A)}(N) \cup f(p)$ has a model, and $f(p)$ is a type of N over $f(A)$. It follows that f takes any basic open set $[G(\underline{x}, \underline{a})]$ of $S_n^M(A)$ to $[G(\underline{x}, f(\underline{a}))]$ where the second is a basic open set of $S_n^N(f(A))$, so f is open. The proof that f is continuous is similar. If p and q are different types in $S_n^M(A)$, there is a formula F in p but not q, and then $\neg F \in q$ since q is complete. Then f takes F to a formula F' in $f(p)$, and $\neg F'$ is in $f(q)$, so f is one–one. So $S_n^M(A)$ is homeomorphic to $S_n^N(f(A))$.

A type p is isolated if and only if $\{p\}$ is open.[16] We are going to show that the following three claims are equivalent: (1) p is isolated; (2) $\{p\}$ = [F] for some formula F of L_A (F is said to isolate p); and (3) there is a formula $F(\underline{x})$ in p such that for every formula $G(\underline{x})$ of L_A, $G(\underline{x})$ is in p if and only if $F(\underline{x}) \rightarrow G(\underline{x})$ follows from $Th_A(M)$. To infer (2) from (1), suppose p is isolated. Then $\{p\}$ is open, so it is a union of basic open sets. A singleton is a union of a set if and only if it is the only nonempty member of the set. So $\{p\}$ is a basic open set, and thus it is [F] for some formula F of L_A. To infer (3) from (2), suppose $\{p\}$ = [F] for some formula F. Assume first that $G(\underline{x})$ is in p but $F(\underline{x}) \rightarrow G(\underline{x})$ does not follow from $Th_A(M)$. Then by compactness there is an elementary extension N of M and a tuple $\underline{a}$ in $D(N)$ such that $F(\underline{a}) \wedge \neg G(\underline{a})$ is true in N. Since M is an elementary submodel of N, $Th_A(M) = Th_A(N)$, so $S_n^M(A) = S_n^N(A)$. Let $q = tp^N(\underline{a} \mid A)$. The $q \in S_n^N(A) = S_n^M(A)$. Since $F(\underline{x}) \in q$ and p is the only type of which $F(\underline{x})$ is a member, p = q. But $\neg G(\underline{x}) \in q$ while $G(\underline{x}) \in$ p, which is impossible. Assume second that $G(\underline{x})$ is not in p. Since p is complete, $\neg G(\underline{x})$ is in p, so by what we just proved, $F(\underline{x}) \rightarrow \neg G(\underline{x})$ follows from $Th_A(M)$. Then since $Th_A(M) \cup \{F(\underline{x})\}$ is a subset of $Th_A(M) \cup$ p and $Th_A(M) \cup$ p is satisfiable, $F(\underline{x}) \rightarrow G(\underline{x})$ does not follow from $Th_A(M)$. To infer (1) from (3), suppose there is an F in p such that for all G of L_A, G is in p if and only if $F \rightarrow G$ follows from $Th_A(M)$. We have $F \in$ p, so $p \in$ [F]. Suppose $q \in$ [F] and G is a formula of L_A. If $G \in$ p, $F \rightarrow G$ follows from $Th_A(M)$, so $G \in q$ since complete types are closed under consequence; while if $G \notin$ p, then $\neg G \in$ p and then as before $\neg G \in q$, so $G \notin q$. Hence p = q, so p is isolated. An isolated type is like a maximally specific kind with a finite nature.

Suppose $A \subseteq D(M)$ and $\underline{a},\underline{b}$ is an (m+n)-tuple of members of $D(M)$ that realizes an isolated type in $S_{m+n}^M(A)$. We will show $tp^M(\underline{a} \mid A)$ is isolated. For suppose $F(\underline{x}, \underline{z})$ isolates $tp_{m+n}^M(\underline{a}, \underline{b} \mid A)$. Then we can show $(\exists \underline{z})$ $F(\underline{x}, \underline{z})$ isolates $tp^M(\underline{a} \mid A)$. Let $G(\underline{x})$ be an L_A formula in $tp^M(\underline{a} \mid A)$, so

---

[16] Isolated types are also called principal.

$G(\underline{a})$ is true in M. If $(\exists \underline{z})F(\underline{x}, \underline{z}) \rightarrow G(\underline{x})$ does not follow from $Th_A(M)$, then there is an m-tuple $\underline{c}$ such that $(\exists \underline{z})F(\underline{c}, \underline{z}) \wedge \neg G(\underline{c})$ is true in M. Then there is an n-tuple $\underline{d}$ such that $F(\underline{c}, \underline{d}) \wedge \neg G(\underline{c})$ is true in M. Since $F(\underline{x}, \underline{z})$ isolates $tp^M(\underline{a}, \underline{b} \mid A)$, $F(\underline{x}, \underline{z}) \rightarrow G(\underline{x})$ follows from $Th_A(M)$. But this is impossible because $G(\underline{x})$ is in $tp^M(\underline{a} \mid A)$, which is a subset of $tp^M(\underline{a}, \underline{b} \mid A)$.

A subset of a topological space is closed if and only if its complement is open. A topology can be given in terms of closed sets: any intersection of closed sets is closed; and any finite union of closed sets is closed. In terms of closed sets, compactness says that every set of closed sets with empty intersection has a finite subset with empty intersection. For suppose C is a set of closed sets with empty intersection. Then the set of complements of sets in C is an open cover, so by compactness, it has a finite subcover; the set of their complements is a finite subset of C with empty intersection. (Conversely, if C is an open cover, the complements are closed sets with empty intersection, so a finite subset of it has empty intersection, and then its complements are a finite open cover.) The complement of the basic open set [F] is [¬F]. Since [¬F] is also a basic open set, [F] is also closed. Sets that are both open and closed are sometimes called clopen. A subset X of a topological space is dense if and only if there is a member of X in every nonempty open set. A subset X of the set of real numbers is a basic open set if and only if there are reals a,b such that a < b and X is the set of all reals greater than a and less than b. The set of rationals is a dense subset of the reals, because there is a rational in every basic open set of reals.

Let L be a countable language. A theory is a set of sentences. Let T be a complete theory with infinite models whose language is L. Let κ be an infinite cardinal. Then T is κ-stable if and only if when M is a model for T and A is a subset of $D(M)$ of cardinal κ, then the cardinal of $S_n^M(A)$ is κ.[17] M is κ-stable if and only if $Th(M)$ is κ-stable. We are going to show that if T is ω-stable, then for all models M of T and all $A \subseteq D(M)$, the isolated types in $S_n^M(A)$ are dense. It suffices to show that for any nonempty basic open set [F] of $S_n^M(A)$, there is an isolated type in [F]. So suppose for reductio [F] is a nonempty basic open set that contains no isolated types. If there were only one type in [F], it would be isolated,

---

[17] Morley introduced ω-stability in his proof of his categoricity theorem. If a and b are different members of A, then x = a is in $tp^M(a \mid A)$ but not in $tp^M(b \mid A)$, so when T is κ-stable, $S_n^M(A)$ is as small as possible. We will usually consider ω-stability. Stability is central to modern model theory.

so there are at least two different types p and q in [F]. Since $p \neq q$, there is a formula G such that $G \in p$ and $G \notin q$, so $\neg G \in q$ since q is complete. Thus $[F \wedge G]$ and $[F \wedge \neg G]$ are each nonempty, and since [F] is their union, neither contains an isolated type. We have split [F].

Next we iterate this split infinitely often. Let Σ be the set of finite sequences of zeroes and ones, that is, the functions whose domain is some $n \in \omega$ and whose range is 2. For σ in Σ, $\sigma 0$ is $\sigma \cup \{<n, 0>\}$ and $\sigma 1$ is $\sigma \cup \{<n, 1>\}$. We will assign to each $\sigma \in \Sigma$ a formula $F(\sigma)$ such that: (1) $[F(\sigma)]$ is nonempty but contains no isolated type; (2) if $\sigma \subseteq \tau$, then $F(\sigma)$ follows from $F(\tau)$, so $[F(\tau)]$ is a subset of $[F(\sigma)]$; and (3) $F(\sigma 0) \wedge F(\sigma 1)$ has no models. We are given a formula F such that [F] is non-empty but contains no isolated types. Let $F(\varnothing)$ be F (where $\varnothing \in \Sigma$). Given $F(\sigma)$ such that $[F(\sigma)]$ is nonempty and contains no isolated types, then as in the last paragraph there is a formula G such that neither $[F(\sigma) \wedge G]$ nor $[F(\sigma) \wedge \neg G]$ is empty or contains an isolated type. Then $F(\sigma 0)$ is $F(\sigma) \wedge G$ and $F(\sigma 1)$ is $F(\sigma) \wedge \neg G$.

The set of all functions from ω into 2 is the set of all countable sequences of zeroes and ones, and these are in effect the decimals in binary notation for the reals from 0 to 1 and the characteristic functions of the sets of natural numbers, so there are continuum many such functions. For any such f, let $f \restriction n$ be f restricted to n, so $f \restriction n \in \Sigma$. For any $F(\sigma)$ let n be the domain of σ; n is the level of $F(\sigma)$. There are 2^n formulae of level n, and in each only finitely many members of A are mentioned. So if A_0 is the set of all members of A mentioned at any level, A_0 is at most countably infinite. For any $f : \omega \to 2$, $[F(f \restriction n)]$ is a sequence of closed sets such that $[F(f \restriction (n + 1))] \subseteq [F(f \restriction n)]$. For any finite subsequence there is a largest p such that $[F(f \restriction p)]$ is contained in them all, so since $[F(f \restriction p)]$ is nonempty, the intersection of the finite subsequence is nonempty. So since $S_n^M(A_0)$ is compact, there is a type p_f in the intersection of all the $[F(f \restriction n)]$. For different f and g from ω to 2, there is a least m such that $f(m) \neq g(m)$. Then $F(f \restriction (m + 1)) \wedge F(g \restriction (m + 1))$ has no models. So $p_f \neq p_g$. Hence $S_n^M(A_0)$ has continuum members, which is impossible, since T is ω-stable. This completes the proof. (This has been a binary tree argument.)

If M is a model for T and A is a subset of D(M), then M is prime over A if and only if whenever N is a model for T and $f : A \to D(N)$ is partial elementary, then there is a $g : D(M) \to D(N)$ that is elementary and extends f. (To say g is elementary means it is an isomorphism between M and an elementary submodel of N.) Suppose that T is ω-stable, M is a model for T, and A is a subset of D(M). We will show that there is an elementary submodel M_0 of M that is prime over A, where every member of $D(M_0)$ realizes an isolated type over A. $D(M)$ is a set and so has a cardinal κ. Let a map κ one–one onto $D(M)$, and write $a(\alpha)$ as a_α for $\alpha < \kappa$. Let $A_0 = A$, and for any limit $\lambda < \kappa$, let A_λ be the union of the A_α for $\alpha < \lambda$; if there is a member of $M - A_\alpha$ that realizes an isolated type over A_α, let β be the least ordinal such that a_β does so, and set $A_{\alpha+1} = A_\alpha \cup \{a_\beta\}$, while if there is none, let $A_{\alpha+1} = A_\alpha$. Then there is a least γ such that $A_\gamma = A_{\gamma+1}$. The domain of M_0 will be A_γ. For $b \in D(M)$ such that $b = c^M$ for some constant c of L, $tp^M(b)$ is isolated by x = c, so $b \in A_\gamma$. The relations and functions of M_0 are the restrictions of those of M to $D(M_0) = A_\gamma$. So M_0 is a submodel of M. We use the Tarski–Vaught test to show that M_0 is an elementary submodel of M. Suppose that $F(b, \underline{a})$ is true in M where $\underline{a}$ is in $D(M_0)$. By the previous result, the isolated types in $S^M(A_\gamma)$ are dense. So there is a c in $D(M)$ such that $F(c, \underline{a})$ is true in M and $tp^M(c \mid A_\gamma)$ is isolated. Then $c \in A_\gamma$. So by the Tarski–Vaught test, M_0 is an elementary submodel of M. Next we show that M_0 is a prime over A. So suppose N is a model for T and $f : A \to D(N)$ is partial elementary. We will build a sequence of partial elementary maps. Let f_0 be f and for any limit $\lambda \leq \gamma$, let f_λ be the union of the f_α for $\alpha < \lambda$. Given $f_\alpha : A_\alpha \to D(N)$ that is partial elementary, there is a formula $F(x, \underline{a})$ that isolates $t_p^{M_0}(a_\alpha \mid A_\alpha)$. Then f_α is a homeomorphism, so $f_\alpha(t_p^{M_0}(a_\alpha \mid A_\alpha))$ is a type in $S_1^N(f_\alpha(A))$, and $F(x, f_\alpha(\underline{a}))$, isolates it. But $F(a_\alpha, \underline{a})$ is true in M_0, so $(\exists x)F(x, \underline{a})$ is true in M_0, so since F_α is partial elementary, $(\exists x)F(x, f_\alpha(\underline{a}))$ is true in N, so there is a b in $D(N)$ such that $F(b, f_\alpha(\underline{a}))$ is true in N. So if we set $f_{\alpha+1} = f_\alpha \cup \{<a_\alpha, b>\}$, then $f : A_{\alpha+1} \to D(N)$ is partial elementary. So $f_\gamma : D(M_0) \to D(N)$ is elementary and extends f. Thus M_0 is prime over A.

We show last that every tuple $\underline{a}$ of members of $D(M_0)$ realizes an isolated type over A. Each $\underline{a}$ is in A_α for some α, and we prove the claim by induction on α. When $a_1,..., a_p$ is a p-tuple of members of $A_0 = A$, then the formula $x_1 = a_1 \wedge ... \wedge x_p = a_p$ isolates $tp^M(\underline{a} \mid A)$ and $\underline{a}$ realizes it. When $\underline{a}$ is in A_λ, $\underline{a}$ is in A_α for some $\alpha < \lambda$, since $\underline{a}$ is finite, so the claim holds by induction. Suppose $\underline{a}$ is a tuple of members of $A_{\alpha+1}$ in which a_α occurs. There are $\underline{b}$ in A_α such that $F(x, \underline{b})$ isolates $tp^M(a_\alpha \mid A_\alpha)$ and some $G(z)$ isolates $tp^M(\underline{b} \mid A)$ by the induction hypothesis. We show that $F(x, \underline{z}) \wedge G(\underline{z})$ isolates $tp^M(a_\alpha, \underline{b} \mid A)$. Suppose $H(x, \underline{z})$ is in $tp^M(a_\alpha, \underline{b} \mid A)$, so $H(a_\alpha, \underline{b})$ is true in M. Then $F(x, \underline{b}) \to H(x, \underline{b})$ follows from $Th_A(M)$, so $(\forall x)(F(x, \underline{b}) \to H(x, \underline{b}))$ does too. Then $G(\underline{z}) \to (\forall x)(F(x, \underline{z}) \to H(x, \underline{z}))$ follows from $Th_A(M)$ because $G(\underline{z})$ isolates $tp^M(\underline{b} \mid A)$. Hence $(F(x, \underline{z}) \wedge G(\underline{z})) \to H(x, \underline{z})$ follows from $Th_A(M)$, and $tp^M(a_\alpha, \underline{b} \mid A)$ is isolated by $F(x, \underline{z}) \wedge G(\underline{z})$. So by what we proved six paragraphs ago, $tp^M(a_\alpha \mid A)$ is isolated. Then the conjunction of a formula isolating the type of $\underline{a}$ without a_α over A and a formula isolating the type of a_α over A isolates $tp^M(\underline{a} \mid A)$.

Recall that T is assumed to be a complete theory with a countable language and infinite models. Let κ be an infinite cardinal. A model M of T is κ-homogeneous if and only if for any subset A of D(M) of cardinal less than κ, any partial elementary $f : A \to D(M)$ and any a in D(M), there is a g extending f that maps $A \cup \{a\}$ into D(M) and is partial elementary. M is homogeneous if and only if it is κ-homogeneous where κ is the cardinal of D(M).[18] $S_n(T)$ is the set of complete n-types such that $T \cup p$ has a model. Since T is complete, $T = Th_\varnothing(M)$, so $S_n(T)$ is $S_n^M(\varnothing)$. We will show that if M and N are countable homogeneous models of T and realize the same members of $S_n(T)$, then M and N are isomorphic. Let $a_0, a_1, \ldots$ be an enumeration of D(M) and $b_0, b_1, \ldots$, an enumeration of D(N). We will build a sequence of partial elementary maps whose union will be the required isomorphism. Let f_0 be $\varnothing$. Then f_0 maps $\varnothing \subseteq D(M)$ one–one onto $\varnothing \subseteq D(N)$ so that for any 0-tuple and any 0-place formula F, that is, sentence, F is true in M if and only if F is true in N, because T is complete. Suppose f_{2p+2} is a partial elementary map (from a finite subset of D(M) to a finite subset of D(N)) and that for i < p, a_i is in the domain of f_{2p+2} and b_i is in its range. We give two extensions of f_{2p+2}, the first adding a_p to the domain, and the second adding b_p to the range. Let $\underline{a}$ be the domain of f_{2p+2} and let $\underline{b}$ be its range. Let q be $tp^M(\underline{a}, a_p)$. M and N realize the same types, so there are $\underline{c},d$ in D(N) such that $tp^N(\underline{c}, d)$ is q. Then $tp^M(\underline{a}) = tp^N(\underline{c})$, and $tp^M(\underline{a}) = tp^N(\underline{b})$, since f_{2p+2} is partial elementary. Thus $tp^N(\underline{c}) = tp^N(\underline{b})$. So since N is homogeneous, there is an e in D(N) such that $tp^N(\underline{b}, e) = tp^N(\underline{c}, d) = q$. So we set $f_{2p+3} = f_{2p+2} \cup \{<a_p, e>\}$. Then f_{2p+3} is partial elementary, and a_p is in its domain. To add b_p to the range, let q be $tp^N(\underline{b}, b_p)$. There are $\underline{c}$, d in D(M) such that $tp^M(\underline{c}, d)$ is q. Then $tp^N(\underline{b}) = tp^M(\underline{c})$, so since $tp^N(\underline{b}) = tp^M(\underline{a})$, $tp^M(\underline{a}) = tp^M(\underline{c})$. Thus there is an e in D(M) such that $tp^M(\underline{a}, e) = tp^M(\underline{c}, d) = q$. Let f_{2p+4} be $f_{2p+3} \cup \{<e, b_p>\}$. Then f_{2p+4} is partial elementary, and b_p is in its

---

[18] Poizat, *Course in Model Theory*, 202, credits homogeneity to Bjarni Jonsson, "Universal Relational Systems," *Mathematica Scandinavica* 4 (1956): 193–208, and "Homogeneous Universal Relational Systems," *Mathematica Scandinavica* 8 (1960): 178–86. J. L. Bell and A. B. Slomson, *Models and Ultraproducts: An Introduction* (Amsterdam: North-Holland, 1969), 207, credit homogeneity to George Wilmers.

range. Then if f is the union of all the f_p for all natural numbers p, f is an isomorphism between M and N.[19]

We turn next to Vaught's two-cardinal version of the Löwenheim–Skolem theorem.[20] If M is an interpretation of a language L and F is an n-ary formula of L, let F(M) be the set of n-tuples $\underline{a}$ of members of D(M) such that F($\underline{a}$) is true in M. Suppose κ and μ are infinite cardinals and $\kappa > \mu$. Then a model M for a theory T is a κ,μ model if and only if D(M) has κ members and for some formula F of the language of T, F(M) has μ members.[21] Vaught's two-cardinal theorem says that when T has a κ,μ model, it has an $\omega(1),\omega$ model. A key motion for us will be that of a Vaught pair of models for a theory. We say that N and M are a Vaught pair of models for T if and only if both are models for T, M is an elementary submodel of N, D(M) $\neq$ D(N), and for some formula F, F(M) is infinite and F(M) = F(N).

First we show that if T has a κ,μ model, then it has a Vaught pair of models. For suppose N is a κ,μ model for T and for some F, X = F(N) has μ members. By the Löwenheim–Skolem theorem, there is an elementary submodel M of N such that X $\subseteq$ D(M) and D(M) has μ members. Thus D(M) $\neq$ D(N), and F(N) = F(M), since M is an elementary submodel of N. So N and M are a Vaught pair of models for T.

Suppose M is a substructure of N. We want a way to tack on M behind N to make a single structure (N, M). To do so we pick a single unary predicate U(x) not in the language L that M and N interpret, and form L' by adding U(x) to L. The new predicate lets us keep track of M in (N, M). We associate with each formula F($\underline{x}$) of L a formula $F^U(\underline{x})$ of L'. If $F(x_1,\ldots,x_n)$ is atomic, then $F^U(\underline{x})$ is $U(x_1) \wedge \ldots \wedge U(x_n) \wedge F(\underline{x})$. If F is ¬G, then F^U is ¬G^U, and if F is G $\wedge$ H, then F^U is $G^U \wedge H^U$. If F is $(\exists x)G(x)$, then F^U is $(\exists x)(U(x) \wedge G^U(x))$. The extension of U in (N, M) is D(M). Then for any $\underline{a}$ from D(M), F($\underline{a}$) is true in M if and only if $F^U(\underline{a})$ is true in (N, M). Suppose N and M are a Vaught pair of models for T. We will show that there are N_0 and M_0 that are a Vaught pair of models

[19] This is a back-and-forth argument. Cantor gave the first back-and-forth argument when he proved that the theory of dense linear orders without endpoints is ω-categorical. Cantor, *Contributions*, 124.

[20] Robert L. Vaught, *A Löwenheim–Skolem Theorem for Cardinals Far Apart* (Amsterdam: North-Holland, 1977).

[21] If T has a κ,μ model M, it is not κ-categorical. For we may add constants c_α for $\alpha < \kappa$ to the language of T plus $c_\alpha \neq c_\beta$ for $\alpha \neq \beta$ and F($\underline{c}$) for tuples of these constants. M is a model for any finite subset of this expansion of T, so it has a model N of cardinal κ in which F(N) has κ members. So M and N are not isomorphic.

for T and $D(N_0)$ is countable. We have a formula F of L such that $F(M)$ is infinite and $F(M) = F(N)$. Let $\underline{m}$ be the members of $D(M)$ mentioned in F. By the Löwenheim–Skolem theorem there is an interpretation (N_0, M_0) of L' such that $D(N_0)$ is countable, $m \in D(M_0)$, and (N_0, M_0) is an elementary submodel of (N, M). Since M is an elementary submodel of N, for any formula G of L, $(\forall x_1,..., x_n)((U(x_1) \wedge ... \wedge U(x_n) \wedge G(\underline{x})) \rightarrow G^U(x))$ is true in (N, M). Since (N_0, M_0) is an elementary submodel of (N, M), these sentences are true in (N_0, M_0), and thus M_0 is an elementary submodel of N_0. Let p be the polyadicity of F and let $\underline{x}_1, \underline{x}_2,...$ be an enumeration of the p-tuples of variables. For $\underline{x}_i$ and $\underline{x}_j$, let $\underline{x}_i \neq \underline{x}_j$ be the disjunction of $y \neq z$ for y among $\underline{x}_i$ and z among $\underline{x}_j$, and for all n let $C(\underline{x}_1,..., \underline{x}_n)$ be the conjunction of $\underline{x}_i \neq \underline{x}_j$ for $i \neq j$ among $1,..., n$. Then for all n, $(\exists \underline{x}_1,..., \exists \underline{x}_n)(C(\underline{x}_1,..., \underline{x}_n) \wedge F(\underline{x}_1) \wedge ... \wedge F(\underline{x}_n))$ is true in (N, M), as are $(\exists x)\neg U(x)$ and $(\forall x_1,..., x_p)(F(x_1,..., x_p) \rightarrow (U(x_1) \wedge ... \wedge U(x_p))$. So these sentences are true in (N_0, M_0). So N_0 and M_0 are a Vaught pair.

Suppose N_0 and M_0 are countable models for T and M_0 is an elementary submodel of N_0. We will argue that there are countable, homogeneous M and N that realize the same types in $S_n(T)$, so M and N are isomorphic, such that (N_0, M_0) is an elementary submodel of (N, M). This argument has several steps. In step one we first show that if $\underline{a}$ is in $D(M_0)$ and p in $S_n^{M_0}(\underline{a})$ is realized in N_0, then there are countable N' and M' such that p is realized in M' and (N_0, M_0) is an elementary submodel of (N', M'). Let ED be the elementary diagram of (N_0, M_0), and let $\Gamma(\underline{x})$ be the union of $\{F^U(\underline{x}, \underline{a}) \mid F(\underline{x}, \underline{a}) \in p\}$ and ED. If $F_1,..., F_m$ are in p, then $(\exists \underline{x})(F_1(\underline{x}, \underline{a}) \wedge ... \wedge F_m(\underline{x}, \underline{a}))$ is true in N_0 because p is realized in N_0, so it is true in M_0 because M_0 is an elementary submodel of N_0, and thus $(\exists \underline{x})(F_1^U(\underline{x}, \underline{a}) \wedge ... \wedge F_m^U(\underline{x}, \underline{a}))$ is true in (N_0, M_0). Thus $\Gamma(\underline{x})$ is finitely satisfiable (in (N_0, M_0)), so it is satisfiable. So there is a countable (N', M') realizing $\Gamma(\underline{x})$ such that (N_0, M_0) is an elementary submodel of (N', M') and p is realized in M'. Repeating, there are countable N^* and M^* such that for every $\underline{a}$ in $D(M_0)$ and p in $S_n^{M_0}(\underline{a})$ realized in N_0, p is realized in M^* and (N_0, M_0) is an elementary submodel of (N^*, M^*). This completes step one. In step two, we first show that if $\underline{b}$ is in $D(N_0)$ and p is in $S_n^{N_0}(\underline{b})$, then there are countable N' and M' such that p is realized in N' and (N_0, M_0) is an elementary submodel of (N', M'). Let ED be the elementary diagram of (N_0, M_0) and let $\Gamma(\underline{x})$ be the union of ED and p. For $F_1,..., F_m$ in p, $(\exists \underline{x})(F_1(\underline{x}, \underline{b}) \wedge ... \wedge F_m(\underline{x}, \underline{b}))$ is true in N_0. So $\Gamma(\underline{x})$ is finitely satisfiable (in (N_0, M_0)). So there is a countable (N', M') realizing $\Gamma(\underline{x})$ such that (N_0, M_0) is an elementary submodel of (N', M') and p is realized in N'. This completes step two.

In step three, we interleave steps one and two to build an elementary chain (N_i, M_i) of countable models. We let (N_0, M_0) be our original (N_0, M_0). The inductive step has three parts. Given (N_{3i}, M_{3i}) we use step one to get (N_{3i+1}, M_{3i+1}), a countable elementary extension of (N_{3i}, M_{3i}) such that any type in $S_n(T)$ realized in N_{3i} is realized in M_{3i+1}. Suppose we have (N_{3i+1}, M_{3i+1}), that $\underline{a}$, $\underline{b}$, and c are in $D(M_{3i+1})$, and $tp^{M_{3i+1}}(\underline{a}) = tp^{M_{3i+1}}(\underline{b})$. Then $tp^{M_{3i+1}}(\underline{a}, c)$ is realized in N_{3i+1} because M_{3i+1} is an elementary sub-model of N_{3i+1}, so by step one there is a countable elementary extension (N_{3i+2}, M_{3i+2}) of (N_{3i+1}, M_{3i+1}) and a d in $D(M_{3i+2})$ such that $tp^{M_{3i+2}}(\underline{a}, c) = tp^{M_{3i+2}}(\underline{b}, d)$. Suppose, third, we have (N_{3i+2}, M_{3i+2}), that $\underline{a}$, $\underline{b}$, c are in N_{3i+2} and $tp^{N_{3i+2}}(\underline{a}) = tp^{N_{3i+2}}(\underline{b})$. Then by step two, $tp^{N_{3i+2}}(\underline{a}, c)$ is realized in N_{3i+2}, so there is a countable elementary extension (N_{3i+3}, M_{3i+3}) of (N_{3i+2}, M_{3i+2}) and a d in $D(N_{3i+3})$ such that $tp^{N_{3i+3}}(\underline{a}, c) = tp^{N_{3i+3}}(\underline{b}, d)$. In the last step we let (N, M) be the union of the elementary chain (N_i, M_i). Then (N_0, M_0) is an elementary submodel of (N, M), and N and M are each countable. By the first part of the inductive step, M and N realize the same types in $S_n(T)$, and by the second and third parts, M and N are both homogeneous. Hence M and N are isomorphic. Moreover, it is clear that if M_0 and N_0 are a Vaught pair, so are M and N.

Now we can prove Vaught's two-cardinal theorem. Suppose T has a κ,μ model. Then by what we have done so far, there is a Vaught pair of countable models M and N for T that are homogeneous and realize the same types in $S_n(T)$, so M and N are isomorphic. We will build an elementary chain N_α, $\alpha < \omega(1)$, such that for all α, N_α is isomorphic to N and $(N_{\alpha+1}, N_\alpha)$ is isomorphic to (N, M). Let $N_0 = N$. When λ is a limit, let N_λ be the union of the N_α for $\alpha < \lambda$. Then N_α is an elementary submodel of N_λ when $\alpha < \lambda$. N_λ is homogeneous. For suppose $\underline{a}$,b are in $D(N_\lambda)$ and $f : \underline{a} \rightarrow D(N_\lambda)$ is partial elementary. Then $\underline{a}$,b are in $D(N_\alpha)$ for some $\alpha < \lambda$. Since f is partial elementary, $tp^{N_\alpha}(\underline{a}) = tp^{N_\alpha}(\underline{fa})$, so since N_α is homogeneous, there is a d in $D(N_\alpha)$ such that $tp^{N_\alpha}(\underline{a}, b) = tp^{N_\alpha}(\underline{fa}, d)$. Let $f^* = f \cup \{<b, d>\}$. Then f^* is partial elementary, so N_λ is homogeneous. N and N_λ realize the same types. For if N_λ realizes p, then for some $\alpha < \lambda$, N_α realizes p, so N realizes p since N_α is isomorphic to N. Conversely, if N realizes p, then for any $\alpha < \lambda$, N_α realizes p, so N_λ realizes p. Hence N_λ is isomorphic to N. For the successor case, suppose N_α is isomorphic to N. Then since N is isomorphic to M, there is a countable proper elementary extension N^* of N_α such that (N, M) is isomorphic to (N^*, N_α). For if $\Gamma(x)$ is the union of the elementary diagram of N_α, the unit set of $\neg F(x)$, and the set of formulae $x \neq a$ for $a \in D(N_\alpha)$, then any finite subset of $\Gamma(x)$ is satisfiable in N_α, and we may take N^*

to be a countable elementary extension of N_α in which every formula in $\Gamma(x)$ is satisfied. We let $N_{\alpha+1}$ be N^*. Let N' be the union of the N_α for $\alpha < \omega(1)$. Then $D(N')$ has $\omega(1)$ members, but for all $\underline{a}$ in $D(N')$, if $F(\underline{a})$ is true in N', then $F(\underline{a})$ is true in M. So since $F(M)$ is countable, N' is an $\omega(1),\omega$ model of T. This completes the proof of Vaught's two-cardinal theorem.

We want to prove a partial converse to Vaught's theorem for ω-stable theories. To this end we will argue that if M is an uncountable model for an ω-stable theory, then there is a proper elementary extension N of M such that any countable type over $D(M)$ realized in N is realized in M. We begin by showing that there is a formula $F(x)$ of $L_{D(M)}$ such that $[F(x)]$ is uncountable but for all formulae $G(x)$ of $L_{D(M)}$, one of $[F(x) \wedge G(x)]$ and $[F(x) \wedge \neg G(x)]$ is at most countably infinite. For suppose not. Then for any $F(x)$ such that $[F(x)]$ is uncountable and some $G(x)$, both $[F(x) \wedge G(x)]$ and $[F(x) \wedge \neg G(x)]$ are uncountable. This sets us up for a binary tree argument. For distinct a and b in $D(M)$, x = a is in $tp^M(a \mid D(M))$ but not in $tp^M(b \mid D(M))$, so $tp^M(a \mid D(M)) \neq tp^M(b \mid D(M))$. Let $F_\varnothing(x)$ be x = x. Then for all a in $D(M)$, $tp^M(a \mid D(M))$ is in $[F_\varnothing(x)]$, so it is uncountable. For any finite sequence σ of zeroes and ones such that $[F_\sigma(x)]$ is uncountable, there is a $G(x)$ such that both $[F_\sigma(x) \wedge G(x)]$ and $[F_\sigma(x) \wedge \neg G(x)]$ are uncountable, and we let $F_{\sigma 0}(x)$ be such a $G(x)$ and $F_{\sigma 1}(x)$ be $\neg G(x)$. Then for all finite sequences σ of zeroes and ones, $[F_\sigma(x)]$ is uncountable and $[F_{\sigma 0}(x)] \cap [F_{\sigma 1}(x)]$ is empty. Then, as when we showed the isolated types of an ω-stable theory to be dense, we let A be the set of members of $D(M)$ mentioned in any $F_\sigma(x)$. Then A is at most countably infinite, but $S_1^M(A)$ has continuum many members, contrary to the ω-stability of T.

Thus there is a formula $F(x)$ such that $[F(x)]$ is uncountable and for all formulae $G(x)$, one of $[F(x) \wedge G(x)]$ and $[F(x) \wedge \neg G(x)]$ is at most countably infinite, while the other is uncountable. Let p be the set of all formulae $G(x)$ such that $[F(x) \wedge G(x)]$ is uncountable and $[F(x) \wedge \neg G(x)]$ is at most countably infinite. If $G_1(x),..., G_m(x)$ are in p, then $[F(x) \wedge \neg G_1(x)],..., [F(x) \wedge \neg G_m(x)]$ are at most countably infinite. Thus their union is at most countably infinite, and this union is $[F(x) \wedge \neg(G_1(x) \wedge ... \wedge G_m(x))]$. So $G_1(x) \wedge ... \wedge G_m(x)$ is in p, and p is finitely satisfiable. For any $G(x)$, either $G(x)$ is in p or $\neg G(x)$ is in p. Hence p is a complete type over $D(M)$. Let M' be an elementary extension of M where some c in $D(M')$ realizes p. For each a in $D(M)$, the formula x = a isolates the type of a over $D(M)$, so $[x = a]$ is a unit set. Thus $[F(x) \wedge x = a]$ is empty or a unit set, and $[F(x) \wedge x \neq a]$ is uncountable.

Thus the formula x ≠ a is in p, so since M′ realizes p, M′ is a proper extension of M. Since T is ω-stable, there is an elementary extension N of M′ that is prime over $D(M) \cup \{c\}$ and such that every $\underline{a}$ in D(N) realizes an isolated type over $D(M) \cup \{c\}$.

Now let $\Gamma(\underline{x})$ be a countable type over D(M) realized by $\underline{b}$ in D(N). We must show $\Gamma(\underline{x})$ realized in M. There is a formula $G(\underline{x}, y)$ in $L_{D(M)}$ such that $G(\underline{x}, c)$ isolates $tp^N(\underline{b} \mid D(M) \cup \{c\})$. Since $(\exists\underline{x})G(\underline{x}, y)$ is in $tp^N(c \mid D(M) \cup \{c\})$, the formula $(\exists\underline{x})G(\underline{x}, y)$ is in p. Moreover, for an $H(\underline{x})$ in Γ, $(\forall\underline{x})G(\underline{x}, y) \rightarrow H(\underline{x})$ is in p. For if not, $(\exists\underline{x})(G(\underline{x}, y) \wedge \neg H(\underline{x}))$ is in p, and then $(\exists\underline{x})(G(\underline{x}, c) \wedge \neg H(\underline{x}))$ is true in M′ and so in N too. But $H(\underline{x})$ is in Γ, and $\underline{b}$ realizes Γ in N, so $H(\underline{b})$ is true in N. Then since $G(\underline{x}, c)$ isolates $tp^N(\underline{b} \mid D(M) \cup \{c\})$, $G(\underline{x}, c) \rightarrow H(\underline{x})$ follows from $Th_N(D(M) \cup \{c\})$, so $(\forall\underline{x})G(\underline{x}, c) \rightarrow H(\underline{x})$ follows too, and thus is true in N, and we have a contradiction. Let Δ be the union of the unit set of $(\exists\underline{x})G(\underline{x}, y)$ and the set of all of $(\forall\underline{x})G(\underline{x}, y) \rightarrow H(\underline{x})$ for $H(\underline{x})$ in Γ. Thus Δ is countable, and if c′ realizes Δ in M, then $(\exists\underline{x})(G(\underline{x}, c')$ is true in M, so for some $\underline{b}'$ in D(M), $G(\underline{b}', c')$ is true in M and $\underline{b}'$ realizes Γ in M. Let $\delta_0(y), \delta_1(y),...$ be an enumeration of Δ. Since $(\exists\underline{x})(G(\underline{x}, y))$ is in p and for all $H(\underline{x})$ in Γ, $(\forall\underline{x})(G(\underline{x}, y) \rightarrow H(\underline{x}))$ is in p, then for all i, $\delta_i(y)$ is in p and so for all n, $\delta_0(y) \wedge ... \wedge \delta_n(y)$ is in p. Hence for all n, $\{y \in D(M) \mid F(y) \wedge \neg(\delta_0(y) \wedge ... \wedge \delta_n(y))\}$ is at most countably infinite. Hence so is the union of these countably many sets. This union is $\{y \in D(M) \mid F(y) \wedge y$ does not realize $\Delta\}$. Thus uncountably many members of D(M) realize Δ, and thus Γ is realized in M.

We can now prove our partial converse to Vaught's theorem. We want to show that if T is ω-stable and has an ω(1),ω model, then for any cardinal κ greater than ω(1), T has a κ,ω model. So suppose M is a model for T such that D(M) has ω(1) members and F is a formula such that F(M) has ω members. By what we just proved, there is a proper elementary extension N of M such that any countable type over D(M) realized in N is realized in M. Then consider the type $\Gamma(x)$ that is the union of the unit set of F(x) and the set of all formulae x ≠ m for all m in D(M) such that F(m) is true in M. This type is countable and omitted in M, so it is omitted in N and F(M) = F(N). Now we iterate through the α < κ. Let M_0 be M, and $M_{\alpha+1}$ be a proper elementary extension of M_α such that $F(M_{\alpha+1}) = F(M_\alpha) = F(M)$, and take unions at limits less than κ. Let N be the union of the chain M_α for α < κ. Then N is a κ,ω model of T.

Next we take up Ehrenfeucht–Mostowski models built from order indiscernibles. This subject begins with Ramsey's theorem. His theorem is an elaboration of the pigeonhole principle. One finite pigeonhole principle says that if n pigeons roost on fewer than n perches, then there is a perch on which more than one pigeon roosts. One infinite pigeonhole principle says that if infinitely many objects are distributed among finitely many sets, then there is a set containing infinitely many of the objects. Our version of Ramsey's theorem generalizes an infinitary pigeonhole principle. Suppose X is a set with ω members, and let $(X)^n$ be the set of all subsets of X with n members. Then if f maps $(X)^n$ into k, there is an infinite $Y \subseteq X$ such that f is constant on $(Y)^n$. The proof is by induction on n. For n = 1, f distributes the ω unit sets of members of X into k boxes, so by the pigeonhole principle there is an infinite Y such that f is constant on Y. For the induction step, suppose the claim holds for n. We may take ω for X. Suppose f maps $(\omega)^{n+1}$ into k. For each a in ω, let f_a map $(\omega - \{a\})^n$ into k so that for $A \in (\omega - \{a\})^n$, $f_a(A) = f(A \cup \{a\})$. We define sequences $a_0, a_1, \ldots$ and $X_0, X_1, \ldots$ such that $a_0 < a_1 < \ldots$, $X_0 \supseteq X_1 \supseteq \ldots$, and X_i is infinite. We set $a_0 = 0$, and $X_0 = \omega$. Then f_{a_i} maps $(X_i - \{a_0, a_1, \ldots, a_i\})$ into k, so there is an infinite $Y \subseteq (X_i - \{a_0, a_1, \ldots, a_i\})$ such that f_{a_i} is constant on Y. We set $X_{i+1} = Y$ and let a_{i+1} be the least member of X_{i+1}. For each A in $(X_{i+1})^n$, let c_i be $f_{a_i}(A)$. $(X_{i+1})^n$ is infinite, so by the pigeonhole principle, there is a c < k such that f_a maps infinitely many A in $(X_{i+1})^n$ to c. Let Y be $\{a_i \mid c_i = c\}$. Then f is constant on $(Y)^{n+1}$. For if $x_1, \ldots, x_n, x_{n+1}$ are in Y and $x_1 < \ldots < x_n < x_{n+1}$, then $x_1 = a_i$ for some i and $x_2, \ldots, x_n, x_{n+1} \in X_{i+1}$. So

$$f(\{x_1, \ldots, x_n, x_{n+1}\}) = f_{x_1}(\{x_2, \ldots, x_n, x_{n+1}\}) = c_i = c.$$

This completes the proof of our infinitary version of Ramsey's theorem.[22]

---

[22] One finitary version of Ramsey's theorem says that for all n, k, and m there is a p such that if f maps $(p)^n$ into k, then for some subset Y of p, f is constant on $(Y)^n$, Y has at least m members, and if y is the least member of Y, then Y has at least y members. This finitary version follows from our infinitary version and can be formalized as a sentence in the language of our theory S of natural numbers in Chapter 5, but cannot be proved in S if S is consistent. So it is an example of an undecidable sentence of S with accessible numerical content. The fact that it is not a theorem of S is called the Paris–Harrington theorem, and there is a proof of it in Marker, *Model Theory*, 196–201.

Ramsey first proved his finitary version of his theorem in "On a Problem of Formal Logic," reprinted in his *The Foundations of Mathematics*, ed. R. B. Braithwaite (Paterson, N.J.: Littlefield, Adams, 1960), 82–111. Ramsey wanted his theorem to show that there is an algorithm for the validity of quantificational formulae with prenex equivalents having an existential quantifier in the scope of a universal in the prenex. A tree for the negation of $(\forall x)(\exists \underline{z})F(x, \underline{z})$ is always finite (assuming function signs have been eliminated). Ronald L. Graham, Bruce L. Rothschild, and Joel H. Spenser, *Ramsey Theory* (New York: Wiley, 1980), is about finitary versions of Ramsey's theorem and their applications.

Let I be an infinite set and let < be a linear order of I. Let M be an interpretation of a language L and let $m : I \to D(M)$ be such that for distinct i and j in I, $m(i) \neq m(j)$. Then m is a sequence of order indiscernibles if and only if for any formula $F(x_1,..., x_n)$ of L and finite sequences $i_1 < ... < i_n$ and $j_1 < ... < j_n$ from I, $F(m(i_1),..., m(i_n))$ is true in M if and only if $F(m(j_1),..., m(j_n))$ is true in M. I need not be a subset of D(M), nor need < be the extension of a formula of L. Let T be a theory with infinite models. Then for any infinite I with a linear order, there is a model M of T and a sequence $m : I \to D(M)$ of order indiscernibles. Let L' be L plus a new constant c_i for each i in I. Let Γ be the union of T, the different sentences $c_i \neq c_j$ for distinct i and j in I, and for all formulae $F(x_1,..., x_n)$ of L and finite $i_1 < ... < i_n$ and $j_1 < ... < j_n$ from I, the conditional $F(c_{i_1},..., c_{i_n}) \to F(c_{j_1},..., c_{j_n})$. A model for Γ provides a sequence of order indiscernibles, so we show Γ finitely satisfiable. Let Δ be a finite subset of Γ, and let I_0 be the finite subset of I such that $i \in I_0$ if and only if c_i occurs in a member of Δ. Let $F_1,..., F_m$ be the formulae of L whose indiscernibility conditionals occur in Δ, and let $x_1,..., x_n$ be the free variables in $F_1,..., F_m$. Let M be an infinite model of T and let < be a linear order of D(M). We define a map f from $(D(M))^n$ to the set of all subsets of $\{1,..., m\}$. For $A = \{a_1,..., a_n\}$ where $a_1 < ... < a_n$, let f(A) be the set of those i such that $F_i(a_1,..., a_n)$ is true in M. We can map the set of subsets of $\{1,..., m\}$ one–one onto 2^m, so we may think of f as mapping $(D(M))^n$ into 2^m, so by Ramsey's theorem there is an infinite $X \subseteq D(M)$ such that f is constant on X. Let s be the subset of $\{1,..., m\}$ that is the value of f on all subsets of X with n members. Since X is infinite, for each i in I_0, there is an x_i in X such that $x_i < x_j$ if and only if $i < j$ (where the first < is the total order of D(M), and the second, the total order of I). Then for increasing $i_1 < ... < i_n$ and $j_1 < ... < j_n$, we have $F_k(x_{i_1}, ..., x_{i_n})$ true in M if and only if $F_k(x_{j_1}, ..., x_{j_n})$ is true in M. So if we extend M by letting c_i denote x_i for i in I_0, we get a model for Δ. This completes the proof that T has a model with a sequence of order indiscernibles.

We used Skolem hulls in Chapter 6 when we proved the Löwenheim–Skolem theorem. To review, let M be an interpretation of a language L. A Skolem function for an existential formula $(\exists x)(F(\underline{z}, x)$ of L is a function f such that for $\underline{a}$ in D(M), if $(\exists x)(F(\underline{a}, x)$ is true in M, then so is $F(\underline{a}, f(\underline{a}))$. We used the axiom of choice to show that there are Skolem functions. Let X be a subset of D(M). Let X_0 be X with the distinguished members of M tossed in, and let D(N) be the closure of X_0 under the functions of M and the Skolem functions. Let N be the structure whose domain is D(N), whose distinguished individuals are those of M, and whose distinguished relations and functions are the restrictions of those of M to D(N). Then N is the Skolem hull of M over X, and it is an elementary submodel of M. An Ehrenfeucht–Mostowski model is the Skolem hull of a model over a sequence of order indiscernibles for it.[23] Suppose L is a countable language, so there are only countably many existential formulae of L, and T is a theory whose language is L. We may form a countable expansion L^* of L by adding to L new and distinct function signs such that for every existential formula $(\exists x)(F(\underline{z}, x))$ of L^* there is a function sign f of L^* such that T^* is T plus $(\exists x)(F(\underline{z}, x)) \to F(\underline{z}, f(\underline{z}))$. We do this in waves, first forming L_1 and T_1 by adding Skolem function signs and axioms to L and T, then forming L_2 and T_2 by so expanding L_1 and T_1, and so on through the natural numbers. L^* and T^* are the unions of the L_n and the T_n. Given a model M of T we can expand it to a model M^* for T^* by adding Skolem functions to interpret the new signs in L^*. Nowadays the Skolem hull is usually formed by closing X under the Skolem functions of L^* and M^*.

Let T be a theory with a countable language and infinite models. We are going to show that for all infinite cardinals κ there is a model M for T^* such that D(M) has κ members and for all $A \subseteq D(M)$, if α is the number of members of A, then M realizes at most $\alpha + \omega$ types in $S_n^M(A)$. It suffices to show this for n = 1, for if M realizes more than $\alpha + \omega$ types $p(x_1, x_2)$ in $S_2^M(A)$, then there are a_p in A such that M realizes more than $\alpha + \omega$ types $p(x_1, a_p)$ in $S_1^M(A)$, and similarly for larger n. Let I be a set with κ members and let < be a total order of I isomorphic to the well-order of κ by $\in$. Let N be an infinite model of T. Form L^* and T^* as earlier. Let N_1 be a model for T^* containing a sequence $m : I \to N_1$ of order indiscernibles, and let M be the Skolem hull of N_1 over m(I). D(M) has κ members.

Pick $A \subseteq D(M)$. For each a in A, there is a term $t_a(\underline{x})$ of L^* and a tuple $\underline{m}_a$ of members of A such that a is the denotation in M of $t_a(\underline{m}_a)$. Let X be the set of m(i), $i \in I$, such that m(i) is in a tuple $\underline{m}_a$ for some a $\in$ A. If A is finite, so is X, and then it has fewer than $\omega = \alpha + \omega$ members; while if A is infinite, X has at most α members, and so no more than $\alpha + \omega$ members. So the number of members of X is at most $\alpha + \omega$.

If b = m(i) and d = m(j), we shift < from I to D(M) by saying b < d if and only if i < j. Let $b_1 < \ldots < b_n$ and $d_1 < \ldots < d_n$ be <-increasing

[23] Andrzej Ehrenfeucht and Andrzej Mostowski, "Models of Axiomatic Theories Admitting Automorphisms," *Fundamenta Mathematica* 43 (1956): 50–68.

n-tuples of order indiscernibles of M.[24] Then $\underline{b} \sim_x \underline{d}$ if and only if for all $i = 1, \ldots, n$ and all x in X, $b_i < x$ if and only if $d_i < x$ and $b_i = x$ if and only if $d_i = x$. So $\underline{b} \sim_x \underline{d}$ if and only if $\underline{b}$ and $\underline{d}$ match in the $<$ order of X. Then for any term $t(\underline{z})$ and $\underline{b} \sim_x \underline{d}$, $t^M(\underline{b})$ and $t^M(\underline{d})$ realize the same type in $S_1^M(A)$. To show this, let $F(y, a_1, \ldots, a_m)$ be a formula of L_A^* where the members of $\underline{a}$ are in A. Then

$$F(t^M(\underline{b}), a_1, \ldots, a_m) \text{ is true in M}$$
$$\text{iff } F(t^M(\underline{b}), t_{a_1}(\underline{m}_{a_1}), \ldots, t_{a_n}(\underline{m}_{a_n})) \text{ is true in M}$$
$$\text{iff } F(t^M(\underline{d}), t_{a_1}(\underline{m}_{a_1}), \ldots, t_{a_n}(\underline{m}_{a_n})) \text{ is true in M}$$
$$\text{iff } F(t^M(\underline{d}), a_1, \ldots, a_n) \text{ is true in M}$$

where the equivalence between the second and third holds by indiscernibility because $\underline{b}$ and $\underline{d}$ match in the $<$ order of X and all of $\underline{m}_{a_1}, \ldots, \underline{m}_{a_n}$ are in X.

So to show that there are at most $\alpha + \omega$ types in $S_1^M(A)$, it suffices to show that $\sim_x$ partitions $<$ increasing n-tuples of $J = \{m(i) \mid i \in I\}$ into at most $\alpha + \omega$ equivalence classes. For $y \in J - X$, let C_y be the set of the x in X such that $x < y$. Then for increasing n-tuples $\underline{b}$ and $\underline{d}$, $\underline{b} \sim_x \underline{d}$ if and only if for $i = 1, \ldots, n$, first, if b_i is in X, then d_i is in X; and, second, if b_i is not in X, then d_i is not in X and $C_{b_i} = C_{d_i}$. So the number of equivalence classes is determined by the number of cuts. But $<$ well-orders J. So cuts C_y and C_z can differ only if either one is empty (but the other is not) or else the greatest lower bound of the m(i) in J greater than all members of C_y differs from the greatest lower bound of the m(i) in J greater than all members of C_z, and in the second case there is a member of X in one of C_y and C_z but not the other. So the number of cuts is at most 1 plus the number of members of X, which is no bigger than $\alpha + \omega$. Hence the number of $\sim_x$ equivalence classes is no bigger than $\alpha + \omega$, and so M realizes no more than $\alpha + \omega$ types in $S_n^M(A)$.

Suppose T is a complete theory with a countable language and infinite models, and let κ be an uncountable cardinal. Then if T is κ-categorical, T is ω-stable. For suppose T is not ω-stable. Then by the Löwenheim–Skolem theorem it has a countable model M such that for some $A \subseteq D(M)$, $S_n^M(A)$ is uncountable. So by compactness there is an elementary extension N_1 of M such that $D(N_1)$ has κ members and N_1 realizes uncountably many types in $S_n^M(A)$. But by what we just

---

[24] By rewriting variables we may consider only increasing sequences of objects. See J. L. Bell and M. Machover, *A Course in Mathematical Logic* (Amsterdam: North-Holland, 1977), 221.

showed using Ehrenfeucht–Mostowski models, there is a model N_2 of T such that $D(N_2)$ has κ members and for all countable $B \subseteq D(N_2)$, N_2 realizes at most ω types over B. Hence N_1 and N_2 are not isomorphic, so T is not κ-categorical. So if T is κ-categorical, it is ω-stable. It then follows that if T is κ-categorical, there are no Vaught pairs of models of T, and thus no κ,μ model (where μ is infinite and $\mu < \kappa$). For suppose T is κ-categorical. Then by the first part of this paragraph, T is ω-stable. If there were a Vaught pair of models for T, then by how we proved Vaught's two-cardinal theorem there would be an $\omega(1),\omega$ model for T. Since T is ω-stable, by the partial converse of Vaught's theorem, there would be a κ,ω model of T. But by compactness there is a model of T whose domain has κ members and in which every infinite set defined by a formula has κ members. Hence T is not κ-categorical. So if T is κ-categorical, it has no Vaught pairs and thus no κ,μ model.

We turn next to minimality. Recall that when M is an interpretation of a language L and F is an n-ary formula of L, then F(M) is the set of n-tuples $\underline{a}$ of members of D(M) such that $F(\underline{a})$ is true in M. A relation among members of D(M) is definable if and only if there is a formula F of $L_{D(M)}$ such that the relation is F(M). Suppose D is an infinite definable relation; then D is minimal in M if and only if the only definable subsets of D are either finite or cofinite. (A subset X of D is cofinite if and only if $D - X$ is finite.) Since we can mention members of D(M) in definitions, the finite and cofinite subsets of D are definable, so a minimal set has as few definable subsets as possible. If D is minimal in M and D is $F(M, \underline{a})$, then the formula $F(\underline{x}, \underline{a})$ is called minimal too. D and F are strongly minimal when F is minimal in any elementary extension of M.

Suppose D is strongly minimal in M. For $A \subseteq D$, we say that $b \in D$ is algebraic over A if and only if there is a formula $F(x, \underline{a})$ such that $F(b, \underline{a})$ is true in M, $\underline{a}$ is in A, and $F(D, \underline{a})$ is finite. (This is a bit like b being the solution to an equation with coefficients in A.) For $A \subseteq D$, acl(A) is the set of all members of D algebraic over A. For $a \in A$, a = a is true in M and = (D, a) is a unit set, so $A \subseteq$ acl(A). If b is algebraic over A by $F(x, \underline{a})$, c by $F(y, \underline{a}')$, and d is algebraic over {b, c} by H(z, b, c), then d is algebraic over A by $(\exists y, z)(H(x, y, z) \wedge F(y, \underline{a}) \wedge G(z, \underline{a}'))$, so acl(A) = acl(acl(A)). Since formulae are finite, any a in acl(A) is in $acl(A_0)$ for some finite subset A_0 of A. These three claims hold for any D.

Minimality figures in the exchange principle. Suppose D is minimal, A is a subset of D, and a and b are members of D. The exchange principle says that if a is algebraic over $A \cup \{b\}$ but not over A, then b is algebraic over $A \cup \{a\}$. This is like solving an equation for a coefficient.

Suppose F(a, b) is true in M, where members of A may be mentioned in F(x, y) and n is the number of members of F(D, b). Let G(y) be the formula of L_A saying that there are exactly n members of D in F(D, y).[25] Since G(b) is true in M, if G(D) is finite, then b is algebraic over A, so a is algebraic over A, contrary to our hypothesis. Thus, since G(D) is a definable subset of D and D is minimal, G(D) is cofinite. F(a, b) ∧ G(b) is true in M, so if F(a, D) ∧ G(D) is finite, b is algebraic over A ∪ {a} and we are home. So suppose for reductio that F(a, D) ∧ G(D) is cofinite. Let m be the number of members of D − (F(a, D) ∧ G(D)), and let H(x) be the formula of L_A saying that there are exactly m members of D in D − (F(x, D) ∧ G(D)). Since H(a) is true in M, if H(D) is finite, then a is algebraic over A, contrary to our hypothesis. So H(D) is cofinite. Thus there are $a_1, ..., a_{n+1}$ in D such that H(a_i) is true in M for i = 1, ..., n + 1. Let B_i be F(a_i, D) ∧ G(D). Since H(D) is cofinite, each B_i is cofinite, so there is a b* in all the B_i. Then for each i, F(a_i, b*) is true in M, so there are at least n + 1 members of D in F(D, b*), contradicting the truth of G(b*) in M. This completes the proof of the exchange principle.

Now suppose D is strongly minimal. A subset A of D is independent if no a in A is algebraic over A − {a}. For a subset C of D, we say A is independent over C if no a in A is algebraic over C ∪ (A − {a}), so even allowing mention of members of C will not get you a. We are going to show that an infinite independent set is a set of indiscernibles. (Note that here we need no order of the indiscernibles.) To this end, we return to types. So suppose that M_0 is an elementary submodel of both M and N, that A is a subset of D(M_0), and that F(x) is a strongly minimal formula in which any individuals mentioned come from A. We will argue that if the n members of a are in F(M) and are independent over A, and the n members of b are in F(N) and are independent over A, then tp^M(a | A) is tp^N(b | A). The proof is by induction on n. For n = 1, let a in F(M) not be algebraic over A and b in F(N) not be algebraic over A. Let G(x) be a formula of L_A. Suppose G(a) is true in M. Then since a is not algebraic over A, F(M) ∧ G(M) is infinite. Because F is minimal, F(M) ∧ ¬G(M) is finite. So there is a unique n such that F(M) ∧ ¬G(M) has n members, and if S says this, S is true in M. If ¬G(b) were true in

---

[25] ¬(∃x)Fx says there are exactly zero Fs, and if N_x(Fx) says there are exactly n Fs, then (∃y)(Fy ∧ N_x(Fx ∧ x ≠ y)) says there are exactly n + 1 Fs. Let D(x_1, x_2) be x_1 ≠ x_2, and let D($x_1, ..., x_n, x_{n+1}$) be D($x_1, ..., x_n$) ∧ x_1 ≠ x_{n+1} ∧ ... ∧ x_n ≠ x_{n+1}. Then (∃$x_1, ..., x_n$) (Fx_1 ∧ ... ∧ Fx_n ∧ D($x_1, ..., x_n$)) says there are at least n Fs. (∀$x_1, ..., x_n, x_{n+1}$)((Fx_n ∧ ... ∧ Fx_n ∧ Fx_{n+1}) → (x_{n+1} = x_1 ∨ ... ∨ x_{n+1} = x_n)) says there are at most n Fs.

N, it would be true in M_0 and M, so since $\neg G(A)$ is a finite subset of $F(M)$, b would be algebraic over A. Since it is not, $tp^M(a \mid A)$ is $tp^N(b \mid A)$. Now suppose the claim holds for n, and that $a_1,..., a_{n+1} \in F(M)$ and by $b_1,..., b_{n+1} \in F(N)$ are independent over A. Let $\underline{a}$ be $a_1,..., a_n$ and $\underline{b}$ be $b_1,..., b_n$. Then $tp^M(\underline{a} \mid A) = tp^N(\underline{b} \mid A)$. Let $G(\underline{z}, x)$ be an (n+1)-ary formula of L_A such that $G(\underline{a}, a_{n+1})$ is true in M. Since $a_1,..., a_n, a_{n+1}$ is independent over A, a_{n+1} is not algebraic over $A \cup \{a_1,..., a_n\}$, so as before $F(M) \wedge G(\underline{a}, M)$ is infinite and $F(M) \wedge \neg G(\underline{a}, M)$ is finite. So there is an m such that the sentence S saying $F(M) \wedge \neg G(\underline{a}, M)$ has m members is true in M. Then since $tp^M(\underline{a} \mid A) = tp^N(\underline{b} \mid A)$ and M_0 is an elementary submodel of M and N, the sentence S' saying $F(N) \wedge \neg G(\underline{b}, M)$ has m members is true in N. As before, since b_{n+1} is not algebraic over $A \cup \{b_1,..., b_n\}$, $G(\underline{b}, b_{n+1})$ is true in N. So $tp^M(\underline{a}, a_{n+1} \mid A) = tp^N(\underline{b}, b_{n+1} \mid A)$. Hence, if M_0 is an elementary submodel of M and N, A is a subset of $D(M_0)$, F is a strongly minimal formula of L_A, B is an infinite subset of $F(M)$ independent over A, and C is an infinite subset of $F(N)$ independent over A, then B and C are infinite sets of indiscernibles such that for any n-ary formula F of L_A and n-tuples $\underline{b}$ from B and $\underline{c}$ from C, $F(\underline{b})$ is true in M if and only if $F(\underline{c})$ is true in N.

If D is strongly minimal and X is a subset of D, then A is a basis for X just in case A is a subset of X, A is independent, and A has the same algebraic closure as X. In a system of coordinates C for a space S, every point in S is a combination of points in C, but no point in C is a combination of points in the rest of C. A basis for a subset of D is like a system of coordinates for a space. We argue that X has a basis by Zorn's lemma. Suppose B is a set of sets. A chain in B is a subset of B totally ordered by inclusion, and a maximal member of B is a member of B with no proper supersets in B. Zorn's lemma says that if the union of any chain in B is a member of B, then B has a maximal member. Since B is a set, there is a d not in B, and by the axiom of choice some relation R well-orders B. For each ordinal α, let $f(\alpha)$ be the R-least proper superset in B of every set in $f(\beta)$ for any $\beta < \alpha$ if there is such a proper superset, but d if there is not. Since B is a set, there is a least α such that $f(\alpha)$ is d. Then the set of $f(\beta)$ for $\beta < \alpha$ is a chain in B, so its union is in B. This union is maximal, for if not we could extend the chain of the $f(\beta)$. Then if B is the set of independent subsets of X, the union of any chain in B is an element of B, so B has a maximal member, and this is a basis for X.

We want to show that any two bases for the same set have the same number of members. We consider independent subsets A and B of D such that A is included in acl(B). First, we suppose $A_0 \subseteq A$, $B_0 \subseteq B$,

$A_0 \cup B_0$ is a basis for B, and $a \in A - A_0$, and we show there is a $b \in B_0$ such that $A_0 \cup \{a\} \cup (B_0 - \{b\})$ is a basis for B. Since $A_0 \cup B_0$ is a basis for B and $a \in A \subseteq acl(B)$, there is a $C \subseteq B_0$ such that $a \in acl(A_0 \cup C)$. Let C^* be such a C of smallest size. Since A is independent, C^* has at least one member, so there is a b in C^*. Then a is algebraic over $A_0 \cup C^*$, but by the leastness of the size of C^* and since $b \in C^*$, a is not algebraic over $A \cup (C^* - \{b\})$. So by the exchange principle, b is algebraic over $A_0 \cup \{a\} \cup (C^* - \{b\})$. So the algebraic closure of $A_0 \cup \{a\} \cup (B_0 - \{b\})$ is that of B. To show independence, suppose for reductio that a is algebraic over $A_0 \cup (B_0 - \{b\})$. Then since b is algebraic over $A_0 \cup \{a\} \cup (C^* - \{b\})$, b is algebraic over $A_0 \cup (B_0 - \{b\})$; just get a from $A_0 \cup (B_0 - \{b\})$, and then get b. But since $A_0 \cup B_0$ is a basis, it is independent, so b is not algebraic over $A_0 \cup (B_0 - \{b\})$. Second, we argue that A is not bigger than B. If B is finite, suppose it has n members and assume for reductio that $a_1, \ldots, a_{n+1}$ are distinct members of A. Let A_0 be $\varnothing$ and B_0 be B. Using the first thing we showed n times, there are distinct $b_1, \ldots, b_n$ in B such that $\{a_1, \ldots, a_n\} \cup (B - \{b_1, \ldots, b_n\})$ is a basis for B. But then $\{a_1, \ldots, a_n\}$ is a basis for B, and since $a_{n+1} \in A \subseteq acl(B)$, this contradicts the independence of A. If B is infinite, then since our language is countable, acl(B) is no bigger than B, and then because A is included in acl(B), A is no bigger than B. Hence any two bases for $X \subseteq D$ have the same number of members, which is called the dimension of X. Note that since our language is countable, acl(A) is countable for any countable $A \subseteq D$, so if D is uncountable, the dimension of D is its cardinal.

Let us return to the situation where M_0 is an elementary submodel of M and N, $A \subseteq D(M_0)$, and F is a strongly minimal formula of L_A. We will show that if F(M) and F(N) are of the same dimension, then there is a partial elementary map from one to the other. Let B and C be bases for F(M) and F(N). Then B and C have the same number of members; there is a one–one correspondence f from B to C. Since B and C are sets of indiscernibles, f is partial elementary. Let S be the set of partial elementary maps g extending f such that if B′ is the domain of g and C′ is its range, then $B \subseteq B′ \subseteq F(M)$ and $C \subseteq C′ \subseteq F(N)$. The union of a chain in S is an element of S. So by Zorn's lemma, there is a maximal $g : B′ \to C′$ in S. Suppose $b \in F(M) - B′$. Since $B \subseteq B′$ is a basis for F(M), b is algebraic over B′. So there is a formula G(x) of $L_{B′}$ such that G(b) is true in M and G(M) is finite. Let $d_1, \ldots, d_n$ be the members of G(M) such that $tp^M(b \mid B′) \neq tp^M(d_i \mid B′)$. Then there are formulae H_i in $tp^M(b \mid B′)$ but not in $tp^M(d_i \mid B′)$. So $G(x) \wedge H_1(x) \wedge \ldots \wedge H_n(x)$ isolates $tp^M(b \mid B′)$. This formula is $J(x, \underline{d})$, where J(x, y) is a formula of L and the members of $\underline{d}$ are in B′. $(\exists x)(F(x) \wedge J(x, \underline{d}))$ is true in M and $g : B′ \to C′$ is partial elementary, so $(\exists x)(F(x) \wedge J(x, g(\underline{d})))$ is true in N. Thus there is a c in F(N) such that $J(c, g(\underline{d}))$ is true in N. Then $\mathrm{tp}^M(b \mid B′) = \mathrm{tp}^N(c \mid C′)$, so $g \cup \{<b, c>\}$ is a member of S properly extending g, contrary to the maximality of g. Hence B′ is F(M), and similarly, C′ is F(N).

If T is ω-stable and M is an infinite model of T, then there is a formula F in $L_{D(M)}$ such that F(M) is a minimal subset of D(M). For if not, then for every F there is a G such that both $F(M) \wedge G(M)$ and $F(M) \wedge \neg G(M)$ are infinite. So we can build a binary tree. Let $F_\varnothing$ be the formula x = x. For any finite sequence σ of zeroes and ones, there is a G such that $F_\sigma(M) \wedge G(M)$ and $F_\sigma(M) \wedge \neg G(M)$ are both infinite, so let $F_{\sigma 0}$ be $F_\sigma \wedge G$ and $F_{\sigma 1}$ be $F_\sigma \wedge \neg G$. For all σ, $F_\sigma(M)$ is infinite, and for a in $F_\sigma(M)$, $\mathrm{tp}^M(a) \in [F_\sigma]$. The intersection of $[F_\tau]$ for $\tau \subseteq \sigma$ is $[F_\sigma]$, and thus nonempty. Hence by compactness for each $f : \omega \to 2$ there is a type p_f in the intersection of all the $[F_\sigma]$ where $\sigma \subseteq f$, and when $g \neq f$, $p_g \neq p_f$. Let A be the set of all members of D(M) mentioned in any F_σ. Then A is at most countably infinite, but $S_n^M(A)$ has continuum many members, contrary to the ω-stability of T.

Infinite models of ω-stable theories supply minimal formulae. We will show that if the theory has no Vaught pairs, its minimal formulae are strongly minimal. This works because when there are no Vaught pairs, we can for any F say that there are infinitely many Fs. More specifically, suppose T has no Vaught pairs and M is an infinite model of T. Let $F(x_1,..., x_p, z_1,..., z_m)$ be a formula of $L_{D(M)}$. Then there is an n such that for any m-tuple $\underline{a}$ in D(M), if $F(M, \underline{a})$ has more than n members (which we can say first-order), then $F(M, \underline{a})$ is infinite. For suppose not. Then for each n there is an m-tuple $\underline{a}_n$ such that $F(M, \underline{a}_n)$ is finite and has at least n elements. Recall the unary predicate U(x) we introduced when N and M were a Vaught pair and we used U to keep track of M when we tacked M on behind N to make a single structure (N, M). Add U to the language L of T. Let $\Gamma(\underline{z})$ be the set of formulae of this language that includes T, the formulae saying U picks out in L a proper elementary submodel of what T describes, the conjunction $U(z_1) \wedge ... \wedge U(z_m)$, sentences saying there are infinitely many p-tuples $\underline{x}$ such that $F(\underline{x}, \underline{z})$, and $F(\underline{x}, \underline{z}) \to (U(x_1) \wedge ... \wedge U(x_p))$. Let N be any proper elementary extension of M. Since $F(M, \underline{a}_n)$ is finite and M is an elementary submodel of N, $F(M, \underline{a}_n) = F(N, \underline{a}_n)$. Let Δ be a finite subset of Γ. Then for n big enough, $\underline{a}_n$ realizes Δ in (N, M), for there will be in Δ only finitely many of the infinitely many sentences in Γ we need to say there are infinitely many $\underline{x}$ such that $F(\underline{x}, \underline{z})$, and we can take n big enough to provide the finitely many things Δ requires. So by compactness, $\Gamma(\underline{z})$ is a type. Hence there is an elementary extension (N', M') of (N, M) and an m-tuple $\underline{a}$ in $D(N')$ that realizes Γ. Then M' is a model of T and N' is a proper elementary extension of M'. As well, $F(M', \underline{a})$ is infinite, and $F(N', \underline{a}) = F(M', \underline{a})$. So contrary to our supposition, N' and M' are a Vaught pair for T.

It follows that if T has no Vaught pairs, then all its minimal formulae are strongly minimal. Suppose that T has no Vaught pairs, that M is a model of T, and that $F(\underline{x})$ is a formula of $L_{D(M)}$ such that $F(M)$ is minimal. Assume for reductio that there is an elementary extension N of M and a formula $G(\underline{x}, \underline{z})$ of the language of T such that for some tuple $\underline{b}$ in $D(N)$, $G(N, \underline{b})$ is a subset of $F(N)$ that is both infinite and coinfinite. We just proved that there is an n such that for any elementary extension N^* of M and tuple $\underline{b}^*$ in $D(N^*)$, $G(N^*, \underline{b}^*)$ is an infinite coinfinite subset of $F(N^*)$ if and only if both $F(N^*) \wedge G(N^*, \underline{b}^*)$ and $F(N^*) \wedge \neg G(N^*, \underline{b}^*)$ have more than n members. We can take n big enough so that if $H(\underline{z})$ is the first-order formula saying there are at most n $\underline{x}$ such that $F(\underline{x}) \wedge G(\underline{x}, \underline{z})$ and $J(\underline{z})$ is the first-order formula saying there are at most n $\underline{x}$ such that $F(\underline{x}) \wedge \neg G(\underline{x}, \underline{z})$, then the sentence $(\forall \underline{z})(H(\underline{z}) \vee J(\underline{z}))$ is true in M. So it is true in N. But in letting N^* be N, both $H(\underline{b})$ and $J(\underline{b})$ fail in N.

Suppose T is ω-stable, M is a model of T, and A is a subset of $D(M)$. We have seen that there is an elementary submodel M' of M that is prime over A. This means that if N is a model for T, then any partial elementary map from A into $D(N)$ extends to an isomorphism from M to an elementary submodel of N. But for any M, $\varnothing \subseteq D(M)$ and for any N, $\varnothing$ is a partial elementary map from $\varnothing$ into $D(N)$. So for any model N of T, M' is isomorphic to an elementary submodel of N. Such a model is called prime. If T is ω-stable, has no Vaught pairs, and M' is a prime model of T, then there is a strongly minimal formula in $L_{D(M')}$. Suppose next that T has no Vaught pairs, M is an infinite model of T, and R is an infinite definable relation on $D(M)$. We show that no proper elementary submodel of M includes R. For if $F(\underline{x})$ defines R in M, and N is a proper elementary submodel of M including R, then $F(N) = R = F(M)$, so M and N are a Vaught pair. If T is also ω-stable, then M is prime over R. For M has an elementary submodel N that is prime over R, and then since T has no Vaught pairs, N is M and M is prime over R.

We are now ready to prove the Baldwin–Lachlan characterization of uncountably categorical theories. T is a complete theory with a countable language and infinite models, and κ is an uncountable cardinal.

Then T is κ-categorical if and only if T is ω-stable and has no Vaught pairs. We used Ehrenfeucht–Mostowski models to prove that if T is κ-categorical, then T is ω-stable and has no Vaught pairs. So suppose, conversely, that T is ω-stable and has no Vaught pairs. Let M_1 and N_1 be models of T whose domains have κ members. T is ω-stable, so it has a prime model M'. Let M and N be the models isomorphic to M_1 and N_1, respectively, formed by replacing the prime elementary submodels in M_1 and N_1, with M'. There is a strongly minimal formula $F(x)$ of $L_{D(M')}$. Then $F(M)$ and $F(N)$ both have κ members. For if either of them, say $F(M)$, had μ members for some $\mu < \kappa$, then by the Löwenheim–Skolem theorem M would have an elementary submodel M^* such that $D(M^*)$ has μ members and $F(M) = F(M^*)$. Then M and N are a Vaught pair for T, contrary to our hypothesis. Then $F(M)$ and $F(N)$ are both of dimension κ. So there is a partial elementary f mapping $F(M)$ one–one onto $F(N)$. By the end of the last paragraph, M is prime over $F(M)$. So we can extend f to a partial elementary g mapping M into N. But by the last paragraph, no proper elementary submodel of N includes $F(N)$. Thus g is an isomorphism from M to N. The Baldwin–Lachlan characterization of κ-categoricity, ω-stability plus no Vaught pairs, is independent of κ, and thus yields Morley's theorem that a theory categorical in one uncountable cardinal is categorical to all.[26]

---

[26] Our exposition follows David Marker. It is common knowledge at his university that he is a superb teacher, and his book *Model Theory: An Introduction* puts superb teaching on the page in a way that shines it into the reader's mind. Marker's book is a math book from which a patient philosopher can learn with pleasure (but one needs the courage to correct misprints). Saturated models, ones that realize many types, are an important theme we left out, because we did not need them. The Baldwin–Lachlan proof of Morley's theorem avoids rank, a notion crucial in Morley's original proof, and central in Saharon Shelah's later analysis of stability (*Classification Theory and the Number of Non-isomorphic Models* [Amsterdam: North-Holland, 1978]), but Poizat, *Course in Model Theory*, 236–37, says, "It could hardly be recommended to a novice, even a gifted one, since its author's trying style makes it almost totally incomprehensible even to an experienced logician." Marker's book is a place to make a start on rank.

TEN

✦

The Zoology of Reality

Logic, I should maintain, must no more admit a unicorn than zoology
can; for logic is concerned with the real world just as truly as zoology,
though with its more abstract and general features.

Russell, *Introduction to Mathematical Philosophy*, 169

In the last four chapters, we reviewed four major monuments of twentieth-century logic. These four results are less familiar to philosophers
than Gödel's proof of the incompleteness of arithmetic. It would be
a shame if philosophy lost touch with logic. From Dedekind, Cantor,
and Frege until World War II, the signal logicians were almost always
both signal mathematicians and signal philosophers. It is not as if after
the war such people suddenly vanished; they did not. But increasingly,
mathematical logic became a recognized subdiscipline of mathematics.
It is rare for our four results to be taught in a philosophy department,
and mathematics courses usually move very swiftly for philosophers.
Equally, many philosophers know first-rate logicians in their mathematics departments who are philosophically acute but shy about speaking
up among philosophers. (A former colleague called philosophy a blood
sport.) If the philosophers do not keep up as the mathematicians move
on, it is inevitable that they will lose touch.

But why should a philosopher put in the significant effort needed to
keep up with the mathematicians? Since the renaissance of logic in the
nineteenth century, philosophers have been intrigued by its metaphysical and epistemological intimations. One thing it revealed was a whole
new kind of objects, sets. Sets have more than earned their credentials
in unifying and organizing disparate subjects and tracts of knowledge,
so much so that by now, no education in abstract pursuits is adequate
without some familiarity with sets. It can sometimes feel as if we had

268

found a sixth and more primitive sort of vertebrate that makes sense of fish, amphibians, reptiles, birds, and mammals.

When a new sort of object is introduced, one wants to know what basic assumptions objects of that sort are supposed to meet. One also wants to know what can be done with them, what new insights they yield. Then one also wants to know what they leave open. In the case of sets, the intriguing basic principles include power set, replacement, choice, infinity, and perhaps foundation. Perhaps their most striking omission is whether Cantor's continuum hypothesis is true, whether there are sets larger than the natural numbers but smaller than the reals.

The natural way to understand Gödel's proof of the consistency of the continuum hypothesis (with set theory, if set theory is itself consistent) is in terms of the constructible sets. Gödel shows us a new realm L of sets where set theory, the axiom of choice, and the continuum hypothesis are all true. Set theory does not prove that L is new, but anyone with a robust conception of sets is likely to think L is too thin to exhaust the sets. The natural way to understand Cohen's proof of the independence of the continuum hypothesis (from set theory, if set theory is consistent) is in terms of generic sets and forcing. These reveal worlds (models) in which set theory holds but choice fails, and others in which set theory and choice hold, but we can make the continuum almost any size we like.

The experience of working through Gödel's and Cohen's proofs is like learning what a new sort of thing is like, and this platonist impression should be trusted. At the same time, in each case there are natural philosophical questions about what these new things, constructible and generic sets, are. Consider first the constructible sets. One philosophical view is that a set is the extension of a predicate. If we allow just any old predicates, we get problems like the paradoxes of set theory. So let us be puritanical and restrict ourselves to predicates in a first-order language with identity whose only extralogical predicate is the epsilon of set membership. (This puritanical view limits the applicability of set theory.) We will allow ourselves, to begin with, only the empty set. But then let us liberalize slightly and allow ourselves to insert into these predicates constants denoting sets we have already got. The word "already" here suggests an ordering; at one stage we got A, and at another, later stage we use A to get B. We let ourselves take these stages as given by the ordinals; otherwise, we will never get versions of the transfinite cardinals, and so will not be able to address the continuum hypothesis.

The constructible sets are what we get by iterating this collections-of-extensions-of-a-predicate-allowing-constant-for-extensions-got-earlier through the ordinals. There have been people who think these really are the sets, and "really" marks this thought as a philosophical view. Burt Dreben once said in lecture that the only reason set theorists do not generally buy this view is that it would put them out of business by settling their open questions. The controversial side of this conception of sets is the claim that the constructible sets exhaust the sets. This claim is congenial to a view that sets must conform to (an idealization of) our description of them, which might in turn be congenial to a kind of idealism about sets. One who is more platonist about sets, who thinks sets and quasars are just there and it is our problem to figure them out, can advance two considerations. First, the dominant iterative conception of sets pictures them arranged starting from the empty set, taking power sets at successor ordinals and unions at limits. This conception breaks with the constructible sets at level $\omega + 1$. At level ω, both agree that we have the countable set of hereditary finite sets. So there are only countably many constructible sets in order $\omega + 1$, but there are continuum many members in rank $\omega + 1$ of the cumulative hierarchy. While set theory does not refute the claim that all the sets of the cumulative hierarchy turn up eventually among the constructible sets in orders higher than their ranks in the hierarchy, the constructible sets look like a thinner world than the received cumulative hierarchy.

Second, recall how Gödel shows that the continuum hypothesis holds in the constructible sets. His main lemma here is that a constructible subset of order $\omega(\alpha)$ is an element of order $\omega(\alpha + 1)$. The proof of this lemma is an application of the Löwenheim–Skolem theorem. That theorem fixes the size of the Skolem hull in terms of the size of the language (and the number of members of the original domain we pick). This sensitivity to the size of the language may give one pause that showing the continuum hypothesis holds in the constructible sets is much real support for the continuum hypothesis in the real world, for the size of the real continuum need not depend on our linguistic resources. This second consideration is really the first come again, but it is perhaps worth remarking that the continuum hypothesis is not taken to have been settled by Gödel's proof that it holds in the constructible sets.

In Cohen's proof of the independence of the axiom of choice and the continuum hypothesis, a philosopher will want to get clear about forcing and truth. Truth is a relation between interpretations and sentences, while forcing is a relation between conditions and (to begin with, limited) sentences. So these are relations between, on the left, interpretations or conditions and, on the right, sentences. Both have inductive definitions, and in each case, the induction is on the complexity of the sentence on the right. Ignoring the left-hand sides, these inductions look very similar, except perhaps for their respective treatments of negation, and this similarity can lead one to wonder whether forcing is a variant of truth. Moreover, forcing yields the models in which set theory is true but also, depending on what we force, the axiom of choice is false or else choice is true but the continuum hypothesis is false.

But there are intricacies in how forcing yields truth. An interpretation settles whether a sentence is true or false only if the interpretation provides extensions for all the extralogical signs in the sentence. In the case of forcing, we begin with constants we intend eventually to denote generic sets, but at the outset these constants are without extensions, and we do not know what the generic sets will turn out to be. Looking on the left, an interpretation in which set theory comes out true will have an infinite domain because set theory includes the axiom of infinity. But on the left of forcing are the conditions, and these are finite. Generic sets are sets of natural numbers, and a particular condition says of finitely many numbers that they are to wind up in such and such generic set, of finitely many other numbers that they are to stay out, and that none should be both in and out. A condition says this even though we do not yet have anything like a definition of these generic sets; instead, each condition provides only finitely much information about which numbers are to be in and which out, but no condition specifies the whole of a generic set.

Our exposition of Cohen's argument was special (and simplified) partly because we concentrated on countable models and, thus, countable languages. It then follows that there is a countable sequence of conditions that is complete. This means that for every natural number n and every generic set a we hope to specify, eventually and indeed finitely far along, the sequence has a condition that settles ever after whether n is or is not to be in a. Then the generic set a is the set of numbers the sequence eventually says should be in a. Once we have the generic sets, they are assigned to the hitherto vacuous constants as their denotations. We then take the minimal countable structure of sets constructible given these generic sets. This structure is the interpretation in which forcing yields truth. The limited sentences true in this structure are exactly those forced by the complete sequence.

Arriving at a generic set can remind one of Baron Munchausen pulling himself out of the swamp by his own bootstraps; first we recite the incantation of the set we want, and then, poof, it appears. To be sure, something like this has been around set theory since its inception.[1] The axiom of comprehension guarantees the existence of sets that are the extensions of predicates we provide (subject, later on, to various restrictions), and a skeptic might take those predicates as incantations supposed to conjure up sets. But forcing does not yield generic sets in the same way comprehension yields sets. Comprehension starts from predicates, while forcing starts from constants. A typical specification in a definition of forcing states desiderata that denotations of these constants should meet, so these desiderata are reminiscent of simultaneous equations in high school algebra. A complete sequence of conditions then suffices to solve these equations; the generic set denoted by a constant is the set of numbers supposed by the conditions in the complete sequence to be in the desired set. So it is comprehension that gets generic sets from complete sequences.

So the existence of generic sets is derived from the existence of complete sequences. But where do complete sequences come from? The main properties a nested sequence of conditions needs in order to be complete are, first, that for each natural number n and each generic set a in view, some member of the sequence settles whether n is or is not to be in a, and, second, that for each limited sentence, some condition forces it or its negation. It is the second feature that gives us a model that makes true what we set out to force. Note that it is how forcing treats negation that yields the second condition. For if no extension of a condition C forces a limited sentence s, then by how forcing for negations is defined, C forces the negation of s. So to get a complete sequence we start with the empty set and then inductively keep on taking extensions that force more sentences and settle for more numbers which generic sets they are to go into. Thus the treatment of negation in forcing is crucial in getting complete sequences, and so generic sets.

Forcing is the nub. Forcing is consistent, because a condition never forces both a sentence and its negation, and it is cumulative, because a condition forces a sentence if one of its subsets does. But otherwise, there are few constraints on what can be forced. We can almost (but not quite) force the cardinal of continuum to be any uncountable cardinal.[1]

---

[1] The applications of forcing are legion. Thomas Jech, *Set Theory*, 3rd ed., rev. and exp. (Berlin: Springer, 2003), is full of examples. Chapters 15 and 28 are devoted to them, but they occur elsewhere too. Easton's theorem (p. 232, 15.18) is the one showing that the cardinal of the continuum can be pretty much what we please.

One is left with the impression of vast ranges of questions left open by received set theory. The message seems to be that if we are ever to settle questions like the continuum hypothesis, we will need deep new insights into the world of sets, and while that would be a delight, one cannot count on delights.[2]

Gödel proved that (if set theory is consistent) we cannot refute the continuum hypothesis, and Cohen proved that (if set theory is consistent) we cannot prove it either. Together they show that the hypothesis is independent of set theory. Modern logic's seminal independence result was Gödel's 1931 proof that elementary number theory is incomplete (if it is ω-consistent). In 1936 Church proved that theory is undecidable (if it is consistent). Indeed, any consistent, axiomatic theory in which all recursive relations are expressible is undecidable, and therefore, by a result of Post's, incomplete. So undecidability and incompleteness are endemic among interesting theories that are axiomatic and consistent.

Turing showed us how to make real mathematics out of the subjunctive conditional that if we could compute (number theoretic function) f, then we could compute g. By 1944 Post noticed that any two known undecidable axiomatic theories were equally undecidable, for from an algorithm for theoremhood in one we could construct such an algorithm for the other. He asked whether this is true of any two undecidable axiomatic theories; are they all of the same degree of undecidability? That is Post's problem. Friedberg and Muchnik proved that there is an axiomatic theory that is undecidable but of different degree from the theories known in 1944 to be undecidable. Put more abstractly, this says that there is an r.e. degree Turing above 0, the degree of the decidable theories, but Turing below 0′, the degree of, say, elementary number theory. It is then natural to ask what the structure of the r.e. degrees under Turing reducibility is. Sacks showed that the r.e. degrees are dense, that is, if b is above a, there is a c strictly between them. Moreover, given such a and b, we can show that any partially ordered countable set has a copy in the r.e. degrees above a and below b.[3]

The structure of the r.e. degrees seems to be very complex – so much so that it would be understandable for mathematical logicians to pick

[2] W. Hugh Woodin thinks we will be able to refute the continuum hypothesis. Patrick Dehornoy's "Recent Progress on the Continuum Hypothesis (After Woodin)" is an online paper attempting to give some idea of Woodin's work: www.math.unicaen. fr/~dehornoy/Surveys/DgtUS.pdf.

[3] See Robert I. Soare, *Recursively Enumerable Sets and Degrees* (Berlin: Springer, 1987), 147, ex. VIII.4.10.

more tractable research problems. But it would be a shame to give up. For the r.e. degrees have their philosophical interest. Philosophical fascination with reason is as old as philosophy. But while one can pick up a handful of sand and examine it, reason is not available for direct examination. Instead, reasoning is the available manifestation of reason, and deductive theories are among the most developed examples of reasoning available to us. R.e. degrees are abstract forms of deductive theories, and the totality of r.e. degrees is an abstract form of all the deductive theories reason could produce. So understanding the structure of the r.e. degrees should yield insight into the nature of reason.

The r.e. degrees represent all possible axiomatic theories, whether produced by people, or by Kantian rational beings very different from us, or never produced by any sentient beings. But all the deductive theories actually produced by people have either been decidable, or else have been of the same degree as elementary number theory and the first-order predicate calculus. The latter is the Turing highest of all the r.e. degrees; if we could decide theoremhood in any theory of that degree, then we could decide theoremhood in any axiomatic theory. Why should human reason always devise axiomatic theories only of the lowest or of the highest possible degree but never of any of the wealth of intermediate degrees? Or could this be merely a distortion induced by our mode of representation? That is, an r.e. set is an abstract representation of an axiomatic theory. But could it be that this representation lets in too much, the excess showing up in the intermediate r.e. degrees, while if we could articulate extra features of genuine axiomatic theories, these would exclude the intermediate degrees, and all the fruits of reason would fall into one of the two familiar baskets? The answer is no; Feferman showed that in each degree, there is (the set of gödel numbers of) a theory, and this theory is axiomatic if the degree is r.e.[4]

The r.e. degrees represent theories that have axiomatic presentation. That is only countably many degrees, and there are continuum many degrees that are not r.e. at all. We have familiar, usually semantic, presentations of theories that have no axiomatic presentations. First-order number theoretic truth and second-order logic are examples known to philosophers. Arithmetic truth lies infinitely many jumps above provability in arithmetic, and that gives a hint of how much less controllable truth is than provability. We argued that because second-order set

---

[4] Solomon Feferman, "Degrees of Unsolvability Associated with Classes of Formalized Theories," *Journal of Symbolic Logic* 22 (1957): 161–75.

theory is finitely axiomatized, if we could decide second-order validity, then we could decide what follows from second-order set theory. The converse is probably true too. This puts second-order logic and second-order set theory in the same degree. This degree is in all likelihood extremely high, but we do not seem to have a perspicuous precise way of measuring how high. Is there a way to iterate the jump into the transfinite far enough to reach this degree? The number of jumps might also measure how many grains of salt to take with philosophical claims for the significance of second-order presentations.

The Baldwin–Lachlan proof of Morley's theorem splits uncountable categoricity into ω-stability and lacking Vaught pairs. (This proves the theorem because the factors are independent of cardinality, so a theory categorical in one uncountable power is categorical in all.) A complete theory with a countable language is ω-stable just in case for any countable subset A of the domain of a model for T, there are countably many complete n-types of M over A (that is, allowing constants for members of A). Each member of A fixes a distinct 1-type, so since A has to be countable, there will always be at least countably many types. So Morley's notion of an ω-stable theory is one that has the fewest types possible over countable subsets of domains of its models. This means that an ω-stable theory shrinks the number of different sorts of models it has sharply.

The n-types of M over A form a topological space. Moreover, this space is compact, one of the richest topological properties. There are appealing visualizable ways to extend logical specification (splitting condition A into $A \wedge B$ or $A \wedge \neg B$) into a continuum of branches on a binary tree, which makes it vivid why 2^ω is the continuum, and then via a reductio to ω-stability. To anyone alive between the ears, this structure is irresistible.

Models N and M for a complete theory T with a countable language are a Vaught pair just in case M is an elementary submodel of N, and M and N are distinct, but there is a formula of the language of T that has the same extension in M and N. If T is both ω-stable and has no Vaught pair, then for any model M of T there is a formula F of the language of T that is strongly minimal over M, that is, that has only the definable subsets it must have in any elementary extension of M (namely, its finite and cofinite subsets). Such strongly minimal sets form bases that impart dimension to the model. Here basis and dimension are the algebraic notions from vector space theory that generalize an aspect of geometry. Once again, the emergence of algebraic structure in models is irresistible.

Dimension fixes the structure of a model and is a linchpin in getting from ω-stability and lacking a Vaught pair to uncountable categoricity. We go the other way, from uncountable categoricity to ω-stability and lacking a Vaught pair, through Ramsey's theorem and its development in Ehrenfeucht–Mostowski models. Ramsey's theorem is a sort of polyadic generalization of the pigeonhole principle, and so inherits the charm of that principle. Ramsey's theorem enables us to add arbitrarily long sequences of order-indiscernibles to a model, and Ehrenfeucht–Mostowski models are the Skolem hulls of those models taken over the order-indiscernibles. The indiscernibles reduce the number of distinct types. Ehrenfeucht–Mostowski models dramatize the object-indifference of formal logic.

For each of these four results, its proof introduced us to objects of a new kind: Gödel's constructible sets, Cohen's generic sets, Friedberg's and Muchnik's r.e. degrees above the degree of decidable theories but below that of, say, number theory and the first-order predicate calculus, and Morley's ω-stable theories, strongly minimal sets, and Ehrenfeucht–Mostowski models. That is, each of these arguments invokes the existence of rather striking objects. In the terms of this chapter's epigraph from Russell, each of these arguments expands our zoology of reality. They expand our knowledge of what there is, and how it fits together, as zoology does of animals.

A perennial and basic philosophical problem about mathematics is now known as Benacerraf's dilemma.[5] The dilemma is an antimony between the claims of truth and those of knowledge. On the one horn, truth is most naturally taken, to put it the old way, as correspondence to fact, or, to put it a new way after Tarski, to require reference to objects, most notably the values of the variables of quantification. But, next, mathematics, including mathematical logic, is a body of truths; it has long been taken as the system of the most absolute truths of which we have the surest knowledge. These two observations already have the consequence that there are mathematical objects; it is *true* that there are infinitely many primes only if there *are* infinitely many primes. This upshot already begins to raise metaphysical hackles.

This anxiety becomes more acute when we add that the objects required for mathematical truth are nonmental, nonphysical abstract

[5] Paul Benacerraf, "Mathematical Truth," reprinted in W. D. Hart, ed., *The Philosophy of Mathematics* (Oxford: Oxford University Press, 1996), 14–30. Benacerraf there relied on Alvin Goldman's causal analysis of knowledge, a view that has not found favor. For a version of the dilemma without so restrictive an analysis of knowledge, see my "Benacerraf's Dilemma," *Crítica* 23 (1991): 87–103.

objects; this lands us in metaphysical platonism, the doctrine that there are nonmental, nonphysical abstract objects. Besides its obviousness, we can give two arguments for our third addition. The first goes back to Frege's argument against the formalists.[6] A common way to assuage metaphysical anxiety is to try to replace abstract objects with ones to which we have familiar perceptual or introspective access. A formalist, for example, might surrender numbers in favor of numerals, but to allay his anxiety these should be concrete, physical inscriptions and utterances. (The alternatives proposed to abstracta are legion.) But, as Frege points out, at each moment in our history we will have inscribed or uttered only finitely many numerals, while there are infinitely many numbers. (To shift to merely possible inscriptions or types without tokens is to sink back into metaphysical anxiety.)

The other argument is modal. No physical object exists necessarily; for each physical object, we can imagine its environs without it. Nor does anything mental exist necessarily. Indeed, most of us believe that for most of its history, the universe was devoid of sentient life. But it is an ancient and honorable view that the objects of pure mathematics exist necessarily. It follows that mathematical objects are neither physical nor mental, which leaves abstract. (This argument is only as good as its ancient and honorable premiss, and one might wonder about it.)

Why do abstract objects raise metaphysical hackles? There are two lines to pursue here. The first is epistemological. We are happiest attributing knowledge to a person when we can make out a connection between the person and what he or she is said to know; call this the contact principle. The only generally accepted mode of contact that yields knowledge is perception. This is where empiricism comes from. But, as Grice argued, perception is by its nature causal.[7] The rub is that very abstract objects like Ehrenfeucht–Mostowski models are utterly inert. So what makes mathematical truth possible, abstract objects, makes mathematical knowledge impossible. That is the epistemological version of Benacerraf's dilemma.

It also has a cosmological version. Traditionally, metaphysics was divided into two parts. Ontology was about which sorts of things are basic. Most of us nowadays think matter is basic. It is an ontological question whether minds (or people) could be disembodied, and it is

---

[6] Gottlob Frege, *Translations from the Philosophical Writings of Gottlob Frege*, ed. Peter Geach and Max Black (Oxford: Basil Blackwell, 1960), 222.

[7] H. P. Grice, "The Causal Theory of Perception," reprinted in *Perceiving, Sensing, and Knowing*, ed. Robert J. Swartz (Garden City, N.Y.: Doubleday Anchor, 1965), 438–72.

another whether there are nonmental, nonphysical abstract objects. We also expect the universe to form a unified system, and (before physicists hijacked the word) cosmology was about what form such a system takes. Our favored cosmology is naturalist; as Hume put it, causation is the cement of the universe.[8] This cosmology can go without saying (and so escape critical attention) and yet govern our ontology. The most pressing objection to Descartes's dualism (we could be disembodied, so mind is no less basic than matter) has always been his inarticulateness about how mind and matter can interact causally. One push toward a materialism about people is an inability to make out how immaterial people could interact with their material bodies. Here too the utter inertness of abstracta rears its head. For if inert abstracta are among the denizens of the universe, then the prospects for a thoroughgoing causal cosmology of the universe are doomed; numbers will form an isolated chaos. That is the cosmological version of the dilemma.

Something has got to give. In the epistemological version, the contact principle deserves scrutiny. Hume famously derived all ideas from impressions.[9] So, if we have no impression of our selves or of necessitation, we have no idea either, and there is no such thing over and above the bundle of the contents of consciousness or constant conjunction between kinds of events. Such a narrow empiricism, tying as it does each legitimate idea down to defining sense experience, did not survive the maturation of the natural sciences after Hume's day.[10] Most of us believe there once were dinosaurs, but none of us has ever seen one in the flesh. Instead, many of us have seen fossils. These are usually not bones but bone-shaped rocks made of minerals other than calcium. They resemble the bones of no creature with whom we now share the planet, but sometimes they come in larger groups that can be assembled into (most of) skeletons. These skeletons also are unlike those of present-day animals. How can we explain these fossils? We suppose there once were unfamiliar animals, dinosaurs. Sometimes, when they died, their bodies were buried. The soft tissue rotted away, and ground water leeched the calcium from their bones, replacing it with other minerals. Though we never perceive dinosaurs, we infer to their past existence as

[8] David Hume, *A Treatise of Human Nature*, ed. L. A. Selby-Bigge, 2nd ed., ed. P. H. Nidditch (Oxford: Clarendon Press, 1978), 662.

[9] Ibid., 1.

[10] W. V. Quine, "Five Milestones of Empiricism," in his *Theories and Things* (Cambridge, Mass.: Belknap Press of Harvard University Press, 1981), 67–72.

our best explanation of what we do perceive.[11] The idea of a dinosaur cannot be reduced to perceptions of fossils.

W. V. Quine and Hilary Putnam argued that we have the same kind of reason for believing in numbers and some other mathematical objects as we have for believing in dinosaurs and dark matter. We observe none of them, but we need them to do the science that explains what we do observe. Anyone who has worked with a science text is familiar with mathematics put to work there, and at least that much mathematics acquires thereby the sort of justification we have for dinosaurs; we need it to make sense of what we see.[12] This is a positive construction; it is not intended by itself to show there are no other ways, like the light of reason, by which we justify mathematical belief. It shows how, by loosening the contact principle enough to legitimate knowledge of natural scientific theory, we can also legitimate knowledge based on experience of some mathematics. It solves the epistemological version of Benacerraf's dilemma by reconciling platonism and empiricism.

One might wonder just how much mathematics we actually need in order to do natural science, and, if it is only a small part, how the rest could be justified. It does seem that the part actually needed is indeed small.[13] Then again, if one is out to systematize Tycho Brahe's observations of the motions of the planets, Kepler's laws of planetary motion will do. But we do not stop here. We want to know why Kepler's are the laws of the planets. Newton's laws of motion plus his law of universal gravitation explain Kepler's, and thus the confirmation Tycho gives Kepler is transmitted to Newton. There is no evident stopping place to such a pattern of generalization, explanation, and systematization (allowing for revision) in natural science. Similarly, the awkward bare minimum of mathematics needed in natural science calls for generalization, explanation, and systematization doubtless through many

---

[11] The recognition of the importance of this mode of inference goes back at least to Charles Sanders Peirce. The name "inference to the best explanation" comes from Gilbert Harman's paper of that title in the *Philosophical Review* 74 (1965): 88–95.

[12] W. V. Quine, "On What There Is" and "Two Dogmas of Empiricism," reprinted in his *From a Logical Point of View*, 2nd ed. rev. (Cambridge, Mass.: Harvard University Press, 1961), 1–19 and 20–46. Hilary Putnam, *Philosophy of Logic* (New York: Harper, 1971). See also my "Access and Inference," in Hart, *Philosophy of Mathematics*, 52–62.

[13] Solomon Feferman, "Why a Little Bit Goes a Long Way: Logical Foundations of Scientifically Applicable Mathematics," reprinted in his *In the Light of Logic* (Oxford: Oxford University Press, 1998), 284–98.

levels. By the mid-twentieth century, the upshot was probably Zermelo–
Fraenkel set theory with the axiom of choice, and by now may include
lots of large cardinals beyond the ken of ZFC.

Let us turn now to the cosmological version of Benacerraf's dilemma.
Quine devoted much of his work in logic to the development of mathematics in set theory.[14] Quine was never an essentialist; he was not
claiming that the number 17 really is this particular set (say, Zermelo's
17-fold iteration of unit set starting from the empty set). His point was
rather the economy that is achieved in abstract studies by presenting
them within set theory. We might extend this economy into cosmology.
Begin by denying the naturalist cosmology that causation is the one
and only cement of the universe. To be sure, it unifies the physical (and
perhaps the mental) side of the universe. But there is a second cement;
it is set membership that unifies the (economical version of the) abstract
(and much bigger) side of the universe. It also cements concreta to the
sets of which they are members. So we can solve the cosmological version of Benacerraf's dilemma by admitting two cements of the universe,
the second uniting its side of the universe to the other side.

The solutions described here to both versions of the dilemma leave
the platonist horn alone and modify the other. Doubtless some will
prefer an opposed strategy, and it is up to them to convince us that
the modifications of truth they propose are worth making. But the
beings, like constructible sets, generic sets, intermediate r.e. degrees,
and ω-stable theories, who emerged in our last four results, are glories
one should be reluctant to abandon or interpret into mere specters of
themselves. They are more exotic than most of the beings that emerged
earlier, like formalized languages, the semantic conception of truth,
the completeness of quantification theory, and the incompleteness of
arithmetic, though the uncountable infinities and the paradoxes of set
theory may match them in wonder. Put the paradoxes to one side; we
still do not really know what to make of them. The other exotica all lie
on the abstract side of our cosmology and are unified set theoretically
(though the set theory may be a bit stronger than ZFC in some cases).
Speaking epistemically, we recognize them in elaborations of theory
that, like all sound theory, is justified ultimately by making sense of
experience.

---

[14] The reference here is really to Quine's whole logical corpus, but his *Set Theory and
Its Logic*, rev. ed. (Cambridge, Mass.: Belknap Press of Harvard University Press,
1969), is a late flower.

Bibliography

Editions cited are largely those in my own library. Where I know of later editions, they are indicated at the end of the citation in square brackets.

Aczel, Peter. *Non-Well-Founded Sets*. Stanford: Center for the Study of Language and Information, 1988.

Alchourrón, Carlos E. "On the Philosophical Adequacy of Set Theories." *Theoria*, 2nd series, year 2 (1986–87): 567–74. Reprinted as "Sobre la adecuación filosófica de las teorías de conjuntos." In Moretti and Hurtado, *La Paradoja de Orayen*, 61–69.

Baldwin, J. T., and A. H. Lachlan. "On Strongly Minimal Sets." *Journal of Symbolic Logic* 36 (1971): 71–96.

Barwise, Jon. *Admissible Sets and Structures: An Approach to Definability Theory*. Berlin: Springer, 1975.

Barwise, Jon, and John Etchemendy. *The Liar: An Essay on Truth and Circularity*. New York: Oxford University Press, 1987.

Bell, J. L., and M. Machover. *A Course in Mathematical Logic*. Amsterdam: North-Holland, 1977.

Bell, J. L., and A. B. Slomson. *Models and Ultraproducts: An Introduction*. Amsterdam: North-Holland, 1969. [2006]

Benacerraf, Paul. "Mathematical Truth." Reprinted in *Philosophy of Mathematics: Selected Readings*, edited by Paul Benacerraf and Hilary Putnam, 403–20. 2nd edition. Cambridge: Cambridge University Press, 1983. Also reprinted in Hart, *Philosophy of Mathematics*, 14–30.

"What Numbers Could Not Be." Reprinted in his *Philosophy of Mathematics*, 272–94.

Beth, Evert W. *The Foundations of Mathematics: A Study in the Philosophy of Science*. Revised edition. New York: Harper Torchbooks, 1964.

Birkhoff, George David, and Ralph Beatley. *Basic Geometry*. 3rd edition. New York: Chelsea, 1959. [1999]

Boolos, George. "The Iterative Conception of Set." Reprinted in his *Logic, Logic, and Logic*, edited by Richard Jeffrey, 13–29. Cambridge, Mass.: Harvard University Press, 1998.

"On Second-Order Logic." Reprinted in *Logic, Logic, and Logic*, 37–53.

The Unprovability of Consistency: An Essay in Modal Logic.
Cambridge: Cambridge University Press, 1979. Fully rewritten and updated
2nd edition, *The Logic of Provability* (1993).

Brady, Geraldine. *From Peirce to Skolem: A Neglected Chapter in the History of
Logic.* Amsterdam and New York: North-Holland/Elsevier, 2000.

Burge, Tyler. *Truth, Thought, Reason: Essays on Frege.* Oxford: Clarendon Press,
2005.

"Frege on Sense and Linguistic Meaning." In *Truth, Thought, Reason,*
242–69.

"Frege on Truth." In *Truth, Thought, Reason,* 83–132.

"Semantical Paradox." Reprinted in Martin, *Recent Essays,* 83–117.

Cantor, Georg. *Contributions to the Founding of the Theory of Transfinite
Numbers.* Translated by Philip E. B. Jourdain. New York: Dover, [1952].
Reprint of 1915 translation.

Gesammelte Abhandlungen mathematischen und philosophischen Inhalts.
Edited by Ernst Zermelo. Hildesheim: Georg Olms, 1962. Reprint of 1932
edition. [1980]

Carnap, Rudolf. "Carnap's Intellectual Autobiography." In *The Philosophy of
Rudolf Carnap,* edited by Paul Arthur Schilpp, 3–84. La Salle, Ill.: Open
Court, 1963.

Der logische Aufbau der Welt. Berlin-Schlachtensee: Weltkreis-verlag, 1928.
Published in English as *The Logical Structure of the World: Pseudoproblems
in Philosophy.* Translated by Rolf A. George. Berkeley: University of
California Press, 1967. [2003]

Chang, C. C., and H. Jerome Keisler. *Model Theory.* Amsterdam: North-Holland,
1973. [1990]

Chellas, Brian F. *Modal Logic: An Introduction.* Cambridge: Cambridge University
Press, 1980.

Chong, C.-T. *Techniques of Admissible Recursion Theory.* Berlin: Springer,
1984.

Church, Alonzo. "A Note on the Entscheidungsproblem." Reprinted in Davis,
Undecidable, 108–15.

"An Unsolvable Problem of Elementary Number Theory." Reprinted in Davis,
Undecidable, 89–107.

Introduction to Mathematical Logic. Vol. 1. Princeton: Princeton University
Press, 1956.

Cohen, Paul J. *Set Theory and the Continuum Hypothesis.* New York: W. A.
Benjamin, 1966. [2008]

Davis, Martin. *Computability and Unsolvability.* New York: McGraw-Hill, 1958.
[1982]

ed. *The Undecidable: Basic Papers on Undecidable Propositions, Unsolvable
Problems, and Computable Functions.* Hewlett, N.Y.: Raven Press, 1965.
[2004]

Dedekind, Richard. "The Nature and Meaning of Numbers." In his *Essays on the
Theory of Numbers,* 31–115. New York: Dover, 1963.

Dehornoy, Patrick. "*Recent Progress on the Continuum Hypothesis (after Woodin).*"
www.math.unicaen.fr/~dehornoy/Surveys/DgtUS.pdf.

De Morgan, Augustus. "On the Syllogism IV." Reprinted in his *On the Syllogism, and Other Logical Writings*, edited by Peter Heath, 208–46. London: Routledge & Kegan Paul, 1966.

Dipert, Randall R. "The Life and Logical Contributions of O. H. Mitchell, Peirce's Gifted Student." *Transactions of the Charles S. Peirce Society* 30 (1994): 515–42.

Duhem, Pierre. *The Aim and Structure of Physical Theory*. Translated by Philip P. Wiener. Princeton: Princeton University Press, 1954. [1974]

Ehrenfeucht, Andrzej, and Andrzej Mostowski. "Models of Axiomatic Theories Admitting Automorphisms." *Fundamenta Mathematica* 43 (1956): 50–68.

Feferman, Solomon. "Degrees of Unsolvability Associated with Classes of Formalized Theories." *Journal of Symbolic Logic* 22 (1957): 161–75.

 "Why a Little Bit Goes a Long Way: Logical Foundations of Scientifically Applicable Mathematics." Reprinted in his *In the Light of Logic*, 284–98. New York: Oxford University Press, 1998.

Ferreirós, José. *Labyrinth of Thought: A History of Set Theory and Its Role in Modern Mathematics*. 2nd edition. Basel: Birkhäuser, 2007.

Field, Hartry. "Tarski's Theory of Truth." *Journal of Philosophy* 64 (1972): 347–75.

Forster, T. E. *Set Theory with a Universal Set: Exploring an Untyped Universe*. 2nd edition. Oxford: Clarendon Press, 1995.

Frege, Gottlob. *The Foundations of Arithmetic: A Logico-mathematical Enquiry into the Concept of Number*. Translated by J. L. Austin. Oxford: Basil Blackwell, 1959. [1980] Original German edition *Grundlagen der Arithmetik* (1884).

 "On Sense and Reference." In *Translations from the Philosophical Writings of Gottlob Frege*, 56–62.

 Philosophical and Mathematical Correspondence. Edited by Gottfried Gabriel et al. Translated by Hans Kaal. Oxford: Basil Blackwell, 1980.

 Translations from the Philosophical Writings of Gottlob Frege. Edited by Peter Geach and Max Black. Oxford: Basil Blackwell, 1960. [1980]

Friedberg, Richard. *An Adventurer's Guide to Number Theory*. New York: Dover, 1994.

 "Three Theorems on Recursive Enumeration: I. Decomposition; II. Maximal Set; III. Enumeration without Duplication." *Journal of Symbolic Logic* 23 (1958): 309–16.

 "Two Recursively Enumerable Sets of Incomparable Degrees of Unsolvability (Solution of Post's Problem 1944)." *Proceedings of the National Academy of Sciences* 43 (1957): 236–38.

Geach, Peter. *Mental Acts: Their Content and Their Objects*. London: Routledge & Kegan Paul, 1957. [1971, 2002]

Gödel, Kurt. *Collected Works*. 5 vols. Edited by Solomon Feferman et al. New York and Oxford: Oxford University Press and Clarendon Press, 1986–2003. Vol. 1, *Publications 1929–1936*, 1986; Vol. 2, *Publications 1938–1974*, 1990.

 "An Interpretation of the Intuitionist Propositional Calculus." Reprinted in *Collected Works*, 1: 301–03.

The Consistency of the Axiom of Choice and of the Generalized Continuum Hypothesis with the Axioms of Set Theory. Princeton: Princeton University Press, 1940. Reprinted in *Collected Works,* 2: 33–101.

"The Consistency of the Generalized Continuum Hypothesis" (1939). Reprinted in *Collected Works,* 2: 27.

"Consistency Proof for the Generalized Continuum Hypothesis" (1939). Reprinted in *Collected Works,* 2: 28–32.

"On the Completeness of the Calculus of Logic" (1929). Reprinted in *Collected Works,* 1: 61–101.

"On Formally Undecidable Propositions of Principia Mathematica and Related Systems I" (1931). Translated by Stefan Bauer-Mengelberg. Reprinted in van Heijenoort, *From Frege to Gödel,* 596–616. Reprinted in *Collected Works,* 1: 145–95.

"Remarks Before the Princeton Bicentennial Conference on Problems in Mathematics." Reprinted in Davis, *Undecidable,* 84.

"Russell's Mathematical Logic" (1944). Reprinted in *Collected Works,* 2: 119–41.

"What Is Cantor's Continuum Problem?" (1947). Reprinted in *Collected Works,* 2: 176–87.

Goldblatt, Robert. *Lectures on the Hyperreals: An Introduction to Nonstandard Analysis.* New York: Springer, 1998.

Graham, Ronald L., Bruce L. Rothschild, and Joel H. Spenser. *Ramsey Theory.* New York: Wiley, 1980. [1990]

Grice, H. P. "The Causal Theory of Perception." *Proceedings of the Aristotelian Society, Supplementary Volume* 35 (1961): 121–52. Reprinted in part in *Perceiving, Sensing, and Knowing: A Book of Readings from Twentieth-Century Sources in the Philosophy of Perception,* edited by Robert J. Swartz, 438–72. Garden City, N.Y.: Doubleday Anchor, 1965.

Gupta, Anil. "Remarks on Definitions and the Concept of Truth." *Proceedings of the Aristotelian Society* 89 (1988–89): 227–46.

Hájek, Petr, and Pavel Pudlák. *Metamathematics of First-Order Arithmetic.* Berlin: Springer, 1993.

Harman, Gilbert. "Inference to the Best Explanation." *Philosophical Review* 74 (1965): 88–95.

"Logical Form." *Foundations of Language* 9 (1972): 38–65.

Hart, W. D. "Access and Inference." In Hart, *Philosophy of Mathematics,* 52–62.

"Benacerraf's Dilemma." *Crítica* 23 (1991): 87–103.

The Engines of the Soul. Cambridge: Cambridge University Press, 1988. [2009]

"For Anil Gupta." *Proceedings of the Aristotelian Society* 90 (1989–90): 161–64.

"Interpolación y relevancia." *Análisis filosófico* 13 (May 1993): 55–56.

"Invincible Ignorance." In Salerno, *New Essays on the Knowability Paradox,* 320–23.

"Long Decimals." In *Future Pasts: The Analytic Tradition in Twentieth-Century Philosophy,* edited by Juliet Floyd and Sanford Shieh, 359–67. Oxford: Oxford University Press, 2001.

"On Non-Well-Founded Sets." *Crítica* 24 (December 1992): 3–21.

ed. *The Philosophy of Mathematics*. Oxford: Oxford University Press, 1996.

"Russell and Ramsey." *Pacific Philosophical Quarterly* 64 (1984): 193–210.

"The Syntax of the World." *Crítica* 28 (April 1996): 13–24.

"The Whole Sense of the Tractatus." *Journal of Philosophy* 68 (6 May 1971): 273–88.

Henkin, Leon. "The Completeness of the First-Order Functional Calculus." *Journal of Symbolic Logic* 14 (1949): 159–66.

Herzberger, Hans G. "New Paradoxes for Old." *Proceedings of the Aristotelian Society* 81 (1980–81): 109–23.

Hewitt, Edwin. "The Rôle of Compactness in Classical Analysis." *American Mathematical Monthly* 67 (1960): 499–516.

Hilbert, David. *The Foundations of Geometry*. Translated by E. J. Townsend. Chicago: Open Court, 1902. [2007] Original German edition *Grundlagen der Geometrie* (1899).

Hilbert, David, and Wilhelm Ackermann. *Grundzüge der theoretischen Logik*. Berlin: Springer, 1928. [1972]

Hinman, Peter G. *Fundamentals of Mathematical Logic*. Wellesley, Mass.: A. K. Peters, 2005.

Hodges, Wilfrid. *A Shorter Model Theory*. Cambridge: Cambridge University Press, 1997.

Logic. Harmondsworth: Penguin, 1977.

Holmes, M. Randall. *Elementary Set Theory with a Universal Set*. Cahiers du Centre de Logique, vol. 10 (Louvain-la-Neuve, Belgium: Academia, n.d.).

Hume, David. *A Treatise of Human Nature*. Edited by L. A. Selby-Bigge. 2nd edition edited by P. H. Nidditch. Oxford: Clarendon Press, 1978. First published 1739–40.

Dialogues Concerning Natural Religion. Edited by Henry D. Aiken. New York: Hafner, 1948. First published 1779.

Isaacson, Daniel. "Arithmetical Truth and Hidden Higher-Order Concepts." Reprinted in Hart, *Philosophy of Mathematics*, 203–24.

Jech, Thomas. *Set Theory*. 3rd edition, revised and expanded. Berlin: Springer, 2003.

Jeffrey, Richard C. *The Logic of Decision*. 2nd edition. Chicago: University of Chicago Press, 1983.

Jonsson, Bjarni. "Homogeneous Universal Relational Systems." *Mathematica Scandinavica* 8 (1960): 178–86.

"Universal Relational Systems." *Mathematica Scandinavica* 4 (1956): 193–208.

Kanamori, Akihiro. "Cohen and Set Theory." *Bulletin of Symbolic Logic* 14 (September 2008): 351–78.

Kant, Immanuel. *Critique of Pure Reason*. Translated by Norman Kemp Smith. London: Macmillan, 1963. [2003] First published 1781.

Prolegomenon to Any Future Metaphysics That Will Be Able to Come Forward as Science. Paul Carus translation revised by James W. Ellington. Indianapolis: Hackett, 1977. First published 1783.

Kleene, Stephen Cole. *Introduction to Metamathematics*. Princeton: D. Van Nostrand, 1952.

"Recursive Predicates and Quantifiers." Reprinted in Davis, *Undecidable*, 255–87.

Kneale, William, and Martha Kneale. *The Development of Logic*. Oxford: Clarendon Press, 1962. [1984]

Kreisel, Georg, and Gerald E. Sacks. "Metarecursive Sets." *Journal of Symbolic Logic* 30 (1965): 318–38.

Kripke, Saul A. *Naming and Necessity*. Cambridge, Mass.: Harvard University Press, 1980. [1998]

"Outline of a Theory of Truth." Reprinted in Martin, *Recent Essays*, 53–81.

Kučera, A. "An Alternative Priority-Free Solution to Post's Problem." In *Twelfth Symposium Held in Bratislava, Czechoslovakia, August 25–29, 1968*. Lecture Notes in Computer Science No. 233, Proceedings, Mathematical Foundations of Computer Science '86, edited by J. Gruska et al. Heidelberg: Springer, 1986.

Lawvere, F. William. "The Category of Categories as a Foundation for Mathematics." In *Proceedings of the Conference on Categorical Algebra, La Jolla*, edited by S. Eilenberg et al., 1–21. New York: Springer, 1966.

Lipton, Peter. *Inference to the Best Explanation*. London: Routledge, 1991. [2004]

Łoś, Jerzy. "On the Categoricity in Power of Elementary Deductive Systems and Some Related Problems." *Colloquium Mathematicum* 3 (1954): 58–62.

Löwenheim, Leopold. "On Possibilities in the Calculus of Relatives" (1915). Translated by Stefan Bauer-Mengelberg. In van Heijenoort, *From Frege to Gödel*, 228–51.

Lyndon, Roger C. *Notes on Logic*. Princeton: Van Nostrand, 1966.

Marker, David. *Model Theory: An Introduction*. New York: Springer, 2002.

Martin, D. A. "Completeness, the Recursion Theorem, and Effectively Simple Sets." *Proceedings of the American Mathematical Society* 17 (1966): 838–42.

Review of Set Theory and Its Logic, revised edition, by W. V. Quine. *Journal of Philosophy* 67 (26 February 1970): 111–14.

Martin, Robert L., ed. *Recent Essays on Truth and the Liar Paradox*. Oxford: Clarendon Press, 1984.

Mates, Benson. *Elementary Logic*. 2nd edition. New York: Oxford University Press, 1972.

Mendelson, Elliott. *Introduction to Mathematical Logic*. 4th edition. New York: Chapman & Hall, 1997. [2009]

Monk, J. Donald. *Introduction to Set Theory*. New York: McGraw-Hill, 1969. [1980]

Montague, Richard, and R. K. Vaught. "Natural Models of Set Theory." *Fundamenta Mathematica* 47 (1959): 219–42.

Moore, Gregory H. "The Emergence of First-Order Logic." In *History and Philosophy of Modern Mathematics*, edited by William Aspray and Philip Kitcher, 95–135. Minneapolis: University of Minnesota Press, 1988.

Moretti, Alberto, and Guillermo Hurtado, eds. *La Paradoja de Orayen*. Buenos Aires: Eudeba, 2003.

Morley, Michael. "Categoricity in Power." *Transactions of the American Mathematical Society* 114 (1965): 514–38.

Morley, Michael, and Robert Vaught. "Homogeneous Universal Models." *Mathematica Scandinavica* 11 (1962): 37–57.

Muchnik, A. A. "On the Unsolvability of the Problem of Reducibility in the Theory of Algorithms." *Doklady Akademii Nauk SSSR*, n.s. 108 (1956): 194–97.

Myhill, John. "The Lattice of Recursively Enumerable Sets." *Journal of Symbolic Logic* 21 (1956): 215, 220 (abstract).

"The Undefinability of the Set of Natural Numbers in the Ramified *Principia*." In *Bertrand Russell's Philosophy*, edited by George Nakhnikian, 19–27. New York: Barnes & Noble, 1974.

Orayen, Raúl. "Una paradoja en la semántica de la teoría de conjuntos." In Moretti and Hurtado, *La Paradoja de Orayen*, 35–59.

Pap, Arthur. "Are All Necessary Propositions Analytic?" *Philosophy Review* 50 (1949): 299–320.

Elements of Analytic Philosophy. New York: Macmillan, 1949. [1972]

"Logical Nonsense." *Philosophy and Phenomenological Research* 9 (1948): 262–83.

"Once More: Colors and the Synthetic A Priori." *Philosophical Review* 66 (1957): 94–99.

Parsons, Charles. "The Liar Paradox." Reprinted in Martin, *Recent Essays*, 9–45.

Peckhaus, Volker. "Paradoxes in Göttingen." In *One Hundred Years of Russell's Paradox: Mathematics, Logic, Philosophy*, edited by Godehard Link, 501–16. Berlin: Walter de Gruyter, 2004.

Poizat, Bruno. *A Course in Model Theory: An Introduction to Contemporary Mathematical Logic*. Translated by Moses Klein. New York: Springer, 2000.

Post, Emil. "Recursively Enumerable Sets of Positive Integers and Their Decision Problems." Reprinted in Davis, *Undecidable*, 304–37.

Priest, Graham. *In Contradiction: A Study of the Transconsistent*. Expanded edition. Oxford: Clarendon Press, 2006. First published 1987.

Putnam, Hilary. *Philosophy of Logic*. New York: Harper & Row, 1971.

"Red and Green All Over Again: A Rejoinder to Arthur Pap." *Philosophical Review* 66 (1957): 100–03.

"Reds, Greens, and Logical Analysis." *Philosophical Review* 65 (1956): 206–17.

Quine, W. V. "Five Milestones of Empiricism." In his *Theories and Things*, 67–72. Cambridge, Mass.: Belknap Press of Harvard University Press, 1981.

From a Logical Point of View. 2nd edition revised. Cambridge, Mass.: Harvard University Press, 1961. [1980]

"*The Inception of 'New Foundations.*'" Reprinted in his *Selected Logic Papers*, 288. Enlarged edition. Cambridge, Mass.: Harvard University Press, 1995.

"Logic and the Reification of Universals." Reprinted in *From a Logical Point of View*, 102–29.

Mathematical Logic. Revised edition. New York: Harper Torchbooks, 1962; reprint of 1951 revised edition of 1940 edition.

Methods of Logic. Revised edition. New York: Henry Holt, 1959.

"Necessary Truth." Reprinted in his *The Ways of Paradox and Other Essays*, 68–76. Revised and enlarged edition. Cambridge, Mass.: Harvard University Press, 1976.

"New Foundations for Mathematical Logic." Reprinted in *From a Logical Point of View*, 80–101.

"Notes on the Theory of Reference." Reprinted in *From a Logical Point of View*, 130–38.

"On What There Is." Reprinted in *From a Logical Point of View*, 1–19.

"Peirce's Logic." In *Selected Logic Papers*, 258–65.

Philosophy of Logic. Englewood Cliffs, N.J.: Prentice-Hall, 1970. [1986]

Reply to Donald A. Martin's review of Set Theory and Its Logic, revised edition. *Journal of Philosophy* 67 (23 April 1970): 247–48.

"Reply to Professor Marcus." Reprinted in *Ways of Paradox*, 177–84.

Set Theory and Its Logic. Cambridge, Mass.: Belknap Press of Harvard University Press, 1963. [Revised edition, 1969]

"Two Dogmas of Empiricism." Reprinted in *From a Logical Point of View*, 20–46.

Word and Object. Cambridge, Mass.: Technology Press of the Massachusetts Institute of Technology, 1960.

Ramsey, F. P. "The Foundations of Mathematics." Reprinted in his *The Foundations of Mathematics and Other Logical Essays*, edited by R. B. Braithwaite, 1–61. Paterson, N.J.: Littlefield, Adams, 1960.

"On a Problem of Formal Logic." Reprinted in *Foundations of Mathematics*, 82–111.

Robinson, Abraham. "Non-Standard Analysis." *Koninklijke Nederlandse Akademie van Wetenschappen* (Amsterdam), *Proceedings*, ser. A, vol. 64 (or *Indigationes mathematicae*, vol. 23) (1961): 432–40.

Rogers, Hartley, Jr. *Theory of Recursive Functions and Effective Computability*. New York: McGraw-Hill, 1967. [1987]

Rosser, J. Barkley. *Logic for Mathematicians*. New York: McGraw-Hill, 1953. [2008]

"The Relative Strength of Zermelo's Set Theory and Quine's New Foundations." In *Proceedings of the International Congress of Mathematicians 1954, Amsterdam, September 2–September 9*, vol. 3 (Groningen and Amsterdam: Erven P. Noordhoff N.V. and North-Holland, 1956), 289–94.

Rosser, J. Barkley, and Hao Wang. "Non-standard Models for Formal Logic." *Journal of Symbolic Logic* 15 (1950): 113–29.

Russell, Bertrand. *Introduction to Mathematical Philosophy*. London: George Allen & Unwin, 1919. [1993]

"Mathematical Logic as Based on the Theory of Types" (1908). Reprinted in his *Logic and Knowledge: Essays, 1901–1950*, edited by Robert Charles Marsh, 57–102. London: George Allen & Unwin, 1956. [2007]

"On Some Difficulties in the Theory of Transfinite Numbers and Order Types" (1905). Reprinted in his *Essays in Analysis*, edited by Douglas Lackey, 135–64. New York: George Braziller, 1973.

Our Knowledge of the External World. London: George Allen & Unwin, 1914. [2009]

The Philosophy of Leibniz. 3rd edition. London: Routledge, 1992.

Principia Mathematica. See Whitehead and Russell.

The Principles of Mathematics. 2nd edition. London: George Allen & Unwin, 1937. First published 1903. [2009]

Ryll-Nardzewski, C. "The Role of the Axiom of Induction in Elementary Arithmetic." *Fundamental Mathematics* 39 (1952): 239–63.

Salerno, Joseph, ed. *New Essays on the Knowability Paradox*. Oxford: Oxford University Press, 2008.

Scott, Dana S. "Axiomatizing Set Theory." In *Axiomatic Set Theory: Proceedings of Symposia in Pure Mathematics*, edited by Dana S. Scott, Vol. 13, 207–14. Providence: American Mathematical Society, 1974.

Shelah, Saharon. *Classification Theory and the Number of Non-isomorphic Models*. Amsterdam: North-Holland, 1978. [1990]

Shepherdson, J. C. "Inner Models for Set Theory." *Journal of Symbolic Logic* 16 (1951): 161–90; 17 (1952): 225–37; 18 (1953): 145–67.

Shoenfield, Joseph R. "A Relative Consistency Proof." *Journal of Symbolic Logic* 18 (1954): 21–28.

Degrees of Unsolvability. Amsterdam: North-Holland, 1971. [1972]

"Measurable Cardinals." In *Logic Colloquium '69*, edited by R. O. Gandy and C. E. M. Yates, 19–49. Amsterdam: North-Holland, 1971.

Mathematical Logic. Reading, Mass.: Addison-Wesley, 1967.

Simmons, George F. *Introduction to Topology and Modern Analysis*. New York: McGraw-Hill, 1963. [1983]

Skolem, Thoralf. "Logico-combinatorial Investigations in the Satisfiability or Provability of Mathematical Propositions: A Simplified Proof of a Theorem by L. Löwenheim and Generalizations of the Theorem" (1920). Translated by Stefan Bauer-Mengelberg. In van Heijenoort, *From Frege to Gödel*, 252–63.

"Some Remarks on Axiomatized Set Theory." In van Heijenoort, *From Frege to Gödel*, 290–301.

Soare, Robert I. *Recursively Enumerable Sets and Degrees: A Study of Computable Functions and Computably Generated Sets*. Berlin: Springer, 1987.

Stevenson, Charles L. "If-iculties." In *Logic and Art: Essays in Honor of Nelson Goodman*, edited by Richard Rudner and Israel Scheffler, 279–309. New York: Bobbs-Merrill, 1972.

Suppes, Patrick. *Axiomatic Set Theory*. Princeton: Van Nostrand, 1960. [1972]

Tarski, Alfred. "On the Concept of Logical Consequence." In his *Logic, Semantics, Metamathematics: Papers from 1923 to 1938*, translated by J. H. Woodger, 409–20. Oxford: Clarendon Press, 1956.

"The Concept of Truth in Formalized Languages." Reprinted in *Logic, Semantics, Metamathematics*, 152–278.

"The Semantic Conception of Truth." Reprinted in *Semantics and the Philosophy of Language: A Collection of Readings*, edited by Leonard Linsky, 13–47. Urbana: University of Illinois Press, 1952.

Tarski, Alfred, in collaboration with Andrzej Mostowski and Raphael M. Robinson. *Undecidable Theories*. Amsterdam: North-Holland, 1953. [1968]

Turing, Alan M. "On Computable Numbers with an Application to the Entscheidungsproblem." Reprinted in Davis, *Undecidable*, 116–54.

Ullian, Joseph. "Quine and the Field of Mathematical Logic." In *The Philosophy of W. V. Quine*, edited by Lewis Edwin Hahn and Paul Arthur Schilpp, 569–89. La Salle, Ill.: Open Court, 1986.

van Heijenoort, Jean, ed. *From Frege to Gödel: A Source Book in Mathematical Logic, 1879–1931*. Cambridge, Mass.: Harvard University Press, 1967.

Vaught, Robert L. *A Löwenheim–Skolem Theorem for Cardinals Far Apart*. Amsterdam: North-Holland, 1977.

Veblen, Oswald. "A System of Axioms for Geometry." *Transactions of the American Mathematical Society* 5 (1904): 343–84.

von Neumann, John. "Über eine Widerspruchsfreiheitsfrage in der axiomatischen Mengenlehre." *Journal für reine und angewandte Mathematik* 160 (1929): 373–91.

von Neumann, John, and Oskar Morgenstern. *Theory of Games and Economic Behavior*. 2nd edition. Princeton: Princeton University Press, 1947. [2007]

Wang, Hao. "A Formal System of Logic." *Journal of Symbolic Logic* 15 (1950): 25–32.

Whitehead, Alfred North, and Bertrand Russell. *Principia Mathematica*. 2nd edition, 3 vols. Cambridge: Cambridge University Press, 1925.

Wittgenstein, Ludwig. *Tractatus Logico-Philosophicus*. Translated by D. F. Pears and B. F. McGuinness. London: Routledge & Kegan Paul, 1961; 1st German edition 1921.

Yandell, Benjamin H. *The Honors Class: Hilbert's Problems and Their Solvers*. Natick, Mass.: A. K. Peters, 2002.

Yates, C. E. M. "Three Theorems on the Degree of Recursively Enumerable Sets." *Duke Mathematical Journal* 32 (1965): 461–68.

Zermelo, Ernst. "Investigations in the Foundations of Set Theory I" (1908). Translated by Stefan Bauer-Mengelberg. In van Heijenoort, *From Frege to Gödel*, 199–215.

Index

Abel, Niels (1802–1829), 11
algebraic over, 261–64
algorithms, 10, 129
  mechanical, 130
  partial, 207
analytic philosophy, 42, 43, 48, 102
Anselm (c. 1033–1109), 41
a posteriori
  knowledge, 31–32, 50
  truth, 37, 38, 39n3, 49–50, 50n9
a priori
  knowledge, 31–32, 39n3
  truth, 50, 50n9
arithmetization
  of analysis, 10, 18, 42
  of syntax, 130
Aristotle (384–322 BC), 19, 35, 94
atomic formulae/sentences, 91–92, 99
Austin, John (1911–1960), 33, 38, 43,
  89–90
axiom
  of choice, 27, 68, 73, 74, 82, 156, 158,
    168, 198–200, 269
    See also ZFC
  of completeness, for the reals, 67
  of comprehension, 4, 47, 52, 66, 68,
    69, 82, 84, 88, 272
  of empty set, 72
  of extensionality, 3, 4, 47, 82, 85, 88,
    154, 168
  of foundation, 74, 79, 82, 154, 168
  of infinity, 68, 73, 74, 82, 154, 168

  of null set, 154, 168
  of pairing, 82
  of power sets, 72, 82, 164, 168
  of reducibility, 66, 67
  of regularity, 79
  of replacement, 76, 82, 154, 160n8,
    168, 171, 194
  schema, 78
  of union set, 72
axioms of closure, 72, 154, 168
  of big union, 72, 82, 154
  of difference, 72, 154
  of intersection, 72, 154
  of singleton, 154
  of union, 72, 154

back-and-forth argument, 352n19
Baldwin, John T.
  Baldwin–Lachlan proof of Morley's
    theorem, 266–67, 267n26, 275
Barbara syllogism, 36
basis, 263–64
Beatley, Ralph, 45
Benacerraf, Paul
  dilemma, 123, 276–80
Berkeley, George (1685–1753), 64, 150
Bernays, Paul (1888–1977), 81, 165
  Bernays–Morse set theory, 81n31
  See also NBG set theory
Bernstein, Felix (1878–1956)
  Cantor–Bernstein–Schroeder theorem,
    28

"Remarks on Definitions and the
Concept of Truth," 119

halting problem, 211–12, 221
Heath, T. L. (1861–1940), 44
Henkin, Leon (1921–2006), 81
Herzberger, Hans
"New Paradoxes for Old," 122
heterological paradox, 62n3, 67
Hilbert, David (1862–1943), 19, 29–30,
44, 52, 59, 100, 139, 153
Foundations of Geometry, The, 42
rule (ω-rule), 144
Hill, Christopher, 199
Hodges, Wilfred, 238
Hume, David (1711–1776), 31, 48
*Dialogues Concerning Natural
Religion*, 41

idealism, in philosophy of mathematics,
64
identity, 2–3
incompleteness of arithmetic. *See* first
incompleteness theorem
independence of the continuum
hypothesis, 200–04
See also Cohen, Paul
independent subset, 262
induced gödelization, 134
inductive definition, 91–92
basis clause, 91–92
extremal clause, 91
inductive clause, 91–92
infinite sets (or systems), 13–17, 73
countably, 13
infinitesimals, 150
infinity, 1, 15, 30
inner model construction, 78–79, 156
interpretation. *See* model
invariance, 166, 172

Jech, Thomas, 162
Jespersen, Otto (1860–1943), 71

Kant, Immanuel (1724–1804), 10,
31–58, 39n3, 59
Critique of Pure Reason, 31–41

*Metaphysical Foundations of Natural
Science, The*, 38
*Prolegomenon to Any Future
Metaphysics*, 31
Kepler, Johannes (1571–1630), 279
Kleene, Stephen Cole (1909–1994), 127,
128, 133
Kneale, Martha, 34
Kneale, William (1905–1990), 38
Kreisel, Georg, 175
Kripke, Saul A., 39n3, 117–18, 119
"Outline of a Theory of Truth," 117
Kuratowski, Kazimierz (1896–1980),
7–8, 103

Lachlan, Alistair H.
Baldwin–Lachlan proof of Morley's
theorem, 266–67, 267n26, 275
language, 97–100
decidable vocabulary, 130
least indescribable ordinal paradox, 63,
67, 71
Leibniz, Gottfried (1646–1716), 6, 9–10,
12–13, 31–33, 34, 39, 43, 148, 150,
245
Lewis, David (1941–2001), 21, 42
liar paradox, 62, 67, 100, 114, 119n59,
122
limit lemma, 229
L-language, 179–85
Locke, John (1632–1704), 32
Łoś, Jerzy, 238
Löwenheim, Leopold (1878–1957), 108
Löwenheim–Skolem theorem, 109,
157–59, 238, 270

Mach, Ernst (1838–1916), 49
Marker, David, 238, 267n26
Martin, D. A., 227
material adequacy condition, 7, 46, 101,
102–03
material implication paradoxes, 55
maximal sets, 227n17
membership, 2
Mendelson, Elliott, 106, 125, 136
ML (after Quine, *Mathematical Logic*),
88

Breinigsville, PA USA
22 March 2011
258135BV00003B/2/P